A Practitioner's Guide To THE REGULATION OF THE INTERNET

Consultant Editor

Mark Haftke
Partner
KLegal

2nd Edition

City & Financial Publishing

City & Financial Publishing
8 Westminster Court
Hipley Street
Old Woking
Surrey GU22 9LG
United Kingdom
Tel: 01483 720707 Fax: 01483 727928
www.cityandfinancial.com

This Guide has been compiled from the contributions of the authors indicated on the table of contents. The views expressed by such authors do not necessarily reflect the views of their respective firm. Further, since this Guide is intended as a general guide only, its application to specific situations will depend upon the particular circumstances involved and it should not be relied upon as a substitute for obtaining appropriate professional advice.

Throughout this Guide the male pronoun has been used to cover references to both male and female.

Editor
Louise C E Travers

ISBN 1 898830 51 7

British Library Cataloguing-in-Publication Data. A catalogue record for this Guide is available from the British Library.

Printed and bound in Great Britain by Biddles Limited Guildford and King's Lynn.

BIOGRAPHIES

Lars Davies is a CMT Analyst at Ashurst Morris Crisp. He joined Ashursts in 1997 and, since then has been heavily involved in a range of regulatory issues related to licensing, interconnection, public procurement, and Internet related matters. He has published in various journals including Computer Law & Practice, International Business Lawyer, Journal of Business Law, Consumer Policy Review, and Compliance Monitor on media and telecommunications issues. He is at present a Research Fellow with the Information Technology Law Unit at the Centre for Commercial Law Studies at Queen Mary and Westfield College. His research and teaching duties include teaching in the Information Technology Law, Internet Law, Telecommunications Law, and European Competition Law options on the University of London Intercollegiate LL.M course.

Alistair Payne is a Senior Associate in the Telecommunications and Intellectual Property Group of Mallesons Stephen Jaques in Melbourne where he represents clients in all aspects of contentious and non-contentious intellectual property and information technology law matters. He holds a BA/LLB from the University of Auckland and an LLM (Int. Prop.) from the University of London.

Mark Haftke leads the 12 strong E-commerce and Digital Media Group in KLegal. He has practiced exclusively in the Internet domain since 1995. His field of expertise covers online advertising and sponsorship, contracts for the complete e-enabled supply chain including B2B exchanges and P2P distribution, e-contracts, PKI, e-payment, privacy and data protection, technology licensing, consumer protection legislation, intellectual property rights, content clearance (including rights licensing, defamation and advertising), m-commerce and T-commerce deals, digital music, Internet radio licensing, joint ventures and EU initiatives covering the regulation of E-commerce. Mark is listed as a leading e-commerce lawyer in the various independent legal directories.

Christopher Millard (LL.B., M.A., LL.M.) is a Partner in the Communications Media and Technology Group at Clifford Chance. His practice is focussed on e-commerce, e-business and data protection compliance projects. He is responsible for NextLaw®, a Clifford Chance online service providing guidance on managing legal and regulatory risks in multi-jurisdictional e-business projects. As a Visiting Professorial Fellow of QMW, University of London, he teaches on LL.M. courses in Internet Law, Information Technology Law and Telecommunications Law. He is a frequent speaker at international conferences and is a visiting lecturer at several universities. He is a past Chairman of the Society for Computers and Law and a past President of the International Federation of Computer Law Associations.

Rafi Azim-Khan heads up McDermott, Will & Emery's e-business and marketing practices in Europe. He has considerable experience of advising media, marketing and leading brand clients on a wide range of advertising/sales promotions and intellectual property issues and on all aspects of e-commerce, particularly in relation to conducting full legal site "audits" for various multinationals, major ISP start-ups, B2B and B2C exchanges and auctions, e-partner agreements, site creation and disclaimers, Pan-EU online contracting, jurisdictional issues, net-shopping and marketing and net betting/gaming.

Rafi is listed as a leading individual in Chambers Directory 2000 – 2001 and Legal Experts 2000 and is further listed as one of the "digital dozen" UK specialists in the 2000 E-Commerce Guide to Legal Services. Rafi also lectures and writes regularly on intellectual property, media, Internet, marketing and related topics.

Margaret Jordan served her articles at (what is now) Cameron McKenna and became a partner there in 1979. Following her husband's move to Belgium, she joined the firm's Brussels office in 1983. She worked on a part-time basis until 1990, becoming a partner in the firm in 1995. Margaret specialises in EU regulatory law and has particular expertise in EU financial services law. Having been based in Brussels for over 15 years, Margaret has a wealth of experience in dealing with the Community institutions.

Nieves La Casta qualified as an Abogado in 1986. She has worked at the European Court of Justice in Luxembourg as a "referendaire" (Legal Secretary) to the Spanish Judge. She became an official of the European Commission in 1990 and is currently on leave. Nieves has also been a Lecturer on European Law at the Universidad Carlos III (Madrid) and San Pablo CEU (Madrid) and a Researcher for the British Institute of International and Comparative Law (London).

Nieves joined the London office of Lovells in October 1999 as a Professional Support Lawyer in the EU & Competition Law department. Nieves is a European Registered Lawyer at the Law Society.

Robert Caplehorn was called to the Bar in July 1980. He has held a variety of legal posts in industry and commerce including Office of Fair Trading (1983 – 1987) and National Westminster Bank (1987 – 1994). In April 1994, Robert joined Mondex International as General Counsel and Company Secretary where he was responsible for legal and contractual issues relating to the global development of e-cash. In May 1999, he joined Bolero International (bolero.net) as Senior Counsel dealing with global e-commerce legal issues pertaining to international trade.

Christopher Kuner is an Attorney in the Brussels office of the international law firm Morrison & Foerster LLP, specialising in e-commerce and legal aspects of the Internet. Christopher is a member of the Legal Advisory Board of DG Information Society of the European Commission, and a member of legal working groups on e-commerce issues of the International Chamber of Commerce, the Internet Law and Policy Forum, and the United Nations Commission on International Trade Law. He is also Vice-Chair of Committee R4 of the International Bar Association. The author of numerous articles and the book "Internet für Juristen" (Verlag C.H. Beck), Christopher is a frequent lecturer on Internet-related topics. Christopher created and maintains a website on recent legal developments in Germany in the areas of Internet and e-commerce.

Karen Mason trained as a Solicitor with international law firm Clifford Chance. Shortly after qualifying in 1993 she moved in-house to the BBC. She went on to set-up the legal department at the Press Association. Karen has since worked as Head of Legal at Demon Internet, taking over the whole legal function for Scottish Telecom when it brought Demon, and becoming Chief Legal Officer after Scottish Telecom floated as Thus plc. She joined Andersen Legal (Garretts) in January 2001.

Philip Gershuny is a Partner at Lovells where he is Head of International Tax. Philip advises in connection with M&A, corporate finance, reorganisations, financial transactions and business start-ups, particularly in the area of e-commerce. He was Managing Partner of Lovells New York office until 1998 and retains many clients and contacts in North America. He speaks at conferences on the subject of the taxation of e-commerce on both sides of the Atlantic.

Martin Hollobone heads up KPMG's New Media Regulatory Team. His expertise has been gained from working at the DTI, HM Treasury and the FSA. At the FSA Martin established and headed up the Internet Unit and was also secretary to the FSA E-Commerce Group. Martin has also been involved with international regulatory issues such as EU e-Commerce related directives and was a member of IOSCO Internet Task Force. Since joining KPMG in January 1999, Martin has worked with firms offering global and pan-European online funds, banking and brokerage services and also heads up KPMG's e-Commerce European Regulatory Network.

Emer Cashin is a Solicitor and has many years experience in financial services law and regulation. She has advised clients on financial services authorisation and the application of the SRO's conduct of business rules. Prior to joining KPMG in 1997, she had spent seven years with an international city law firm (Clifford Chance) as well as working for the predecessor to the SFA. Emer now specialises in the application of financial services legislation and regulations including marketing restrictions related to e-Commerce business.

Heather Rowe joined Lovell White Durrant as a banking lawyer, over fourteen years ago. She has specialised in advising in relation to companies in the fields of telecommunications and computers and is now a partner in the Computers, Communications and Media group. Heather has drafted, on a regular basis, turnkey projects in the computer/telecommunications field, outsourcing agreements, agreements relating to hardware and software supply and development, standard terms and conditions of supply/purchase and provision of a wide range of services in the information technology and telecommunications fields, and EDI and network agreements.

Given her banking background, combined with her practice areas, Heather specialises in all aspects of e-commerce.

Another major part of that practice relates to data protection, since the law in all EU Member States was supposed to have changed in 1998 to give effect to an EC Directive on this and there are a number of implementation issues that arise.

She is Chairman of the International Chamber of Commerce's International Working Party on Data Protection and Privacy, as well as having just been appointed the Chairman of ICC UK's Committee on Computing, Telecommunications and Information Policy. She is also Chairman of the Centre for the Study of Financial Innovation's Working Party on Regulation and the Internet.

Heather was, until last year, also Co-Chairman of Committee R, the Technology and E-Commerce Law Committee, of the International Bar Association.

Matthew Redding joined Lovells as a trainee Solicitor in 1999. As part of his training, he spent six months in the Computers, Communications and Media Group of Lovells where he was closely involved with giving advice on telecoms, Internet, data protection and Intellectual Property related matters. He has also been heavily involved with the production of Lovells newsletters on telecoms issues and client notes on legal issues relating to encryption export controls, digital signatures, interception of communications and data protection.

CONTENTS

Chapter 1

WHAT IS THE INTERNET? 1

Lars Davies, Research Fellow, University of London
and CMT Analyst, Ashurst Morris Crisp

Chapter 2

DOMAIN NAMES, TRADE MARKS AND UNFAIR COMPETITION 13

Alistair Payne, Senior Associate
Mallesons Stephen Jaques

Chapter 3

COPYRIGHT AND THE INTERNET 49

Mark Haftke, Partner
KLegal

Chapter 4

THE LEGAL ISSUES OF THE WORLD WIDE WEB 91

Lars Davies, Research Fellow, University of London
and CMT Analyst, Ashurst Morris Crisp

Chapter 5

MAKING CONTRACTS OVER THE INTERNET 105

Mark Haftke, Partner
KLegal

Chapter 6

JURISDICTION 125

Dr Stuart Dutson, Litigation and Arbitration Solicitor
Linklaters – Linklaters & Alliance (London)

CHAPTER 7

DATA PROTECTION 145

Christopher Millard, Partner
Clifford Chance

Chapter 8

ADVERTISING 181

Rafi Azim-Khan, Partner
McDermott, Will & Emery

Chapter 9

SELLING AT A DISTANCE .... .207

Margaret Jordan, Partner
Nieves La Casta, Professional Support Lawyer
Lovells Boesebeck Droste

Chapter 10

PAYMENT SYSTEMS ON THE INTERNET 225

Robert Caplehorn, Senior Counsel
Bolero International Limited

Chapter 11

ELECTRONIC SIGNATURES .251

Christopher Kuner, Attorney at Law
Morrison & Foerster LLP (Brussels)

Chapter 12

CONTENT LIABILITY AND ISPS 265

Karen Mason, Senior Manager (Solicitor)
Andersen Legal Garretts

Chapter 13

TAX IMPLICATIONS OF THE INTERNET 273

Philip Gershuny, Partner
Lovells

Chapter 14

FINANCIAL SERVICES REGULATION 291

Martin Hollobone, Director
Emer Cashin, Manager, New Media Regulatory Team
KPMG

Chapter 15

BEST PRACTICE FOR COMPANIES IN THE USE OF EMAIL, INTERNET COMMUNICATIONS AND ACCESS TO WEBSITES 317

Heather Rowe, Partner
Matthew Redding
Lovells

Chapter 1
WHAT IS THE INTERNET?

Lars Davies
Research Fellow
University of London
and CMT Analyst
Ashurst Morris Crisp

1.1   Introduction

The phenomenal growth of the Internet has given rise to a growing need to define and, if possible, to address the legal issues that arise when dealing across the Internet. Unfortunately it is very difficult to examine these legal issues without some understanding of the basic technology of the Internet. Therefore, in order to define and address these issues properly, the first question that needs to be addressed is what is the Internet? This question is much easier to pose than it is to answer. The problem stems from the fact that the Internet is usually only observed on a superficial level. Users tend only to see a few of the many facets of the Internet and so tend to form their own ideas of what it is. However, such ideas are almost always incomplete and so, for the purpose of analysing the legal implications and principles described later in this Guide, this Chapter will try to give a brief, and yet practical working definition of the Internet.[1]

1.2   What is the Internet?

The word "Internet" is probably best used to refer to the internetworking of networks rather than simply referring to a single network or entity. Contrary to popular belief, no particular network can be pointed to and identified as the Internet. Rather than simply a single network, what does exist is an expanding group of private and public networks, local area networks, wide area networks, and regional and national networks that can interconnect. These interconnect in such a way that any computer on a particular network can communicate with another computer on any other network in a seamless manner. The communications are completely transparent. The fact that computers on different networks can communicate with each other does not, however, mean that the networks together can be regarded as a single network. The whole collection might seem as if it were one, but it is not and must not be regarded as such, as will be seen later. One reason is that the collection of individual and distinct networks raises several legal issues that are quite separate from those that arise from the use of the networks themselves. Just as there is no single network that can be identified as the Internet, so there is no single entity which owns or controls the Internet. Instead, any ownership or control that may exist will simply vest in the individual computers and networks which together make up the Internet, with spheres of ownership or control applying to each discrete component only.

---

[1]   For a more detailed description of the workings of the Internet *see* Krol, "The Whole Internet User's Guide & Catalog", O'Reilly & Associates, Sebastapol CA, 2nd ed., 1994; and Wiggins, "The Internet for Everyone", McGraw-Hill, New York, 1994.

The communications technology that allows these networks to connect with each other consists of a suite of protocols denoted by the acronym TCP/IP.[2] This term, which is the acronym for "transmission control protocol/Internet protocol", is slightly misleading in itself as the protocol suite consists of a set of several protocols.[3] The transmission control protocol ("TCP") and Internet protocol ("IP") are simply two of these. The suite itself consists of layers of protocols: the applications layer protocols, the transport layer protocols, and the network layer protocols. The idea behind the model is very simple and is partly responsible for the rapid growth in the use of the protocol suite. The idea is simply that that each layer provides its own set of functions to the protocols above, and uses the functions provided by the protocols in the layer directly below. The hierarchical structure, which is flexible enough to allow each layer to be independently updated and developed without affecting the integrity of the layers above or below, is often referred to as the "protocol stack".

Though it is disputed whether the exact origins of the Internet were military or civilian, it is generally agreed that one of the main factors in its rapid growth and acceptability was both the power and the free availability of the TCP/IP protocol suite. Anyone could, and still can, use the specifications to create an implementation of the protocol suite for a particular system and so interconnect with other computers running the same suite.

TCP/IP was initially developed from research work sponsored by the US Department of Defense to develop a networking technology that would provide a military computer network that could survive and continue to operate after a nuclear strike on one or more of its components. TCP/IP works by providing functions to break up a piece of digital data into small packets or "datagrams"; it then transports those packets across any combination of networks to their destination. Neither the actual routes taken by each datagram nor the communications hardware which make up those routes matter to the operation of the network communications, as each datagram can take a different route to the others. Should the receiving computer not receive all the datagrams, it can simply request the transmitting computer to re-transmit the missing ones.[4] All that matters to the operation of the network communications is that the transmitting computer can "see" the receiving computer.

---

[2]   For a full explanation of how TCP/IP works *see* Hunt, "TCP/IP Network Administration", O'Reilly & Associates, 2nd ed., 1998; Bearpark, "Protocols for Application Communication", McGraw-Hill, London 1995; and Washburn & Evans, "TCP/IP: running a successful network", Addison-Wesley, Wokingham, 1993.

[3]   A protocol is simply a set of rules and specifications which should be followed. Within TCP/IP each protocol defines a specific set of rules and specifications which set out the way to perform certain communications functions. So long as these rules and specifications are followed then the systems which operate the protocols will be able to communicate. As a consequence, the protocols are hardware and the operating system is independent. Provided that the protocols are correctly implemented, the protocol stacks should be able to communicate.

[4]   The actual process is a little more complex in reality but this explanation will suffice.

The lowest protocol layer[5] – the Internet layer – provides the basic transport and addressing facilities and nothing else. The protocol most commonly used is the IP which provides a connectionless service with no error correction facilities – in effect it is merely "a best efforts protocol". It neither knows nor cares whether or not the data packets arrive at their destination. All it requires is a valid address which it can "see" and to which it can send the packets. The protocol uses a unique 32-bit binary number to create an address – the IP address – for each interface to a protocol stack. A single computer can have more than one interface and so more than one IP address. For the sake of convenience these numbers are often expressed as a series of four octets of eight bits, each of which are written in decimal form (e.g. xxx.xxx.xxx.xxx) rather than in binary representation.[6] This form of addressing, though succinct and utilitarian, is not immediately user friendly and so another system, the Domain Name System ("DNS"), is used to provide an extra addressing layer that is easier to use and a little more friendly.

The next protocol layer up from the Internet layer – the transport layer – provides the link between the application layer protocols and the Internet layer protocols, and adds to the functionality of the latter. The two most common protocols are the TCP and the user datagram protocol ("UDP"). To provide a reliable link between two computers, TCP offers a connection-based service that includes error correction. To ensure reliability, however, the protocol must include a great deal of information about the data and the individual datagrams in each piece of data, and so incurs a large overhead in terms of the processing required for each datagram. Thus more datagrams are required to send a particular piece of data than if it were sent using UDP. TCP cannot be used to broadcast as it can only connect to a single interface. UDP, on the other hand, provides a basic connectionless service without any error-correction facilities. It has a low processing overhead and requires only a small amount of information to be stored in the datagrams that it transmits. Consequently UDP can transmit a given piece of data using fewer datagrams than TCP.

In addition to using the IP address provided by the IP, the transport layer protocols provide an address called a "port" – a 16-bit number – for the application layer protocols to use. Each service provided by the applications layer uses one or more unique ports when transmitting or receiving information. Certain services such as telnet, or hypertext transfer protocol ("HTTP"), have port addresses specified as defaults and these are defined in the specifications of the relevant protocols. Others, such as file transfer protocol ("FTP"), will use both their default ports for any initial communications together with any extra ports that are dynamically allocated to the service as and when they are needed. New services can use any of the available ports that are not already reserved for other services.

---

[5] There are two further layers within the stack – the network hardware layers which interact with the actual network hardware and come below the Internet layer, but these simply apply to the hardware on which the protocol stack operates and not the networking levels themselves. On ethernet networks they include the function of accessing the unique address that each ethernet network point must have and then relating this to the IP address of the protocol stack.

[6] Though decimal notation is easier to read and remember, binary notation is much easier to work with when setting up networks. Entities such as netmasks and subnets are much more easily understood when seen in binary notation.

To create a full numerical TCP/IP address, the port address is appended to the end of the IP address. For example xxx.xxx.xxx.xxx:21 refers to an FTP server on interface xxx.xxx.xxx.xxx, whilst xxx.xxx.xxx.xxx:80 refers to an HTTP server on interface xxx.xxx.xxx.xxx. Rather than using the default values, the ports for various services can also be specifically allocated by a network administrator if necessary, such as for network security purposes. Thus xxx.xxx.xxx.xxx:8000[7] could also refer to an HTTP[8] server or indeed any other service which is configured to use that port.

As the numerical IP addressing system is not particularly user friendly a second form of addressing that uses a set of symbols called the DNS can be used. The addresses formed with this system are those that are most readily recognised by users as Internet addresses, though the TCP/IP suite can only operate through the numerical IP addresses. DNS addresses must therefore be translated to IP addresses before they can be used by the suite.

The DNS is hierarchical in structure and works by using a set of named domains with which a unique address can be constructed. As the DNS is independent in structure from the IP addressing system, domains can be chosen for the convenience of the users or network administrator. Each domain name address can be mapped to an IP address. Indeed, since the IP address merely refers to a single stack interface, more than one DNS address can be mapped to a single IP address. An example of such an address is:

ftp.company.com

and

www.company.com

where both addresses can be mapped to the same IP address. DNS addresses can also be mapped to more than one IP address in a similar way.[9] However, the domain names are not mapped to the individual ports, only the IP address, and so, though each domain refers to the same IP address, as they can refer to different services they may automatically refer to different ports. Given that no numerical port address is specified at the end of the addresses it would probably be safe to assume that each service uses the default port assigned to it. Thus the address "ftp.company.com" may refer to an IP address such as xxx.xxx.xxx.xxx:21, whilst the address "www.company.com" would then correspond to an IP address such as xxx.xxx.xxx.xxx:80.[10]

The DNS, as it is currently set up, uses two distinct naming schemes. One of these is the geographical scheme which uses country code Top Level Domains ("ccTLDs"). In this scheme the uppermost domain such as ".uk", ".io", ".tm", ".to", or ".ru" specifies a country or territory – each has its own unique two letter domain though for historical or political

---

[7]   8000 is a commonly used alternative to the predefined HTTP port number 80.

[8]   Port 8000 is a common substitute for the HTTP service.

[9]   This may be done where a network administrator wants to spread the access load on a particular service by apportioning it out across a set of servers. It may also be done where a particular computer is connected to several distinct networks so that the server has the same DNS address irrespective of the different IP addresses for each of the networks.

[10]   If a non-default port is used this is normally appended to the DNS address leaving a space between the DNS address and the port number.

reasons some have more than one.[11] The next level of domain could be organisational[12] and could use domains to indicate the type of organisation that the address belongs to. For example ".ac" or ".edu" could be used to refer to academic organisations; ".co" or ".com" to refer to commercial organisations; ".gov" to refer to governmental organisations; and so on. The next level of domain refers directly to the network on which the address resides and could be the name of the network provider, the name of an organisation, or another name which the network operator desires. Finally, the Lower Level Domains are decided according to the network users or administrators. The domains within each country are allocated by one or more predetermined national authorities to ensure that each address remains unique. These authorities often operate their own set of guidelines for allocating domains and may well only deal with addresses that fall within certain domains, such as "co.uk", "ac.de", or "co.ru".

The alternative naming scheme is the organisational scheme – where the highest domain defines the type of organisation to which the domain belongs. These are known as generic Top Level Domains ("gTLDs") and are ".com" for commercial, ".edu" for academic or educational, ".gov" for governmental, ".int" for international organisation, and so forth. The Lower Level Domains are partitioned in a similar manner to that described above. This scheme is presently co-ordinated by the Internet Corporation for Assigned Names and Numbers (the "ICANN")[13] (".com", ".net" and ".org"), Internet Assigned Numbers Authority (".int") and Network Solutions Inc. (".edu"). The ".gov" gTLD is reserved for the US Federal Government whilst the ".mil" gTLD is reserved for the US Military. Provisional agreement has been reached by ICANN to approve a further seven suffixes, including ".biz", ".info" and ".pro".

What is important to understand is that the domain does not automatically refer to the country in which the address resides. This is true of the organisational[14] scheme but it is also true of the geographical scheme.[15] All that the address shows is the organisation with which the address is registered and no more.[16] Another important facet is that, though the DNS is an infinite resource – any name may be registered – only one particular instance of a complete name may be registered. Thus a paradox exists whereby the DNS provides an infinite and yet, at the same time, a scarce resource.

---

[11]   Such as ".su" and ".ru".

[12]   The ".us" domain hierarchy, for instance, uses the US Postal Service postal areas as the Second Level Domain.

[13]   *See* www.icann.org.

[14]   A common fallacy is that all organisational domains refer only to US-based organisations when all they show is that the domain holders have registered with the relevant registry. Any organisation which satisfies the registration requirements can obtain an organisational domain, though one or two are reserved for US-based organisations.

[15]   As an example the Indian Ocean domain, ".io" is being used by the Internet One organisation to provide a domain registry which will try to deal with the conflicts that naturally arise between domain name holders and holders of trademarks. For more details *see* the Internet One server at "http://www.io". Other domains are being used in attempts to create offshore domains or trademark-specific domains.

[16]   Any address which an applicant has had to provide when registering a domain, if this is required, is usually that of a contact, rather than the physical address of a computer or network. In many cases, however, the contact address may also refer to the address of a computer or server involved with that particular domain.

The networks themselves cannot provide services of any nature. All that they can do is provide the communications infrastructure over which users provide services to each other. These are the services that provide the information or functions that users see, with each service providing its own set of functions; each service may thus provide a different view of the nature and operation of the Internet. The Internet is best viewed as a communications medium and nothing more. It is neither a computer nor a particular network. It is simply a means by which computers can and do communicate with each other.

1.3 Services over the Internet

1.3.1 Electronic information

Computers store and process data as strings of bits, or ones and zeros. These bits, when taken together, can also be regarded as a single binary number, which is written in ones and zeros. Thus a large file can be viewed as a single string of bits. Almost all types of data or information – whether it is sound, visual, or text-based – can be represented by binary numbers and thus as a string of bits. Computers can transmit and make perfect copies of any binary data easily. The binary nature of any data also means that a computer can slice the string into little pieces or packets, and transmit them to another computer which can then reassemble the bits in the correct order to make a perfect copy of the original string. It is this ability to transmit bits and make perfect copies that gives rise to many of the legal issues that surround the use of the Internet.

1.3.2 Servers and clients

In order to provide and use these services, users must operate servers and/or clients. The computers connected to the Internet are often described as servers or clients – a description which can cause a great deal of confusion. The description does not refer to the size of the computers or to different computers. What the description does refer to is the function of a particular program that runs on a computer. A server is simply a program that is configured and used to provide a service to another program; the program serves up data or information. Where the term is used to describe a computer, it simply refers to a computer that is capable of running programs that act as servers. Given that a great deal of processing power is sometimes required to run some types of server software, these computers are generally more powerful that others that are typically used by the average user.

A client is simply a program that accesses and uses a service provided by a server. A client uses, obtains or interacts with a service. What can be confusing is that a computer can run both clients and servers, and so can often be referred to as both a client and a server. One of the attractions of the Internet is that any computer attached to the Internet can, in theory at least, operate both as a client and a server. Perhaps the easiest way to visualise the distinction is that a program is acting as a server if it provides a service and a client if it uses or accesses a service, even a service provided by a server running on the same computer as the client.

1.3.3   *Electronic mail*

Electronic mail ("email") is the most common service used over the Internet and allows users to communicate with and send information to other users regardless of time zones or geographic location. Its utility and power are almost endless as users can transmit any data that is capable of binary representation. All that is required is some sort of connection between the users.[17] To a user, email simply involves creating a message and then sending it on its way to a recipient. The actual mechanics are slightly more complicated and usually involve the participation of several programs, computers and networks. The sender uses a client program to create a message and then transmits the message to the sender's mail server. This mail server, if it is not also the recipient's mail server, then transmits the message to the recipient's mail server. The message can be transmitted to the destination, either directly or via a series of mail servers. The recipient's mail server then transmits the message to the recipient's client when the recipient's client requests the message. The clients and servers can operate on any computer on the Internet. Users do not need to run email clients on computers to which they have physical access but can run these on computers which they access across the Internet. The location of the users is therefore not necessarily the same as the location of the clients of the mail servers.

Contrary to popular belief, email is neither instantaneous nor totally reliable;[18] such a belief is often rapidly dispelled after a mere few days of using the service. Certainly email can often appear to be instantaneous but the reality can be quite different as senders cannot usually be certain of when the recipient reads or even receives a message. Mail servers can send mail once that client has passed the message to them or, if network traffic is high or the receiving server is not responding, store the message and send it at a later time. This time delay can be anything from a few minutes to several days and is set by the server administrator. Quite apart from the transmission delays come the delays caused by the mail clients, or rather by their use by users. Some users will run their mail clients in the background whilst they carry out other tasks; the mail clients will usually query the mail server at specific time intervals set by the user to automatically retrieve messages. Other users will only run their clients when they wish to check their email box. Thus, even though the sender's message has been received by the recipient's mail server, the recipient may not actually access the mail until some time after.

Messages can be lost in the networks.[19] As the recipient does not usually know that the message is coming, there is no way that it can subsequently ask for the message to be re-transmitted if it is not received. Using a system of email receipts can be just as fraught as these too are transported by the email system and are just as likely to get lost in the system.

---

[17]   Email is such a powerful service that several protocols use its messaging model as a foundation for their own functionality.

[18]   See Stoll, "Silicon Snake Oil: second thoughts on the information highway", Macmillan, London, 1995, Chapter 10 for an interesting comparison between email and the US Postal Service. The book is also a highly readable critique on the over-reliance and over-belief that often surrounds discussions about the Internet as a whole.

[19]   Usually undelivered messages are returned to the sender but sometimes they are "lost" and are deleted without either party becoming aware of the ultimate fate of the message.

If a receipt is received the sender cannot usually be sure of whether the recipient's mail server sent the receipt, or whether the recipient's client sent the receipt. An additional problem is determining whether the receipt was sent after the recipient read the message or when the recipient's client received the message.[20]

1.3.4 Usenet

Usenet, or network news, is a worldwide discussion medium on which users can post information or requests for information in defined areas or news groups, the number of which are growing continuously. The contents of these news groups are transmitted as a whole to designated computers or news servers and it is from these servers that users download the data and read the information contained. Users use special client programs called news readers to access the information or to post information to the news groups and, as with email, any type of digital data can be posted to these news groups. News groups can cover virtually any topic and they do not all need to be publicly available.[21] Any computer can be configured to act as a news server and many closed user groups and organisations use "private" news servers as discussion groups or to disseminate messages efficiently.

Given the contentious content of some news groups it has become quite common for some Internet Service Providers, on-line service providers, companies, and universities to restrict or prohibit access to those news groups that they deem unacceptable, often those news groups concerned with sex. Others refuse to restrict or censor access on the principle of freedom of expression or free speech. The subject of on-line censorship, and the arguments for and against such actions, will remain contentious for a long time to come.

1.3.5 File transfer protocol

The FTP[22] is a basic protocol that provides the ability to transfer data from one computer to another. As with any service that operates over the Internet all that is required to transfer files is a working connection between the computers. Should the transmission be interrupted in mid transfer then the user can usually resume the transfer by starting again and picking up from where the previous transmission was interrupted. Almost any file that can be stored in electronic format can be transferred using this protocol. All that is required is that the file can be read and accessed by the clients and servers.

---

[20]   Some mail filters and pre-processors can be set to automatically send receipts once the mail has been received irrespective of whether the recipient has actually read the messages. The text of the receipts can, however, usually be set to make this clear and simply state that the message has been received but not as yet read.

[21]   News servers are often used to provide a discussion or conferencing system to a closed group of users.

[22]   Other protocols such as file sharing protocol ("FSP") and TFTP have very similar, if not identical functionality, but are used in different circumstances. Some implementations of FSP can create security issues and so are not widely available. TFTP is almost identical to FTP and is used to allow the transfer of a restricted set of files. For almost all intents and purposes FTP and TFTP are interchangeable.

Users simply use an FTP client to access an FTP server. Users then select and transfer the required files. Users are not restricted to transferring files to themselves but can, if permitted to do so, transfer files to the computer on which the server runs. Users can also, if they are sufficiently knowledgeable, use one client on one computer to transfer files between two other computers.

1.3.6 The World Wide Web

The World Wide Web ("WWW"), though probably the most public and recognisable face of the Internet, is not a network at all, despite its name which suggests otherwise. It is simply a service provided over the Internet, and it uses a specific protocol – the HTTP – to access and transfer documents. This is often confused with the HyperText Markup Language ("HTML") which is a document Markup Language and not a protocol. The client program, commonly referred to as the browser, will access the server which will then send a page of data. Browsers can read documents in HTML format – the format of the majority of documents – but are also capable of reading documents in ASCII format.[23]

HTTP can also be used to transfer files in a manner similar to FTP.[24] Unlike FTP, however, which requires a constant connection between the client and server whilst the user accesses the server, HTTP only requires a connection whilst actually transmitting data. Consequently HTTP needs less network resources than some other protocols when transmitting data. Each connection stays up only long enough to transmit the page of data accessed.

The HTTP protocol is surprisingly small and allows the client to access not only HTML pages but also information provided by other protocols (such as FTP, Gopher,[25] and WAIS)[26] either natively or by accessing these protocols themselves. HTTP can therefore be viewed as a multi-service protocol. HTML itself is simply a page formatting language that

---

[23] The original purpose of the web technology was to serve as a document distribution system. It is quite common to come across documents that come across as ASCII but in fact are binary documents (such as video clips, graphics or program codes) that have been misconfigured and transmitted as ASCII. This is often given away by the fact that what the browser displays appears to be rubbish.

[24] Unlike FTP, the functions provided by HTTP file transfer are very basic. HTTP does not allow the user to halt a file transfer and then resume the transfer from that point. The user must instead restart the file transfer from the beginning, regardless of the amount that was previously transferred. This shortcoming will be addressed in future releases of HTTP. HTTP file transfer does, however, make more efficient use of the network band width than FTP, not so much in the number of datagrams transmitted but in the number of ports used and the server workload.

[25] Gopher is a highly efficient service that is used to access electronic data in a structured and hierarchical way. The WWW has effectively superseded Gopher as a document delivery mechanism and gopher servers are no longer as common as they once were.

[26] The Wide Area Information Service ("WAIS") is another document delivery service based on searchable indexes of document collections. It is now becoming less common as the WWW and its search engines perform a similar function.

defines the structure and functionality of the page, and includes the ability to build in links to other pages or services within a page. HTML does not dictate how a page should be displayed. That is a function that is left for the browser to carry out and users can configure their browsers to display colours, fonts, and such like as they wish.[27]

Developments in the wireless arena have extended the reach of the Internet. Though the use of TCP/IP was never limited to systems that interconnected via physical cables, wireless connection was, until recently, something that was somewhat unusual in the consumer market. This has now changed. Though it has always been possible to run a TCP/IP connection over GSM, or any other wireless connection to which a user could connect a modem, such a connection tended to be inefficient due to the limited bandwidth that was and still is available over the wireless connection. The wireless application protocol ("WAP")[28] was developed to address the problem of limited bandwidth, and in its early days was promoted as being capable of delivering Internet content to handheld devices. Unfortunately experience has not lived up to the promise in the initial versions of WAP. However, new versions are being designed and implemented which should address some or all of the problems that have been experienced thus far.

WAP is not strictly a TCP/IP protocol, though it can and does interface with an IP network and does make use of some of the existing standards.[29] WAP uses the Wireless Markup Language ("WML") to display data in much the same way as HTTP uses HTML. Indeed WML is sometimes said to contain a subset of the HTML commands and WML pages can be served by HTTP servers that are configured to do so.[30] HTML pages can be translated into WML pages but information will be lost. That is unavoidable given the differences in bandwidth and screen displays that WAP and WML are designed to work with. Work is underway to remedy the inconsistencies and to try to bring WML and HTML under the same standard but WML will still be limited by its design constraints. Nevertheless an objective view should be taken of these limitations which should not be seen to detract from its usefulness. WAP and WML are designed to work with mobile handsets which have limited displays and limited bandwidth, and as such have been optimised for that purpose. HTML and existing web pages contain far too much information to display on a handset with any ease.

---

[27]   The latest specifications of HTML will include the ability to include style sheets that will allow the authors of the pages to control to a great extent how the browser displays. Some proprietary extensions to HTML also allow the authors to specify what fonts should be used when displaying the page.

[28]   *See* http://www.wapforum.org for more details.

[29]   Future developments will see greater compatibility and support in WAP for more of the TCP/IP protocols such as HTML and HTTP.

[30]   Unfortunately it is not strictly true to state that WML is a subset of HTML. WML is a different Markup Language which shares certain features with HTML. Unlike HTML or other Markup Languages, WML can interact directly with a special class of network server, the Wireless Telephony Applications ("WTA") server to control incoming and outgoing calls, functionality that cannot be obtained by using an HTTP server alone.

1.4 Conclusions

The Internet is itself a vast network of networks that merely interact with one another in a multitude of ways through a multitude of services. The possible uses to which these services lend themselves are immense, as are the possible legal consequences. Jurisdictional analysis and knowledge of the underlying operations of the Internet will always remain important in determining how to deal with the issues that arise.

Under the veneer of different services, the networking technology of the Internet still exists and continues to provide the backbone on which new services are developed. Understanding the overall nature, look and feel of the Internet will help immeasurably when it comes to analysing the legal issues involved with its use.

Chapter 2
DOMAIN NAMES, TRADE MARKS AND UNFAIR COMPETITION

Alistair Payne
Senior Associate
Mallesons Stephen Jaques

2.1 Introduction

Intellectual property rights are essentially national rights. Although various international conventions attempt to harmonise individual laws to assist trade and promote the exchange of intellectual property on a global basis, there is no single worldwide system. While reform of intellectual property regimes has historically been technology driven, they have never before been overtaken to the extent that they have by the Internet.

The fundamental challenge is the creation of a truly borderless and global environment for the exchange of information and commercial transactions. An Internet site can be viewed from anywhere in the world and goods can be purchased instantly from the other side of the world without leaving home. If there was ever any doubt, now there is no question that goodwill and reputation are not confined to national borders and can exist worldwide. Trade marks, whether registered or unregistered, operate in this new environment at an international level. Conflict arises because there is no international law of trade marks and national laws are being relied upon to control a global, electronic marketplace.

There is an important distinction to be made between the "physical" and the "virtual" (or electronic) worlds. The gatekeepers of commerce in the virtual world are domain names not trade marks. Domain names act as identifiers of an entity's site no matter what information or commercial activity is being undertaken from that site. Their function is much broader than merely acting as an identifier of particular goods or services – they provide an entry to an information source, but in doing so may also function as trade marks. Domain names may also attract their own "virtual" goodwill based on their use and reputation as gatekeepers for particular sites. For these reasons they are of crucial importance in the struggle to replicate an entity's physical world economic power in the virtual world.

However, like all good things, the most sought after group of domain names is a limited resource. In a global marketplace it is obviously preferable to obtain a global identifier. There are only a limited number of desirable variables for what up until now have proved the popularly accepted global identifiers – the Top Level Domain ("TLD") names ".com", ".org" and ".net" – and competition has been fierce; registrations in these TLD groups grew, collectively, by more than 217 per cent in 2000.

The Domain Name System ("DNS") makes no provision equivalent to the trade mark system's classification of goods and services, so that, for example, there is no possibility of registering the same ".com" domain name in different fields of activity. The first to register has to date usually obtained prior rights. This leaves trade mark proprietors who consider that they have superior rights to a domain name, by virtue of prior usage or registration of an equivalent trade mark, to rely on the particular registry's domain name dispute resolution policy or to their remedies in national courts. As a result the intersection between domain names, registered trade marks and common law usage rights to a trade name or trade mark has become one of the most controversial and political areas of Internet law.

2.2 Domain names

2.2.1 What is a domain name?

Internet addresses are allocated by the Internet Assigned Numbers Authority (the "IANA") to regional Internet Protocol ("IP") registries and in turn to Internet Service Providers. These addresses have unique IP numbers (in numerical form for each computer linked to the Internet). As strings of numbers are difficult to remember and do not have the recognition value of common language names, alpha-numeric addresses or "domain names" are also assigned for each address.

2.2.2 Generic Top Level Domain names, country code Top Level Domain names and Second Level Domain names

The DNS is hierarchical. At the top of the tree are TLDs. These may be generic Top Level Domain ("gTLDs") names or country code Top Level Domain ("ccTLDs") names. Second Level Domain ("SLDs") names are sub-groupings of the TLDs which may be based on various criteria and include the desired global identifier.

More than 200 countries (including the US) administer or authorise the administration of their own country code DNS using ccTLDs. An example is the ".uk" or the ".au" domain spaces administered in the UK and Australia respectively. Country code systems may also break down their individual registration systems into SLDs based on the type of registrant. For example, the Australian system allocates ".com.au" for commercial entities, ".gov.au" for governmental entities, and ".edu.au" for educational organisations. Some countries base SLD groupings on geographical areas, others have no sub-grouping facility and merely list organisation names directly before the country code. There is considerable variation in the way each system is organised.

Traditionally, gTLDs included the ".com", ".net", ".org", ".gov", ".edu", ".mil" and ".int" domains. The generic DNS for ".com", ".net" and ".org" is administered by the Internet Corporation for Assigned Names and Numbers (the "ICANN") and is available to persons and businesses worldwide. ICANN have recently approved the use and administered the tender process for the registry administration of the new gTLD's – ".aero", ".biz", ".coop", ".info", ".museum", ".name", and ".pro". ICANN, a non-profit organisation, co-ordinates the assignment of Internet domain names and IP address numbers. In addition, ICANN co-ordinates the stable operation of the Internet's root server system.

The ".gov" domain is reserved exclusively for the US Government. The ".edu" domain is reserved for educational institutions and is registered only through Network Solutions Inc. ("NSI"). The ".mil" domain is reserved exclusively for the US Military. The ".int" domain is used only for registering organisations established by international treaties between governments.

The generic DNS and country code DNS operate in parallel, giving people the option to register in individual country systems or in what has up until now come to be regarded as the global option for commerce – the ".com" space of the gTLD system. Significantly, there is no residency requirement for gTLD registrants. This is a considerable advantage over independent national systems which, in many cases, have a residency requirement as a prerequisite to registration.

The IANA is the overall authority for day-to-day administration of the Internet DNS. IANA staff carry out administrative responsibilities for the assignment of IP addresses, autonomous system numbers, TLDs and other unique parameters of the DNS and its protocols.

2.2.3 *The generic Top Level Domain registration system*

There have been recent changes to the registration of the gTLD names ".com" (for commercial organisations), ".org" (for non-profit organisations) and ".net" (for network service providers). Until March 1999, NSI was the sole registrar and registry administrator for these gTLD names. Following an amendment to the cooperative agreement between the US Department of Commerce and NSI in October 1998 it was agreed that a shared registration system would be set up under which an unlimited number of registrars would compete for domain name registration business utilising one shared registry (which would continue to be operated by NSI). All domain name registrars must be accredited by ICANN and ICANN is responsible for establishing uniformity in domain name allocation and dispute resolution that binds all registrars and all domain name registrants. There are currently in excess of 130 accredited domain name registrars and information on each of them can be found at the ICANN website at *http:\\www.icann.org*. Names are allocated on a "first come, first served" basis.

In making an application for registration, the applicant enters into a contract with the relevant registrar and is subject to their terms and conditions. These terms and conditions usually require an indemnity from the applicant in respect of any liability the registrar may incur from the use or registration of the domain name. The registrar usually does not otherwise attempt to determine the legality of an application, the registrant's rights or whether the domain name may infringe a third party's rights. Provided the domain name is not identical to an existing registration it can be registered.

2.2.4 *Uniform dispute resolution policy*

Registrars are required to make it a condition of registration of the ".com", ".net" and ".org" domains that all domain name disputes be subject to the ICANN Uniform Domain Name Dispute Resolution Policy (the "UDRP"), approved by ICANN on 24 October 1999, effective 1 December 1999. The UDRP allows cancellation or transfer of the disputed domain name. The complainant must show under paragraph 4(a) of the UDRP that the domain name:

(a) is identical or confusingly similar to a trade mark or service mark of the complainant; and

(b) holder has no rights or legitimate interests in the domain name; and

(c) has been registered and is being used in bad faith.

The UDRP offers guidance on establishing factor (2) – that there is a legitimate interest in the domain name. Paragraph 4(c) of the UDRP provides that this may be shown where:

(a) there is evidence of the registrant's use of, or demonstrable preparations to use, the domain name with a bona fide offering of goods or services; or

(b) the registrant has been commonly known by the domain name, even if the registrant has not acquired trade mark or service mark rights; or

(c) the registrant is making a legitimate non-commercial or fair use of the domain name, without intent for commercial gain to misleadingly divert consumers or to tarnish the trade mark or service mark at issue.

However these factors are neither conclusive nor exhaustive and any evidence as to a lawful interest in the domain name can be sufficient.

Various panels have held that there has to be a rational relationship between the proposed use and the domain name.[1] For example vague and abstract marketing ideas[2] have been found to be insufficient to support a showing of a legitimate interest. Conversely, the panel in *Digitronics Inventioneering v. @Six.Net Registered*[3] held that evidence that showed the registrant had used and was known by the disputed domain name for four years prior to the decision, even though it did not hold the trade mark or service mark rights to the name, was sufficient to establish a legitimate interest.

Bad faith initially seemed to be a difficult requirement to satisfy, as the complainant had to establish both registration in bad faith and that the domain name was currently being used in bad faith. However, in cases heard to date panellists have taken a reasonably liberal approach. Paragraph 4(b) of the UDRP, sets out examples of activity which will satisfy the bad faith requirement:

(a) circumstances indicating that a registrant has registered or acquired the domain name primarily for the purpose of selling, renting, or otherwise transferring the domain name registration to the complainant or to a competitor of that complainant at a cost in excess of the costs of acquiring the domain name; or

(b) the registrant has registered the domain name in order to prevent the owner of the trade mark or service mark from using the mark in a corresponding domain name (provided that the registrant was engaged in a pattern of such conduct); or

(c) the registrant has registered the domain name primarily for the purpose of disrupting the business of a competitor; or

(d) by using the domain name, the registrant has for commercial gain intentionally attempted to attract people by creating a likelihood of confusion with the complainant's mark as to the source, sponsorship, affiliation, or endorsement of its website by the complainant.

---

[1]   *20th Century Fox Film Corp. v. Risser* NAF Case FA0093761 (decided 15 February 2000).

[2]   *Boardwalk Bank v. Thorogood*, World Intellectual Property Organisation ("WIPO") Case No. D2000-0213 (decided 20 May 2000).

[3]   WIPO case No. D2000–0008 (decided March 2000).

Bad faith is not necessarily limited to positive action.[4] While it is still necessary to prove that the domain name has not only been registered and is being used in bad faith it is possible that, in certain circumstances, inactivity by the registrant can amount to the domain name being used in bad faith.[5] This allows a trade mark owner who believes that a domain name is identical or confusingly similar to its trade mark to use the dispute resolution procedure even where that domain name is not in use.

2.2.5 *Making a complaint under the UDRP*

Complaints are handled by an ICANN approved dispute-resolution service provider. At the time of writing there are five approved service providers: CPR, Institute for Dispute Resolution, eResolution, the National Arbitration Forum and the WIPO. Each service provider has their own set of supplementary rules to which the complainant must comply in addition to the rules of the UDRP.

To commence proceedings a complainant submits a complaint to an approved service provider in the form and containing the detail required by the rules of the UDRP and supplemental rules of the service provider. This complaint must include the grounds on which the complaint is made and supporting documentation including, in particular:

(a) the manner in which the domain name is identical or confusingly similar to the complainant's trade mark or service mark; and

(b) why the registrant should be considered as having no rights to or legitimate interests concerning the disputed domain name; and

(c) why the domain name has been registered and is being used in bad faith.

On receiving the complaint in the appropriate form the service provider will forward the complaint to the registrant of the contested domain name. The registrant has 20 days to provide a response with supporting material. The parties can elect a three member panel or single member panel to adjudicate. The panel decides the conduct of the proceedings and only in exceptional circumstances will there be an oral hearing. Usually the panel will make its decision within 14 days of appointment.

The UDRP does not attempt to prevent complainants from commencing independant court proceedings. If a panel decides that a disputed domain name should be cancelled or transferred, the registrar will wait 10 days before implementing that decision to see if court proceedings are commenced. Where proceedings are commenced, the registrar will take no further action until the proceedings are concluded or settled.

---

4   *Telstra Corporation Limited v. Nuclear Marshmallows*, WIPO Case No. D2000-0003.

5   The policy lists three such circumstances where passive holding can amount to use in bad faith; namely an intention to sell, the domain name to the complainant or complainant's competitor; registering a domain name in order to prevent the owner of the trade mark or service mark from reflecting the mark in a corresponding domain name; or registering a domain name for the primary purpose of disrupting the business of a competitor. This list is not exhaustive and it is conceivable, after the *Telstra* decision that other instances of passive holding can constitute use in bad faith. Other panel decisions are more reserved in expansively defining bad faith *Cf World Wrestling Federation Entertainment Inc. v. Michael Bosman*, WIPO Case No. D99-0001.

2.2.6 *Country code registration systems*

The rules for domain name registration in different countries vary considerably. Some have a residency requirement, while others register on a "first come, first served" basis. More than 50 jurisdictions allow anyone to register a domain, including the UK, the US, South Africa, Switzerland and New Zealand. However, although being open to all comers, each system may impose restrictions. As an example, the Australian system requires that:

(a) the applicant must be a commercial entity operating in Australia, either as a registered body or having rights to the commercial name;

(b) the domain name is directly derived from the legal name of the entity applying for registration;

(c) it is not a generic or highly descriptive word;

(d) it is not an offensive or obscene word;

(e) it is not an unqualified Australian place name; and

(f) the applicant warrants that it does not infringe any third party's rights.

These fairly broad restrictions are specifically imposed to try to ensure that conflict between trade mark, trade name owners and domain name registrants is minimised, and that fraudulent registration is eliminated. Other countries which impose restrictions of similar reason include Ireland and Bulgaria. Both policies preclude the registration of a domain name which is "likely to lead to confusion", such as with famous local names or well-known international marks. This kind of policy places the registries in the position of quasi-statutory controllers of their country's domain name registration system but, if appropriately administered, can limit the number of obvious potential conflicts and help prevent piracy of well-known marks in accordance with international obligations under the Paris and Trade Related Aspects of Intellectual Property Rights ("TRIPs") conventions. Maligned parties still have the opportunity of applying to the courts for relief.

Dispute-resolution policies also vary between different jurisdictions. Many are based on the premise that the registry will play no part in dispute resolution and that the parties must resolve any dispute themselves. Some registries make applicants for domain name agree to submit to a specific dispute-resolution procedure (in the event that a dispute arises) and agree to be bound by that decision. Up-to-date details of worldwide registries and specialised services with experience in domain registration can be found on the IANA website at *http://www.iana.org.*

WIPO has set up a ccTLD program to provide assistance to the administrators of ccTLDs in designing domain name practices and polices, especially in the area of dispute resolution. So far 32 administrators of ccTLDs have relied on WIPO's advice and 14 ccTLDs use WIPO for dispute resolution. WIPO is currently preparing a voluntary set of intellectual property guidelines for the benefit of ccTLD administrators. Information on the status and implementation of these initiatives can be found on the WIPO website at *http:\\www.WIPO.org.*

2.3   Domain name disputes

Since the first edition of this Guide there has been an explosion in reported domain name dispute cases. This is due both to the ever increasing competition worldwide to secure domain name registrations and to the establishment of dedicated dispute resolution organisations.

The majority of reported domain name disputes involve:

(a) well-known trade mark proprietors trying to protect their globally recognised trade marks and brand names against pirates who are attempting to "cybersquat";

(b) competitors seeking to trade on the established proprietor's goodwill and reputation; or

(c) a non-competing business from the same or different jurisdictions who registers its own domain name in good faith, or who specifically chose a domain name as a method of redirecting web traffic to its Internet site.

In general established trade mark owners in categories (a) and (b) have been successful in obtaining a remedy whether through a dispute resolution procedure, or in court, provided they can show that their mark has been used by the domain name owner in bad faith and as a trade mark. However where as in category (c) the parties are not in direct competition and therefore cannot rely on traditional theories of trade mark infringement, their prospects are likely to turn on the domain name owner's intent and whether the use constitutes a dilution of the trade mark owner's rights or unfair competition in a particular jurisdiction. The choice of dispute resolution forum particularly for cases in category (c) may be crucial in determining the final outcome.

2.3.1   *Cybersquatting*

"Cybersquatting" is the term coined for a prior registrant registering a domain name for the purpose of extorting a settlement payment from the bona fide trade mark or trade name owner. In cases where the fraudulent registrant is not providing the same goods and services as the trade mark owner, or is not "using" the trade mark in the requisite sense, traditional trade mark infringement remedies have usually proved ineffective.

The trend in both common law and civil law jurisdictions has been for courts to strive to interpret existing laws to control cybersquatting. Courts have been prepared to grant remedies in passing off or under unfair competition laws. Trade mark owners in the US initially turned to common law, statutory state dilution remedies and, to the Federal Trademark Dilution Act to control uses which allegedly diluted the distinctiveness of their trade marks. More recently they have been able to take advantage of the first tailor made anti-cybersquatting law – the Anticybersquatting Protection Act (the "ACPA").

Although many cybersquatting disputes will now be resolved under the UDRP, in cases where it is not applicable, or either party commences court proceedings, then the parties will need to consider their prospects based on the existing trade mark laws, or cybersquatting specific legislation applicable in that jurisdiction. A description of the US ACPA, some examples of decisions by panellists based on the UDRP and descriptions of some leading decisions follow.

2.3.2   *The US Anti-cybersquatting Protection Act*

The ACPA came into force on 29 November 1999. The Act protects famous and "distinctive" trade marks against a person who registers, traffics in, or uses an identical or confusingly similar domain name in bad faith with an intent to profit from it. Importantly there is no requirement for there to be competition between the parties in relation to the same goods and services, or a likelihood of confusion as required in a US trade mark infringement action. A trade mark owner can seek injunctive relief (including forfeiture, cancellation or transfer of the domain name), and elect either damages and profits, or an award of statutory damages of between $1000 to US$100 000 per domain name at the court's discretion. The Act is retrospective in operation, insofar as it enables an action to be brought against a domain name that was registered before the commencement of the Act, although in these circumstances damages are not available.

As with the UDRP it is the bad faith element which presents the greatest challenge to litigants. The Act sets out a list of nine matters to be considered in determining bad faith. These are:

(a) the intellectual property ownership rights of the domain name holder in the domain name;

(b) the extent to which the domain name consists of the legal name of the domain name holder or is a name which is otherwise commonly used to identify the domain name holder;

(c) the domain name holder's prior use of the domain name in connection with the bona fide offering of any goods or services;

(d) the domain name holder's bona fide non-commercial use or fair use of the mark in a site accessible under the domain name;

(e) the domain name holder's intent to divert consumers from the trade mark owner's online location (whether for commercial gain or to disparage the trade mark) by creating a likelihood of confusion as to the source, sponsorship, affiliation, or endorsement of the site;

(f) offering to resell the domain name to the trade mark owner or a third person for profit without having used or intended to use the domain name to offer any goods or services themselves;

(g) the domain name holder's provision of material and misleading false contact information when applying for registration of the domain name and its intentional failure to correctly maintain this information or a prior pattern of conduct indicating this;

(h) the domain name holder's registration of multiple domain names that are identical or confusingly similar to others' trade marks;

(i) the extent to which a trade mark is incorporated in the domain name and is distinctive or famous.

The Act enables an "in rem" claim to be brought against act of registration of the domain name, instead of against the registrant of a domain name, which overcomes difficulties in locating and proceeding against the domain name owner.

2.3.2.1   *Electronics Boutique Holdings Corp. v. Zuccarini*

A cybersquatter registered dozens of domain names based on the possible misspelling of popular websites. Upon typing in these domain names the Internet surfer was lured into a "mousetrap" in which a series of advertising windows appeared in succession, earning the cybersquatter 10 to 25 cents for each click on the advertisement. The US District Court found that the respondent had registered various misspelled variations of the plaintiff's trade mark which were confusingly similar to it and found that the defendant's registration and use were in bad faith. The Court awarded the maximum statutory damages under the ACPA of $100,000 per domain name, noting the previous suits brought against the respondent and the wide victimisation caused by its business. The judgment shows the seriousness with which courts in the US view cybersquatting and their preparedness in appropriate circumstances to apply the ACPA to its maximum effect.

2.3.3   *ICANN dispute resolution cybersquatting decisions*

The trend overall seems to indicate a strong bias in favour of trade mark owners.[6] A distinctive trade mark or a generic trade mark which has acquired a strong secondary meaning is likely to diminish the domain name registrant's rights or legitimate interests and is more likely to support a finding that the registrant had constructive notice of the trade mark owner's interests at the time of registration and therefore acted in bad faith. Correspondingly, the more generic the domain name, the more likely it is that the domain name registrant has a legitimate interest and has not acted in bad faith. Decisions by different panellists and concerning cases from differing jurisdictions can however result in unpredictable outcomes as is demonstrated by the cases discussed below.

2.3.3.1   *J. Crew International Inc. v. crew.com*[7]

In this case the well known clothing retailer J. Crew International Inc. claimed that the US-based respondent's domain name "*crew.com*" was identical to its CREW trade mark or confusingly similar to its J.CREW trade mark. It alleged that the respondent was a domain name speculator who had no legitimate interest in the domain name and used the domain name in bad faith by purposefully precluding the complainant from registering either trade mark as a domain name. The respondent maintained that its use was legitimate in that it was developing the domain name for its own use and sale to clients and that it had no knowledge of the complainant's trade marks when it registered the domain name. The respondent also alleged that it had an association with the complainant as a member of the complainant's affiliate network and had dealt with the complainant in good faith at least up to the point of the respondent's refusal to sell the domain name to the complainant for a nominal sum.

The majority of the panel found that the respondent had no demonstable plan to use the domain name, had engaged in a pattern of conduct involving speculative registration of domain names and therefore had no legitimate interest to its registration. Further, the respondent had knowingly precluded the complainant from registering domain names identical to its trade mark as it had proceeded with its registration even though it had constructive notice of the complainant's trade mark registration.

---

[6]   De Souza, Chad, "Specific Remedies for Cybersquatting", Part 1, Internet law Bulletin, vol. 3, no. 4, July 2000 and "Specific Remedies for Cybersquatting" Part 2, Internet law Bulletin, vol. 3, no. 5, August 2000.

[7]   WIPO Case No. D2000-0054, 20 April 2000.

The dissenting panellist strongly disagreed with this decision on the grounds that a trade mark owner is not entitled to all domain names which incorporate, or are identical to, its trade mark. Speculation *per se* is not sufficient under the UDRP to support a finding of no legitimate interest and of abusive registration unless there is evidence of infringement, dilution, or a bad faith intent to profit commercially from the trade mark. The panellist points out that with generic terms such as "crew" (as opposed to famous marks or generic marks which have acquired secondary meaning) it is not possible to automatically impute the respondent with a bad faith intent to sell the domain name to the complainant, particularly as in this case where there was no evidence of an attempt to create confusion and in fact the complainant had invited the respondent to link to its website.

The panellist suggests that the UDRP is appropriate for cases involving abusive registrations where there is a bad faith intent to profit commercially from a trade mark but was never intended to govern disputes such as this concerning a legitimate dispute of trade mark interests. In his view the majority decision goes beyond the ambit of the policy in attempting to address a dispute which the UDRP was not designed to handle. In doing so, it wrongly creates a new test focussed on whether the respondent had a bona fide purpose or use in mind prior to acquisition of the domain name rather than following the three-step test mandated by the UDRP.

By contrast the panels in *Allocation Network GmbH v. Steve Gregory*[8] and *General Machine Products Company Inc. v. Prime Domains (a/k/a Telepathy Inc.)*[9] found that the domain name broker respondents were entitled to retain their registrations because in either case they had a legitimate interest in their respective domain names and there was no evidence of bad faith. In both cases the domain names were generic or descriptive words without a demonstrated secondary meaning, there was no evidence that the respondents knew of the complainants' trade mark registrations at the date of domain name registration (there was no question of imputing constructive notice even where both respondents were US-based) and there was no evidence that the domain names had been chosen with intent to profit from or otherwise abuse the complainants' trade mark rights. The emerging principle based on the UDRP test appears to be that a domain name broker's simple act of registration of a generic mark will not be enough to show that it does not have a legitimate interest and some intentional action must be demonstrated to show bad faith.[10]

As can be seen the choice of forum for cybersquatting cases is therefore best determined according to the party's interests concerned and the complexity of issues involved. Where there is no apparent evidence of bad faith or where there are competing interests to be considered it is likely to be preferable, depending on the relevant jurisdiction, to refer the matter to the courts.

2.3.3.2 US – *Intermatic Inc. v. Toeppen*[11]

Prior to the introduction of the Act courts had in some cases taken advantage of anti-dilution statutes in order to prevent cybersquatters from registering domain names for famous marks. The Intermatic case was an early example of this remedy in action.

---

[8] WIPO Case No. D2000-0016, 24 March 2000.

[9] National Arbitration Forum File FA0001000092531.

[10] *See* also the decision in *Cigna Corporation v. JIT Consulting*, AF – 00174, 6 June 2000.

[11] *Intermatic Inc. v. Dennis Toeppen* 947 F. Supp. 12227 (N.D. I11.1996).

Toeppen registered approximately 240 domain names including such well-known business names as *deltaairlines.com, britishairways.com and neiman-marcus.com.* He had also registered *intermatic.com.* The plaintiff had a significant and well-established US-wide business and owned a US trade mark registration for the Intermatic trade mark.

Toeppen had not traded under its domain name or otherwise made use of the Intermatic name or mark. Accordingly there was no infringement because there was no evidence of actual confusion or intent to confuse on this summary judgment claim. However, the court found the mere act of registering *intermatic.com* as a domain name for the purpose of arbitrage was a commercial use and that registration breached the Federal Dilution Act, Section 43(c) of the Lanham Act and the Illinois Anti-Dilution Act because it lessened the capacity of Intermatic (which the court found to be a famous mark) to identify and distinguish goods and services, and it diluted the trade mark by blurring.

2.3.3.3 UK – Marks & Spencer plc v. One In A Million Limited and Others[12]

In jurisdictions such as the UK, where there is no separate theory of trade mark dilution, it was until recently considered very difficult to restrain the activities of domain name arbitragers who have never used the domain name in the same field of activity as the bona fide trade mark owner.[13] Faced with the prospect of having to pay significant sums to purchase variations on their existing domain names or to risk third parties trading on their reputations, a number of well-known trade mark owners in the UK decided to test the state of English law with surprising effect.

Marks & Spencer have a number of domain names including *marks-and-spencer.co.uk* and *marks-and-spencer.com.* One In A Million Limited and its directors operated as dealers in domain names and made a practice of registering the names or trade marks of well-known companies as domain names with the intention of selling the names to a company or third party who would be interested in using the domain name to trade off the reputation and good will attaching to a well-known company's name.

One In A Million Limited registered the domain name *marksandspencer.com* with NSI in the US and *marksandspencer.co.uk* with Nominet in the UK; the only difference between these names and Mark's and Spencer's own domain names being the omission of hyphens. The arbitrageur also registered domain names such as *sainsbury.com, ladbrokes.com* and *virgin.org* amongst others.

The plaintiffs claimed passing off and trade mark infringement under Section 10 (3) of the Trade Marks Act 1994. Although the court noted that mere registration of a domain name is not passing off in itself, it found that the arbitragers' actions were clearly intended to injure Marks & Spencer's frights in the future as it could be assumed that a third party would only wish to purchase the domain name if it sought to pass its products off as Marks & Spencer's. The defendant's arguments that neither the sale of the domain name to Marks

---

12   *Marks & Spencer plc v. One In A Million Limited and Others,* High Court, Chancery Div, 28 November 1997; *see* report at http//www.nic.uk/news/legal/oiam-judgement.html. Affirmed by the Court of Appeal, Chancery Division, report at http://www.nic.uk/news/legal/oiam-appeal-judgement.html.

13   The successful injunction proceedings against an arbitrageur in *Harrods Ltd v. UK Network Services Ltd & Others* (unreported) are not representative as they were undefended. *See* discussion of this case by D Osborne, "Domain Names, Registration and Dispute Resolution and Recent UK Cases" [1997] 11 E.I.P.R. 644.

& Spencer, nor its retention as a blocking mechanism, constituted passing off were rejected on the basis that Marks & Spencer would not be concerned unless there was a potential risk of deception. The final injunction sought by the plaintiff did not require proof of damage; it was enough that the registrations were intended to cause the plaintiff damage in the future.

Relying on Section 10 (3) of the Trade Marks Act 1994, which protects marks with "reputation in the UK" where they are used in a different field of activity, Marks & Spencer alleged that the defendant was infringing its rights by using a similar trade mark which was detrimental to the exclusivity and reputation of its trade mark in the UK. The court rejected the defendant's argument that use of the domain name had not been "in the course of trade" by holding that this did not infer any requirement for use as a trade mark, but merely that the trade mark was used in the course of business such as in the course of the arbitrager's business. While indicating that the likelihood of confusion was not necessarily implied in Section 10 (3), the court found that, even if this was a requirement, members of the public who in the future searched for Marks & Spencer's website were likely to be confused by a third party's registration for *marksandspencer.co.uk*. Therefore mere registration of the similar domain name and the consequent likelihood of future infringement would support an injunction to restrain the defendant's continued arbitrage of these domain names. The defendant was ordered to transfer the domain names back to Marks & Spencer.

This decision has subsequently been affirmed on appeal and offers considerable comfort for UK trade mark owners that they can retrieve confusingly similar domain name registrations from unscrupulous arbitragers in the UK, quite apart from any possibility of seeking relief under a domain name dispute resolution procedure.

2.3.3.4 *DB Breweries Ltd v. The Domain Name Company*

The New Zealand High Court expressly adopted the *One In A Million* case in this decision in August 2000. It involved a passing off action by a well known New Zealand brewing company and the registered proprietor of the DB trade mark, against the domain name holders of *www.db.co.nz*. The Court held that given the well known history of the plaintiff's company and the business of the defendant, it was an "irresistible conclusion" that it was the intention of the defendants to appropriate the good will of the plaintiff, or to enable others to do so. Notwithstanding that there was no actual use of the domain name, by expressly adopting the approach taken in the *One In A Million* case, the Court was prepared to grant interlocutory injunctive relief.

2.3.3.5 *Civil law jurisdictions*

Civil law jurisdictions have the potential to offer more satisfactory remedies against cybersquatters than many common law jurisdictions. EC jurisdictions feature trade mark laws based on the broad protections given in the European Trade Mark Directive[14] and may include protection based on the anti-dilution provision in Article 5(2) of the Directive. They also tend to have well-developed unfair competition laws which usually offer a remedy in the circumstances where the cybersquatter is obviously acting in bad faith, even

---

14   European Trade Mark Directive 89/104.

if the hijacked domains are not in use. The *Epson.de* case demonstrates the use of both the causes of action and the level of protection provided by the German Civil Code[15] for the protection of trading names against unlawful use and unauthorised registration as domain names by third parties.

2.3.3.6 *"Epson.de" Case*[16] *– Germany*

The defendant registered 200 domain names including the names and trade marks of well-known companies and *epson.de* incorporating EPSON, the trade mark of the well known computer manufacturer. The defendant had offered to sell the domain name to the computer manufacturer but, on receiving a better offer from one of its distributors, permitted the distributor to use the domain name on payment of a monthly fee.

The court found that, although merely registered in the domain name as a trade mark does not amount to using the trade mark in the course of trade, there was an imminent danger that a third party would use the domain name in trade and in those circumstances relief should be granted for the trade mark infringement under Section 12 of the German Civil Code. Further, the registration of a domain name for unscrupulous purposes was *contra bonos mores* and contravened the German unfair competition law. The defendant was ordered to cancel the *epson.de* domain name registration.

2.3.4 *Prior domain name registration for use in connection with the same field of activity*

A trade mark or trade name owner may find that someone else has registered a domain name which is very similar, if not identical, to its existing trade mark or business name. The parties may be unwitting bona fide applicants from different jurisdictions or, if from the same jurisdiction, may attempt to claim concurrent rights to the domain name. Alternatively the parties may be competitors seeking to trade off the other's goodwill or to disparage its reputation. The prior trade name (or trade mark) owner seeks the removal of the domain name on the basis of prior usage rights and/or infringement of its trade mark because the defendant is using the mark in the same, or a related, field of activity.

Where a respondent knowingly acted in bad faith in registering a domain name which is similar to a well known or reputed trade mark it is very likely that there will be circumstances which enable a UDRP panel to find that the respondent has acted in bad faith and has no legitimate interest, or in which a court will be justified in granting a remedy based on trade mark infringement, dilution or an unfair competition type remedy.

Where the parties had no apparent intent to trade off the other's reputation, then the same result may not be achievable under the UDRP as in court proceedings as a complainant under the UDRP must show that the respondent acted both in bad faith and had no legitimate interest in the domain name. In addition UDRP complaints which involve complex competing interests, have generally been identified by panellists as being unsuitable for this forum as the panel has no jurisdiction to deal with additional issues. This type of case is more appropriately resolved by the courts.

---

[15]   Section 12 BGB – Guiding Principles from cases decided under this provision suggest that: (a) a domain name will be protected as a trade name against reservation by third parties (LG Frankfurt, 26 February 1997, 2/6 O 633/96; CR 97, 287; Zahrnt, BB97, 1120); (b) use by a third party of a name as a domain name or a sub-domain is unlawful if unauthorised (LG Luneberg, 29 January 1997, 3 O 336/96; GRUR 97, 470; Stromer, CR 97, 288).

[16]   *"Epson.de"* – Landgericht Dusseldorf, 4 April 1997; 34 O 191/96 as reported in [1997] 13 E.I.P.R. at D-11.

2.3.5 Bad faith examples

2.3.5.1 Playboy Enterprises Inc. v. Calvin Designer Label[17]

A Californian website registered in the domain names *playboyxxx.com* and *playmatelive.com*, incorporating the plaintiff's registered trade marks Playmate and Playboy. Playboy Enterprises Inc. ("Playboy") claimed trade mark infringement and unfair competition. The district court found that there was a sufficient likelihood of success on both claims and issued a temporary restraining order requiring the website publisher to cease using the domain names containing Playboy's trade marks and requesting NSI to cancel the domain name registrations and to pass control of the names to the court.

2.3.5.2 Cardservice International Inc. v. McGee[18]

Cardservice International Inc. ("CSI") owned a registered trade mark for Cardservice International in respect of credit and debit card processing services. McGee had attempted to become a representative of CSI without CSI's permission and had registered the domain name *cardservice.com*. The court had previously directed McGee to cease all use of "cardservice" on the Internet and to delete all references from its site. This order was made on the basis that there was a likelihood of confusion between CSI's registered trade mark and McGee's domain name – Internet users accessing McGee's website might believe that they had reached CSI, or even if they did know who they had reached, might take advantage of McGee's services instead of CSI's.

McGee had subsequently registered a new site *csimall.com* which obviously included an acronym derived from SCI's domain name and mark. The court found that McGee, in breach of its earlier injunction, had acted in bad faith and with malicious intent, and granted relief including a substantial award for attorney's fees.

2.3.5.3 Societe Co-operative Agricole Champagne Cereales v. G.J.[19]

This is the first French case in which a court has upheld the rights of an unregistered trade mark owner against a global ".com" domain name registrant. The plaintiff a company called Champagne Cereales had operated under this name for 70 years and had a company registration for this name. The defendant competitor of the plaintiff registered and began using the domain names *champagnecereale.com* and *champagne-cereale.com*. The court found that the use and registration of the names created a likelihood of confusion and traded on the plaintiff company's goodwill. Accordingly the court granted the plaintiff an injunction, damages and fined the defendant.

2.3.5.4 ColArt Fine Art & Graphics Ltd v. Art2 Art LLC[20]

ColArt Fine Art & Graphics Limited owns and operates an art supply business identified for many years by the well known trade mark Winsor & Newton. It owns worldwide trade mark registrations for this mark. Art2Art LLC is also in the art supply business, but did not manufacture goods, instead offering products for sale manufactured by others,

---

[17]   *Playboy Enterprises Inc. v. Calvin Designer Label* No. C-97-3204 (N.D. 8 September 1997).

[18]   *Cardservice International Inc. v. McGee* 950 F. Supp. 737 (E.D. Va. 16 January 1997).

[19]   *Tribunal de Grande Instance de Versailles*, 14 April 1998.

[20]   WIPO Case No. D2000 – 1410.

including by ColArt. Without authorisation Art2Art registered the domain name *windsornewton.com* and used it as a link to its own website until the point at which it received a letter of demand from ColArt.

In spite of the lack of submission by Art2Art, the panel found that Art2Art had no legitimate interest and was prepared to infer bad faith on the basis of Art2Art's conduct in registering a confusingly similar domain name to draw customers to a competing enterprise. The panel ordered that the subject domain name be transferred to ColArt.

2.3.6 *No apparent intent cases*

2.3.6.1 *Gateway 2000 Inc. v. Gateway.com.Inc.*[21]

Gateway 2000 Inc. is a Fortune 500 computer manufacturer and owns a trade mark registration for Gateway 2000. The defendant, a computer service consultancy, had registered *gateway.com* as its domain name six years before the plaintiff brought its claim and a number of years prior to the plaintiff's trade mark registration.

Gateway 2000 Inc. claimed trade mark infringement and dilution. The court found that there was no infringement because the plaintiff had not shown that "Gateway", as opposed to "Gateway 2000", had been used as a mark to identify the company before the defendant's use commenced, and that there was no evidence to suggest that the defendant had in any way chosen to trade on the computer manufacturer's goodwill, or would advantage itself by doing so. In order to succeed in the Federal Trademark Dilution Act claim, the plaintiff had to show that the alleged dilution began after its mark became famous. Although Gateway 2000 was a famous mark at the date of the claim, there was insufficient evidence to suggest that it was famous in 1988 when the defendant began using its domain name.

2.3.6.2 *Pitman Training Limited v. Nominet UK*[22]

Both the plaintiffs – Pitman Training Limited and PTC Oxford Limited (its franchisee in the office skills business) – and the second defendant, Pearson Professional Limited are entitled to trade under the name "Pitman" in the UK. Pearson Professional Limited registered *pitman.co.uk* for its long-established publishing division "Pitman Publishing" but did not attempt to connect its website to the domain name for some months. On doing so it found that the domain had been removed from the server and due to an error by Nominet (the UK Registrar), had been reassigned to PTC Oxford Limited and had been used by that company in good faith for more than six months. Pearson Professional Limited demanded the return of the name from PTC and, when this was refused, requested that Nominet intervene on the basis that Pearson Professional Limited had been the first to register according to Nominet's "first-in-time" policy. Nominet complied with this requests and the plaintiffs brought proceedings to reclaim the domain name, claiming amongst other things that use of the domain name by Pitman Publishing was passing off.

---

[21]   *Gateway 2000 Inc. v. Gateway.com.Inc.* (1997) US Dist. Lexis 2144 (E.D.N.C. 6 February 1997).

[22]   *Pitman Training v. Nominet UK* (1997) F.S.R 797.

At the final hearing the court rejected any suggestion of passing off as Pitman Publishing had been trading under the "Pitman" name for around 150 years. There was no evidence that little more than six months' use of the domain name by PTC had cause the public to associate the domain name with PTC, or had resulted in any confusion other than that resulting from both companies continuing to trade under the "Pitman" name.

2.3.6.3 *Weber-Stephen Products Co. v. Armitage Hardware*[23]

The respondent in this WIPO domain name dispute is a distributor of Weber products and had registered and was using a series of domain names incorporating the complainant's registered trade marks, including the *webergrills.com* domain name for its web page. For several years the respondent also used the complainant's trade mark on its web page in advertising the complainant's products, but clearly stated that it was acting as the Respondent's authorised distributor.

The panel found that the complainant had failed to show that the respondent had acted in bad faith and noted that if there were contractual or other issues which affected the parties' dispute than these should be dealt with in the parallel district court proceedings which would procedurally allow for the resolution of competing contractual and trade mark interests.[24]

2.3.7 *Prior domain name registration for use in connection with different fields of activity*

With increasing frequency, a well-known trade mark or business name owner finds that a company involved in a quite unrelated commercial activity has already registered a domain name which is identical or similar to the first company's business name or trade mark. Consistent with the purpose of the UDRP in defeating cybersquatters, complainants will not succeed in these circumstances if they cannot assert that the domain name registrant has acted in bad faith. Further if the domain name registrant is using the domain name in relation to goods or services which are distinct from those of the plaintiff, then without some element of improper purpose, it will be difficult to assert that the registrant has no legitimate interest in the domain name. In this type of case complainants will need to look to their remedies at law.If the parties are from the same jurisdiction, the proprietor of the well-known name or mark may be able to seek removal of the domain by claiming trade mark dilution or passing off. In the US the dilution remedy is well developed at both state and federal levels for "famous" trade marks.

To date there is no equivalent remedy currently available in the UK. On a literal reading Section 10 (3) of the Trade Marks Act 1994 goes some way towards filling this gap, but to date has been given a restrictive interpretation by English courts and only applies in circumstances where there is a likelihood of confusion between the marks.[25] If, as appears

---

[23]   WIPO Case No. D 2000–0187.

[24]   *See* also the similar example of the panel's decision in *Draw-Tite Inc. v. Plattsburgh Spring Inc.* WIPO Case No. D2000–0017. *See* also the similar factual scenario and result in *Bravilor Bonamat B.V. v. Bouman Hotelbenodigdheden B.V.*, Amsterdam District Court reported in International IT and New Media Update, Freshfields Bruckhaus Deringer.

[25]   BASF plc v. CEP (UK) plc [Knox. J., 26 May 1995, unreported]; *Baywatch Production Co. Inc. v. Home Video Channel* [1997] FSR 22.

to have been the original intention in the preamble to the European Trade Mark Directive[26] (as confirmed by the European Court of Justice in *Sabel B.V. v. Puma*)[27] , the section is not to be restricted to a "likelihood of confusion" analysis, then there may be an effective remedy in these situations in the UK.

German, French and Dutch courts have already demonstrated their readiness to provide a remedy where an established and well-known name or mark is misappropriated by a third party for use in its domain name, whether by means of trade mark law, unfair competition or in the case of law Germany using the relevant provision of the German Civil Code. In general terms, trade mark law remedies for less well-known marks and names are limited and a remedy may only be available in these circumstances where there is obvious evidence of bad faith and where the required elements of unfair competition are present.

2.3.8 *Same jurisdiction cases*

2.3.8.1 *Hasbro Inc. v. Internet Entertainment Group Ltd*[28]

Hasbro Inc. owns the trade mark Candyland; it is registered for a children's game which Hasbro has manufactured for 47 years. The Internet Entertainment Group Ltd registered the domain name *candyland.com* for a sexually explicit adult entertainment site.

Hasbro claimed trade mark dilution under the US federal and state statutes. The court found that Hasbro's claim was likely to succeed on the merits and ordered the defendant not to use "candyland" as a name or mark in connection with its Internet activities and to discontinue use of its domain name.

2.3.8.2 *Toys "Я' Us Inc. v. Akkaoui*[29]

In this case the court issued an injunction preventing the defendant, Akkaoui, from suing the domain name *adultsrus.com*, or any variation of it, for an Internet site and shopping service for adult entertainment products. The court found Toys " Я " Us and Kids " Я " Us to be famous marks which would be tarnished by association with the inconsistent image portrayed by the *adultsrus.com* adult shopping service.

2.3.8.3 *Hasbro Inc. v. Clue Computing Inc.*[30]

Hasbro Inc. the owner of the trade mark "Clue" in relation to a popular board game claimed that the defendant had infringed and diluted its trade mark by registering the domain name *www.clue.com* for promotion of the defendant's computer consulting business. The court found that there was no likelihood of confusion to support an infringement claim, the mark did not meet the "famous" prerequisite for relief under the Federal Trade Mark Dilution Act and there had in any event been no dilution in the

---

26   European Trade Mark Directive 89/104.

27   *Sabel B.V. v. Puma*, C-251/95 [unreported 11 November 1997].

28   *Hasbro Inc. v. Internet Entertainment Group Ltd*, 40 U.S.P.Q 2d 1479 (W.D. Wash. 9 February 1996).

29   *Toys 'Я" Us v. Akkaoui* No. 96-3381 CW, 1996 US Dist. Lexis 17090 (N.D. Cal. 29 October 1996).

30   66F. Supp. 2d 117 (D. Mass. 1999).

requisite sense. This case supports the proposition that well known mark owners are not entitled as of right to a domain name based on the registration. A "first-in-time" domain name registrant, even of a well known mark, will be able to protect that registration in the US provided that there is no evidence of trade mark infringement or dilution.

2.3.8.4 *Virtual Works Inc. v. Network Solutions Inc. and Volkswagen of America Inc.*[31]

The plaintiff is a website development, hosting an e-commerce company which registered the domain name *www.vw.net* and commenced a site under this domain name advertising its services. At some point the plaintiff had offered to sell its domain name to the defendant, and had once posted a disparaging remark about the defendant on its website. The plaintiff did not trade under the mark VW and did not have an equivalent trade mark registration and there was some evidence of consumer confusion. In these circumstances the court found that the plaintiff's conduct in registering and using the domain name amounted to cyberpiracy, trade mark dilution and trade mark infringement.

2.3.8.5 *L'Affaire St. Tropez*

In L'Affaire St. Tropez,[32] the St. Tropez city authorities held various trade mark registrations for Saint Tropez and had registered a domain name in French domain space under the name *nova.fr/saint-tropez>*.

A French company involved in computer communications, which had previously assisted the city authorities in setting up its website, registered *saint-tropez.com* with the NSI. The St. Tropez city authorities claimed trade mark infringement and unfair competition in that the French company had unlawfully traded on its goodwill. In finding for the city authorities the court accepted jurisdiction because the information on the *saint-tropez.com* site was accessible to the French public. The court indirectly referred to the parties' previous working relationship and the defendant's bad faith in choosing its domain name and ruled that, for the purposes of infringement, even though the city's trade mark registrations did not extend to computer communications, there was still a sufficient likelihood of people confusing the domains and sties in spite of any differences between the TLDs. Although the general principle of French trade mark law appears to be that, unless a mark is well known, a competing field of activity is a prerequisite to a finding of trade mark infringement,[33] the city authority's claim for unfair competition did not require similar fields of activity and, in view of the previous relationship between the parties and Eurovirtuel's bad faith, the court was prepared to find that Eurovirtuel had unlawfully traded on the plaintiff's reputation and goodwill. The defendant company has appealed against the decision.

---

[31]   2000 US Dist. Lexis 2670 (E.D. Va. 24 February 2000).

[32]   *L'Affaire Saint-Tropez*, 21 August 1997, Tribunal de Grande Instance de Draguignan reported at http://www.legalis.net/ jnet/decisions/marques/tgi_sttropez.htm.

[33]   *See* L713-5 cpi; ETAM case, TGI Paris, 25 November 1993.

2.3.8.6   *"Krupp.de"*[34] – *Germany*

Mr Krupp, a private individual, registered the domain name *krupp.de* and used it to offer Internet services under the name "Krupp Kommunikation" over an 18-month period. The plaintiff was the well-known steel manufacturer "Krupp" and owned a trade mark for its name, but was unable to obtain a domain name in the German domain space because of the defendant's prior registration. The plaintiff sued for infringement of rights to its name.

The court emphasised the notoriety of the "Krupp" name in connection with the steel manufacturer and found as a result there was a likelihood under the German civil code[35] that the public would associate Krupp Kommunikation with the steel manufacturer. As the plaintiff's name was so well known, there was likelihood that the defendant's business would be associated with the plaintiff's or that the public would incorrectly infer some commercial relationship, even though the respective businesses operated in quite different fields of activity. In the circumstances the rights of the well-known name holder overcame the rights of the third party to use its own name and the defendant was restricted from using his own name without an appropriate identifier and was ordered to case using the domain name. The decision has subsequently been affirmed on appeal.[36]

2.3.8.7   *Labouchere case*[37]

IMG Holland NV ("IMG") advises investors on financial products. It registered domain names in the ".com" domain space using the trade marks and trade names of six of the largest Dutch insurance companies and banks, and set up websites under each domain name giving information on each organisation but with a clear indication that the information was provided by IMG. The organisations brought proceedings for trade mark infringement.

Even thought the use by IMG was in the nature of a comparative use which did not serve to distinguish IMG's services or products, the court found that there was an infringement of Article 13A.1.d of the Benelux Trade Mark Act (the equivalent to Article 5(5) of the Directive). IMG had used these trade marks in the course of trade in a manner which took unfair advantage of, or was detrimental to, the character or repute of the trade marks. Not only might people assume that the information originated from the banks or insurance companies themselves, but those organisations were precluded from using their own trade marks or trade names as domain names for websites in the ".com" domain space. The conduct was also in breach of Article 5 of the Dutch Trade Names Act as there was a likelihood that people would be confused by the domain names registered by IMG.

---

[34]   "krupp.de" decision of the Landgericht Bochum, 24 April 1997; 14 O 33/97; *see* report in (1997) 13 E.I.P.R. at D-10.

[35]   Cause of action was based on S 12 BGB.

[36]   OLG Koln (21 March 1997, 19 I 174/96).

[37]   Decision of the President of the District Court of Amsterdam, 15 May 1997; IER 1997, No. 44; *see* report at [1997] 13 EIPR D-14.

2.3.9 Different jurisdictions

The UDRP is likely to be of limited use to complainants from different jurisdictions where there is no reasonably obvious evidence of bad faith. However an established and reputed trade mark holder in one jurisdiction may, depending on the particular circumstances, be successful in arguing that a foreign respondent had no legitimate reason to register a confusingly similar domain name and that the panel should infer bad faith. The UDRP will not assist in cases of real honest concurrent use.

Where the parties are from different jurisdictions and operate in different fields of activity then the resolution of an ownership dispute in court is likely to hinge on the registered trade mark rights in each jurisdiction, or the degree of renown resulting from international spillover of the parties' respective reputations. Although a judgment from a foreign jurisdiction may persuade a registry to maintain a registration in favour of one party, ultimately a judgment from the legal regime in which the domain name registry is located will govern the outcome of the case.

A "dilution" or "unfair competition" type remedy may also be available, even where the domain name is registered through a foreign registry. Where a court accepts that nothing more than accessibility will suffice for it to take jurisdiction, it will be able to apply its own law to control use of the domain name in that jurisdiction. The utility of doing so from a plaintiff's perspective depends on whether the defendant has commercial interests or assets in that jurisdiction, or the judgment will suffice to persuade a foreign domain name registry to remove the registration. If the defendant has a pre-existing trade mark registration for the SLD in another jurisdiction, then depending on the relevant registry's domain name dispute resolution policy, a conflicting judgment from a third jurisdiction may ultimate be of little practical use.

2.3.9.1 Prince Sports Group v. Prince plc[38]

Prince plc, a computer services company based in the UK, registered the domain name *prince.com* through NSI (the sole gTLD registrar at that time) and also registered *prince.co.uk* in the UK domain space. Prince Sports Group Inc. the owner of various trade mark registrations for Prince both in the US and in the UK, attempted to register *prince.com* and on discovering that this name was already taken resolved to invoke NSI's dispute resolution policy by sending a letter of demand to Prince plc. The letter threatened litigation unless Prince plc assigned its *prince.com* domain name registration and refrained from using Prince as any part of its new domain name.

Prince Sports Group Inc. forwarded a copy of the letter to NSI and initiated its dispute resolution process whereby Prince plc had 30 days in which to withdraw its registration, produce a valid trade mark registration or file proceedings in the US, failing which NSI would put the domain name on hold. Prince plc did not hold a relevant trade mark registration in either jurisdiction and instead of complying with NSI's dispute resolution procedure, filed proceedings against the sporting goods manufacturer in the UK seeking a declaration under the Trade Marks Act 1994 that *prince.com* did not infringe the sporting goods manufacturer's trade mark rights and that its letter of demand was an unjustifiable threat. NSI did not enforce its policy but instead deposited the domain name registration with the English court pending a declaration. In the meantime the sporting goods manufacturer filed proceedings against both NSI and Prince plc in the US Federal Court.

---

[38] *Prince Sports Group v. Prince plc*, Ch 1997 – P2355 (Mr Justice Neuberger – action filed on 30 July 1997).

The English court held that the threat was unjustified and ordered the sporting goods manufacturer to refrain from making further threats, but refused to make any declaration concerning infringement in the UK, or in respect of ownership of the domain name because this might interfere in the pending US lawsuit.

2.3.9.2　Concertconcept.com case

MCN, a Kansas City based Internet services firm, registered the domain name *concertconcept.com*. A German company brought interim injunction proceedings in the German courts for infringement of its trade name and trade mark in Germany. The German court considered that the only justification required for it to take jurisdiction was the accessibility of the website – the fact that the host computer or domain registration was based in the US was irrelevant. The court held that the German company's rights had been infringed and issued an injunction preventing MCN from using its NSI registered domain name or variations of it, including *concertconcept.de* in the German domain space.[39]

2.3.9.3　Olly's B.V. v. CPS Korea[40]

CPS Korea Corp., a South-Korean company based in Seoul, registered the domain name *oilily.com* for intended use in connection with an an online fresh produce and flower business in Korea. Olly's B.V., a Netherlands based corporation manufactures, distributes and retails apparel and cosmetics under the trade mark Oilily and has worldwide trade mark registrations for this mark.

Olly's B.V. asserted that CPS obtained the domain name registration with full knowledge of the Complainant's long prior use and ownership of the Oilily trade mark and to obtain financial gain from the goodwill attaching to the mark. CPS maintained that Olly's trade mark was not well recognised in Korea and that it had no knowledge of the trade mark and devised and registered the domain name independantly.

The panel found that the domain name was essentially identical to Olly's mark, however CPS had a legitimate interest in its domain name and was not acting in bad faith as the panel accepted that CPS had independently devised the name in preparation of commencing an unrelated business. On this basis Olly's request for transfer of the domain name was refused.

2.3.10　*Domain name registration strategies*

The importance of undertaking both domain name and, in high-risk cases, trade mark searches, prior to making an application for the registration of a domain name, should not be underestimated. Minimise potential liability by searching as much as possible.

Provided that there are no conflicts, register immediately. "First-in-time" registration is paramount. For trade marks, trade names and brands which are used internationally consider registration in all relevant generic domain spaces and in all relevant country code domain spaces, but ensure that the domain names are not just placemarkers and are

---

[39]　Landgericht Berlin, 20 November 1996, 5 U 659/97, 97 0 193/96 (confirmed on appeal on 25 March 1997).

[40]　WIPO Case No. D2000-0203.

actually in "use". Ensure that all trade names and brand names which function as trade marks are registered as word marks exactly as they appear in the SLD so that the trade mark and SLD are clearly identical or confusingly similar.

Where appropriate consider the possibility of registering variations of each domain name, particularly in jurisdictions which have not yet shown a propensity to give the level of protection against dilution and unfair competition which appears to be available in the US and many European civil law jurisdictions. This will help prevent opportunists from registering obvious variations either in an effort to use the pulling power of the domain name for unrelated third party advertising or in an attempt to sell a competing product or service.

In some jurisdictions, domain names can also be registered as trade marks in their own right. Registrations usually include the SLD together with the ".com" TLD. The US Patent and Trade Mark Office and the UK Trade Marks Registry treats the ".com" portion of the domain as a generic feature.[41] Provided that the SLD is sufficiently distinctive in its own right and does not appear to function merely as an address, it will be registrable as a mark for providing information services of the specified kind. Registration in this manner might, in limited circumstances, be a useful additional safeguard in dissuading potential registrants or infringers, but it is likely to be of limited additional value if all appropriate domain name registrations and a base supporting trade mark registration for the identical SLD have been obtained.

In a global marketplace, rights will be best preserved by obtaining "first-in-time" domain name registration in relevant domain name spaces and by registering appropriate trade marks in every major jurisdiction and in selected smaller jurisdictions which maintain ccTLDs.

2.3.10.1 *Conflicting registrations and choosing a dispute forum*

If searches reveal a conflicting registration then consider whether the relevant domain space requires registrants to agree to the UDRP or to a particular dispute resolution forum. The advantage of the UDRP for resolving disputes is that it is generally cheaper than litigation, is cross-jurisdictional and offers a relatively short decision time. The disadvantage is that it is only appropriate for a limited class of circumstances and failure to assess these circumstances may result in a complainant wasting time and resources which could more usefully have been expended in commencing court proceedings.

If the UDRP does apply, then potential complainants should consider whether this is a case of "cybersquatting" in the sense described in the introduction to Section 2.3, or an example of a competitor seeking to trade on the first domain registrant's goodwill and reputation. If the case fits into either category then it may be worthwhile making a complaint under the UDRP or at least considering its application.

Key considerations in deciding whether to make a complaint (after establishing that the domain is confusingly similar and is in "use") will be whether the registrant is using the domain name in bad faith, or whether the registrant has a legitimate interest in using the

---

[41]   For USPTO guidelines *see* http://www.uspto.gov/web/offices/tac/notices/guide299.htm. The UK Trade Marks Registry issued a statement concerning "Registration of Internet Domain Names As Trade Marks" in the UK Trade Marks Journal, No. 6166, 12 March 1997 and the statement is discussed by Jeremy Morton, "Opinion.Com" [1997] 9 E.I.P.R. 496.

domain name. If the dispute potentially involves complex trade mark or contractual issues then it may be preferable to consider proceeding in court. UDRP complainants are only likely to be successful where the registrant is cybersquatting, or has obviously acted in bad faith.

If the case involves competing businesses from the same jurisdiction then it is likely that there will be some element of bad faith which may suffice to ground a complaint under the UDRP. At any stage during these proceedings the parties will still have the opportunity to choose to commence court proceedings for trade mark infringement, dilution or unfair competition remedies as may be appropriate.

If the case involves non-competing businesses, whether from the same or different jurisdictions, with no apparent evidence of bad faith then complainants are unlikely to be successful under the UDRP. In these circumstances complainants are better advised to consider bringing proceedings for trade mark infringement, dilution or unfair competition remedies in relevant forums.

2.4   Trade marks

2.4.1   *The "virtual world" trade mark problem*

The international trade mark system was conceived in an age when international trade was clearly defined and controlled by national borders. It was intended as a means of protecting the identifiers of goods and services in a trader's home country and in individual jurisdictions to which the trader sought to export its goods and services. Goodwill attaching to the mark in each country could be protected on a jurisdiction-by-jurisdiction basis and it was relatively straightforward to ensure that trade marks which infringed in one jurisdiction were not used in that jurisdiction.

The position became a little blurred with the development of modern broadcasting, telecommunications and mass cross-border media dissemination. Suddenly it was difficult to control the jurisdictions in which marks were used and goodwill (at least for famous marks) could not be contained behind national borders from spilling over into neighbouring countries. To this point communications were initiated by the broadcaster in a defined timeframe and were directed at identifiable groups. Although some philosophical modification was required, particularly as a result of the changing nature of international trade and advertising techniques, it was still appropriate and possible for trade marks to be regulated on a jurisdiction-by-jurisdiction basis because each activity was directed at a specified jurisdiction and could be identified, monitored and individually controlled within the jurisdiction's borders.

Enter the Internet – a new paradigm for trade mark law because it creates a truly international marketplace without recognising national borders. Sites may be accessed from anywhere, at any time, affording trade marks and service marks an international role without regard for whether a third party is already using that mark, or a confusingly similar mark in the viewer's jurisdiction. But how is the site owner or content provider to know whether a mark may or may not be used in a particular jurisdiction? And how can use be controlled where the user has no links with a jurisdiction to enable effective enforcement of an order restraining infringement?

The Internet, as an environment for marketing products and conducting business, cuts right across the traditional concept of an international marketplace separated by physical borders which underpins existing trade mark law. It creates a new environment for trading and marketing in which services and products attract an international goodwill and reputation and require a new kind of trade mark protection. The commercialisation of Internet technology has moved too far too soon for the law to properly harness the concept of this global, virtual marketplace.

The result is a digital marketplace retarded by artificial segmentation arising from the courts taking an overly robust view of their own jurisdiction. The hallmark of this environment is uncertainty. Uncertainty for website owners in assessing whether trade mark rights will be infringed in a foreign jurisdiction, or as a result of the use of new Internet technologies, and uncertainty for trade mark owners in attempting to properly protect their marks and brand equity in a virtual environment. The only guidelines for Internet users and trade mark owners are to take account of the developing approaches of individual national courts. In default of Internet-specific regulation, market behaviour will come to be dictated by the standards of the most highly developed and strictly regulated players in the trade mark marketplace. There is already a discernible trend in Internet behaviour toward conformity with contemporary US trade mark law rules.

2.4.2 *Application of physical world trade mark principles in a virtual environment*

Trade mark laws apply to the World Wide Web in the same way that they apply to the physical world. The only difference is that trade marks on a website potentially function in every jurisdiction in which the website can be viewed. There are no longer discrete physical borders separating individual trade mark regimes. The consequence is that infringement can occur in a foreign jurisdiction just as readily than in the trade mark owner's home jurisdiction. While the trade mark owner will necessarily check the home marketplace at the time of registration and subsequently maintain a market watch strategy, it is probably unlikely, unless the trade mark is famous, that it will do so elsewhere. In addition a mark which may not infringe under the laws of its home jurisdiction may well be illegal under foreign trade mark law regimes.

The threshold test before infringement theories come into play is whether the foreign court will take jurisdiction. Experience to date suggests that most courts will strive to assert their jurisdiction to bring the foreign party to court. In general these proceedings will only be of concern to the foreign defendant and of benefit to the plaintiff, if the defendant has assets, is trading in the jurisdiction, or hopes to do so in the future. The option of subsequently obtaining and enforcing judgment in the defendant's home territory, even if possible, will usually be futile in cases like these where the primary remedy sought is injunctive relief.

Many jurisdiction cases concerning trade marks have to date come from the US. They turn on American personal jurisdiction principles under the due process clause or on the application of the so-called "long arm" jurisdiction statutes in particular states. While an in-depth consideration of jurisdiction principles is made elsewhere in this Guide, it is useful to briefly review a sampling of cases to establish a senses of the growing globalisation of trade mark law and the developing trends as to when foreign trade mark principles may need to be taken into account.

The high watermark of these decisions is *Playboy Enterprises Inc. v. Chuckleberry Publishing Inc.*[42] in which an American court (although qualifying its earlier decision by upholding an earlier injunction) was prepared to take jurisdiction over a website for the Italian magazine *Playmen* because it found that as the website invited people to view and subscribe to the magazine and was accessible from the US, it constituted a distribution of products in that country. Consequently the court issued an injunction restricting the website owner from using the trade mark *Playmen* which previously (but before the creation of the website) had been held by the court to infringe Playboy Enterprise Inc's US trade marks.

By contrast, in *Bensusan Restaurant Corp. v. King*,[43] jurisdiction was refused in a trade mark infringement suit brought by The Blue Note jazz club in New York in circumstances where a club of the same name in Missouri owned a website which was found to be merely a passive information source for the benefit of local customers. The site was obviously aimed at local consumers and featured no means of purchasing tickets or making enquiries over the Internet and was therefore neither present in New York State nor aimed at New York citizens.

At the opposite end of the spectrum is *Zippo Manufacturing Co. v. Zippo Dot Com Inc.*[44] in which a California-based defendant was held to be subject to jurisdiction in Pennsylvania because it had sold 3,000 passwords to subscribers in Pennsylvania and entered into contracts with access providers in Pennsylvania to service customers in that state. The court found that much of the alleged trade mark infringement and dilution had occurred in that state and summarised the three situations for assessing jurisdiction (as subsequently confirmed in *Weber v. Jolly Hotels*)[45] as follows:

(a) active business on the Internet (jurisdiction almost certain);

(b) where there is an exchange of information between computers depending on the level of interactivity of the defendant's site and the commercial nature of the site (jurisdiction likely but depends on the particular nature of the site); or

(c) where the website is merely passive and does little more than provide information (jurisdiction unlikely).

Based on these principles, the key elements at least in the US are interactivity and intention. The more passive the website the less likely that courts will take jurisdiction; on the other hand if a website allows immediate re-transmission of information back to the site, offers a means of communication such as a toll free telephone number and is obviously aimed at a relevant audience then the court may well accept jurisdiction. However there are potential risks even for passive websites, depending on the jurisdiction concerned.[46]

---

[42]   *Playboy Enterprises Inc. v. Chuckleberry Publishing Inc.* consequently 1996 US Dist LEXIS 8435 (S.D.N.Y. 19 June 1996).

[43]   *Bensusan Restaurant Corp. v. King*, 937 F Supp. 295 (S.D.N.Y. 1996).

[44]   *Zippo Manufacturing Co. v. Zippo Dot Com Inc.*, 952 F. Supp. 1119 (W.D. Pa. 1997).

[45]   *Weber v. Jolly Hotels*, 1997 US Dist. LEXIS 14036 (D.M.J. 9/12/97).

[46]   *Telco Telecommunications Group Inc. v. An Apple A Day Inc.*, 1997 US Dist. LEXIS 14543 (E.D. Va 9/24/97) – this was not a trade mark case but concerned defamatory statements made on the defendant's website which were not necessarily aimed at residents in the court's jurisdiction. Nevertheless, based on the specific requirements of Virginia's jurisdiction statute, the court took jurisdiction.

The moral is that there is a potential risk of infringement in any foreign jurisdiction if a website is aimed at the jurisdiction or in any way permits or induces consumers to deal with the website owner in commerce. Website owners need to carefully assess these factors and review trade mark use on their site before conducting commerce on the Internet. Fairly extensive trade mark searching facilities are available on the Internet in key jurisdictions, as are domain name directory search facilities.[47] Failure to take precautions may risk a quite unexpected trade mark infringement, dilution or even unfair competition action in a remote location.

2.4.3   *Trade mark use*

In the virtual world, as in the physical world, a mark or sign must be used as a trade mark before use constitutes "infringing use". Merely referring to a trade mark or a domain name containing a trade mark in a descriptive sense is not trade mark use. For example, as a domain name functions as a descriptor for a home page's address, the use of a domain name as a plain text hyperlink purely to navigate to the domain name owner's home page is unlikely to constitute trade mark use.[48] However, use of a trade mark on its own as a plain text hyperlink to a site controlled by the trade mark owner arguably goes beyond mere descriptive use to constitute use as a trade mark.[49]

Subject to any defences available to a trade mark owner in individual jurisdictions,[50] the right to use the trade mark in relation to the owner's goods or services is *prima facie* exclusive to the trade mark owner and use by a third party is use as a trade mark. However, regardless of the niceties of individual trade mark regimes, the prudent website owner in an international marketplace is well advised to keep in mind that all unauthorised use of a trade mark in a commercial context may constitute trade mark use.

2.4.4   *Trade mark infringement*

Infringement in most jurisdictions requires a finding of unauthorised use of an identical (or confusingly similar) trade mark for the same (or similar) goods or services.[51] In the context of the Internet, infringements can arise in a number of ways depending on the nature of trade mark use. The possibilities based on cases to date are set out below:

---

[47]   *See* for example the Thomson & Thomson site at www.thomson-thomsom.com for details of Saegis – the online trade mark research service.

[48]   In principle, it is unlikely even if a domain name contains a registered trade mark or is registered as a trade mark, that descriptive use for its primary function as a website locator could amount to use as a trade mark.

[49]   Infringement in these circumstances is jurisdiction specified. For example, while in the US it appears (based on the settlement in *The Washington Post v. Total News*) that such use would constitute trade mark infringement, it has been argued in Australia that this would not constitute trade mark use (*see* Margaret Ryan, "Shetlands Islands Showdown – The Legality of Hyperlinks and Framing Technology on The Web", Journal of the Intellectual Property Society of Australia and New Zealand, September 1997, pages 26 to 33.

[50]   Statutory defences (such as for use in good faith to refer to a characteristic of the goods and services or for comparative advertising purposes) may prevail in individual cases.

[51]   In the US the test under the Lanham Act requires a finding of "likelihood of confusion".

(a) unauthorised electronic use of a trade mark on a website;

(b) unauthorised use of a trade mark in a domain name;

(c) use of a trade mark as a link to a site operated or authorised by the trade mark owner;

(d) use of a trade mark as a link to a site not authorised by the trade mark owner;

(e) use of a framing device to obscure the framed site's trade marks;

(f) use of a third party's trade mark as a "metatag"; and

(g) use of a third party's trade mark as a "keyword" to bring up banner advertising.

The trade mark infringement analysis in each case will, of course, depend on the particular law of the jurisdiction concerned but it is vital to recognise that multi-national trade mark owners are often in a position to "forum shop" for the jurisdiction which offers the most sympathetic trade mark infringement analysis and the greatest breadth of possible relief. For this reason, any guidelines for the use of trade marks on the Internet need to take into account the full range of protection mechanisms available in different jurisdictions, including those in which extended protection for well-known marks, dilution and unfair competition type remedies are available.

2.4.5 *Well-known trade marks*

Proper protection for famous trade marks with truly international renown is required in most jurisdictions by international convention[52] and is, in addition, the subject of regional conventions.[53] To fulfil international obligations, the trade mark laws of most developed nations provide special protection for these marks,[54] or make some other kind of provision (often by means of unfair competition laws) for protecting the integrity of famous marks against use in unrelated fields of activity which may damage the interests of the trade mark owner. Unauthorised commercial use on the Internet of a famous mark in relation to the same or dissimilar goods or services will almost inevitably result in an infringement or unfair competition action. Where the mark is similar but not identical to a famous mark and is used for dissimilar goods or services the level of protection is more restricted, but dilution or unfair competition law remedies may still be available in jurisdictions such as the US and a number of European countries.

2.4.6 *Trade mark dilution*

Under the relevant state or federal statutes in the US, a well-known trade mark which has been used for a significant period of time in the US, may be diluted by a mark which is used for dissimilar goods or services, even where there is no competition between the marks and no resulting confusion. In general, dilution has been held to occur under state dilution statues in cases where there is a "tarnishment" or "blurring" of the well-known mark. "Blurring" occurs where the defendant uses the well-known mark in a modified form in relation to its goods or services such that it is likely to lose its distinctiveness in

---

[52] Article 6bis, Paris Convention for Industrial Property; Articles 16(3) TRIPS Agreement.

[53] For example, Article 2(d) EC Trade Mark Directive 89/104.

[54] For example, by Sections 10(3) and 56 of the Trade Marks Act 1994 (UK) or by specific additional remedies such as the Federal Dilution Act in the US.

relation to the well-known mark.[55] "Tarnishment" occurs where the well-known mark is used in association with inferior or unwholesome goods or services.[56] It also appears that courts are prepared to extend the remedy to cases where the second mark is merely imitating the first.[57] As discussed earlier, dilution remedies have proved a very effective means of protecting well-known marks used as domain names by third parties. It has also proved useful in the context of new Internet technologies as discussed in Section 2.4.8.

2.4.7   *Unfair competition*

Most jurisdictions also feature unfair competition laws in a variety of forms. At the most fundamental level of development is the common law tort of "passing off" which in its modern formulation extends to situations where there may be no confusion but a likelihood of association by the public between the plaintiff's and the defendant's marks.[58] A recent UK decision suggests that a "passing off" action can protect goodwill attaching to a trade name or trade mark against third party use of that name or mark on the Internet no matter where the website on which the conduct takes place is based, or where the parties come from. This decision underlines the cross-jurisdictional conflict of trade mark rights in a virtual world and points to the potential scope for "passing off" and unfair competition actions to play a significant role in controlling trade mark use on the Internet.

2.4.7.1   *Mecklermedia Corp. v. DC Congress GmbH* [59]

DC Congress GmbH owned a German trade mark registration for Internet World and initiated trade mark infringement proceedings in Germany against the plaintiff's German licensee. Meanwhile Meckermedia Corp., a US-based corporation, brought proceedings against the defendant German company in the UK alleging that the defendant had passed off the American Company's goodwill and reputation by using Internet World, *inter alia*, as a trade mark on its website based in Germany. On an interlocutory application concerning jurisdiction, the English High Court found that the plaintiff had considerable goodwill and reputation in the UK in connection with Internet World, and that there was evidence to suggest that the defendant was clearly attempting to attract custom from the UK. The Court was prepared to accept jurisdiction on the basis that harm was being done to the plaintiff's goodwill in the UK quite separately from any claim by the defendant of trade mark infringement in Germany.

---

[55]   *Deere & Co. v. MTD Prods Inc.*, 41 F.3d 39, 43 (2d Cir. 1994).

[56]   *See* for example *Toys "Я" Us v. Akkaoui*, 40 U.S.P.Q.2d (BNA) 1836 (N.d. Cal. 1996).

[57]   *Wawa Inc. v. Haaf*, 1996 WL 460083 (E.D. Pa. 1996), in which the court found that HAHA diluted the famous WAWA trade mark.

[58]   For example, *see Lego System Akteiseklab v. Lego M Lemelstrich Ltd* (1983) F.S.R. 155 (Ch. D.) in the UK and *Hutchence v. South Seas Bubble Co. Pty Ltd*, (1986), 6 I/P.R. 473 at 482 in Australia.

[59]   High Court TLR 3/27/97.

Statutory enactments in various common law countries also prohibit trade mark activity which amounts to false sponsorship, endorsement, designation of origin or misleading conduct in circumstances where there is no requirement to prove damage and consequently no necessity for the parties to be operating in a competitive relationship.[60]

Civil unfair competition laws generally operate on the basis of, or are at least significantly influenced by, the breach of a moral code of conduct and in the most blatant circumstances will provide a remedy where there is little evidence of a competitive relationship between the parties.[61] Provided that the plaintiff's mark has a reputation within the jurisdiction which appears to be damaging the defendant's conduct (whether as a result of confusion, false association or sponsorship, or activity roughly equivalent to the US concepts of "blurring" or "tarnishment") there may be a remedy available under the jurisdiction's unfair competition laws.

American plaintiffs have been the first to make claims in relation to new Internet technologies based on a range of trade mark, dilution and unfair competition causes of action.

2.4.8   *New Internet technologies*

"Linking" is the basis facility for navigating the Internet. "Framing" is a type of "linking" which permits viewing of one site from within another. "Metatags" are search terms which, when used by someone searching the web, enable location of a programmed site. All these new technologies provide enhanced scope for the infringement and dilution of trade marks, and offer opportunities for the website owner to take unfair advantage of competitor's website and business activities.

2.4.9   *Linking*

Two types of "linking" are used on the Internet. The first and most ubiquitous is "hypertext reference linking", in which a user is transported to another site by clicking on a highlighted piece of text. The user's web browser retrieves and makes a copy of the linked document which is displayed on the user's screen. The second type of link is called an "inline link", in which images originating at another source appears as an integral image within the viewer's website. With this type of "linking", a command in one document instructs the automatic retrieval of the image and incorporation into the host page.

Linking cases tend to be primarily motivated by the facility of links to jump over another site's home page and, in doing so, lead consumers directly into the site, bypassing the site owner's advertising. Although such links may be convenient for users, the resultant reduction in traffic past the website owner's advertising space results in a reduction in the potential value of the site. The first linking case was *Ticketmaster Corp. v. Microsoft Corp.*[62]

---

[60]   An example is Sections 52 and 53 of the Trade Practices Act 1974 in Australia and the corresponding sections of the Fair Trading Act 1985 in New Zealand which were broadly modelled on Sections 43 and 43(a) of the Lanham Act in the US.

[61]   A case in point is Concept (*concept.com*) discussed earlier.

[62]   *Ticketmaster Corp. v. Microsoft Corp.*, No. 97-3055 DDP, C.D. Cal. 12 April 1997.

2.4.9.1 *Ticketmaster Corp. v. Microsoft Corp*

Ticketmaster, the largest entertainment ticket seller in the US, initiated proceedings against Microsoft for having linked the "Sidewalk" service available on its website to the Ticketmaster site. Sidewalk features information about live events and Microsoft arranged the link so that people could link directly from Sidewalk to the appropriate page for the event in Ticketmaster's site, bypassing Ticketmaster's front door (and advertising).

Ticketmaster alleged that Microsoft had diluted the value of Ticketmaster's marks and business, falsely associated its Sidewalk site with Ticketmaster and engaged in unfair competition by accessing the Ticketmaster site without approval (negotiations for exactly this service had previously failed between the parties). Microsoft alleged that it was merely "linking", that Ticketmaster could have prevented the link had it chosen to, and that in any event its use was non-commercial. Furthermore, in accordance with the basic Microsoft principles of interoperability and to enable the proper functioning of the Internet, Microsoft argued that this kind of "linking" must be permissible. It also argued that a business with a presence on the Internet invites others to use its Internet address to contact it, and that third parties accordingly have an implied licence to link to the business site. In response, Ticketmaster altered the structure of its website to prevent Sidewalk from linking in this way and posted a message for Microsoft customers inviting them to come through the "front door".

Ticketmaster has more recently revisited deep linking issues in a case which appears to support the right to hyperlink.

2.4.9.2 *Ticketmaster v. Ticket.com*[63]

Ticket.com provided a ticketing information site and sold tickets for a limited number of events from its site. Where it was unable to sell Tickets directly it provided a "deeplink" to Ticketmaster's site and displayed a statement for viewers that the tickets were sold by another ticketing company. Ticketmaster sought an injunction against Tickets.com to prevent the company from deep linking to the Ticketmaster.com website and using "spiders" to extract information from the site. Ticketmaster alleged copyright infringement, unfair competition, trespass and breach of contract.

Ticketmaster argued that deep linking to an interior page caused damage because users bypassed its home page where most of its advertising was displayed. The court found that hyperlinking did not involve copyright infringement as there was no copying involved in linking a user to the Ticketmaster site. Furthermore there was no deception because the user was clearly told that they were being transferred to another site. As far as unfair competition was concerned it was noted that deep linking, without confusion of source would not necessarily amount to unfair competition.[64]

---

63   2000 US Dist LEXIS 4553 (C.D. Cal. 2000).

64   "Deep Linking Your Way to a Lawsuit" *Ticketmaster Corp., et al. v. Tickets.Com Inc.* (27 March 2000) http://www.gigalaw.com/library/ticketmaster-tickets-2000-03-27.html.

The claim for trespass also failed as Tickets.com's spiders did not harm or obstruct Ticketmaster's computers or business. Ticketmaster had also alleged that Tickets.com violated the terms and conditions of the website by deep linking however the court found users were not required to click on the terms and agreement box before proceeding to the rest of the site and therefore no contract was created.[65]

Even following this case it is still safest for commercial website owners to only link to another site's homepage. To avoid unfair competition claims website owners are well advised to use a notice to inform users that they are being linked to another website. It is preferable to avoid using logos or trade marks to take users to a linked site and where a link is to a competitor's site then it is still best to negotiate a linking agreement.

2.4.10 *Framing*

"Framing" is similar to "inline linking" in which a framed segment of a third party's site is imported into a local website, effectively allowing viewers to look through one site into another. Website owners can use frames to incorporate entire websites produced by others, or portions of such sites, and to surround them with their own advertising. In this way advertisers can gain increased exposure because their advertising remains in view while the viewer proceeds through the framed site.

It can be difficult to tell whether the content is attributable to the framed site or to a third party, as the remote site is framed under the Universal Resource Locater (the "URL") of the displayed site and there may be no obvious delineation between the respective images. This may lead to claims of unfair competition or misappropriation because the viewer is unaware that the material comes from a framed site and may incorrectly assume that it is provided by the owners of the displayed site. If the trade marks or logos of the framed site are visible side-by-side with the trade marks of the displayed site, then this has the potential to falsely represent approval or affiliation by the displayed site owner when this is not the case.

Further, if the framed site's advertising is visible on the displayed site, the frame may be created in such a way that the advertising is not portrayed as initially intended or in a way which devalues it. Alternatively, if framing results in the framed site appearing to have an association with the displayed site, or with competitive advertisers on the displayed site, then this may also give rise to an unfair competition action.

Trade mark infringement can arise both where the trade marks on the displayed site appear beside the content of the framed site and where trade marks of the framed site appear next to content of the displayed site. In the first scenario – where the framed site's trade marks are obscured – there is no "use" of the framed site owner's trade marks, but in circumstances where there exists a specific prohibition on obscuring trade marks this can amount to infringement. For example in the US, if viewers could assume that the displayed site owner was in some way associated with the framed site owner, this may constitute trade mark dilution. In the second scenario there is an unauthorised use of the framed site owner's trade marks which, if held to be in relation to the goods or services of the displayed site, may constitute infringement. While there is as yet no guidance on these issues from the courts, the leading example of a framing action, *Washington Post Co. v. Total News Inc.* demonstrates the potential causes of action in the US.

---

[65]   "Hyperlinking and Deep-linking" Tammy Bortz (June 2000)
         http://www.mbendi.co.za/werksmns/techwks8.htm.

2.4.10.1 *Washington Post Co. v. Total News Inc.*[66]

Total News Inc. operated a news website which provided links to a variety of news sources including the Washington Post website. Internet users of the Total News website could view the Washington Post website displayed in a frame as part of the Total News site. The Washington Post content did not take up the whole screen. Remaining sections were filled with three Total News frames, including advertisements framed simultaneously with the Washington Post news site. Viewers only saw the Total News URL. The Total News site obscured other elements of each framed Washington Post page including its advertising.

Washington Post sued, alleging trade mark infringement, dilution and unfair competition, and misappropriation of the plaintiff's intellectual property. In June 1997, the claim was settled on the basis that Total News would cease framing the Washington Post website or causing any of the Washington Post website to appear on a user's computer screen together with materials supplied by Total News. Total News also agreed that any link from its website would only be a plain text hyperlink and that the linking website would not include any Washington Post logo or graphics. In settling the case, the Washington Post entered into a "linking agreement" which unusually extended to plain text hyperlinks.

The linking agreement entered into in this case raises a serious question as to whether consent could be required for a plain text hyperlink, at least in the US. Obviously, if this is the case, there are significant consequences for all website owners and users.

More recently there is a suggestion in *Futuredontics Inc. v. Applied Anagramics Inc.*[67] a decision of the US District Court on a motion to dismiss that a framed website could be protectable as a "derivative work" under the US Copyright Act if the framed web page could be characterised as being in a concrete or permanent form. However it seems unlikely that a framed website could be characterised in this way.

2.4.11 *Metatags*

"Metatags" are key terms used by website owners and search engine coders to enable Internet search engines to match a website to a search query. "Metatags" have proved a useful device in enabling site owners to maximise the number of visits to their sites by listing all possible search terms of their sites and not just words or content appearing on the site. However "metatags" are also a useful tool for people wanting to take unfair advantage of the reputation of other businesses. By entering the name or trade mark of the business, the website owner ensures that its site reference comes up in the list of search results for the site and in this way increase the chances of its site being viewed. Unscrupulous website owners will use this opportunity to offer competing goods or services to those offered by the well-known site owner. Courts in the US, UK and Netherlands[68] have considered whether the use of metatags in these circumstances constitutes trade mark infringement or some kind of false association or endorsement. The first examples of metatag cases are from the US.

---

[66] *Washington Post Co. v. Total News Inc.*, 97 Civ. 1190 (S.D.N.Y., 20 February 1997) and *see* "Stipulation and Order Settlement and Dismissal" at at AOL Legal Department site http://legal.web.aol.com/decisions/dlip/washorde.html.

[67] Case No. CV97-6991 ABC (Manx), 1998 US Dist. Lexis 2265 (C.D. Cal. 30 January 1998).

[68] *Deutz v. ADT vd Heuvel* – a Dutch court found that the defendant's use of *Deutz* in a metatag was a trade mark infringement under Dutch law (contravention of Article 13, Part 13 sub d BMW).

2.4.11.1   *Playboy Enterprises Inc. v. Calvin Designer Label*[69]

Playboy Enterprises Inc. ("Playboy") sued Calvin Designer Label for operating pornographic websites (*Playboy XXX.com and Playmatelive.com*) and for including terms such as "Playboy" and "Playmate" as programmed metatags. In this case, people searching under the term "Playboy" would have located the Calvin Designer Label site even though it had no affiliation with Playboy Enterprises Inc. Playboy demanded that the website's names should be changed and that its trade marks should be removed from Calvin's programmed metatags. The court issued a preliminary injunction against Calvin, temporarily shutting down its sites.

Prior to this decision, there was no certainty as to whether courts would treat the unauthorised use of trade marks as metatags as trade mark infringement. In the first case of this kind to be brought by a law firm[70] (which incidentally operated domain name registration devices) against Internet business operators who included the firm's name in their metatags hoping to pick up additional business, the Internet business complied with the firm's demand and the case was settled. The Playboy decision makes it clear that in the US the unauthorised use of metatags could constitute trade mark infringement. However, a subsequent case brought by Playboy confirms that the unauthorised but descriptive use of trade marks as metatags may not in certain circumstances constitute an infringing use.

2.4.11.2   *Playboy Enterprises Inc. v. Terri Welles*[71]

Terri Welles was "Playmate of the Year" in 1981 and developed her own website selling autographed photos, promoting a newsletter and advertising membership of her fan club. The site included references to her career and to her past successes as "Playmate of the Year" and "Playmate of the Month" for Playboy magazine. Ms Welles had also used these terms as metatags in the code for her site. Her site included a clear disclaimer indicating that it was not endorsed by Playboy.

At a preliminary hearing the Federal Court found that Ms Welles was entitled to make fair use of these trade marks and that there was no dilution of Playboy Enterprises Inc's trade marks. Her use was limited to describing her career and identifying her site, and was not intended to imply any association with Playboy magazine. The metatags were merely index guides to the content of her site which had been used in good faith by Ms Welles to help guide web surfers to the site.

The later *Niton* case is an example of courts restraining the use of metatags to prevent false association or endorsement between competitors.

2.4.11.3   *Niton Corp. v. Radiation Monitoring Devices Inc.*[72]

Niton Corp. and Radiation Monitoring Devices Inc. are competitors in the market for detection of lead paint. Niton discovered that the metatag descriptions of various pages of Radiation's website falsely stated that they were the "Home page of Niton corporation, makers of the finest lead, radon and multi-element detectors". This description appeared

---

[69]   *Playboy Enterprises Inc. v. Calvin Designer Label*, 44 US PQ. 2d 1156 (N.D. Cal. 1997).

[70]   *Oppedahl & Larson; see* report at http://www.bna.com/e-law/cases/oppensi.htm.

[71]   *Playboy Enterprises Inc. v. Terri Welles.* 1998 US Dist. LEXIS 9180 (S.D. Cal. 18 May 1998).

[72]   27F. Supp. 2d 102 (D.Mass. 1998).

in various search engine results that linked to Radiation's website and would obviously lead potential Niton customers to Radiation's website or permit customers to assume that there was some kind of affiliation between the parties. Niton obtained an injunction preventing Radiation from continuing to represent that it was associated with the plaintiff in its metatags. This decision does not appear to be based on trade mark infringement, but rather on the ability of the court to prevent the defendant from falsely holding itself and its website out as having some affiliation with the plaintiff.[73]

The unauthorised use of trade marks as "metatags" in other jurisdictions may also constitute trade mark infringement. Where national laws include a statutory prohibition on misleading representations, false association or endorsement (or an unfair competition law prohibiting "parasitic" activities) then the trade mark owner may be able to rely on these as additional remedies. A "passing off" action in its extended modern form may also assist, provided that a court is prepared to accept that use of the trade mark as a metatag results in the viewer incorrectly assuming that there is some connection between the trade mark owner and the website owner. Recently a English court has considered trade mark infringement and passing off in the context of metatags.

2.4.11.4 *Roadtech Computers Limited v. Mandata (Management and data services) Limited*[74]

The plaintiff and defendant are competitor computer companies. Roadtech had invested considerable resources into its website and had been successful in attracting custom. Mandata used Roadtech's trade marks as metatags over a two-month period without authorisation in an attempt to attract Roadtech's potential customers. Roadtech obtained summary judgment in passing off and trade mark infringement but interestingly failed on its diversion of trade claim because there was insufficient evidence of the number of people who found themselves in the Mandata site having used the "Roadrunner" or "Roadtech" metatags.

2.4.12 *Keyword advertising*

"Keyword" advertising is where banner advertisements are linked to search terms so that an advertisement appears whenever a particular search term is typed into a search engine. Search engine owners "sell" the key words to advertisers. Viewers who click on the banner advertisement are then taken directly to the advertiser's web page.

Provided that consumers are not confused by the practice there is unlikely to be any way of restricting it. However where non-generic trade marks are used or where the websurfing consumer is suddenly transported to a competitor's site there may be grounds to support a cause of action in trade mark infringement, dilution or unfair competition. The following American case shows that these causes of action are unlikely to be successful where the trade mark concerned is generic.

---

[73]   *Niton Corp v. Radiation Monitoring Devices Inc.*, 27F. Supp. 2d 102 (D. Mass. 1998).

[74]   High Court, Chancery Division, Case No. HC 199904573, Decision of Master Bowman.

2.4.12.1   Playboy Enterprises Inc. v. Netscape Communications Corp.[75]

In this case of "keyword advertising" Playboy Enterprises brought preliminary injunction proceedings against Netscape to prevent the practice of "keying" advertisements to the word "playboy" and "playmate". The plaintiff held federal trade mark registrations for both words but the court found no evidence of actual consumer confusion and because both words were generic found that there was no likelihood of confusion to support an infringement claim. The plaintiff's dilution claim was also rejected on the grounds that there was no evidence of blurring, tarnishment, nor any other damage to the plaintiff's marks when advertising for goods and services. Finally, the court found that the defendant's use of "playboy" and "playmate" in keying was both a permitted fair use of the plaintiff's marks and a use permitted by the first Amendment.

2.5   Strategies for protecting trade marks and minimising liability for trade mark infringement and unfair competition

Hopefully this list of "do's" and "don'ts" based on how the law has developed to date will provide some useful guidelines for advising clients who are planning or already using websites, and for trade mark owners seeking advice on protecting their marks in the virtual world.

(a) *Obtain permission* – the fundamental step for website owners is to obtain licences and permission for the use of materials referring to trade names and trade marks other than in a descriptive way.

(b) *Avoid other's trade marks and logos* – the website owners should avoid the unauthorised use of someone else's trade mark or logo as a hyperlink, as this may amount to trade mark infringement.

(c) *Linking framing* – ideally, permission should be sought before linking or framing. Although a plain text hyperlink using a URL is unlikely to constitute trade mark infringement, if in doubt obtain the domain name owner's permission. A linking agreement is the safest course for inline linking and framing.

(d) *Link directly to a home page* – when arranging a link without permission preferably make it link directly to a home page in order to avoid by-passing a website owner's home page and advertising.

(e) *Disclaimer* – clearly identify the website as not being associated with any sites to which it is linked or framed if there is no such association. A disclaimer to this effect is appropriate.

(f) *Metatags* – use of trade names or trade marks as metatags should be avoided. Such use is likely to be a trade mark infringement or may breach unfair competition laws.

(g) *Keywords* – avoid use of keywords which comprise distinctive trade marks or non-generic words, or of using banner advertisements which could result in consumer confusion.

(h) *Jurisdiction* – the key factors governing whether a foreign court takes jurisdiction appear to be the degree of commercial interactivity and the intention of the site owner to reach a foreign audience. A minimalist, passive website is highly unlikely to attract

---

[75]   55F Supp.2d (1999).

liability but, in reality, many websites are specifically trying to facilitate commerce and to make their site more interactive. Where appropriate, it would be useful to implement a user registration process which has two main benefits:

(i) it enables the site owner to obtain the user's agreement to contract out of the law of the foreign jurisdiction where possible; and

(ii) it allows users from certain jurisdictions to filter out.

   Interactivity could also be reduced by directing customers to off-line processing of orders.

(i) *Trade mark and web searches* – trade mark owners should undertake searches in foreign target market jurisdictions to assess whether conflicting marks are used or registered in that jurisdiction in an attempt to pre-empt infringement claims. Prudent trade mark owners should monitor search engines for evidence of conflicting domain name registrations and for use of their trade marks as metatags by third parties.

Chapter 3
COPYRIGHT AND THE INTERNET

Mark Haftke
Partner
KLegal

3.1　　　　Introduction

UK copyright subsists in classes of work when they are recorded, in writing or otherwise. No formalities are required, such as registration. The classes of work are as follows:[1]

(a) literary, dramatic, musical and artistic works;

(b) films, sound recordings, broadcasts and cable program services; and

(c) the typographical arrangement of published editions.

To be protected, the work must fall into one of the categories of protected work that the Copyright, Design and Patents Act 1988 (the "CDPA") sets out. Literary works include tables and compilations, databases, computer programs and their preparatory design materials.[2] Dramatic works include those of dance or mime.[3] Musical works do not include the words intended to be spoken or sung with the music. These constitute a literary work separate from the musical work. A sound recording or film will usually comprise more than one copyright as there may be copyright in any works embodied in them (e.g. a musical work such as a song or a literary work such as the lyrics or a script).

The work must be original to be protected. A work will generally be considered original if it is created without slavish copying – a modicum of independent effort is often enough. Thus, a work which amounts to an infringement of another's work may itself be protected by copyright.

The first owner of the copyright in a work is the person who creates it and is referred to as the "author".[4] In the case of sound recordings, the author is taken to be the producer.[5] In the case of films it is taken to be the producer and the principal director.[6]

---

[1]　　　Section 1(1).

[2]　　　Section 3(1).

[3]　　　Section 3(1).

[4]　　　Section 11(1).

[5]　　　Section 9(2)(aa).

[6]　　　Section 9(2)(ab).

In the case of a broadcast the author is the person who made it.[7] In the case of a cable program service the author is the person who provided it.[8] In the case of typographical arrangements, the first owner of copyright is taken to be the publisher.[9] There may be more than one author of a work in which case the work will be one of "joint authorship".[10]

If the person who created the work did so in the course of their employment then the copyright will be first owned by their employer subject to any contrary agreement.

Legal ownership of a copyright can only be transferred to another person by one of the following methods:[11]

(a) an assignment;

(b) testamentary disposition (e.g. in a will); or

(c) by operation of law.

The most common way of assigning copyright is the first. To validly transfer the legal title to a copyright the assignment from A to B must be in writing and signed by A.[12] Ideally it should use the words "I [A] hereby assign to [B] the copyright in..." and specify the work and the territory (e.g. the UK or the world and so on).

Instead of assigning the copyright the owner can simply grant a third party the right to exercise any of the copyright owner's exclusive rights. Such a licence can be exclusive to the licensee or non-exclusive. A non-exclusive licensee has no automatic rights to bring an action for copyright infringement.

An exclusive licensee can sue copyright infringers just as if he were the copyright owner but he must join the copyright owner as a party to the action. In any copyright infringement action by an exclusive licensee, it is an absolute defence that the act complained of was authorised by the copyright owner (even though the copyright owner gave that authority in breach of the exclusive licence). To be valid, an exclusive licence must be in writing and signed by the licensor.[13]

It will be necessary in a copyright action to identify when a work was recorded and copyright in it came into existence. In a dispute about whose work was created first and who must have copied whom, it will be useful to identify the work's "birth date". One way of doing this is for the author to seal it in an envelope (for future reference, write on the front what is inside), seal the envelope (with wax or some other seal) and then post it to themselves or a solicitor. It should then remain unopened. The post mark should be clearly visible. In the event of a dispute it can be opened for the first time in the presence of a reliable witness (e.g. a solicitor). This will prove that it was in existence (in the envelope) at the time it was posted.

---

7   Section 9(2)(b).

8   Section 9(2)(c).

9   Section 9(2)(d).

10   Section 10.

11   Section 11(2).

12   Section 90(1).

13   Section 90(3).

Copyright gives the owner the exclusive right to perform certain acts in the UK in relation to protected works. The infringing acts must fall into one of the acts defined in the CDPA as restricted by the copyright. A person who performs those acts in relation to the whole or a substantial part of the work without permission infringes the copyright in it. There are two different classes of infringement: primary infringements and secondary infringements. The rules about them are different.

The main difference between them is that with primary infringements the state of knowledge or intention of the infringer is irrelevant so that innocence is no defence. In the case of secondary infringements the infringer must have had the requisite knowledge (or the reasonable grounds for it) set out in the CDPA.

The owner has the following exclusive rights which if performed by another without authority amount to a primary infringement. They are the right to:

(a) copy the work;

(b) issue to the public copies of the work not previously in circulation (sometimes called the right of first sale or the distribution right);

(c) to rent or lend the work to the public;

(d) to perform, show or play the work in public;

(e) to broadcast or include the work in a cable program service;

(f) to make an adaptation of the work or do any of the above in relation to an adaptation.

The restricted act must have been performed in the UK in order to infringe the UK copyright.

It is also a primary infringement to authorise another to do any of the acts restricted by the copyright even if that authority has been given abroad so long as the restricted act was performed in the UK.

Secondary infringements are committed by those who do the following:

(a) perform certain acts in relation to articles that the perpetrator knows or has reason to believe are infringing copies or are specifically designed or adapted for making copies of a particular work;

(b) transmit the work by means of a telecommunications system (otherwise than by broadcasting or inclusion in a cable program service) knowing, or having reason to believe, that infringing copies of the work will be made by means of the reception of the transmission in the UK or elsewhere;

(c) give permission for use of a place at which copyright is infringed by public performance unless when giving it they have reasonable grounds to believe that the performance would not infringe;

(d) supply apparatus used to infringe copyright by playing/showing a work knowing, or having reason to believe, that it would be so used or with the same knowledge allow the apparatus to be brought onto premises of which they are the occupier;

(e) supply a copy of a sound recording or film knowing, or having reason to believe, at the time that the copy (or a copy made from it) would be likely to be used so as to infringe copyright.

The biggest difficulty with the application of copyright law to Internet communication is defining digital files and Internet applications in terms provided by an Act that was passed in a world that was then primarily concerned with the distribution of copyright works in tangible form.

Copyright is changing rapidly. The pressure for change in the EU arises, in part, out of the need for some harmonisation measures in the single market. However, the EU's recent "Proposal for a Draft Directive on Copyright in the Information Society" has highlighted the further pressure for change to balance the vested interests of copyright owners and the prospective interests of Information Society Service Providers.

The difficulties faced by owners and users of copyright can be summarised as follows:

(a) creative works have become digitalised so that use, in many cases, has come to necessitate copying;

(b) due to digitalisation, traditional barriers to dealing in works on a commercial scale have disappeared and even the activities of non-commercial individuals can pose a substantial economic threat;

(c) digitalisation has helped to shrink the globe;

(d) the Internet, specifically, has empowered users to publish on a global scale thereby exposing works to exploitation in countries with systems offering weak protection; and

(e) the Internet presents owners and users of copyrights with a global marketplace fragmented by differing national laws.

In addition, the Internet has special applications: hypertext links and framing services; on-demand digital streams; chat rooms; newsgroups; interactive networked games; email and so on. These have created brand new difficulties that require existing legislation to be considered in a new light.

Copyright is a national right. National systems of copyright protection vary. This Chapter is concerned with UK copyright law and references to "copyright" are to UK copyright, unless otherwise stated. However, it is unrealistic to operate in the online digital space without reference to what is going on at other levels. Such reference is made in this Chapter to the extent necessary.

This Chapter approaches the subject of copyright and the Internet in the following way:

(a) the international legislative framework;

(b) UK copyright law and Internet issues; and

(c) World Intellectual Property Organisation ("WIPO") and EU initiatives to deal with the copyright and Internet issues.

3.2   The current international legislative framework

The UK copyright issues created by use of the Internet are best considered in the context of the international legislative framework. That framework is based on the following copyright conventions and treaties:

(a) The Berne Convention;

(b) The Universal Copyright Convention;

(c) The Rome Convention;

(d) The Geneva Convention; and

(e) General Agreement on Tariffs and Trade ("GATT") and Trade Related Aspects of Intellectual Property ("TRIPs").

3.2.1   The Berne Convention

The Berne Convention for the Protection of Literary and Artistic Works has a long history stretching back to the last century and is administered by WIPO (an organisation of the United Nations). It applies to literary and artistic works[14] (published and unpublished) whose authors are nationals of a Convention country or to works first published in a Convention country. Such works include musical works, with and without words. It does not cover sound recordings. The Convention grants authors moral rights of paternity (to be identified as the author) and of integrity (viz. distortions and mutilations).[15]

It also grants authors exclusive rights over the following:

(a) translation of literary and artistic works;[16]

(b) reproduction in any form of literary and artistic works;[17]

(c) public performance by any means or process and the communication to the public of a performance of dramatic, dramatico-musical and musical works;[18]

(d) broadcasting of literary or artistic works or their communication to the public by any other means of wireless diffusion;[19]

(e) any communication to the public by wire or by rebroadcast;[20]

---

[14]   Including "every production in the literary, scientific and artistic domain, whatever may be the mode or form of its expression...".

[15]   Article 6 bis.

[16]   Article 8.

[17]   Article 9.

[18]   Article 11.

[19]   Article 11 bis(1).

[20]   Article 11 bis(1).

(f) authorising adaptations, arrangements and other alterations of literary or artistic works;[21]

(g) cinematographic adaptation and reproduction of literary and artistic works, their distribution, their public performance and their communication to the public by wire.[22]

It is worth noting in the context of what follows that under the Convention:

(a) the extent of protection and the means of redress afforded are governed exclusively by the laws of the country where protection is claimed.[23] Thus, the process of enforcement is territorially fragmented; and

(b) the communication by wire of literary or artistic works is expressly not an act of publication.[24]

Convention countries may permit the reproduction (by others) of literary and artistic works subject to a "three-step test": it applies only to "special cases" where the reproduction does not "conflict with a normal exploitation of a work" and "does not unreasonably prejudice the legitimate interests of the author".[25] This relates to the "fair use exception" and, because it permits individual arrangements on a country-by-country basis, has become a major headache for EU harmonisation in the Internal Market.

The Convention countries constitute a union referred to as the Berne Union.[26]

3.2.2 *Universal Copyright Convention*

For many years, the provisions of the Berne Convention were unacceptable to a number of economically important countries, especially the US, which refused to join the Berne Union. In particular, they objected to the term of protection and the absence of any formalities (such as registration) for the creation of copyright protection. To include such countries within the fold of international protection, and to allow their nationals to benefit from international protection, a halfway house was created in 1952 in the form of the Universal Copyright Convention (the "UCC") which was updated in 1971. Since then the Berne Union has grown (e.g. by the inclusion of the US) with membership having retrospective effect. As a result the UCC has become less important in the international legislative framework.

The UCC covers the same types of works as the Berne Convention but takes effect without prejudice to it. It offers a narrower scope of protection, a shorter minimum term of copyright protection (life plus 25 years) and permits UCC member countries to mandate registration requirements as a precondition of copyright subsistence. The power of UCC countries to create exceptions to these exclusive rights is less restricted than under the Berne Convention. It is enough that the exceptions "...do not conflict with the spirit and the provisions of this Convention...".

---

[21]   Article 12.

[22]   Article 14.

[23]   Article 5.

[24]   Article 3.

[25]   Article 9(2).

[26]   The members of the Berne Union current as at 19 January 1998 are listed in Schedule 1.

It is worth noting in the context of what follows that under the UCC:

(a) publication means "reproduction in tangible form";[27]

(b) UCC Convention countries are obliged to consider their conditions of copyright as satisfied if "...from the time of the first publication all the copies of the work" (published with authority) bear the symbol © accompanied by the name of the proprietor and the year of first publication "...placed in such manner and location as to give reasonable notice of claim of copyright";[28] and

(c) the UCC obviously retains its relevance in respect of countries that are not members of the Berne Union.[29]

3.2.3   *The Rome Convention*

The International Convention for the Protection of Performers, Producers of Phonograms and Broadcasting Organisations was signed in Rome in 1961. By virtue of it, Contracting States[30] grant to each other national treatment in respect of performances, phonograms and broadcasts.

"Phonogram" means any exclusively aural fixation of sounds of a performance or of other sounds; "publication" means offering copies of a phonogram to the public; "reproduction" means the making of a copy or copies of a fixation; "broadcasting" means transmission of sounds or of images; and "sounds by wireless" means for public reception.[31]

It protects against:

(a) the unauthorised "...broadcasting and communication to the public...", fixation or reproduction of a fixation of a performance;[32]

(b) the unauthorised direct or indirect reproduction of phonograms;[33]

(c) the unauthorised rebroadcasting or fixation of broadcasts, or the reproduction of unauthorised fixations of broadcasts;

(d) the communication to the public of television broadcasts in places charging an entrance fee.

The minimum term of protection is 20 years from the end of the year of fixation, performance or broadcast.

---

27   Article VI.

28   Article III.

29   UCC countries not a part of the Berne Union are listed in Schedule 2.

30   *See* Schedule 3 for a list of Contracting States as at 6 March 1998 – note the US is not a member.

31   Article 3.

32   Article 7.

33   Article 10.

National conditions for the subsistence of copyright are fulfilled if "...all the copies in commerce of the published phonogram or their containers bear a notice consisting of the symbol © accompanied by the year date of first publication placed in such a manner as to give reasonable notice of claim of protection".[34]

As well as the same kind of exceptions as they provide in respect of literary and artistic works, Contracting States may also provide for exceptions to protection as regards:

(a) private use;

(b) use of short excerpts in connection with the reporting of current events;

(c) ephemeral fixation by a broadcasting organisation by means of its own facilities and for its own broadcasts;

(d) use solely for the purposes of teaching or scientific research.[35]

3.2.4   *The Geneva Convention*

The Convention for the Protection of Producers of Phonograms Against Unauthorised Duplication of Their Phonograms of 1971 protects producers of phonograms against unauthorised duplication which will then benefit the performers and authors involved with phonograms.

It does not limit or prejudice any domestic law or other international agreement (including the Rome Convention 1961). The protection (if any) and the conditions of protection for the performers whose performances are fixed in phonograms is a matter for each Contracting State's domestic law.

Article 2 of the Convention provides that each Contracting State[36] shall protect producers of phonograms who are nationals of other Contracting States against:

(a) the making of duplicates without the consent of the producer (for purposes of public distribution);

(b) the importation of such duplicates for public distribution; and

(c) the distribution of duplicates to the public.

The means by which the Convention is implemented and the duration of the protection given is a matter for each Contracting State's domestic law, though a minimum of 20 years is set. Compulsory licences in certain circumstances are permitted.

3.2.5   *GATT-TRIPs*

The World Trade Organisation Agreement, passed in Geneva in December 1993, is a multinational agreement intended to promote international trade. It contains the GATT and an individual agreement called the TRIPs Agreement specifically drafted to address Trade Related Aspects of Intellectual Property. It covers many different types of intellectual

---

[34]   Article 11.

[35]   Article 15.

[36]   *See* Schedule 4 for a list of Contracting States as at 10 December 1997.

property including patents, trademarks and copyright. It sets levels of protection and (unlike earlier conventions) obligations with respect to enforcement of those rights against infringement. It (and GATT) are administered by the World Trade Organisation (the "WTO") and are subject to its arbitration process. What follows is concerned with the TRIPs Agreement.

None of TRIPs derogates from the Berne or Rome Conventions (UCC is not mentioned). Its principal, relevant features are:

(a) members are obliged to comply with Articles 1–21 of and the Appendix to the Berne Convention except in respect of moral rights;

(b) computer programs are protected as literary works;

(c) compilations of data which constitute intellectual creations by reason of the selection or arrangement of their contents are protected as such;

(d) the minimum term of copyright protection for non-life of author calculations is 50 years (applying various start dates);

(e) performers have the "possibility of preventing" the unauthorised fixation of unfixed performances, the broadcasting by wireless means and communication to the public of their live performances;

(f) producers of phonograms have the right to authorise or prohibit the direct or indirect reproduction of their phonograms;

(g) broadcasting organisations have the right to prohibit the unauthorised fixation, reproduction of fixations, the wireless rebroadcasting of broadcasts and the communication to the public of television broadcasts "of the same";

(h) existing systems of equitable remuneration for phonogram rental may continue;

(i) exceptions permitted by the Rome Convention may be provided by Member countries; and

(j) members' national laws must make available fair and equitable enforcement procedures against infringement of rights covered by TRIPs including expeditious remedies of a preventative and deterrent kind applied to avoid barriers to trade and which are not unnecessarily complicated or costly and do not entail unreasonable time-limits or unwarranted delays.

In the event of a dispute about a Member State's compliance with TRIPs, recourse may be had to the arbitration process of WTO. To a certain extent this has limited the ability of some "strong intellectual property" Member States to unilaterally impose trade sanctions on weaker ones.

In the US, the US Trade Representative maintains a list of countries[37] whose adequacy of intellectual property protection merits action or continuing review.

---

[37]   Special 301 provisions of the Omnibus Trade and Competitiveness Act 1988.

Interestingly, though agreed in 1993, the Agreement did not address the particular problems posed by the new media.

It is in the context of this prevailing, international, legislative framework of copyright protection that copyright and the Internet must be considered.

3.3 UK Law

In the UK the copyright does not need to be registered to come into existence. However, certain criteria do need to be met for copyright to subsist in a work. If copyright does subsist in a work then separate tests determine whether that right has been infringed by any given act performed in relation to that work.

In determining whether copyright protects a work and who owns it, regard must be had to the work in force at the time of its creation. The UK has had three principal Copyright Acts: those of 1911, 1956 and 1988. For the sake of relative simplicity and brevity, reference is made below to the provisions of the 1988 Act since that applies to resolving all issues of what acts constitute infringement since that Act came into force.

This Section looks at copyright in the following parts:

(a) subsistence of copyright issues;

(b) infringement of copyright issues;

(c) particular Internet issues.

The liabilities of Internet Service Providers ("ISPs") which have an increasingly special regime, are considered elsewhere in this Guide.

A website will usually constitute a compilation on the basis that it is the author's intellectual creation. It may contain databases and will certainly contain other copyright works such as computer graphics and photographs (even though the photographic images are electronically held), sound recordings, musical works and films. The site will also contain literary works in the form of editorial and computer programs. However, identifying what is and is not a computer program is not always easy when it comes to the Web which includes technologies such as mark-up languages and protocols. For example, the CDPA does not define "computer program".

In respect of such intellectual property the author's rights will include moral rights and copyright.

3.3.1 Moral rights

In addition to the copyright, the author of certain works has certain "moral" rights, some of which first need to be asserted in writing, all of which may be waived and none of which can be assigned to another party. The rights are:

(a) to be identified as the author or director (which must be first asserted in writing);

(b) the right to object to a derogatory treatment of the work (which includes mutilating it or treating it in some way prejudicial to the reputation of the author);

(c) not to have authorship of a work falsely attributed to him; and

(d) the right to privacy in respect of photographs and films commissioned for private and domestic purposes.

3.3.2 *Copyright subsistence*

There are a number of problems with using an analogue system of copyright protection in the digital domain. They include the following subsistence issues.

3.3.2.1 *Fixation (subsistence of copyright)*

The Berne Convention leaves it to individual members of the Union to decide if works must be fixed to qualify for copyright. The Rome Convention requires that in respect of phonograms the sounds be "fixed".

If fixation of the work is required for it to qualify for protection then what degree of permanence is required? Is it sufficient if the works are temporarily stored in a computer's temporary Random Access Memory ("RAM")?

If a person extemporises a speech or a jazz musician improvises a rendition no copyright work comes into existence unless and until it is recorded (or broadcast – i.e. by wireless means). If it is streamed over a digital, wired network, with no permanent copy being stored, is there "fixation"? There may be in some countries but not others – where national laws diverge – as the data travels the network. If not, no copyright in a musical work or sound recording is created.

3.3.2.2 *Publication (subsistence of copyright)*

Copyright can protect both published and unpublished literary and artistic works and sound recordings.

Published musical works whose authors are not qualifying nationals would be protected under the Berne Convention if the work is:

(a) first published in a qualifying country; or

(b) if first published outside a union country, simultaneously published in a qualifying country.

Under Berne, the meaning of "published works" means "works published with the consent of their authors, whatever may be the means of manufacture of the copies provided that the availability of such copies has been such as to satisfy the reasonable requirements of the public, having regard to the nature of the work".[38]

Under the Rome Convention, "phonograms" are protected if first published or first fixed in a contracting state (states may elect). If first published in a non-contracting state they still qualify for protection if subsequently published in a contracting state within 30 days. "Publication" means "the offering of copies of a phonogram to the public in reasonable quantity".[39]

It is increasingly common for companies to make literary, musical and artistic works and films and sound recordings first available via the Internet.

---

[38]   Article 3(3).

[39]   *See* footnote 18.

It is possible that such works have not been previously published in the atomic world. If not "authored" by a qualifying author then copyright will exist only if the first publication or fixation condition is fulfilled.

If a work is stored on a server awaiting access but is not accessed, is it published? Has there been any "offering" or any offering "of copies"? Has such offering been to "the public"?

If the work is "published" where is it first published? In the state where the user's computer is located? Could it be said to have been first published in a state where a network server is located (over which the data may pass) even though Internet data may travel in separately routed data packets? How could an owner realistically know?

The Berne Convention makes clear that wired communication itself is not publication; publication under the UCC requires a tangible reproduction; the Rome Convention depends on fixation for the concept of publication in respect of sound recordings.

Thus, at the international level, the new digital products may not easily qualify for copyright where its subsistence depends on publication and place of first publication. The Rome Convention permits contracting countries to choose between the place of first fixation and that of first publication, allowing greater national divergence.[40]

3.4   Copyright infringement

"If the qualification requirements of this Chapter, or Section 163 [Crown], 165 [Parliament] or 168 [international organisations] are once satisfied in respect of a work, copyright does not cease to subsist by reason of any subsequent event."[41] Thus, putting a work on the Internet does not remove its qualification for copyright protection.

3.4.1   *Copying*

It is an infringement of copyright to copy the work.[42] Copying in relation to a literary, dramatic, musical or artistic work means reproducing the work in any material form.[43]

This includes storing the work in any medium by electronic means.[44] In relation to any description of work, copying includes the making of copies that are transient or incidental to some other use of the work.[45]

This clearly covers permanent storage in such media as hard drives, as well as temporary storage in RAM. The same is true under US law.[46]

---

[40]   The UK's DTI looked at the issue of changing, *see* report by NERA "Copyright Protection of Foreign Sound Recordings" HMSO 1989.

[41]   Section 153(1).

[42]   Section 17(1).

[43]   Section 17(2).

[44]   Section 17(2).

[45]   Section 17(6).

[46]   *Sega Enterprises v MAPHIA* 857 F Supp 679 (ND Cal 1994) – a position now enshrined in the Digital Millennium Copyright Act 1998 - *see* Section 3.7.1.

The same issue is raised in the EC's Directive harmonising the law applicable to computer programs (Directive 91/250/EEC on the Legal Protection of Computer Programs). It provides that copying includes the "...permanent or temporary reproduction of a computer program by any means and in any form..." and that "insofar as loading, displaying, running, transmission, or storage of the computer program necessitate such reproduction, such acts shall be subject to authorisation by the rightholder".[47] There is English authority that even the copying of a work on-screen can amount to an infringement.[48]

This does create difficulties for those operating equipment that forms part of the Internet infrastructure, such as ISPs. Copies are continually being made on their servers as part of the everyday, authorised transmission of copyright works.

3.4.1.1 Derogation from grant

In what circumstances may a user be liable for using copyright works on the Internet? Clearly, downloading another's work to a server will create a copy that will infringe copyright if made in the UK. Will the user be liable for downloading a copy of the work or receiving it as a bitstream where the transmission is not expressly authorised by the owner? If the transmission is by the owner he will be unable to complain that the necessary and consequential copy made by the user infringes his copyright. The principle of non-derogation from grant has the authority of the House of Lords[49] and would appear to apply to situations where the owner of a work makes it available from a website. The owner will know that a copy will be made by the person accessing it, at least in RAM, and he can hardly complain when that happens. However, how far does that principle extend? Does it mean that the owner cannot complain if the user prints off a permanent copy, or stores the work permanently on his hard drive, or stores it on the local network through which he accessed the site (e.g. a corporate intranet)? Can the owner complain that browser cache copies are being made if his site is viewable by a browser that is known to have a cache function? The owner would be well advised to create an express licence making such matters clear. If the user steps beyond the authority given to him by the owner or the law then he may infringe copyright if he commits a restricted act. The difficulties of categorising such acts are examined below.

3.4.1.2 Permitted acts

The user may still not infringe the copyright in a work even though he does not have the express permission of the owner or the benefit of the "derogation from grant" principle because he comes within the provisions of the CDPA dealing with "permitted acts".[50] There are a variety of them and they include the following:

---

[47]   Article 4.

[48]   *Bookmakers' Afternoon Greyhound Services Ltd v. Wilf Gilbert (Staffordshire) Ltd* [1994] FSR 723 – a decision made under the 1956 Copyright Act.

[49]   *British Leyland Motor Corporation Ltd v. Armstrong Patents Co Ltd* [1986] 1All E.R. 850.

[50]   Sections 28 et seq.

(a) fair dealing with a literary, dramatic, musical or artistic work (or in the case of a published work, in the typographical arrangement) for the purposes of research or private study does not infringe any copyright in the work[51] (except that in the case of a database the source must be indicated);[52]

(b) fair dealing in a work for the purpose of criticism or review, of that or another work or of a performance of a work, does not infringe any copyright in the work provided that it is accompanied by a sufficient acknowledgement;[53]

(c) fair dealing with a work (other than a photograph) for the purpose of reporting current events does not infringe any copyright in the work provided that it is accompanied by a sufficient acknowledgement (not required for sound recordings, films, broadcasts or cable programs);[54]

(d) lawful users of a copy of a computer program making a back-up copy of it which it is necessary for them to have for the purposes of their lawful use;[55]

(e) the performance of any act that is necessary for the purpose of access to and use of the contents of a database in exercise of a right to such access and use.[56]

In respect of acts of fair dealing it is necessary that the dealing is both fair and necessary. Subject to that there is no reason why a criticism of a poem, for example, could not be posted to a website by the reviewer including a few lines from the poem. However, the question arises as to whether anyone could lawfully read it. The owner will not have authorised its presence on the Web. The reviewer cannot authorise the performance of any restricted acts. The site visitor is not reviewing or criticising the work and cannot be said to be undertaking any "fair dealing" as a result. The same problem would not affect the reader of a magazine in which a similar review appeared as the reader is not making a "copy" in any conventional sense when they read it. However, to access the Internet version they must make a copy on screen and in RAM which, for reasons set out above, would amount to an infringement.

3.4.2 *Issuing copies to the public*

The issue to the public of copies of a work is an act restricted by the copyright. The meaning of "issuing copies" and "the public" has been touched on in the context of qualification rather than infringement of copyright. CDPA Section 175(1)(b) applies a definition of what amounts to issuing copies to the public for the purposes of defining "publication" under Section 177, not for the purposes of defining it as an infringement under Section 18. It is, therefore, unclear whether making a work available from an electronic retrieval system could amount to "issuing copies to the public" within the meaning of CDPA Section 18. There are complications in treating "electronic files" as copies in connection with the "exhaustion of rights" principle.

---

51   Section 29(1).

52   Section 29(1A).

53   Section 30(1).

54   Section 30(2).

55   Section 50A(1).

56   Section 50D(1).

3.4.2.1   *Exhaustion of rights*

Goods that are *unlawfully* on the market are dealt with according to specific provisions of the CDPA. CDPA Section 22 prohibits the importation of infringing copies of works into the UK.[57] By virtue of Section 27(3) an infringing copy includes a copy which would have been infringing if made in the UK and which is, or is proposed to be, imported into the UK.[58]

As a result, if goods have been manufactured either without the consent of the copyright owner, or with the owner's consent to do so only outside the UK, then those goods may not be imported into the UK without the copyright owner's permission. This is true whether or not the importation is from within or outside the EU. However, what is the position where goods are lawfully on the market of the EU with the owner's consent?

The principle of exhaustion of rights means that once a copy of a work has been placed lawfully on the market with the owner's consent, he becomes unable to assert his copyright in order to prevent the subsequent distribution or sale of that copy, subject to certain conditions. In the 1971 case of *Deutsche Grammophon v. Metro*[59] (which was concerned with the distribution of physical goods) the European Court of Justice (the "ECJ") held that:

(a) although Article 36 of the Treaty of Rome permits prohibitions on the free movement of goods, it does so only to the extent that they are justified "for the protection of the rights that form the specific object" of the property; and

(b) therefore it would conflict with the principle of free movement if a copyright owner could use his exclusive distribution right to prevent the marketing of his goods in one Member State which had been sold by him or with his consent in another Member State.

The Court did not identify what it meant by the "specific object" of the property.

Copyright is really a bundle of rights. This leads to the possibility that the rights of an owner of a copyright work may be exhausted in some respects but not in others. Consequently, the issue of parallel importation of copyright works is concerned not simply with the exhaustion of copyright but with the exhaustion of the individual rights of which it is comprised.

This distinction is critical as shown by the first of the two *Coditel* cases to come before the ECJ.[60] In it, the ECJ considered whether the right to show a film in one Member State could be used to prevent its cable re-broadcast in that same member sourced from a television

---

[57]   "The copyright in a work is infringed by a person who, without the licence of the copyright owner, imports into the UK, otherwise than for his private and domestic use, an article which is, and which he knows or has reason to believe is, an infringing copy of the work."

[58]   "An article is also an infringing copy if (a) it has been or is proposed to be imported into the UK, and (b) its making in the UK would have constituted an infringement of the copyright in the work in question, or a breach of an exclusive licence agreement relating to that work."

[59]   *Deutsche Grammophon GmbH v. Metro-SB-Grossmarkte GmbH & Co KG*, Case 78/70 [1971] ECR 487.

[60]   SA Compagnie Generale Pour La Diffusion De La Television, *Coditel & Ors v. SA Cine Vog Films* (case 62/79)[1981] 2 CMLR 362 and *Coditel SA & Ors v. Cone Vog Films SA & Ors* (No 2) (case 262/81) [1983] FSR 148.

showing of it in another Member State. The ECJ decided that films were in a different category to goods as they are made publicly available by repeated performance. The economic benefit to a copyright owner whose works are embodied in goods is in the sale of those goods to the public. However, the economic value of a performance work, such as a film, lies in the copyright owner's ability to continue authorising its performance. In the case of a film this would be by its repeated broadcast to different audiences.

Consequently, the copyright owner could exercise his exclusive, national right to authorise performance of a work in order to prevent the showing of that work in a Member State, notwithstanding that it had already been lawfully shown in another Member State.

If a work is lawfully digitalised, stored on a network server for public access (e.g. a world wide website) and transmitted to a browsing member of the public, the question arises whether the owner's rights have been exhausted. If so, then that and any other copies sent by him could be lawfully transmitted throughout the EU by others as parallel imports. By contrast, if the transmission is treated as the performance of a work or a service then the principle of *Coditel* will apply. As such the owner could prevent the further transmission of those "copies" within the EU.

3.4.3 *Rental and lending*

It is an act restricted by the copyright in a work to rent or lend it to the public.[61] "Rental" means "making a copy of the work available for use, on terms that it will or may be returned for direct or indirect economic or commercial advantage...".[62] "Lending" means "making a copy of the work available for use, on terms that it will or may be returned, otherwise than for direct or indirect economic or commercial advantage, through an establishment which is accessible to the public."[63]

The contrast with the wording of CDPA Section 18 is to be noted. There the Act speaks of "the issue to the public of copies" whereas here we are concerned with "making them available". Whilst the latter expression may better suit the operation of file serving, CDPA Section 18A poses a different problem with the requirement that the work will or may be "returned". Obviously it is possible that files could be made to self-erase after a period of time, but that is not the same thing as being returned. Furthermore, in relation to lending, the expression "establishment which is accessible to the public" is unhelpful in the online context. Though intended to cover "bricks and mortar" operations, it is unclear if this would include a shopping mall, for example.

There still remains the problematic concept of "copies". In this respect one would expect CDPA Sections 18 and 18A to be treated consistently.

---

61   Section 18A(1).

62   Section 18A(2)(a).

63   Section 18A(2)(b).

3.4.4 *Performing, showing or playing in public*

CDPA Section 19 provides that the performance of a literary, dramatic or musical work in public is a restricted act. "Performance" includes "in general, any mode of visual or acoustic presentation, including presentation by means of a sound recording, film, broadcast or cable program of the work." In relation to sound recordings, films, broadcasts or cable programs the playing or showing of the work in public is restricted by the copyright.

The application of this Section provides little difficulty in cyberspace because sub-Section 19(4) provides that:

> "Where copyright in a work is infringed by its being performed, played or shown in public by means of apparatus for receiving visual images or sounds conveyed by electronic means, the person by whom the visual images or sounds are sent, and in the case of a performance the performers, shall not be regarded as responsible for the infringement."

Accordingly, the owner will not be able to sue the person sending the data for infringement by performance, playing or showing in public solely on the basis of him having sent it. Of course, it may have been necessary to copy the work or it may have been included in a cable program service but these are different infringements to that covered by CDPA Section 19.

There are questions about whether those who are peripherally involved in the transmission of the data but are not the original sender of the data would be liable. CDPA Section 19 refers in the singular to "the person by whom" it is sent which tends to refer to the originator rather than others involved in the routing process or Internet Service Provision. However, it is to be borne in mind that Section 19 of CDPA is concerned with the acts of performing, playing or showing in public and it is unlikely that the activities of these others would involve that.

A difficulty that arises in CDPA Section 19 as well as in other parts of the CDPA is the notion of "the public". There is a considerable body of case law on the meaning of that phrase, a consideration of which is beyond this Chapter. The interested reader is referred to the standard reference works on the subject. However, what is clear is that domestic or quasi-domestic audiences will not be covered and that otherwise the question must be judged by looking at the nature of the audience without imposing an unnecessarily strict interpretation on the meaning.[64]

3.4.5 *Broadcasts and cable program services*

3.4.5.1 *Broadcasts*

CDPA Section 6 defines "broadcast" as "...a transmission by wireless telegraphy of visual images, sounds or other information which:

(a) is capable of being lawfully received by members of the public, or

(b) is transmitted for presentation to members of the public;...."

---

[64] *See* "The Modern Law of Copyright and Designs" 2nd Ed p. 407.

It follows that if Internet transmissions do not amount to communication to the "public" (*see* above), then it will not amount to a broadcast under CDPA Section 6(1)(b). Section 6(1)(a) is primarily aimed at encrypted transmissions where the reception in the UK is authorised. By analogy, an encrypted transmission over the Internet which was unlawfully unencrypted and re-broadcast would not amount to a broadcast under Section 6(1)(a). Even if it were lawful it would still need to be by "wireless" means. There is no reason why an Internet transmission has to be by wired communication with the prevalence of satellite and mobile telephony but it is likely to at least involve wired communication at some point in the data packet's journey. It is unclear whether a court would characterise one transmission as being in part a broadcast and in another part a wired communication but it is possible.

The consequences of the transmission being a broadcast are that other Sections of the CDPA will come into play – principally those that provide exemptions and a scheme of compulsory licensing for the inclusion of works in broadcasts. These include the right to make ephemeral copies and to include certain works in the broadcast.

3.4.5.2   *Cable program services*

The Internet existed at the time the CDPA came into force but it does not appear that it was in the mind of the Government. What was recognised is that digital and online services would need to be catered for. To this end, provision was made for the delivery of works via cable and telecommunications systems and it was acknowledged that these services could be interactive. Therefore, by luck, judgement or a combination of both, Parliament managed to pass a definition of cable program service which fairly neatly defined Internet transmissions. It is a quirk of English law that online transmissions are covered by such a provision. This produces both good and bad consequences. On the one hand, it means that it is less imperative to introduce a more appropriate definition than if there had been a complete vacuum. Whilst many services are therefore within the CDPA they must be shoehorned into a definition that might have been better worded had it been bespoke drafted for online transmissions. It also means that many provisions intended to cover cable programs also incidentally include website transmissions, which does not necessarily suit the owners of copyright works.

CDPA Section 7, so far as relevant, provides:

> "(1) In this Part – "cable program" means any item included in a cable program service; and "cable program service means a service which consists wholly or mainly in sending visual images, sounds or other information by means of a telecommunications system, otherwise than by wireless telegraphy, for reception –
>
> (a)   at two or more places (whether for simultaneous reception or at different times in response to requests by different users), or
>
> (b)   for presentation to members of the public,
>
>   and which is not, or so far as it is not, excepted by or under the following provisions of this Section."

There is an exception set out in sub-Section 7(2)(a) which covers:

"a service or part of a service of which it is an essential feature that while visual images, sounds or other information are being conveyed by the person providing the service there will or may be sent from each place of reception, by means of the same system or (as the case may be) the same part of it, information (other than signals sent for the operation or control of the service) for reception by the person providing the service or other persons receiving it."[65]

Sub-Section 7(5) provides:

"References in this Part to the inclusion of a cable program or work in a cable program service are to its transmission as part of the service; and references to the person including it are to the person providing the service."

It is therefore important to note that though websites may be held to fall within Section 7(1) it will not always be the case that the same website remains a cable program service. Sometimes it may be and sometimes not depending on its mode of operation. Thus, a bank's website might be a cable program service until it is used but at the point that a customer uses it to receive a service it will be excepted from that definition.

This has important repercussions because of what flows from classifying websites as cable program services (or broadcasts). For example, the CDPA provides that the following do not amount to infringements in respect of cable program services: timeshift recording;[66] free showing in public of a cable program;[67] and to make an ephemeral recording for the purposes of transmission.[68]

The question of whether websites are cable program services was raised but not answered in the undecided, *Shetland Times* case, (considered above). The point remains undecided.

3.4.6   Adaptations

In the case of literary or dramatic works, "adaptation" includes a translation of the work.[69] This would include a translation from analogue into digital form. However, since an adaptation is made only when recorded it is arguable that this process of change is not an infringement when it occurs in a modem as the signal is not "recorded". Computer programs are covered by provisions specific to them and include translating the work from one level of language to another.

---

[65]   The application of this exception is unclear. During the Bill's passage through Parliament it was said in the House of Lords by Lord Young of Graffham: "However, what should not come within Clause 7 are those elements of a service which are genuinely interactive in the sense that input from the user modifies what is contained in or sent through the system....The result in relation to Prestel and similar services, for example, is that, in their normal mode of presenting information to the user, they will fall within Clause 7 but, when they are used for purposes of ordering goods or conducting banking transactions, they will not".

[66]   Section 70.

[67]   Section 72.

[68]   Section 68(2).

[69]   Section 21(3)(a)(i).

3.4.7   *Authorisation*

It is a primary infringement to authorise outside the UK the commission of an act in the UK which is restricted by the copyright. "Authorisation" implies that the person purports to have authority to permit the act to be done. This is to be distinguished from mere facilitation. If a website makes works available without authority on servers outside the UK it may be difficult for the proprietor to argue that he was not implicitly holding out that a copy could be made in the UK when a surfer located in it accessed the work. However, a website that merely has user operated links to infringing works may only be facilitating an infringement authorised by the proprietor of the linked-to website.

3.4.8   *Secondary infringements*

Secondary infringements require a degree of guilty knowledge: the infringer must know, or have reason to believe, that the matter complained of is an infringing thing. The Act speaks of "articles" and "copies". Sections 22–26 inclusive set out the range of secondary infringements. Some would appear to have a potential impact on Internet transmissions whilst others do not.

3.4.9   *Dealings with articles*

CDPA Section 22 is concerned with the importation into the UK of "articles" which are infringing copies (or which the importer knows or has reason to believe are infringing copies) other than for private or domestic use. If an electronic file is a copy for the purposes of CDPA Section 18, is there any reason why it should not be for the purposes of Section 22? Articles do not include, for example, broadcast signals. Should wire communications be treated differently? If so, then identifying the importer becomes relevant. Section 22 does not apply to the recipient's private and domestic use.

CDPA Section 23 applies to the act of possessing or dealing with infringing copies and covers:

(a) possession in the course of a business;

(b) selling/letting for hire/offering or exposing for sale or hire;

(c) in the course of a business exhibiting in public or distributing; and

(d) distributing otherwise than in the course of a business to such an extent as to prejudicially affect the owner of the copyright;

(e) an article which is, and which he knows or has reason to believe is, an infringing copy of a work.

If the act of distribution applies to tangible copies then the parts of this Section referring to that activity are unlikely to apply to electronic transmission. As to the other acts covered there does not appear to be any reason why they could not affect hosts and transmitters of such works in digital form.

3.4.10   *Providing the means for making infringing copies*

Whilst CDPA 1988 Section 24(1) deals with articles used for making copies, it refers to articles "specifically adapted" for that purpose which suggests it is aimed at something more than items that are no more than copies. The provisions of Section 24(2) applies where Section 7 (cable programs) does not. It prohibits the unauthorised transmission of a work by means of a telecommunications system by a person who knows, or has reason to believe, that an infringing copy will be made by means of the reception of the transmission in the UK or elsewhere. The infringing copy must be made by virtue of the reception alone. If the recipient does not make a permanent copy an action under CDPA Section 24(2) may depend on the arguments about whether RAM and cache copies are infringing copies.

3.5   Linking

Hypertext links are addresses of files located on the Internet. They are embedded in the text of the page and are usually disguised by a different phrase, often highlighted. The links can be to a page or to a particular work deep in the website. In any event, the work arrives at the recipient's computer without a copy of the work(s) being made on the linking site. Links can be executed manually by the viewer or automatically. A link can be used to bring to the visitor's screen a composite made up of information from the linking site and information from the linked site. As a result, a visitor may perceive information from different sites appearing as one page of the linking site without knowing that some of the work is actually being transmitted from a different site. As no copying is being done by the owner of the linking site, can copyright be used to prevent such linking from occurring?

It might be thought effective for the owner of the linked site to impose licence terms which prohibit accessing the site by a link at all or accessing other than by a link to the home page. Would this make accessing by unauthorised links an infringement? Arguably not. First of all, absent any restriction, it is likely that a website owner grants an implied licence to access the works in a website. Otherwise, why would they be there? A website owner may seek to impose the terms of an express licence. The licence need not be a contract, just a simple permission. It is true that in respect of primary infringing acts, innocence is no defence as liability is strict. However, it might be thought unfeasible to hold that the terms of a copyright licence could be secret. If so, a sufficient attempt would have to be made to draw them to the attention of the prospective licencee. By the time visitors using a link see the page on which the terms are displayed it is too late to retrospectively impose terms of use on them. It might be possible for the licence to state that if the user does not agree to the terms then he should proceed no further. But if the visitor does then proceed to access works in a manner beyond the scope of the licence the causal link to the linking site proprietor has been broken and no authorisation could be said to have been given by that person.

Even if the initial access by the visitor via a link could amount to a breach of a licence governing the use of the linked site, the claim for infringement would be against the visitor. A claim of authorisation might be made against the person making the link but the act of linking might be said to amount only to facilitation rather than authorisation. The former is not actionable.[70] Arguably, the linked site does more than facilitate because the excution of the link compels the making of a copy of the linked work by the visitor. It might be inferred from that fact that the proprietor of the linked site purported to have authority to make a copy of the linked work. Were that the case, the linking party would still have the same defences based on ignorance of the licence terms as the visitor would have in order to defeat any allegation of infringement or authorisation of it.

If the link itself is a copy of another's work then an infringement under CDPA Section 17 may follow. In the *Shetland Times* case,[71] it was not disputed that the headlines forming the link could be protected by copyright.

---

70   *CBS Songs Inc v. Amstrad Consumer Electronics plc.* [1988] AC 1013.

71   *Shetland Times Ltd v. Wills* [1997] EMLR 277.

In the absence of copying, the proprietor of the linked site might have a claim under CDPA Section 20. That was the alternative claim in the *Shetland Times* case, on which the pursuers succeeded at the interim hearing stage. The court's reasoning is unclear and it is not obvious that such a claim will always succeed. Section 20 provides:

> "The broadcasting of a work or its inclusion in a cable program service is an act restricted by the copyright in –
>
> (a)   a literary, dramatic, musical or artistic work;
>
> (b)   a sound recording or film; or
>
> (c)   a broadcast or cable program."

The argument is that the work or works in the linked site are included, without permission, in a cable program service by the person creating the link.

In the *Shetland Times* case the user had to click on the link to execute it. At that point he was taken from the linking site to the linked site. It is arguable that when he became connected to the linked site and the data flowed to him from that site the work was being transmitted as part of the service represented by the linked site not the linking site.

Realistically, if the linking site is the service then what is included within it if a manual link is established? The address of the file. If that amounts to including, within the linking site service, the work to which that link points, then it is difficult to know where the chain stops. By implication there is also included all the works which are pointed at by the linked site and so on.

Alternatively, one must argue that the address itself represents an item that has been included in the service. However, it does not seem sensible to argue that. Otherwise the test for originality that creates a threshold for deserving works is defeated. It is also inconsistent with other parts of the Act, such as the wording of Section 72.

If the link is an automatic link then the linked site's work may appear as part of the linking site. Here it is easier to see that the work might be included as part of the linking site service. The question derived from sub-Section 7(5) is whether the linked work is transmitted as part of the linking site service. Arguably it is not as there are simply two services being provided: one by the linked site and one by the linking site. This same reasoning applies to frames.[72]

3.5.1   *Newsgroups*

Newsgroups arguably have a special place because the duplication and onward transmission of the contents of the Newsgroups is undertaken automatically by software without any human intervention. In the *RTC Church of Scientology v. Netcom*[73] case, which concerned the reproduction of copyright materials over Newsgroups, the court found missing the "volitional" or causal elements necessary to hold the operator directly liable for copying which is automatic and caused by a subscriber.

---

[72]   Litigation in the US has addressed some of these isues: *Ticketmaster v. Microsoft* suit filed 28 April 1997 and *The Washington Post Co. v. Total News Inc.*, DC SNY 97 Civ 1190 (PKL) – settled.

[73]   *Church of Scientology Religious Technology Center v. Netcom On-Line Communication Services Inc.*, US District Court for the Northern District of California, 21 November 1995.

3.5.2 Databases

3.5.2.1 Copyright protection of databases

The Copyright and Rights in Databases Regulations came into force in the UK on 1 January 1998 and implement the EU Directive on the legal protection of databases. They do so by amending the CDPA 1988.

Originality is a precondition of copyright subsistence. In the UK, for example, the test for originality is whether the work has been produced by the owner's "sweat of the brow". In other countries, originality demands some intellectual creativity. Thus, there is disparity with the consequence that some works protected in the UK would not be protected in other jurisdictions.

The Directive (and the Regulations which implement them in the UK) are intended to harmonise this discordance and seek to do so by:

(a) amending the existing rules of copyright regarding the copyright protection of databases; and

(b) creating a brand new right specific to databases which gives them protection against certain acts for a term of 15 years.

UK law protected databases by copyright under the CDPA 1988 as literary works, though when passed, that Act did not specifically refer to them (though it does refer to tables and compilations).[74]

The Regulations amend Section 3(1) of the CDPA 1988 so that databases on the one hand, and tables/compilations on the other, are unequivocally identified as different types of protected, literary works.

The meaning of "database" is now defined in Section 3A of the CDPA 1988. It means:

"...a collection of independent works, data or other materials which –

(a) are arranged in a systematic or methodical way, and

(b) are individually accessible by electronic or other means."

The same Section goes on to state that:

"...a literary work consisting of a database is original if, and only if, by reason of the selection or arrangement of the contents of the database the database constitutes the author's own intellectual creation."

This has fundamentally affected the copyright protection of databases under UK law for the future. Because of this, "saving" provisions are included within the Regulations to protect many existing databases (*see* Section 3.5.2.2).

In future, a database will only qualify for UK copyright protection if it is, in accordance with Section 3A, by reason of the selection or arrangement of the contents of the database, the author's own intellectual creation.

---

[74]   Section 3(1)(a).

There are various other amendments in copyright terms: for example, the infringing act of "adapting" in relation to a database now means "...an arrangement or altered version of the program or a translation of it";[75] fair dealing in databases excludes anything done for a commercial purpose.[76]

The Regulations provide that if the database had been created and was protected in an EC Member State, on or before 27 March 1996, but does not fulfill the "intellectual creation" requirement of originality then, nevertheless, the remaining term of the protection it had enjoyed should continue unaffected.

Therefore, any computer generated databases protected by UK copyright on 27 March 1996 will enjoy the remainder of their term. Those created after 27 March 1996 will not be protected by UK copyright as from 1 January 1998.

3.5.2.2 *New database right*

The database right introduced into the UK by the Regulations is a brand new right which did not previously exist under UK law. It only protects databases made on or after 1 January 1983.

The database right subsists where there has been a substantial investment of financial, human or technical resources in obtaining, verifying or presenting the contents of a database. Substantiality is to be judged by quantity and/or quality.

The right first belongs to the person who takes the initiative in making a database and assumes the risk of investing in its making (subject to the usual rule about employers and their employees).

Subject to specific exceptions, the right protects against:

(a) the permanent or temporary transfer of all or a substantial part of the contents of a database to another medium by any means or in any form ("extraction"); and

(b) making all or a substantial part of the contents of a database available to the public by any means ("re-utilisation").

The Regulations also provide that repeated and systematic extraction or re-utilisation of insubstantial parts of the contents may amount to the doing of those acts in relation to a substantial part.

There is a fair dealing right for non-commercial extraction (teaching and research) which does not apply to re-utilisation.

The term of protection for database rights is 15 years from the end of the year in which the database was completed. If during that 15-year period the database is made available to the public then the term expires 15 years from the end of the year in which it was first made available. Any changes to the database that would result in the database being considered to be a substantial new investment qualify that database for its own term of protection.

---

[75]   Section 21(3)(ac).

[76]   For example Sections 29(1A) and 29(5).

3.6 The legal initiatives

To address the problems outlined above and some others arising in other jurisdictions, initiatives are taking place at several levels, including WIPO and the EU, that are likely to affect the future direction of UK copyright law in this area. This Section looks at initiatives at WIPO and in the EU.

3.6.1 WIPO

The United Nations, through the auspices of WIPO, considered the need to improve the protection of certain intellectual property rights in the digital age. The consultations amongst members of the WIPO culminated in Geneva in 1996 with the proposal of three new instruments: the first, an amendment to the Berne Convention (the "Berne Amendment Treaty"); the second, a New Instrument which is not associated with any other Treaty but does state that it shall not derogate from any other (e.g. the Rome Convention and the "Phonograms Treaty") and the third, a new Treaty on databases (the "Database Treaty"). This last could not be agreed upon and was dropped. The other two were unanimously approved by those present (after amendment).[77]

One of the key compromises on the Berne Amendment Treaty concerned whether transient copies are infringing copies which consequently impacted on ISP liability. A proposed article to the effect that the reproduction right gave the owner the exclusive right to make even transient copies was strongly objected to and in the end dropped in order to achieve unanimity. Instead an agreed statement noted that the reproduction right covered by the Berne Convention includes the right to make digital copies. The scope and effect of that statement are unclear.

3.6.1.1 The Berne Amendment Treaty

In relation to literary works the Treaty begins by clarifying points which have been in issue in some jurisdictions by expressly providing that: computer programs are protected as literary works (Article 4) and compilations of data or other material whose content selection/arrangement makes them intellectual creations are protected as such (Article 5).

There is also confirmation that authors of literary and artistic works have the exclusive right of authorising the making available to the public of the original and copies of their works through sale or other transfer (Article 6).

Article 7 confirms that the authors of computer programs, cinematographic works and works embodied in phonograms enjoy an exclusive rental right.

The Treaty creates an exclusive right of authorising communication to the public of works by wire or wireless means (including in on demand services) (Article 8).

Article 10 permits individual countries to provide exceptions to these rights but subject to the three-step test set out in Article 9(2) of the Berne Convention.

It proscribes interference with protective devices and systems for managing information about rights ownership (Article 11). Article 12 requires Member States to provide adequate and effective legal remedies against those who interfere in certain ways with rights

---

[77] Those WIPO members who are signatories to the two Treaties as at 18 March 1998 are listed in Schedule 5.

management information ("RMI") systems or deal in copies whose RMI systems have been removed or altered knowing or having reason to believe that it will induce, enable, facilitate or conceal an infringement of any right under this Treaty or the Berne Convention.

3.6.1.2 *The Phonograms Treaty*

The Treaty on performers and producers of phonograms effectively creates a new moral right of paternity for performers in respect of their live and recorded performances (Article 5). In addition, they acquire the right to authorise the broadcast, communication to the public and fixation of their unfixed performances (Article 6).

The Treaty grants to performers an exclusive right to authorise reproduction (Article 7), distribution (Article 8) and rental of copies of their recorded performances (Article 9) and to make available their recorded performances "online" whether by wire or wireless means (including in an on demand service) paralleling the Treaty on literary works (Article 10).

Producers of phonograms (that is the entity that takes the initiative and has the responsibility for the first fixation of the sounds) shall enjoy the exclusive right of authorising the direct or indirect reproduction of their phonograms in any manner or form (Article 11).

Article 12 confirms that producers of phonograms shall have the exclusive right of authorising the making available to the public of the original and copies of the phonograms. However, individual states are left to determine the conditions under which exhaustion shall apply.

The treaty provides that to the extent that a system is already in place for the equitable remuneration of performers and producers of phonograms, that system may be maintained if it does not materially impair their exclusive rights of reproduction.

Article 15 provides that performers and producers of phonograms shall be entitled to a single equitable remuneration for the direct or indirect use of phonograms published for commercial purposes, for broadcasting, or for any communication to the public. National legislatures may provide that the remuneration may be claimed from the user by the performer or producer or both. States may introduce exceptions consistent with the three-step test.

It contains the same provisions for technological measures and RMI as the Bernen Amendment Treaty. The Treaties will come into effect three months after 30 states have ratified or acceded to them.

By these two proposals the members of the WIPO have attempted to amend, clarify and add to existing international conventions to address potential shortcomings concerned with reproductions and on-demand communications to the public.

However, there was no resolution of the temporary reproduction issue. The right to create exceptions under the Treaties (the three-step test) remains as wide as ever creating little hope for a common approach to the protection of rights.

3.6.2   ***The European Union***

3.6.2.1   *Harmonisation of copyright generally*

There is a tremendous amount of activity at EU level to harmonise copyright protection throughout Europe which is beyond the scope of this Chapter. It encompasses the issuing of the following Directives:

(a) 91/250/EEC on the legal protection of computer programs;

(b) 92/100/EEC on rental rights and lending rights and certain related rights;

(c) 93/83 on the coordination of certain rules applicable to satellite broadcasting and cable retransmissions;

(d) 93/98 on the harmonisation of the term of protection and certain related rights; and

(e) 96/9 on the legal protection of databases.

Computer programs are a prominent feature of online and offline works. They are transmitted over networks as much as any other form of literary work.

The issues of transient reproduction and the exceptions to it which face music rights owners have already been addressed in two of these Directives.

The Computer Programs Directive defined protected acts of reproductions as all "permanent or temporary reproduction...by any means and in any form...".[78] The same approach was taken in the Database Directive.[79] The defining provisions are those relevant to the authors' rights – not the neighboring rights. Both Directives also harmonise within the EU the exceptions to the right of reproduction.

However, there is doubt about exactly which reproduction rights are protected and there is still some disparity between Member States since harmonisation has only been achieved to a small extent.

3.6.2.2   *The EU and the Information Society*

One of the first significant steps in this area was the report of the high-level group on the Information Society to the Corfu European Council (the "Bangemann Group"). It concluded that a common regulatory approach should be developed to promote a competitive market for information services. It was followed by the Green Paper on Copyright and Related Rights in the Information Society[80] that identified a number of areas of copyright law that required consideration and raised a number of questions:

(a) how to ascertain where an act of infringement in the process of digital transmission takes place (i.e. whose law should apply)?;

(b) whether the copyright owner should be able to prevent the distribution of a work in other territories once it has been transmitted into an EU state?;

(c) whether the act of digitisation should constitute an infringing act of reproduction?;

---

[78]   Article 4(a).

[79]   Article 5.

[80]   COM (96) 568 final.

(d) when should transmissions be regarded as private/to the public at large?;

(e) whether a consent to digitisation is a waiver of moral rights?;

(f) whether there should be a centralised system of rights clearances with a scheme of management rules?; and

(g) whether the copyright should include a specific right to control digital dissemination?

After a number of responses had been received the Economic and Social Committee adopted an Opinion on the Green Paper on 31 January 1996. The Opinion identified as main priorities the following issues: the applicable law; the exhaustion principle; the protection of the right of digitalisation as part of the right of reproduction; identifying when there is a communication to the public in a network transmission; the harmonisation of moral rights; and balancing the interests of owners, users and consumers.

On 20 November 1996, pre-empting the WIPO Geneva conference, the EU Commission adopted a communication on Copyright and Related Rights in the Information Society as a follow-up to the Green Paper. It identified the initiatives required to achieve a level playing field of protection throughout the Internal Market. They covered the reproduction right (and harmonisation of its exceptions); the right of communication to the public; the legal protection of anti-copying systems; and the distribution right in respect of goods only (including EU harmonisation on the principle of exhaustion).

3.6.2.3 *The Proposal for a Draft Directive on Copyright and Related Rights in the Information Society*

On 10 December 1997, a new Proposal for a Draft Directive was adopted for the harmonisation of certain aspects of copyright and related rights in the Information Society (COM (97) 628 final).

The Commission appeared to be following the path of international direction at WIPO level, whilst providing for legislation along the same lines to ensure market harmonisation across the EU.

3.6.3 *Reproduction right*

On the issue of reproduction the Proposal (*see* Section 3.6.2.3) left the tendentious issue of the exceptions to this right to individual Member States. However, it did provide for obligatory exceptions to the reproduction right for certain technical acts of reproduction dictated by technology having no separate economic significance of their own (i.e. cache copies created during transmission).

The exceptions left to individual Member States were:

(a) reprographic rights;

(b) private copying; and

(c) copying by libraries.

This left the way open for Member States to introduce private copying levies (the UK, Eire and Luxembourg do not have them; Sweden and Portugal are introducing them).

3.6.4 Communication to the public

In respect of the communication of works to the public the Proposal focused on the act of offering to the public the restricted service. The proposal sought to harmonise the rights applicable to on-demand transmissions (as distinct from broadcasts and private communications).

The Proposal set out an exhaustive list of exceptions which, in addition to those listed in respect of the reproduction right, included teaching and scientific research; non-commercial use for the visually and hearing impaired; excerpts for reporting current events; and the use of quotations for criticism or literary review, administrative and judicial procedures.

3.6.5 Distribution and exhaustion

The Proposal addressed the distribution right and the issue of exhaustion. This did not apply to services in general or online. The Proposal provided for a system of Community-wide exhaustion in respect of tangible goods (e.g. CDs, CD ROMs and tapes).

3.6.6 Protection devices and RMI systems

The Proposal also required Member States to legislate against devices that circumvent anti-copying protection and against alteration of RMI systems.

3.6.7 Longer-term issues

There were a number of areas identified by the Commission as suitable not for short-term action but appropriate for further consideration. They were as follows:

(a) *the broadcasting right* – it is recognised that the impact of multi-channel broadcasting may promote this medium to the position of a primary market for music rights. The Commission intended to continue evaluation in this field;

(b) *applicable law and enforcement* – this is a matter of such complexity that the Commission intended to introduce a separate communication dealing with it;

(c) *management of rights* – the Commission proposed to continue to monitor this area;

(d) *moral rights* – the Commission intended to further consider whether, and if so, what further harmonisation is required;

(e) *ISP liability* – the EU's approach was to separate ISP liability from the copyright Proposal since it is a horizontal issue cutting across a number of other areas such as defamation, privacy, pornography and so on to be looked at separately (now dealt with in the Draft E-Commerce Directive).[81]

3.6.8 The amendments of the Legal Affairs and Citizen's Rights Committee

On 21 January 1998 the Commission submitted a proposal for a Directive. Parliament referred it to its Legal Affairs Committee (as well as the Committees on Environment, on Culture and on Economic and Monetary affairs). A draft report of Roberto Barzanti was considered by the Legal Affairs Committee that approved the draft legislative resolution unanimously.

---

81   European Parliament and Council Directive 2000/31/EC, OJ 2000 L178/1.

As a result, a Legislative proposal was made subject to a number of amendments seeking to alter existing draft recitals and articles and introduce new ones. The highlights were as follows:

Recital 3 was altered to emphasise the need for a high level of protection for intellectual property but not at the expense of the fundamental principles of an open and modern society in which freedom of expression and the public interest must be fully achieved.

Recital 9 was altered to recognise that producers should be properly rewarded for financing the creative work of authors and artists.

Recital 10(a) acknowledged that a consistent application of technical measures to protect works is ultimately the way to ensure that the legal principles are effective.

Recital 12 noted that the other directives such as that on e-commerce addressing the issue of liability for network environment activities should be put into force in conjunction with this one.

Recital 12(a) noted the necessity for transparency and rationalisation amongst collection societies as regards competition rules.

Recital 16 suggested that there be a harmonised exclusive right to make works available in an on-demand environment and that the mere fact that a transmission is between just two people does not, of itself, make it private.

Recital 23 was amended so that ephemeral copies are permitted as an exception to the right of reproduction to the extent that they are "transient and incidental reproduction forming an integral part and essential to a technological process carried out for the sole purpose of enabling the use of a work ...which is authorised or permitted by the law and which has no separate economic significance for the rightholders". This could also include caching or browsing.

Recital 26 provided that Member States should be allowed to provide for private copying subject to fair compensation being paid but it also envisaged a two-tier regime: the current one applying to analogue copying (e.g. the current blank tape levy) and a new one to apply to digital copying.

Recital 28(a) envisaged a study to improve new legal ways of solving disputes where there are accusations of infringements of authors' rights.

Recital 33(a) suggested that greater consumer confidence will ensue from more legal certainty as to the legitimate identity of a specific Internet site from which copyrighted materials may be obtained.

A new Article 2(2) implicitly recognised that in the digital world "use" amounts to copying and stated that, where contractual or statutory authorisation for use is given, it shall carry with it the right of reproduction if it is required for a merely incidental purpose and possesses no independent economic significance.

A new Article 3(4) provided that the mere provision of equipment does not amount to a communication.

New Article 3(5) recognized that some broadcasts may be predominantly made up of phonograms in such a way as to conflict with the normal exploitation of phonograms and prejudice the legitimate interests of phonogram producers in which case they shall have a right to equitable remuneration.

Whereas old Article 5(1) referred to "temporary" acts of reproduction, amended Article 5(1) referred to acts of reproduction that are "transient and incidental" and an integral and "essential" part of a technological process for the sole purpose of enabling a work to be used. Such acts were exempted from the exclusive right of reproduction subject to the further new condition that the use must be authorised by the rightholders or permitted by law and must have no economic significance for the rightholders.

Article 5(2) allowed Member States to create limitations to the reproduction right established by Article 2 in a series of specified circumstances. They were modified in the following way:

(a) an amendment excluded sheet music from the exception applying to reproductions on paper or a similar medium effected by any kind of photographic technique. It also imposed a right to receive fair compensation;

(b) it imposed a right to receive fair compensation in respect of reproductions on audio/visual/audio-visual recording media made by a natural person for private use and non-commercial ends;

(c) a new Article proposed a further circumstance where the right of reproduction may be limited – namely, where there does not exist any reliable and effective technical means capable of protecting the interests of the beneficiaries;

(d) the library type exception to the right of reproduction was specifically limited to acts of documentation or conservation;

(e) a specific exception to the reproduction right was proposed in respect of ephemeral recordings for the sole purpose of legitimate broadcasts; and

(f) a number of fair dealing type exceptions were proposed, for example for current events reporting purposes in respect of the analogous use of individual works from daily newspapers and radio and for the purposes of criticism or review.

By an addition to Article 5(4) these exceptions and limitations were not to prevent the use of technological means of protection.

Under a new Article 5(5) broadcasting organisations got the right to use, or authorise others to use, their archive productions produced or commissioned and financed by them for new broadcasting, on-demand or other multimedia services subject to payment of equitable remuneration to those that contributed to it (e.g. performers and authors).

Article 6(2) was revamped to deal with devices for circumventing copy protection. Member States would be required to provide against the manufacture or distribution of devices, products or components or the provision of services which:

(a) are promoted, advertised or marketed for the purpose of circumvention;

(b) have only a limited commercially significant other purpose; or

(c) are primarily designed, produced, adapted or performed to enable or facilitate circumvention.

A technical measure (not to be interfered with) is one designed to protect copyright or any related right and it is effective if access is enabled as a result only with the authority of the rightholder.

By a new Article 9(5), an author was entitled to receive reasonable remuneration proportional to the revenue from the exploitation of his work when he cedes or transfers his right of reproduction, communication to the public or distribution, and he may not renounce that right.

3.6.9 *Communication from the Commission to the European Parliament*

Subsequently, the Council adopted a common position on this proposal on 28 September 2000 following which the Commission gave an opinion on the Council's common position (27 November 2000) fully endorsing it. A summary of the Council's common position, as endorsed, is as follows:

Article 1 – the Directive will not affect those concerning computer programs, rental and lending rights, satellite and cable retransmission, term of protection or databases.

Article 2 – the following persons will have the exclusive right to authorise or prohibit direct or indirect, temporary or permanent reproduction by any means and in any form, in whole or in part:

(a) authors of their works;

(b) performers of fixations of their performances;

(c) phonogram producers of their phonograms;

(d) producers of first fixations of their films, in respect of the original and copies of their films;

(e) broadcasting organisations in respect of fixations of their broadcasts whether transmitted by wire or over air by cable or satellite.

Article 3 – to the same class of persons in respect of the same works the Directive grants an exclusive right in respect of communication to the public by wire or wireless means and provides that such right shall not be exhausted by any act of communication.

Article 4 – subject to exhaustion of rights there is an exclusive right to distribute to the public by sale or otherwise.

Article 5 – temporary acts of reproduction referred to in Article 2 which are transient or incidental and an integral and essential part of a technological process, whose sole purpose is to enable a transmission in a network between third parties by an intermediary or a lawful use and having no independent economic significance are exempted from the right of reproduction. Member States may provide for exceptions and limitations to the reproduction right (and where they do equally in respect of the distribution right) subject to certain conditions which include the Berne three-step test (*see* Section 3.6.1.1 above).

Article 6 – there is an obligation on Member States to create adequate legal protection against the circumvention of any effective technological measures carried out in the knowledge or with reasonable grounds to know that objective is being pursued. A similar requirement exists in relation to the manufacture, importation, distribution, sale (and so on) of products and devices the purpose of which is to achieve circumvention. In addition to, absent voluntary measures, Member States must ensure that the beneficiaries of exceptions and limitations are given the means to enjoy them. Such provision may also be made where private copying is impossible subject to rightholders being able to limit the number of reproductions.

Article 7 – Member States shall provide for adequate legal protection against certain acts affecting the integrity of rights management information.

3.6.10 *The Parliament's legislative resolution on the Council's common position ("second reading")*

On 14 February 2001, as part of the codecision procedure, the Parliament voted on amendments to the Council's common position. The focus of the amendments was on exceptions and limitations: the private copying exception featured strongly in light of the coincidental litigation against Napster in the US (*see* below). Ignoring the amendments that were proposed but not adopted, the amendments may be summarized as follows:

Aritcle 6 assures protection of technological measures but also empowers Member States to ensure this does not prevent the public's enjoyment of the benefits of exceptions and limitations. A proposed new Recital 52(a) clarifies that this empowerment does not apply, in the case of access via online interactive services, where the services are governed by contractual arrangements.

The exceptions to the right of reproduction set out in Article 5(2) include that of private copying in sub-paragraph (b). The wording "in respect of reproductions on any medium made for the private use of a natural person and for non-commercial ends" is proposed to be amended to "...by a natural person for private use and for ends that are neither directly nor indirectly commercial". In remains subject to a principle of fair compensation. This amendment clarifies that exceptions could not be aimed at a commercial or indirectly commercial operation like Napster. Whether Napster would themselves be liable for breach of the right of reproduction is a different question considered below.

In relation to the exceptions associated with teaching and scientific research, news reporting, literary criticism or review and political speeches (Articles 5(3)(a), (c), (d) and (f) respectively), the obligation has become one to indicate the source unless this is impossible rather than whenever possible.

One amendment excludes "any other commercial use" from the exception provisions of Article 5(3)(j) relating to use of works for advertising public exhibitions or sales or artistic works.

There is also an amendment to examine the impact of the Directive on the functioning of the internal market and to highlight any difficulties.

3.7   The US

3.7.1   The Digital Millennium Copyright Act 1998 (the "DCMA")

The DCMA is a statutory work of considerable complexity that can be summarised in the following way:

(a) Part I is concerned with the implementation of the WIPO Treaties;

(b) Part II is concerned with online copyright liability limitation. It seeks to set up a series of safe harbours for the benefit of ISPs in respect of some of their activities subject to them meeting certain conditions. If the ISP can enter the safe harbour then it is protected from claims for damages and injunctive relief[82] in respect of allegations of copyright infringement;

Routing – the conditions to be met are that the transmission is automatic and that there is no selection of recipients, no copies held longer than is necessary and no modification of the work.

Temporary storage – the safe harbour exists where the material was made available on-line by a third party, and was sent to and at the request of another third party, where the storage was automatic and for this purpose if the following conditions are also met. There is no modification of the material, the service provider complies with the originator's requirements as to refreshing etc., does not interfere with the technology's ability to report use of the work, has met any conditions imposed as regards access to the work and if, in certain circumstances, the service provider moves expeditiously to remove the work.

Hosting – service providers providing hosting services have a safe harbour where they do not have actual or constructive knowledge and on getting it to act quickly to remove the work; they do not receive remuneration directly attributable to the infringing activity in a case where it has the right and ability to control the activity. To deal with the "take down" requirements imposed on service providers as a condition of limited liability, the DCMA sets up a system for notification of claimed infringement that establishes a dialogue between the owner, the provider and the source of the alleged infringing version.

Linking – there is a safe harbour in respect of linking subject to the usual conditions as to knowledge, financial benefits and acting expeditiously to remove material. On condition that the service provider complies with a number of conditions it will not be liable for taking down information or denying subscribers access to the network. Subpoenas may be issued at the request of copyright owners against service providers for identification of an alleged infringer.

(c) Part III covers copyright issues arising out of computer maintenance; and

(d) Part IV deals with miscellaneous matters including rights in sound recordings and provides as follows:

---

[82]   Other than in respect of routing, providing connections, or transient storage in the course thereof, a court may grant injunctions restraining the provision of access to works, access to a subscriber, or as the court may see fit, to prevent copyright infringement at a particular location if that is the least burdensome of all comparable remedies.

In respect of certain digital audio transmissions[83] that are not part of an interactive service, the public performance of sound recordings is made subject to the scheme of statutory licensing if a number of conditions – set out in complex detail – are met.

3.8   Napster

It is perhaps worth considering – in the context of UK law – the high-profile case decided in the US involving the Internet service "Napster".

Napster had made available software that enabled users to file-swap between their Personal Computers ("PCs") on a peer-to-peer basis, sound recordings compressed in MP3 format. The argument advanced by the Recording Industry Association of America (as plaintiff) was that the majority of such files were unlawfully made copies of popular sound recordings and that as a result Napster was liable for contributory and vicarious copyright infringement. To succeed it had to show direct infringement by a third party (the users) and that Napster, with knowledge of such infringement, induced, caused or materially contributed to the infringing conduct. It succeeded in obtaining an injunction on that basis though that was stayed on an appeal. On appeal the US Court of Appeals for the Ninth Circuit upheld the injunction in amended form, continued the stay until the lower court amended its order and remanded the case back to the lower court for that purpose. The Appeal Court agreed that Napster users infringe the US copyright owner's rights of reproduction (downloaders) and distribution (uploaders). It agreed that the fair use defence did not apply. It found that Napster knowingly encourages and assists the infringement of copyrights. However, it took a different view on whether the system could be used for commercially significant non-infringing uses. Nor did it impute the requisite level of knowledge to Napster merely because peer to peer technology may lead to copyright infringements. In this connection it endorsed the decision in the *Netcom* case (*see* Section 3.5 above). However, it agreed that on the facts the plaintiffs would be likely to prevail on the issue of whether Napster knew or had reason to know of its users' infringements. It endorsed the view that Napster had actual knowledge of specific infringements and that it could block access but failed to do so. It also concluded that Napster materially contributes to the infringements by providing the site and facilities for that to happen. The Appeal Court also accepted the lower court's finding of a likelihood of success in establishing vicarious liability.

The original injunction compelled Napster to ensure copyright infringing acts did not occur on its system. That was changed to oblige the owners to notify Napster of infringements as a condition of its obligation to block access to the offending content. There are two problems with that: users can call the files what they like making identification difficult; and Napster does not have access to user's files.

What makes the case interesting from a UK perspective is that English law is phrased in terms of infringing or authorising infringement, where authorisation implies that the giver has power or authority to give permission for the use complained of.

The Napster software, effectively matches bargains so that if a user logged onto the server requests a file available from another user logged onto the server at that time the file is downloaded from the latter to the former. The files are not stored on or downloaded from the Napster server.

---

[83]   That is, those that are: (a) subscription digital audio; (b) non-subscription transmissions; or (c) non-exempt satellite digital audio radio services.

Despite the allegation that the service was mainly used for swapping infringing copies, it did not have to be used wholly or mainly for that purpose.

It is clear that the copies complained of were not being made with the permission of their purported owners. Were they infringing copies? If made outside the UK then such acts of copying did not amount to infringements of English law. However, transmitting them into the UK might amount to an infringement under the CDPA Section 7 and resulting copies made in the UK would be infringing.

It is also possible that the transmissions would be secondary infringements under the CDPA Section 22. It is unlikely that any of the exceptions created by the CDPA (such as Section 70 and the fair dealing defences) would apply.

It then follows whether Napster would be said to be liable for the acts of infringement committed in the UK by its users. In the case of *CBS Songs v. Amstrad Consumer Electronics plc. ("Amstrad")*, the House of Lords drew a distinction between "authorisation" in the sense explained above and mere facilitation. On that basis it might be said that Napster is responsible for facilitation only and not for authorising the infringements. However, there are two bases on which that view might fail to prevail.

First, looking again at the question in the age of the Internet the House of Lords might not follow itself. Second, in the *Amstrad* case, attention was given to the effect of the defendant having control over the infringers. Reference was made to an authority for the proposition that a person who has under their control the means by which an infringement may be committed, who makes it available to others, knowing or having reason to suspect that it is likely to be used for the purpose of committing an infringement, not taking steps to limit its use to legitimate purposes, would authorise any infringement that resulted from such use.[84] It is possible that the House of Lords would apply that doctrine to Napster and find it liable as a result.

The Internet poses a number of challenges to a system developed for an analogue world and how it will be applied judicially is unclear.

---

[84] *per* Gibbs J in *Moorhouse v. University of New South Wales* [1976] RPC 657.

Schedule 1

*Berne Convention Members
as at 19 January 1998*

Albania

Algeria

Argentina

Australia

Austria

Bahamas

Bahrain

Barbados

Belarus

Belgium

Benin

Bolivia

Bosnia and Herzegovina

Botswana

Brazil

Bulgaria

Burkina Faso

Cameroon

Canada

Cape Verde

Central African Republic

Chad

Chile

China

Colombia

Congo

Costa Rica

Côte d'Ivoire

Croatia

Cuba

Cyprus

Czech Republic

Democratic Republic of the Congo

Denmark

Dominican Republic

Ecuador

Egypt

El Salvador

Equatorial Guinea

Estonia

Fiji

Finland

France

Gabon

Gambia

Georgia

Germany

Ghana

Greece

Guatemala

Guinea

Guinea-Bissau

Guyana

Haiti

Holy See

Honduras	Morocco
Hungary	Namibia
Iceland	Netherlands
India	New Zealand
Indonesia	Niger
Ireland	Nigeria
Israel	Norway
Italy	Pakistan
Jamaica	Panama
Japan	Paraguay
Kenya	Peru
Latvia	Philippines
Lebanon	Poland
Lesotho	Portugal
Liberia	Republic of Korea
Libya	Republic of Moldova
Liechtenstein	Romania
Lithuania	Russian Federation
Luxembourg	Rwanda
Madagascar	Saint Kitts and Nevis
Malawi	Saint Lucia
Malaysia	Saint Vincent and the Grenadines
Mali	Senegal
Malta	Slovakia
Mauritania	Slovenia
Mauritius	South Africa
Mexico	Spain
Monaco	Sri Lanka
Mongolia	Suriname

Sweden

Switzerland

Thailand

The former Yugoslav

Republic of Macedonia

Togo

Trinidad and Tobago

Tunisia

Turkey

Ukraine

United Kingdom

United Republic of Tanzania

United States of America

Uruguay

Venezuela

Yugoslavia

Zambia

Zimbabwe

Schedule 2

Universal Copyright Convention Members who are not members of the Berne Convention as at 21 October 1996

Bangladesh

Belize

Cambodia

Kazakstan

Laos

Saudi Arabia

Tajikistan

Schedule 3

Rome Convention Members as at 6 March 1998

Argentina

Australia

Austria

Barbados

Bolivia

Brazil

Bulgaria

Burkina Faso

Canada

Cape Verde

Chile

Colombia

Congo

Costa Rica

Czech Republic

Denmark

Dominican Republic

Ecuador

El Salvador

Fiji

Finland

France

Germany

Greece

Guatemala

Honduras

Hungary

Iceland

Ireland

Italy

Jamaica

Japan

Lebanon

Lesotho

Luxembourg

Mexico

Monaco

Netherlands

Niger

Nigeria

Norway

Panama

Paraguay

Peru

Philippines

Poland

Republic of Moldova

Saint Lucia

Slovakia

Slovenia

Spain

Sweden

Switzerland

The former Yugoslav Republic of Macedonia

United Kingdom

Uruguay

Venezuela

Schedule 4
Geneva Convention Members as at 10 December 1997

Argentina

Australia

Austria

Barbados

Brazil

Bulgaria

Burkina Faso

Chile

China

Colombia

Costa Rica

Cyprus

Czech Republic

Democratic Republic of the Congo

Denmark

Ecuador

Egypt

El Salvador

Fiji

Finland

France

Germany

Greece

Guatemala

Holy See

Honduras

Hungary

India

Israel

Italy

Jamaica

Japan

Kenya

Latvia

Luxembourg

Mexico

Monaco

Netherlands

Peru

Republic of Korea

Russian Federation

Slovakia

Slovenia

Spain

Sweden

Switzerland

Trinidad and Tobago

United Kingdom

United States of America

Uruguay

Venezuela

Schedule 5

WIPO Members who are signatories to the "Berne Amendment Treaty" and the "Phonograms Treaty" as at 18 March 1998

Argentina

Austria

Belarus

Belgium

Bolivia

Burkina Faso

Canada

Chile

Columbia

Costa Rica

Croatia

Denmark

Ecuador

Estonia

Finland

France

Germany

Ghana

Greece

Hungary

Indonesia[85]

Ireland

Israel

---

[85]   This State has ratified the Berne Amendment Treaty.

Italy

Kazakhstan[86]

Kenya

Kyrgyzstan

Luxembourg

Mexico

Monaco

Mongolia

Namibia

Netherlands

Nigeria

Panama

Portugal

Republic of Moldova[87]

Romania

Senegal

Slovakia

Slovenia

South Africa

Spain

Sweden

Switzerland

Togo

United Kingdom

United States of America

Uruguay

Venezuela

European Communities

---

[86]   This State is a signatory to the Berne Amendment Treaty only.

[87]   This State has ratified both Treaties.

Chapter 4
THE LEGAL ISSUES OF THE WORLD WIDE WEB

Lars Davies
Research Fellow
University of London
and CMT Analyst
Ashurst Morris Crisp

4.1 Introduction

The World Wide Web is a rather strange entity. It is perhaps the most recognisable face of the Internet, and yet it is a very recent development. Its immense power comes not from the protocol which controls the service, but rather from its utility. However, just as it is one of the most used services, so it is one of the most misunderstood. Indeed, a common misconception is that the World Wide Web is the Internet, or if it is not, then that it is a separate network. It is none of these. Instead the World Wide Web is simply a service that is provided across the Internet, albeit a very powerful one.

The World Wide Web, in its most basic form is simply a set of hypertext links which link documents together. The user operates a special client program called a browser to access the documents or other pieces of data. The documents themselves are usually in the form of ASCII text or structured using the HyperText Markup Language ("HTML"). The HTML itself is a simple and yet powerful language which defines the various components of the document. Indeed it is powerful enough to enable authors to link in data from different resources and so build complex documents from several parts. These parts can reside on the same computer or can reside on different computers on the Internet.

Early browsers were simply text based, but over the past decade browsers were developed to display the text graphically, and then to display graphic images themselves. The result has been the development of a completely new on-line publishing media which is highly graphical and rich in content. Authors are now able to influence how their pages appear in a user's browser by using style sheets, embedded fonts and other technologies. The modern World Wide Web is years ahead of its text only beginning.

From its inception the World Wide Web was designed to enable authors to share their publications, or information in a seamless manner across a network with others without needing to resort to any complex operations. Such power of the World Wide Web comes from its primary protocol, the hypertext transfer protocol ("HTTP"). At first glance this protocol may seem very complex given all that it seems to achieve, but it is in fact very small and incredibly simple. Its power comes from the fact that the protocol concentrates on transferring data in a particular manner and actually allows browsers to access to other protocols aside from HTTP should the user or author prefer the data to be retrieved by other means. Thus the power of the World Wide Web comes not from a single protocol but the combination of several different protocols, all of which are designed to perform certain tasks.

The HTTP uses a set of unique addresses to find the documents or their components.[1] These addresses, which are known as Uniform Resource Locators ("URLs") simply point to the location of a particular piece of data. The address usually consists of three parts, the first detailing the protocol to use to fetch the data, the second relates to the computer on which the data resides, and the third refers to the location of the data in that computer system. Such an address could look like:

http://www.company.com/location/page.html

ftp://www.company.com/another_location/page.html

The first address stipulates that the client or browser should use the HTTP to access the data in page.html whilst the second instructs the client to obtain data using the file transfer protocol ("FTP").[2] The flexibility with which a user can access almost any information or service using a World Wide Web browser means that a user can, for the most part use such a browser as the sole gateway to the Internet.[3] Thus the World Wide Web can be said to encompass a great part of the Internet.

The technology behind the World Wide Web has developed rapidly since its initial inception and is now almost unrecognisable from the original text only presentation. Authors can not only control the appearance of their pages but can also incorporate applets or small pieces of code which can directly interact with users, and create systems which generate pages individually and in real time in response to users' requests and requirements.

Unfortunately, the flexibility of the World Wide Web has an unwelcome side effect. This flexibility is such that the legal issues raised by the use of the World Wide Web are such that they can also be said to encompass most of the issues raised by the use of the Internet. As a consequence the legal issues of the Internet are those of the World Wide Web. This though does not, however, help to identify the individual issues or point to where or when they occur. In order to do this the issues are probably best separated into two categories, those to do with the operational structure of the World Wide Web, and those to do with the actual content or data itself. To some degree these two categories overlap but they do at least help to gain some degree of focus on the problems and issues that must be dealt with.

Intellectual property will obviously play a great part in raising the legal issues related to content. So too, however, do the areas of criminal law, defamation, advertising, consumer protection, contract, gaming and so on. Indeed there is almost no limit to the number of regulatory areas which apply to the content of the World Wide Web. This, in fact, becomes

---

[1]   The following discussion is a simplification of what actually happens but it is sufficient to understand the basic mechanics of the World Wide Web.

[2]   The HTTP and FTP servers could easily be configured so that the location of the data is the same for both services. By doing this the administrators would give users the option of using either protocol to download the data. FTP is usually quicker than HTTP to transfer data but requires more network and server resources for the same task. A web server is distinct from other data servers in that it uses HTTP to serve or transfer data. FTP servers can be used for the same purpose but these are not web servers in the true sense.

[3]   Such use will not be the most efficient as the different protocols usually work best with their dedicated client programmes. However, the user may prefer the convenience over seeking the highest performance, especially when, for most part, the differences are not all that great.

obvious when the true nature of the Internet and the World Wide Web are taken into account. The World Wide Web is simply a service for transmitting information across the Internet, and as such any regulations that apply to the particular information if it is electronically transmitted will apply equally to the information transmitted using the World Wide Web. The World Wide Web does not really change the applicability of the laws and regulations. If they apply to information in an electronic form then they apply to the World Wide Web.

The World Wide Web is global and consequently the laws of every jurisdiction covered by the Internet will apply however unwelcome that may be. Whether the laws can be enforced is another matter entirely. There are however, certain aspects of the World Wide Web that give rise to particular issues that do need specific mention and it is the purpose of this Chapter to attempt to illustrate a few of these. Due to the global nature of the World Wide Web and the huge variety of issues that arise through its use this Chapter cannot cover every circumstance. Rather it will simply attempt to illustrate some of the main issues and show how they may be dealt with.

4.2   Caching and its consequences

Given the vast geographic distances and the multitude of servers on which the data resides it does seem quite remarkable that the World Wide Web can operate at the speed at which it does. This is partly a consequence of the structure and operation of the Internet, but it is also a consequence of a process called caching. Rather than constantly access the original data some browsers and servers cache the information that they have recently accessed, that is they store copies of the information locally. When a request is received for information in a cache this is accessed rather than a new copy from the original location. However, the browsers or servers will usually place an initial request to check whether the local copy is still current or whether the information on the originating server has been updated. They will then access whichever copy is the most up-to-date.

The activity of caching has obvious implications so far as copyright is concerned. Any information which is a qualifying publication under copyright law automatically attracts copyright protection. A great deal of information on the World Wide Web will attract copyright and caches store copies of this information. The length of time the information has been stored does not matter as any transient copying of protected information is an infringement of copyright.[4] Currently the generally accepted position on this matter is that information placed on the World Wide Web comes with an implicit licence that allows basic electronic copying in order to read the information, and includes the right to cache

---

[4]   For example in the UK *see* Section 17(6) Copyright Designs and Patent Act 1986.

the information. Caching, and indeed the entire operation of the Internet rests on this understanding.[5] This position can of course be altered by explicit statements such as allowing the right to read the information but not to print the information, and several sites do state explicitly to what use the information may be put.[6]

The operation of a cache does not exempt the operator from copyright law. Should copyright holders determine that a cache contains information which infringes their copyright then they can demand that the cache operator remove that information. Up to that instance, if the cache operator is unaware of the existence of infringing information then they would not be held liable for primary[7] or secondary copyright infringement. Once the operator is put on notice, however, they must act to remove this information or they may be found liable from that moment on.

4.3 Obscenity and defamation

Caching also raises other issues which will give cause for concern as does the storing of information in general. Information might be inadvertently stored which contravenes other regulations such as those governing obscene material or defamation. Again were the operator to be unaware of the existence of the information then they would not be held liable. However, once informed of its existence the operator should act as swiftly as possible to remove the information, or at the very least to post a notice warning of its defamatory nature. Though this has not caused too much concern where the information has been of an obscene nature where operators have usually been only too willing to remove such information, it has raised some argument, especially in the area of defamation.

Though there is little argument as to liability where an individual is the primary author of defamatory material, Internet Service Providers ("ISPs") and server operators are very much opposed to being treated in the same manner as distributors or publishers when it comes to defamatory material placed on the Internet by a user, anonymous or otherwise. Most cases of defamation on the Internet have involved email or usenet,[8] and the judgments have caused a great deal of concern within the Internet community, especially where server operators or ISPs have been found liable even though the material originated from third parties.

---

[5]   Unfortunately the initial drafts of the Proposal for a European Parliament and Council Directive on the harmonization of certain aspects of copyright and related rights in the Information Society would included provisions that threatened the practice of caching information on the World Wide Web and effectively required operators to seek the permission of copyright holders before they could cache data. This obviously introduces a heavy burden on operators that would render caching impossible and as a result of heavy lobbying the provisions were amended. Unfortunately, though the amendment seems to offer an exemption the wording is such that it is debatable whether or not the issue has been solved. The US, on the other hand, has taken a more direct approach and has exempted caching from copyright infringement, provided that any restrictions on the use of any copyright material are followed (Section 202 Digital Millennium Copyright Act). Essentially this provision codifies what is or was the general position on caching.

[6]   In addition to using explicit license terms authors can easily use features of HTML and HTTP to prevent caching.

[7]   This of course only applies where the operator is not responsible for placing the infringing information on the World Wide Web in the first instance, which would hold true were they unaware of the existence of the information.

[8]   *See* for instance the recent case of *Laurence Godfrey v. Demon Internet Ltd* (1999) QBD.

The World Wide Web differs from these services in one major respect. Information on the World Wide Web, unlike that in email or usenet, is rarely transient. Rather it is semi-permanent in that it is stored on a server or servers until deleted by either the author or server operator. However, the volume of information on the World Wide Web, like that on the usenet or email services, is immense and constantly changing, especially on servers where the information is supplied and posted by third parties. Consequently it could be very difficult for operators to monitor all the information successfully, though it would be easier to monitor than email or usenet. Whether the web server operator is more likely to be found to be a publisher or distributor of the material than the administrator of an email or usenet service is a moot point. What is clear is that ignorance of the material does not provide a defence if the operators are made aware of the material itself.[9] Once the operators know of the material they should act immediately. Whether this is to remove the material or post a notice warning of the defamatory nature of the material will depend on the policies of the operators and the information itself. What is clear is that doing nothing once they are put on notice will not afford operators protection[10] against an action for defamation. This obviously places the operators in some difficulty. The disparity in resources that will exist between the operators on the one-hand and the individual users on the other is a great cause for concern. Any aggrieved party will, if the law permits, seek to take action against the party with the greater resources. This is usually the operator.

The operator will face a dilemma on receipt of a notice that information on the service may be of a defamatory nature. The main dilemma will be what constitutes an actionable notice? Does an email message or facsimile from the aggrieved party constitute proper notice, or must the notice be in the form of a solicitor's letter? The issue is a real one for if the operator acts to remove a message which then turns out not to be defamatory then the question arises as to will they be in breach of the rights, whether contractual, intellectual property, or otherwise of the originating party? If so then what will be the limit of their liability? If they refuse to act then they risk being held liable to the aggrieved party. The position is an uncomfortable one and is symptomatic of the difficulties caused by the law surrounding defamation.

Arguments that removing such information may constitute an attack on free speech have little weight. Some operators passionately believe that the Internet must remain an area where freedom of speech has absolute effect. Whether or not this is desirable, it is not the legal position and the law must and indeed does take precedence over emotion. The laws concerning defamation and obscenity are most certainly enforceable. Operators must decide on what action they will take on receipt of a notice. They may even attempt to clarify matters by publishing their policy on the matter declaring the form of notice that they will act upon and detailing what actions they will take on receipt of such a notice. What they cannot do is to state that they will take no responsibility for the information content. They can certainly state that they do not monitor the information content on their services. They cannot, however, expect that this will provide any protection once they are informed of the existence of the information.

---

[9]   The position is altered where the operators hold themselves out as providing a family oriented service or where they claim to provide screened or moderated information content. In these circumstances they could not claim to have no knowledge of the information prior to being informed of its defamatory content.

[10]   *Laurence Godfrey v. Demon Internet Ltd.*

4.4 **Web pages, frames, links and the confusion they cause**

One of the attractions of the World Wide Web, and indeed one of the attractions of using HTML over ASCII is that pages can themselves be constructed from a variety of different sources, each of which is independently read by a browser before the page is constructed and displayed in all of its glory. That at least is the theory. The technology allows for a completely new way of providing information as text, graphics, moving images and so forth can be assembled together to provide very rich content. Unfortunately this can also lead to a number of issues which must be addressed.

Just as it is easy for users to construct a page of information from a number of their own sources so it is just as easy for users to incorporate content that belongs to others. This practice will obviously raise issues of copyright infringement. Whilst there remains the understanding that, unless otherwise indicated, there is an implicit licence to copy data on the World Wide Web for the purpose of reading it on-line, it cannot be said that an implicit right exists to use the same material in any other manner, such as incorporating it into another page. If the implicit right to copy does exist then it is almost certainly restricted to accessing and reading the information as the original author intended. Of course the author may grant a licence to use the information in other ways such as to incorporate the information into another page but this is not an implicit right. This holds whether individual parcels of information are incorporated, or whether an entire page is incorporated into another page, such as where the page is displayed in a frame within another page.

Displaying pages in frames that are themselves within a page is a common and powerful way of displaying information. The act of incorporating pages from other sources into a frame creates a new work which could appear as if it were part of the same system and same authors' work, unless the source were acknowledged in a prominent manner. This has two consequences. The first is that it would almost certainly constitute copying for the purposes of copyright infringement as a substantial part would have been copied.[11] This would hold true regardless of what was actually copied, whether it be text, an image, or the entire contents of a page, so long as the part copied was a substantial part of a copyright protected work.

The second consequence would be that the users incorporating the page in a frame could be liable for passing off. By incorporating the page in a frame it could quite reasonably seem to the user accessing the resultant page, that of the page with the frame and the contents of the frame itself, were inextricably linked, even though the actual pages were from distinct and unconnected systems. The author of the incorporated page might not wish to be associated in any way with the author or system of the incorporating page and would instead prefer to maintain a distinct identity. Were the source of the incorporated page to be fully acknowledged then no such association or confusion should arise. Such acknowledgement would possibly protect against the possibility of a passing off action. It is doubtful whether it would protect against an action for copyright infringement if such copying has been prohibited by the copyright holder.

---

[11]   If a work is copied then it is almost a substantial part – why would an unsubstantial part be copied. The question concerns the qualitative and not the quantitative nature of the part that is copied.

Similar confusion or association could also arise where a URL or embedded link in a page links to information on another system in a manner which would suggest some form of approval by the author. Users browsing the pages might believe that the original authors or administrators were somehow connected to, or indeed approved of the subsequent information accessed through the link. For this reason many systems notify users when they are about to leave their systems and access information held on servers that are not under their control. These notices usually indicate that the authors take no responsibility for the information on the external servers. Such a notice will help to prevent confusion as to authorship and also break any link that might otherwise form in the browsing user's mind. It could thus serve to protect the author of the linking page from liability over the information content of the pages accessed by the link, though such protection would only be afforded if the declaration was in good faith rather than an artificial device to attempt to circumvent liability.

4.5   Liability for the invisible

Just as incorporating a page or piece of information into another page could result in an action for passing off so too could the use of a particular piece of information which is not actually displayed by a browser. Metatags[12] were originally designed to enable authors to include in a page some information that should not be displayed when the page itself is displayed. The information which these tags can contain is user definable and may be anything from authorship and version, to information which a web server may analyse and process when passing the page to the accessing client.

Web indexing engines can quite easily scan the entire contents of web page which they encounter. This would, however, entail a large processing overhead so they are usually configured to scan the first few lines of each page. One use of metatags is thus to include information which authors wish indexing engines to use to classify or index the pages such as key words and other pertinent information. Most users will only include information that refers solely to their pages. However, any text information can be placed in these metatags and as such other users can quite easily insert data into their pages which would result in indexing engines preferring their pages in preference to those of others. Indeed it is a trivial process to incorporate trading names, trade marks, or product or service descriptions of rivals. Indeed by repeated use of such information the user can thus effectively persuade an indexing engine to re-direct an inquiry for a rival to themselves. This is because with most indexing tools, the more times a particular word or phrase is discovered in the few lines that they index the higher the rating that page will receive, regardless of the actual visible content of the page.

This practice has proved to be highly controversial and as such operators have been able to configure modern indexing engines to ignore metatags and simply scan the visible text content. These engines can analyse the metatags or compare the metatags and content in an attempt to ascertain whether metatag loading is taking place.[13] Authors could attempt

---

12   Metatags are very simple in structure and take the form <META *(information)* >. They are not displayed by browsers despite the fact that they do form part of the HTML specifications and are an integral part of any page that contains them.

13   Simply loading the metatag above with multiple instances of a particular word or phrase could increase the effective hit rate of an indexing engine. Sophisticated indexing engines can be configured to counteract and even penalise such deliberate loading of metatags but these will not defeat the problem completely. However these will not remove the problem of false loading completely.

to circumvent this analysis and filtering by simply inserting the names or marks of competitors into metatags in order to redirect inquiries to their own pages. Such an action might possibly constitute passing off if the loading of the metatags and the eventual site reached effectively represented a supposed connection with the actual site originally intended though this would depend on the surrounding facts.

4.6   Uniform Resource Locators and their problems

Copyright will almost certainly attach to pages or other works on the World Wide Web such as images, sound files, or moving images. A recent question arose as to whether URLs themselves could attract copyright protection.[14] Should they do so then operators of indexing services which create lists of links and URLs from World Wide Web pages from all over the Internet could be held liable as would authors who include links on their own pages.[15] There is obviously a distinction between URLs which consist simply of the address of a particular piece of information, and URLs which take the form of embedded links but whose description is taken from the page to which they refer. The legal position is uncertain as the courts have yet to decide the matter. It is doubtful that they will be regarded as substantial enough to attract copyright but until the courts have addressed the issue in a definitive manner it is very difficult to give a definite answer to the question.

4.7   Contracts and advertisements

The World Wide Web is a delightful medium in which commercial entities could construct mechanisms to enter into electronic commerce ("e-commerce") with consumers or other commercial entities. The issues raised contract law will apply as in any other arena.

The location of contracting parties is very important, especially when the contracts are consumer contracts. Within European Union Member States consumer protection law is overriding and will override any terms within a contract which contravenes the provisions of the law. Such terms could themselves constitute a civil offence, and in some cases a criminal offence. In addition to legal requirements regarding the terms and conditions of the consumer contracts the legislation will almost certainly require that the contracts be in the national language of the consumer. Failure to provide for this may not only render the contract void or unenforceable, but in some circumstances could result in the commercial interest committing an offence.

By placing an advertisement of the World Wide Web, a commercial interest is essentially advertising to the world. Though the contents may satisfy the legal requirements of their home jurisdiction, in many cases, such as financial advertising, product advertising, and so forth, that same material will breach regulations in other jurisdictions. The question of course is whether those jurisdictions can enforce their regulations. It is true that many may not be able to do so, but they may still seek to take jurisdiction. Certainly the jurisdictions will assert their jurisdiction if they are able to do so.

---

[14]   *See Shetland Times Ltd v. Dr Jonathan Wills* [1997] FSR 604.

[15]   *See* "Controlling World-Wide Web Links: property rights, access rights and unfair competition", Chris Reed 1998, forthcoming in the Indiana Journal of Global Legal Studies.

Some regulators have begun to sense that automatically asserting jurisdiction will not work and have made clear that they will not regard advertising on the World Wide Web as falling within their jurisdiction providing certain requirements are met.[16] Others, however, still take the view that anything on the Internet, and subsequently the World Wide Web, automatically falls within their remit. In essence the laws of the jurisdictions in which a commercial interest wishes to trade or do business should be checked before placing advertisements which could fall foul of regulation. Technically, it is possible to limit and control access to different areas of information by consumers and other parties from different jurisdictions but these are never totally secure. Most regulators however, do recognise the difficulties involved and are generally satisfied provided that the commercial interests take adequate steps to comply with the regulations.

4.8 Domain names

One component of the Internet that has proved to be one of the most problematic is also one of its most central services, namely the Domain Name System ("DNS") that is used by virtually every user. Indeed such is the reliance put upon it that users and services would often be unable to operate on the Internet without it.

The World Wide Web exacerbates the problem due to its direct use of domain names in the URLs that make up the addressing system used, and by the use to which users put these URLs. The initial development of the World Wide Web intended that the URLs would be hidden with the text of a web page. The URLs were never intended to be as visible nor put to the various uses as they are today. The data in a page would take the form of hypertext and the URLs would be triggered when a user activated a link buried within the text of the page. The linked data would then be uploaded seamlessly without the user being aware of the actual details of the link itself; the embedded links and the underlying structure of the page and its relationship to other pages would be the sole concern of the author of the page. Unfortunately, developments have raced ahead and at the present time URLs have become highly visible. Indeed URLs are now commonly used in and other promotional media, as an indication that a particular company or product has a presence on the Internet. This would in itself not be so much of an issue were it not for the fact that this use of URLs is similar to that which the commercial interests make of trademarks.

The use of similar marks or signs for products or services that are completely dissimilar to those for which a trade mark is registered can have the effect of diluting that mark, so reducing its value and its scope, and this is naturally of great concern to trade mark holders who will almost always instigate usage policies and police these rigidly. These

---

[16] In its recent statement regarding the use of Internet websites to offer securities, solicit securities transactions or advertise investment services offshore, dated 23 March 1998, the US Securities and Exchange Commission ("SEC") seems to go some way to accepting at least part of the principle. In brief the statement of interpretation states that the SEC would not regard websites offering financial services as offering these services in the US provided that they do not specifically target persons in the US. However, the statement makes it clear that this does not hold for fraudulent or manipulative activities. In these cases the SEC will take action regardless of whether any transactions were carried out in the US. The statement is not as helpful as it first appears as the requirement not to specifically target investors in the US includes screening out applications from such investors, not pricing products and services primarily in US dollars, if at all, and other such conditions which are highly impractical at best given the international nature of the Internet. The US dollar is a reference currency against which users on the Internet may compare their own. Limiting the use of this currency as a reference marker would greatly reduce the attractiveness of any financial website.

policies will apply both to the use to which the holders of the trade mark put their marks, and the use which they permit others to make of that mark. The reason for such behaviour is that in drastic cases dilution, if unchecked, can eventually destroy a registered trade mark resulting ultimately in its revocation. Trade marks are diluted not only by the actions of third parties but, importantly, by the actions of the right holders themselves through overuse of their trade mark. As such trade mark holders must be extremely vigilant to the use made of their trade marks on the World Wide Web. Not only must they ensure that their trade marks are not being infringed, either through their use in URLs or domain names, but they must also ensure that their trade marks are not being diluted in any way.

4.9 The Domain Name System and trade marks

It is an unfortunate and ultimately unavoidable fact that the very quality that attracts commercial interests to the use to which they make of the DNS, the use of identifiable and recognisable names as addresses, is the same quality that attracts those same interests to trade marks. This duality is unfortunate because it immediately produces a fundamental conflict between the DNS and trade marks, one which is highly unlikely to be resolved without fundamental legal change in trade mark law, and an equal change in the DNS and its use.

The basic principle behind the administration of DNS addresses was a first come first served approach which ignored the existence of trade marks and instead allowed users to register which ever domain they requested. This principle worked for a time but problems began to occur as commercial interests began to take notice of the commercial potential of the Internet. As this grew so some users began to register a large number of domains using the names of trade marks, corporations, or entities identified with the commercial interests in the hope of selling these domains to the corporate interests at a later date for a profit.

This practice poses several problems for commercial interests in relation to trade marks and their treatment under the law. Though a domain name may contain the name of a trade mark it is important to realise that under the law of trade marks its use by a party other than the right holder does not necessarily result in an infringement of that trade mark. For an infringement to occur the allegedly infringing mark or domain name must be used in the course of trade. In many cases there may be little scope to bring an action for infringement of an existing trade mark or an action for passing off as no such use of the mark has been made.

Though actual trade mark infringement may be difficult to prove, in cases where domain names have been pre-registered for existing trade marks or similar names it may well be possible instead to bring an action to prevent future infringement of the registered trade mark or future passing off.[17] In some civil law jurisdictions, such as those within the EU, there may also be scope for an action based on unfair competition or based on extortion. Any action over an alleged infringement of a trade mark or an action for passing off or unfair competition requires careful and thorough legal advice and should not be undertaken lightly.

---

[17] See *British Telecommunications plc v. One In A Million; Virgin Enterprises Ltd v. One In A Million; J Sainsbury plc v. One In A Million; Ladbroke Group plc v. One In A Million;* and *Marks & Spencer plc v. One In A Million* [1998] FSR 265.

4.10   Classes and domains

A subtle yet often unnoticed point gives rise to one of the fundamental reasons why conflicts will almost certainly continue to occur between trade marks and domain names. The Nice Classification of trade marks outlines 42 separate and distinct classes of trade marks which refer to the goods or services to which the trade marks attach. Prospective right holders must register the class or classes of their marks in addition to the mark itself in order to obtain a trade mark as the protection granted is for the exclusive use of the marks as trade marks to distinguish goods or services of the class or classes against which the marks are registered. A consequence is that different right holders in either the same or different jurisdictions are quite able to register the same or similar mark for different classes. So long as these marks are used for the activities described by the classes there should be no trade mark infringement. The Nice Classification is very important when considering the question of whether one user is infringing another's trade mark. That they may be using the same name is neither here nor there. The requirements for infringement must be met for there to be an infringement of a registered trade mark.

Pre-registered domains cause some concern but this is nothing when compared to the issues that arise from the commercial use of domain names. At first glance the DNS may seem like a limitless resource. Unfortunately in practical terms it is a scarce resource. Within any addressing hierarchy the domain addresses must be absolutely unique. A consequence of this requirement is that only one user may own any one particular domain name at any one time. Given that different commercial interests in different jurisdictions may legitimately own the rights to essentially identical trade marks, it would be safe to assume that in promoting their Internet presence these interests would wish to register, own, and use the same domain name.

The national, or regional scope of trade marks usually means that there is little confusion over the trade mark holder's identity or the trade marks in the jurisdictions in which those marks are registered. Unfortunately, unlike trade marks the Internet and the services provided over it, such as the World Wide Web, do not and cannot limit themselves to the same boundaries. Nor does e-commerce. Regardless of how many entities may be entitled to use the same trade mark in their respective jurisdictions the DNS means that only one right holder can hold a particular domain.

The limitation on domain names matters greatly as only one trade mark can map directly to any one domain. If a single mark holder holds all the registrations for a particular trade mark then there is no problem. The problems arise when more than that one holder legitimately holds a registration to a particular trade mark. There are a limited number of Top Level Domains ("TLDs") and, as would be expected, commercial interests view certain TLDs as more advantageous than others.

For commercial interests this holds especially true for the ".com" generic Top Level Domain ("gTLD"). Due to the perceived advantages of this domain commercial interests are willing to dispute prior registrations for certain domains on the grounds that the registration of the domain and its use infringes their trade mark. Due to the fact that ".com" is seen as the most prestigious domain, US based concerns are especially willing to fight over this domain, though the willingness to bring a dispute stems partly from the rather strange view that litigation is a valid business tool and partly from a misunderstanding of the nature of trade marks. Proof of trade mark infringement is a requirement for successful litigation.

In response to the problems resulting from the clash between domain names and trade marks various domain name registries have attempted to introduce some form of dispute control mechanism and registration controls to deal with the problem though some have more stringent requirements in place than others. Generally speaking users who register have to make a declaration that they intend to make use of the domains that they register. Should they fail to use the domains, usually within a specified time limit, then they will lose the registration. Some registries also require users to agree to indemnify them against any actions brought for trade mark infringement, though whether this will be effective in curbing alleged abuse this has yet to be seen.

Where a bona fide dispute arises, such as between two legitimate right holders from different jurisdictions then the situation is more complex. The actions that a registry might take will depend entirely on its guidelines and agreements with the domain holder. However, if the registration of a domain name is legitimate then the registration should usually stand irrespective of the nationality or size of the holder of the domain.[18]

4.11   Attempts to deal with these issues

The existing situation is far from satisfactory. Litigation over domain names and trade mark infringement is prohibitively expensive and time consuming and the current situation with regard to the disparate dispute resolution mechanisms of the separate domain name registries means that domain holders may receive different treatments at the hands of the various registries. The lack of certainty is completely unsatisfactory.

One possible solution to the problem caused by the scarce capacity of the gTLDs would be to dissolve the ".com" and ".org" domains, instead requiring the right holders to register under the country code Top Level Domains ("ccTLDs") in which they hold registered trade marks. Though this would solve a large section of conflicts where conflicting right holders hold marks in different jurisdictions, it would do little to alleviate the problems caused by the Nice Classification system, or indeed the potential disputes which could arise with well known trade marks. As a realistic proposal it is a non starter. It would fail, however, as domain name holders in the prestigious gTLDs would strongly resist losing their registrations.

Another proposal from the World Intellectual Property Organisation ("WIPO") suggested the creation of a gTLD specifically for registered trade marks with a Second Level Domain ("SLD") of randomly assigned number strings to help differentiate between identical trade marks belonging to separate rights holders. Though most numbers will be randomly generated for memorable number strings the more memorable the number string the higher the registration fee. Unfortunately this again would result in generating conflicts over who could register which SLD with squabbles over certain memorable number strings a certainty.

---

18   *See Prince plc v. Prince Sports Group Inc.* The facts of the case again are illustrative of this point though the case itself turned on a technicality. Though Prince plc, a British company, was much smaller and much less well known than the US group that attempted to take over the domain registration, they had a valid trade mark and, crucially, had registered their domain before the other party. Under the relevant registry's rules a prior registration of a valid trade mark as a domain name by a valid holder of that mark, regardless of the jurisdiction within which that mark was registered, would stand a challenge from a holder of the same or similar mark from another jurisdiction. The case also neatly illustrates the point that a small trade mark holder can successfully ward off a challenge from a larger trade mark holder, even one from the same jurisdiction in which the registry resides.

The proposal which has found many advocates was one which called for the controlled expansion of the numbers of gTLDs that are currently available. Some have even called for a special gTLD for registered trademarks and gTLDs for specific classes of business such as ".firm", ".corp" and ".inc". Though these are seductive arguments the result could be to essentially multiply the domains in which conflict would arise. However, the Internet Corporation for Assigned Names and Numbers (the "ICANN"), which has overall responsibility for the DNS, has investigated the issue of creating new gTLDs and, on 16 November 2000, selected seven new TLDs and started negotiations with various parties to administer these domains.[19] The discussion is not closed and new domains will almost certainly be selected in the future.

The wireless application protocol ("WAP") has often been described as a wireless web. This is not strictly true given the limitations of the platform on which WAP has been designed to operate namely wireless handsets. Nevertheless it does deliver web like information to the handset and allows users to interact with several Internet services. As with any service, the legal issues depend on the service in question. Thus where the user makes use of web like services then the legal issues will be those that also affect the web. Where the user makes use of email services then those legal issues that pertain to email will apply. In essence WAP should simply be seen as yet another protocol or service in the same way that the Internet should be seen as a collection of protocols or services.

---

[19]   The seven new gTLDs are ".aero", ".biz", ".coop", ".info", ".museum", ".name", and ".pro". At the time of writing these were not yet operational and ICANN had not authorised any parties to register domains under these gTLDs. For further information please *see* http://www.icann.org/tlds/.

Chapter 5
MAKING CONTRACTS OVER THE INTERNET

Mark Haftke
Partner
KLegal

5.1   Introduction

The power of the Internet to distribute information may be considered beyond dispute. Its suitability as a medium for trade depends on the resolution of a number of issues. Amongst them is the matter of confidence and, in particular, confidence in the integrity and enforceability of contracts made online for the sale of goods and services. This Chapter applies the principles of English contract law to the sale of goods and services over the Internet, which is referred to below as "e-commerce". The following analysis is divided into three parts: first, the principles of contract law relevant to Internet trade; second, the practical considerations that result; third, the provisions of the EU's E-Commerce Directive. The Distance Selling Directive is dealt with in Chapter 9 of this Guide.

5.2   Free form and uniform systems

There are a number of significant differences between e-commerce and traditional trade. Traders operate in a global medium and international contracts are common. It is impersonal and it may be anonymous. As with traditional mail order, the contracting parties do not normally meet and rarely speak. In contrast with mail order, e-commerce facilitates immediate performance in the delivery of some services and intangibles.

There are different ways of conducting e-commerce. The most common way at present is over the World Wide Web via websites. A essential characteristic of that process is the absence of any prior agreement between retailer and consumer over how they will trade and exchange data. The medium is essentially free form until one party imposes control. How those controls work is the essence of how contract law applies to e-commerce.

5.3   Contracts distinguished

The word "contract" has a distinguishing meaning. First of all, it does not describe mere agreements. Agreements come in all flavours but only those that are intended to have the force of law behind them are "contracts". By way of example, agreements for social engagements, agreements that are "subject to contract", and mere promises are not "contracts". Furthermore, mere permissions are often not contracts. Thus, the consent of a copyright owner to perform an act restricted by the copyright need not be given by way of a contract. It may be that the licence is no more than a voluntary permission, unsupported in any way by the notion of a contract or the principles of contract law.[1]

---

[1]   The issues concerning copyright permissions and pure licences are considered elsewhere in this Guide.

In order to distinguish between mere agreements and contracts, English law requires that the following elements are present in any agreement in order for it to qualify as a contract. There must be in each case:

(a) an offer;

(b) unequivocal acceptance of the offer which is communicated to the offeror;

(c) supporting value for the agreement (called "consideration") moving from the offeree;

(d) an intention to create legal relations and capacity in each party to be legally bound.

If one of these elements is missing then the agreement will not constitute a contract in English law. This Chapter does not consider (c) and (d) for want of any special issues connected with the Internet.

5.3.1 *Contracts "in writing" and "signatures"*

By virtue of a variety of statutes, some contracts must be made in writing. They include dispositions of interests in land, regulated consumer credit agreements, promissory notes and bills of exchange and sale. If not made in writing some will be invalid and others, such as credit agreements, will only be enforceable against the debtor by court order.

By contrast, under the Statute of Frauds 1677, contracts by which a party guarantees the debts or performance of another need to be evidenced in writing – that is their terms can be agreed orally and noted in a memorandum of no particular form. Nevertheless, the memorandum must be signed by the party giving the guarantee.

Under regulations governing commerce in a number of industrial sectors, it is necessary for certain information to be provided by the vendor or supplier in writing (e.g. the financial services and pharmaceuticals industries).

Such considerations give rise to questions about what is required in an e-commerce contract to satisfy requirements of form. The UK Government announced its commitment to remove legal obstacles that stand in the way of e-commerce and to draw up a code of conduct for businesses and consumers trading electronically.[2] That will require a change in legislation that has requirements of form that effectively proscribe electronic documentation. One other vital area that will also need to be addressed as a concomitant part of the sweeping away of such obstacles is a stable and trustworthy infrastructure for digital signatures. The UK's Electronic Communication Act 2000 (which is in force in parts) attempts to wrestle with the infrastructure requirements for digital signatures.[3]

5.4 Making contracts on line

It is a fundamental that when two parties bargain, they must agree before a contract is formed. Thus, the terms of the offer to trade and the acceptance of those terms must match.

---

[2] The Competetiveness White Paper presented to Parliament December 1998.

[3] Considered elsewhere in this Guide.

5.4.1   *The offer*

Identifying the offer and the acceptance is vital for a number of reasons. Without doing so it is impossible to know if there was a "meeting of minds" between the parties over what were the contract terms. Furthermore, neither party has any obligation to perform until the contract is made, so that identifying the moment when the contract is made (by the acceptance of the offer) is important. Moreover, when it comes to enforcing the contract it is necessary to work out which countries' laws apply and this may be determined according to a number of factors, which may include the place where the contract was made.

When does a communication amount to an offer capable of acceptance? Any email should expressly state whether its contents comprise an offer or merely an invitation to the recipient to make one. Statements to this effect are often seen on company notepaper. It is best to include such a statement within the body of the email message rather than as part of any header or attachment which may not be perceptible following transmission.

A website comprises an entire environment and an e-commerce website will have a trading area comprising text, images and a database linked to a variety of back office functions. When a user visits the site they see information about the goods or services for sale. Obviously, if these constituted offers for sale then a number of problems would arise. For instance, it may be an offence in a number of regulated services to offer goods or services for sale without restriction (e.g. in the financial services, pharmaceutical, drinks and tobacco industries).

English law treats the display of goods in a shop not as an offer for sale but as an "invitation to treat".[4] The consequence of this approach is that it is the purchaser's response to the vendor's display that represents the offer. This is also important because it leaves the vendor free to accept or decline the offer as it sees fit. Whilst it is undecided whether the advertisement of goods or services on a website represents an offer for sale or an invitation to treat under English law it is very likely to amount to the latter. However, there is no danger in expressly stating the position in the website.

Some website proprietors will not wish potential purchasers to make offers to purchase goods or services on unacceptable terms. The vendor must preset and control the manner in which an offer can be made and the terms upon which the purchaser may choose to buy from the website. Even where each offer may be different and open to negotiation, for instance where work is being put out to tender – the website proprietor will want to ensure uniformity in the way the offer is presented. This can be achieved by the use of standard forms for accessing the website and standard terms and conditions of trading which apply to any offers made.

Any standard terms of trading that the vendor wishes to impose must apply to the offer. If the offer is made without reference to the vendor's standard terms, the vendor cannot accept it on the basis that his standard terms do apply. Instead, any attempt to subsequently incorporate the standard terms will amount to a counter-offer which the purchaser could then choose to accept. In order that the offer is made on the standard terms, they must be known to the purchaser before the offer is made, otherwise the offer cannot be made subject to them. The purchaser should be made aware that the vendor will

---

4   *Pharmaceutical Society of Great Britain v. Boots Cash Chemists (Southern) Limited* [1953] 1 QB 410.

only contract on its standard terms, that any offers must be made on those terms and will be deemed made subject to those standard terms. In a strictly controlled environment the purchaser will have two choices only: either to submit the offer subject to the standard terms or not submit any offer at all. The crucial element is that the terms and conditions are brought sufficiently to the attention of the purchaser before the offer is sent.

It is important that all the terms of the offer are contained within the offer alone. There should be no place in the electronic form for other terms to be imposed. The only variables should be those expressly envisaged such as colour, quantity, price and so on. Nevertheless, it is possible for the nature of the agreement to be altered in two ways. First, it would be possible for the purchaser to follow up the offer with a separate communication by telephone, post or email. There is little that can be done physically to prevent that. If the revised offer is communicated before the first offer is accepted then the sensible vendor will refuse to accept the offer and request that a new one is resubmitted in the conventional, prescribed manner through the website form. If the original offer is accepted before the revision is communicated to the vendor it will be too late for the purchaser to unilaterally vary the terms of the offer as the contract will have been made. It might be thought possible to state that only offers made via the permitted method will be capable of acceptance. However, there is little to stop the offeror altering the terms of an acceptable offer using some other method of communication if that does come to the attention of the vendor. Any purported prohibition will be of no effect as the revision will have come to the attention of the vendor.

It may be that the vendor himself inadvertently incorporates terms or makes representations upon which the offeror relies when making the offer. The vendor should therefore be careful to ensure that the contents of the website and any other associated materials do not contain actionable misrepresentations or messages that could be construed as other terms of any contract.

It may be a crucial matter when the offer was made and accepted since until that moment either party may vary their position or withdraw entirely from the bargain. To deal with this, English law has developed a set of rules about when communications sent by different media are deemed to have been sent. In the case of the offer, it is fundamental that it is received by the vendor because until then he cannot decide whether or not to accept it (*see* Section 5.4.2).

5.4.2   *The acceptance*

The offer must be accepted without equivocation so the terms of the acceptance must match exactly the terms of the offer. The offer must be accepted before it is revoked or revised. Once accepted the offer is incapable of subsequent variation. If a contract has been formed then, strictly speaking, it is the contract that will be varied but only with the consent of all parties. An offer is capable of acceptance in a number of ways but in each case the acceptance must be communicated to the offeror. The material differences between the ways in which an offer may be accepted are differences of timing and location.

The point at which an offer is accepted will vary according to whether the means of communication is instantaneous or not. Where communication is instantaneous English law deems that the acceptance is communicated at the time and place it is perceived by the offeror. Where the communication is by post the acceptance is deemed communicated at the time of posting.

It is undetermined in English law into which category email falls. Emails are electronic but they are not necessarily instantaneous. When an offeree receives the offer an automatic response may be generated whilst the offeror is still online. The message may appear as script within a website. Alternatively, where there must be some delay between the making and acceptance of the offer then the vendor will need to initiate the communication. If it is by email then the mail may not arrive due to network defects. If it does arrive then it may sit in the recipient's in-box without being opened.

It seems likely that where the purchaser is off-line the communication will not be treated as instantaneous. Does that mean that the courts will apply the rule that an email offer is accepted by email when the email is sent (by analogy with established rules about the post)? One argument in favour of such an approach is that when the vendor accepts the offer it may then conduct itself in a prejudicial way, for instance, by buying supplies. It might be thought wrong for a purchaser to then be able to withdraw the offer when the vendor has prejudiced itself in the belief that the offer has been accepted.

On the other hand, there are good reasons why the courts may prefer an approach that depends on the acceptance having been received. First, there may be reluctance to rely on the posting rule in such an erratic environment. With the Royal Mail there is a general presumption about the reliability of its service that allows for rules that deem a communication delivered if posted and not returned unopened. The Internet is unreliable and its infrastructure variable. There may be intervening service providers. The purchaser's connection may be sporadic or constant. The message may be legible when sent but corrupt and illegible on arrival. The courts could take the view that email is insufficiently reliable and deem such communications as complete only when received.

Second, one of the arguments in favour of adopting the "accepted when posted" rule does not apply to email – namely the evidential difficulty of proving whether an offer has been received. Postmarks do provide some evidence of when "acceptance by posting" occurred. However, in the ordinary postal service there is no equivalent objective evidence of the date or time of receipt. A rule that acceptance takes place at the time of posting avoids the risk of purchasers making self-serving statements about whether the acceptance was received before the offer was revoked. This justification would have less force in the online environment. The time when an email is sent, delivered and opened can be determined. Indeed, a sendor can be notified when an email is opened.

Furthermore, distance selling legislation imposes a "cooling-off period" which will run from when the contract is made. How could the cooling-off period run without the purchaser knowing it has begun?

As an alternative to "written" acceptance, an offer can be accepted by conduct. The conduct may, and often does, amount to performance of the contract. In this way, the vendor's acceptance of the offer and performance of the contract may be simultaneous. Because an offer can be accepted by conduct it is important that the vendor makes it clear what conduct will and will not amount to acceptance since some acts could be misconstrued. For instance, a purchaser will submit the offer and personal data including payment details. It is possible to construe acceptance of this message as acceptance of the offer. The vendor should be careful to stipulate how acceptance will be signified and that certain acts are not intended as a form of acceptance.

A common approach is to state that the offer is not accepted until payment has been taken. The vendor may state as a term of trading that the offer will not be accepted until payment has been taken which will only occur when the goods are ready for dispatch. In this way, the vendor has the right to refuse the order right up to the moment before payment is taken when the goods are ready to be sent out to the purchaser. If acceptance can only take place by the debiting or charging of the purchaser's card (and that does not happen until the goods or services are ready for delivery), there is little chance of the vendor being placed in the difficult position of being unable to perform a binding contract of sale.

The E-Commerce Directive is considered in detail below but it is important to mention that English law on contract formation will be amended by the implementation of the Directive. The earlier drafts contained detailed and difficult preconditions to the creation of a valid click wrap agreement. Those requirements were removed before the Directive was given effect. Nevertheless there remain provisions on the giving of information as part of the contract formation process.

5.4.3   *Capacity*

The anonymity of the Internet means that a number of difficulties may arise over the identity of the parties to a contract made electronically and at a distance. Such difficulties generally fall into two categories: legal capacity and mistake. If a person does not have the legal capacity to make a contract then a question must inevitably arise over the legal enforceability of any agreement. There are two situations in which the issue of the capacity of the purchaser will be relevant: where the purchaser wishes to recover money he has parted with and where the vendor wishes to enforce a contract which the purchaser no longer wishes to complete.

5.4.3.1   *Minors*

There are two broad principles governing contracts with minors. One protects the minor by holding that they are generally unenforceable. The other protects adults who do not seek to take unfair advantage of a minor by upholding contracts that are for "necessaries". The case law in this field is varied in its approach and reflects the tension between protecting the interests of minors against unscrupulous traders and the interests of traders against unscrupulous minors.

Necessaries cover goods and services, and are not limited to necessities[5] but do exclude mere luxuries (as opposed to "luxurious articles of utility").[6] Ultimately the question can be reduced to whether it was reasonable for the minor to be supplied with the goods or services in question. This can hinge on a number of factors such as whether the minor already had an adequate supply of the matter in question. This test may apply irrespective of whether the vendor knew the answer at the time of contracting.[7]

Doubt remains whether a minor can be sued over a contract for necessaries that has yet to be fulfilled. If so, then a vendor could compel performance of it. It is possible, however, that this right only arises where the minor has been supplied with the goods or services in question.

---

5   *Peters v. Fleming* [1840] 6 M&W 42, 46.

6   *Chapple v. Cooper* [1844] 13 M&W 252, 258.

7   *Johnstone v. Marks* [1887] 19 QBD 509.

In respect of certain types of contract (e.g. contracts for and shares in companies) a minor will have the right to choose whether to be bound by it or to avoid it. Such contracts are said to be voidable.

If a contract with a minor is neither valid (e.g. for necessaries) nor voidable then it will not be binding on the minor. However, one rule is worth mentioning in this context. A minor that has performed under the non-binding agreement can only recover money or property transferred under it if he would have been entitled to do so as an adult (i.e. there is some other lawful reason such as a breach amounting to a complete failure of consideration). The courts have power to order a minor to transfer back to a vendor property acquired pursuant to an unenforceable contract.[8]

5.4.3.2 Mental patients

Generally speaking a contract with a mental patient is valid. However, if one contracting party knew of the other's disability then it is voidable by the disabled party who may still have to pay a reasonable price for "necessaries...sold and delivered...".[9]

5.4.3.3 Companies

With a few exceptions, most companies incorporated in England and Wales are created in accordance with the provisions of the applicable Companies Acts. Generally, it is not possible for a company to escape from a contract on the grounds that its purpose was beyond the objects set out in the company's memorandum.[10] A person dealing with such a company will be taken to have dealt with it in good faith believing the company capable of entering into the contract unless the contrary is proved. In that case the contract might be unenforceable by the person acting in bad faith.[11]

5.4.4 Mistake

If a person does have legal capacity to contract but is not in fact the person that the other thinks him to be then a question may arise as to the extent to which that other is bound by the contract made under that mistake and the extent to which it was effective to pass title. Since the transaction will be conducted at a distance it is likely that the parties will never meet. The identity of the contracting parties requires care. It is possible that purchasers may be seeking the goods of one company and will instead mistakenly visit the website of another with a confusingly similar domain name. If they purchase goods or services, are they stuck with them or can they force a refund once they realise their mistake?

The rules regarding "mistake" and its effects in English contract law are complex. In a nutshell, one party's consent to making the agreement may be negatived if their mistake is fundamental. If it is fundamental, then the contract may be void if the mistake also induced the contract and was "operative".

---

8   Minors' Contracts Act 1987 Section 3(1).

9   Sale of Goods Act 1979 Section 3(2).

10   Companies Act 1985 Section 35(1).

11   Companies Act 1985 Section 35A.

A mistake as to identity is fundamental and will therefore negate the purchaser's consent to the making of the contract. For instance, if a purchaser buys goods at a website mistakenly thinking it to be the site of a company with a famous reputation for quality then the mistake will be fundamental.[12] The mistake must have induced the mistaken party to enter the contract. In this example, the mistake will have induced the contract. If, by contrast, the purchaser does not care about the fact over which he is mistaken then it will have no effect. For example, if the purchaser did not care about the identity of the vendor but was merely mistaken as to the quality of the goods being purchased then arguably consent would not be negatived. This might be the case if the purchaser thought he was buying "same day" fresh food which was in fact a day old.[13]

However, even if the mistake did induce the contract, generally speaking the contract will remain valid despite the mistake. The contract will only be void if the mistake is "operative". There are three general circumstances where it will be operative: where a reasonable person could not infer the intention of the parties from the circumstances surrounding the transaction; or where one party knew of the other's mistake; or where one party negligently induced the other's mistake.

For this reason it is sensible for a vendor to clearly state who they are somewhere in the electronic trading area. That way it will be harder for a purchaser to set aside a contract on the basis of mistaken identity.

The notice should appear in the terms of trading. Although there will not usually be any written document signed by both parties it is arguable that if the contract is made on the written terms of trading set out in the website then the purchaser cannot claim that they thought they were contracting with someone else. They will generally be taken to have intended to contract with the person named. In that way, vendors can protect themselves from claims seeking to set aside contracts made where the parties have not met and an allegation of mistake as to identity may be made as a result.

What about the vendor's perspective? If the purchaser can be found then the vendor can sue for the money owed or, in some cases, the return of the goods. However, if the goods have been sold on and are in the possession of a third party then it will be important to establish that the purchaser never acquired title to the goods to pass on to any third party. If the vendor relied on the identity of the purchaser in extending credit (e.g., by assuming him to be someone known to the vendor) then it may be possible to void the contract by applying the principles of "mistake".[14] But if the vendor is not influenced by the identity of the purchaser (because, for example, the vendor has not attributed any quality to the identity, such as creditworthiness), then the contract will not be void and title will pass to the third party.[15]

---

[12]   *Cundy v. Lindsay* [1878] 3 App. Case 459.

[13]   *Smith v. Hughes* [1871] L.R. 6 QB 597.

[14]   *Cundy v. Lindsay See* footnote 12 above.

[15]   *King's Norton Metal Co. v. Edridge, Merrett & Co. Ltd* [1897] 14 TLR 98.

5.5   Consumer protection law

There is a welter of legislation providing consumer protection. Some of it is of general application to consumer retailing and has no special significance in the online environment (such as the provisions of the Consumer Protection Act 1987 dealing with defective goods). However, the application of some laws and a number of voluntary codes of practice dealing with advertising and mail order need separate consideration. What follows is divided into four sections: criminal liability; civil liability; voluntary codes; and the EU directives on distance selling and E-Commerce. There is a question mark over whether and in what circumstances a web page may amount to an advertisement. Statutes and directives vary in what factors are to be considered in answering that question. For the sake of brevity and with deference to commercial reality, it is assumed in what follows that companies will generally consider their web pages to be advertisements in order to err on the side of caution. What follows does not cover regulations affecting particular, regulated industries.

5.5.1   Criminal law

The Mail Order Transactions (Information) Order 1976 states that where payment is made before the goods are supplied the advertisement must state the name and address of the person carrying on the business. It was intended for traditional mail order. It does not apply to adverts sent by TV broadcast, sound or film. It is unclear whether it applies to websites or not. If it is to be implemented the relevant information should appear in the advertisement so this should be borne in mind when deciding on how the terms appear.

The Business Advertisements Disclosure Order 1977 provides that the vendor must make it clear that the goods are offered in the course of business (rather than as a private seller).

The Trade Descriptions Act 1968 prohibits the use of false trade descriptions. That cannot be excluded or limited by the terms and conditions and is a pitfall to be avoided.

The Unsolicited Goods and Services Act 1971 prohibits sending unsolicited goods and then demanding money in payment. The Unsolicited Goods and Services (Invoices etc.) Regulations 1975 contain specific provisions on the layout of invoices not asserting a right to payment.

The Consumer Transactions (Restrictions on Statements) Order 1976 prohibits certain statements seeking to restrict a consumer's rights. It is impermissible to use a notice to avoid the effects of the Unfair Contract Terms Act 1977 or restrict consumers' statutory rights. Hence, it is appropriate, for the avoidance of doubt, to include a notice in the terms of trading to the effect that they do not affect the purchaser's statutory rights.

The Consumer Protection Act 1987 Part III makes it an offence to display misleading prices or methods of calculating the price which are misleading. Therefore, the vendor must not state that:

(a) the price is less than it actually is;

(b) the price depends on factors it does not actually depend on;

(c) the price covers matters for which an extra is actually charged;

(d) the customer expects the price to change when he does not;

(e) price comparisons are valid when they are not.

For the sake of completeness it is worth noting that there is an order related to the Consumer Protection Act 1987 which gives guidance on it regarding incorrect pricing – the Consumer Protection (Code of Practice for Traders on Price Indications) Approval Order 1988.

The Price Indication (Methods of Payment) Regulations 1991 apply where the prices charged vary according to the method of payment used. They apply to an indication of a price given in an advertisement if it contains an invitation to consumers to place orders by means of a telecommunications system for the supply of goods or for the provision of services.[16] They require, amongst other things, that where a vendor gives consumers an indication of a price at which goods or services are available (which is not applicable to all methods of payment accepted) he shall, before the contract is made, make available statements about any method to which the price does not apply and the difference in price.

The Sale of Goods Act 1979 inserts implied terms into a contract of sale. They are called statutory rights. Restricting liability for breaches of the obligations created by the Act can, for example, amount to a an offence under the 1976 Order and be void under the 1977 Unfair Contract Terms Act (*see* below).

5.5.2   *Civil liabilities*

Most importantly the Consumer Protection (Cancellation of Contracts Concluded Away From Business Premises) Regulations 1987 apply to contracts made away from business premises. By analogy, they may well apply to website sales. They state that the consumer is to have a cooling-off period of seven days to cancel the order by notice of cancellation.

Any contract that does not give that right is unenforceable unless (so far as the exceptions apply): the value of the order is under £35 or, if over £35 and concluded on the basis of a trader's catalogue, the catalogue notifies the consumer of their seven day cooling-off right. It also provides for the consequences of such termination – namely that the consumer can return the goods (at their expense if required) or, if they have not been sent, a full refund.

The Distance Selling Regulations now cover this area.

5.5.3   *Voluntary codes*

The British Code of Advertising and Sales Promotion is formulated and regulated by the Committee of Advertising Practice under the auspices of the Advertising Standards Authority (the "ASA"). The effect of a failure to comply is that the ASA may investigate any complaint by the public, make an adverse ruling and publicise its findings. It is intended to be embarrassing if the vendor cares.

The other codes are applied by trade associations against their members. A vendor may be refused advertising in publications of companies that are members if it is not applying the ethical standards of trading that the codes require.

---

[16]   Section 6.

5.6   Terms to be considered

For reasons given above, the supplier using a website for e-commerce will wish to impose terms and conditions of trading on consumers. In addition to those provisions (required pursuant to legislation identified above) the following should also be considered.

5.6.1   *Delivery*

It makes good practical sense to advise consumers how long to wait before they start making enquiries about the progress of their order. Some online services give customers the ability to track their orders in real time and push email notices to them when the order has been dispatched and so on. The Distance Selling Directive addresses the time for delivery issue.

5.6.2   *Warranties*

Certain warranties will be implied by law unless specifically excluded. They include fitness for purpose and satisfactory quality.[17] A warranty as to title will also be readily implied. Consideration should be given as to any further warranties that should be excluded or limited, but regard should be had to the provisions of the Unfair Contract Terms legislation referred to below.

5.6.3   *Refunds and returns*

Consumers will want to, and indeed will, send back goods received. The retailer that does not anticipate or ignores this fact is storing up a great deal of trouble. It is essential to formulate a policy to deal with returns and refunds, and introduce such a scheme as conditions of the consumer contract, thereby limiting the exposure of the supplier to the idiosyncratic demands of consumers. A scheme can be more or less sympathetic to the consumer depending on the supplier's approach to marketing. It must comply with the requirements of the Distance Selling Regulations (dealt with elsewhere in this Guide).

In cases where the goods arrive in faulty condition, the issue for the supplier will be to determine whether the goods were:

(a) faulty when dispatched and therefore the supplier's liability;

(b) damaged in transit and therefore the liability of the courier; or

(c) damaged by the customer in which case the supplier may accept their return or not.

The supplier should have insurance for this type of event and may be obliged to make enquiries in respect of transactions above a certain value.

5.6.4   *Chargebacks and insurance*

Where the goods are paid for by credit card the issuer will have a policy that deals with complaints by its holders in respect of goods purchased with that card. In certain circumstances, the consumer will be given a refund by the card issuer. The issuer will seek

---

[17]   Sale of Goods Act 1979 Section 14. The term "satisfactory quality" applies to contracts made after 3 January 1995 pursuant to the amendments made by the Sale and Supply of Goods Act 1994 replacing, amongst other things, the earlier notion of "merchantable quality".

to recover that sum from the vendor. The amount repaid to the consumer will be inclusive of postage and packaging and the vendor will already have become liable to pay the postage and packaging cost to the third party that delivered the goods. Therefore when the amount is taken from the supplier's account and repaid to the consumer the vendor will be out of pocket. There is very little the supplier can do about this without considerable commercial leverage. The card issuer will usually reserve the right to make chargebacks as it considers appropriate according to its prevailing policy and the party fulfilling delivery will expect payment for shipments delivered (unless the return results from the shipper's breach).

The position is worse where the supplier has received a payment resulting from a fraudulent or unauthorised use of a credit card for which the holder is not liable either pursuant to the Consumer Credit Act 1974 or the Banking Code of Practice. Typically, all credit card issuers will place the risk in "customer-not-present" transactions with the supplier. Therefore the supplier will bear the risk and carry the liability for the unpaid purchase price of goods it has delivered when the card issuer refunds the price to the victim card-holder and applies a chargeback to the supplier's account. Realistically the supplier's remedy lies in an insurance policy against this type of risk.

5.6.5 *Liability clauses*

Whilst the use of standard terms and conditions can minimise the problems of free-form communication, it also has a drawback when it comes to limiting liability. Although English law places great importance on not interfering in contracts that are freely negotiated between parties, it takes a different view where the terms are not freely negotiated. This can arise in at least two ways: where there is an inequality of bargaining power as between, say, a vendor and a consumer; and where one party insists on contracting on its written standard terms of business. In either of those cases, where one party seeks to restrict or exclude their liability to the other, the exemption clause may be completely unenforceable or may be enforceable only if it satisfies the requirement of reasonableness.

Much of the applicable law in this area derives from the Unfair Contract Terms Act 1977 (the "UCTA") and the Unfair Terms in Consumer Contracts Regulations 1994 ("the Regulations").

5.6.5.1 *Unfair Contract Terms Act 1977*

In respect of negligence generally, it is impossible under UCTA to exclude liability for death or personal injury resulting from negligence.[18] As regards other loss and damage, a contract term that seeks to restrict or exclude liability for negligence is unenforceable except insofar as it is reasonable.[19] This is not confined to contracts with consumers.

Where one of the contracting parties deals either as a consumer or on the other's standard terms then the other party (i.e. usually the website vendor) cannot exclude or restrict liability for breach of contract or render substantially different performance than that contracted for or no performance, except insofar as the restriction/exclusion clause is reasonable.[20]

---

[18] Section 2(1).

[19] Section 2(2).

[20] Section 3.

The test of reasonableness also applies to indemnities given by consumers.[21]

It is impossible for a vendor to exclude the warranties as to title implied in contracts for sale or hire-purchase. As regards the implied terms as to fitness for purpose (and conformity of goods with description or sample), liability for breach in contracts with consumers cannot be excluded and can only be excluded in contracts with others insofar as it is reasonable.[22]

There is a good deal of bartering of services on the Internet, particularly in the provision of copyright extracts and advertising. It is worth noting that UCTA Section 7 applies the same provisions to such contracts as those created by UCTA Section 6.

UCTA Section 8 applies the test of reasonableness to clauses restricting or limiting liability for pre-contract misrepresentations.

Detailed consideration of the rules for determining what is reasonable are beyond the scope of this Chapter. In any event, the answer depends on the circumstances of each case. However, it is worth mentioning that UCTA Section 11 provides some guidance. It states that regard shall be had in particular to the following (set out in Schedule 2 to the Act):[23]

(a) the relative strength of the parties' bargaining power;

(b) whether the customer received an inducement to accept the term or could have entered a similar contract without it;

(c) whether the customer ought reasonably to have known of the nature and extent of the exclusion, having regard to custom of the trade and the parties' previous dealings;

(d) if the restriction is conditional on non-compliance with some term, whether at the time of the contract it was reasonable to expect that such compliance would be practicable;

(e) whether the goods were manufactured, processed or adapted to the special order of the customer.

Furthermore, where one party seeks to limit their liability to a specified sum of money, Section 11(4) provides that in determining the reasonableness of the limitation, regard shall be had to:

(a) the resources available to meet the liability; and

(b) how far it was open to cover the liability by insurance.

5.6.5.2   *Unfair terms in Consumer Contracts Regulations 1999*

These regulations revoke the 1994 Regulations of the same title and provide that a contractual term not individually negotiated shall be unfair if it causes a significant imbalance in the parties' rights and obligations under the contract to the detriment of the consumer. It will always apply to a term that has been drafted in advance without

---

[21]   Section 4.

[22]   Section 6.

[23]   Section 11(2).

influence from the consumer on the substance of the term. As such, website terms and conditions are affected. Any written contract must be in plain intelligible language. This poses a problem where it is directed at a country but not written in its native language.

An unfair term is not binding on the consumer. The Regulations apply despite any choice of law clause if the contract has a close connection with an EU Member State (which have similar legislative provisions as this implements an EU Directive). Injunctions may be ordered to prevent the continuing use of unfair terms.

5.7   The E-Commerce Directive[24]

5.7.1   *Scope of the Directive*

The European Union has implemented the E-Commerce Directive. The Directive does not apply to certain types of activity such as tax, gambling, cartels, litigation, laws designed to promote cultural and linguistic diversity or defend pluralism. Insofar as it applies it does so to the provision of "information services", which includes any service that[25] normally provides for remuneration at a distance[26] by electronic means[27] at the individual request of a recipient of services.[28]

The ostensible virtue of the Directive is its provision that Member States may not, for reasons falling within the Directive's "co-ordinated fields", restrict the freedom to provide information society services from another Member State.[29] The effect of this provision is crucial. It means that if the service is lawfully provided in a Member State where the provider is established then its provision in other Member States is also lawful. In effect, a Member State's laws on the provision of information society services become supranational and the provider need only be concerned with the laws of one country not all the countries of the EU individually.

The Directive is subject to derogations from the principle of free movement[30] and expressly does not apply to certain areas set out in its Annexe including:

(a) copyright and neighbouring rights;

(b) e-money;

(c) the freedom of parties to choose their applicable contract law;

(d) contractual obligations concerning consumer contracts;

(e) real estate contracts subject to formal requirement laws where it is located;

(f) unsolicited commercial communications.

---

[24]   "A European Initiative on Electronic Commerce", COM (97) 157 final, 16 April 1997.

[25]   Defined in Article 2.

[26]   When the parties are not simultaneously present when the *service* is provided.

[27]   Sent initially and received by electronic equipment for processing a storage of data, entirely transmitted, conveyed and received by wire, radio, optional or other electromagnetic means.

[28]   Provided through the transmission of data on individual request.

[29]   Article 3.

[30]   Article 22.

Member States may restrict the freedom to provide information society services on condition that such a measure is necessary on grounds of:

(a) public policy (as to race, sex, religion or nationality);

(b) health, security or consumer protection;

It shall be taken against a service which prejudices one of the above or risks doing so and shall be proportionate.[31]

As stated above the Directive does not apply to contractual obligations regarding consumer contracts, a derogation that considerably undermines the purpose of the Directive in attempting to stimulate business investment in online services and provide legal certainty. Service providers will still have to understand the intricacies of each Member States' national consumer protection laws.

5.7.2   *Service providers*

A "service provider" is any natural or legal person providing such services.

The Directive does not apply to services supplied by providers established in a third country.

Member States must ensure that the information society services supplied by providers established in that Member State, comply with national provisions.[32]

A service provider is established where it pursues an economic activity using a fixed establishment for an indeterminate duration. The presence of the technical means and technologies required do not constitute an establishment.[33]

Member States cannot make access to information society services dependent on the permission of an authority unless it is not specifically targeted at information society services.[34]

Member States will have to compel information society services to render easily accessible, in a direct and permanent manner to their recipients and competent authorities certain information including:

(a) name, address of establishment and details for quick and direct contact (i.e. email address);

(b) any registration number or trade register entry;

(c) the activities covered by any applicable authorisation scheme;

(d) as regards regulated professions, any bodies of registration, professional title, rules and places where the service is regularly provided; and

(e) VAT number where applicable.

---

[31]   Article 3.

[32]   Article 3.

[33]   Article 2.

[34]   Article 4.

In addition, they must enact legislation to ensure that prices of information society services are indicated accurately and unequivocally.[35]

Subject to certain conditions, service providers avoid liability, other than for prohibitory injunctions, in respect of certain access, caching and hosting services.

5.7.3 *Information society services*

The provisions directly addressing information society services are concerned with transparency in commercial communications and electronic contracts. They also make provision as regards the regulated professions.

5.7.3.1 *Commercial communications*

A commercial communication is any form of communication designed to promote directly or indirectly goods, services, or the image of a company subject to two exceptions:

(a) means of direct access such as a domain name; or

(b) directory/listing type activities.[36]

Member States are to ensure that such communications comply with the following:

(a) they are clearly identified as such;

(b) it is clear on whose behalf they are issued;

(c) promotional discount offers etc. are clearly identified as such and the conditions attaching to them are easily accessible, presented accurately and unequivocally (with similar rules in respect of games).[37]

An unsolicited commercial communication sent by email must be clearly and unequivocally identifiable as such as soon as it is received. Service providers engaged in such activities will be required to consult opt-out registers.[38]

5.7.3.2 *Regulated professions*

The Directive envisages the supply of information society services by regulated professions and introduces a number of requirements to that end (in addition to information required as to establishment, described above).

Member States will have to provide that information society services may be rendered by regulated professions subject to professional rules about standards being met. Community level codes of conduct are to be encouraged to determine the type of information that may be given in this regard and the Commission may stipulate this.[39]

---

[35]   Article 5.

[36]   Article 2.

[37]   Article 6.

[38]   Article 7.

[39]   Article 8.

5.7.3.3 *Electronic contracts – formation*

With certain exceptions, Member States are obliged to ensure that their legislation allows contracts to be concluded electronically. They must not prevent the effective use of electronic contracts or deprive them of legal effect and validity because they were electronically made. This does not apply to the following:

(a) contracts relating to real estate (other than rental rights);

(b) contracts involving the courts, public authorities etc.;

(c) contracts of suretyship;

(d) contracts governed by family law or the law of succession.[40]

5.7.3.4 *Electronic contracts – information*[41]

Member States are to provide that, except where otherwise agreed by persons who are not consumers, the following information must be provided clearly comprehensibly and unambiguously by the information society service provider and prior to the order being placed by the service recipient. This shall include the following information:

(a) the different technical steps to be taken to conclude the contract;

(b) whether the contract is to be filed/accessible;

(c) the technical means for correcting input errors before the order is placed;

(d) the languages offered for the conclusion of the contract.

The service provider will have to provide information about applicable codes of conduct (unless a non-consumer otherwise agrees).

The two previous paragraphs do not apply to contracts made exclusively by email.

Contract terms and conditions must be available in a way that allows the recipient to store and reproduce them.

5.7.3.5 *Placing the order*[42]

Except when otherwise agreed by a non-consumer, the following applies where the order is placed through technological means:

(a) receipt of the order must be without undue delay and by electronic means;

(b) the order and acknowledgement are deemed received when accessible by the addressees;

(c) there shall be means to correct input errors before order placement;

except that paragraphs (a) and (b) will not apply to email contracts.

---

[40]   Article 9.

[41]   Article 10.

[42]   Article 11.

5.7.3.6   Liability of intermediary service providers[43]

This subject is considered in greater detail beyond the mere scope of the E-Commerce Directive, elsewhere in this Guide. So far as the Directive is concerned the position may be summarized as follows.

(a) *Mere conduits* – in the case of a service that consists of the transmission in a communication network of information provided by a service recipient or the provision of access to it (including the automatic, intermediate and transient storage of the information insofar as this takes place for the sole purpose of carrying out the transmission in the communication network), Member States must ensure the service provider is not liable for the information transmitted on condition that it does not initiate the transmission, select its recipient or select/modify the information contained in the transmission. This will not prevent the judiciary from requiring the termination or prevention of infringements.

(b) *Caching* – the same provision is made as regards the automatic, intermediate and temporary storage of the information performed for the sole purpose of making more efficient the onward transmission of information to other recipients of the service on their request on condition that it:

(i) does not modify the information;

(ii) complies with conditions on access to it and industry standard rules as to updating it;

(iii) does not interfere with the lawful use of technology widely recognized and used by industry to obtain data on use of the information; and

(iv) acts expeditiously to remove or disable access to the information on receipt of actual knowledge that the information at the initial source has been removed from the network, and/or access to the information has been disabled and/or that the same has been ordered by a court or administrative authority.

(c) *Hosting* – the same provision is made as regards the storage of information from a service recipient, on condition that it:

(i) does not have actual knowledge of illegal activity or information and – for damages claims – does not have actual knowledge of the facts or circumstances from which such illegality is apparent; or

(ii) acts expeditiously to remove or disable access to such information on obtaining such knowledge.

---

[43]   Article 12.

5.7.4 *Implementation*

The Directive includes a series of provisions aimed at implementing the following requirements. These include:

(a) the use of codes of conduct which may involve consumer associations inputting on the drafting;[44]

(b) the use of effective out-of-court dispute settlement procedures;[45]

(c) access to rapid court measures to terminate alleged infringements;[46]

(d) co-operation between authorities; and[47]

(e) the national determination of appropriate sanctions for infringements to national legislation.[48]

---

[44]   Article 16.

[45]   Article 17.

[46]   Article 18.

[47]   Article 19.

[48]   Article 20.

Chapter 6
JURISDICTION

Dr Stuart Dutson
Litigation and Arbitration Solicitor
Linklaters – Linklaters & Alliance (London)

6.1   Introduction

From the dawn of the Internet, jurists have been prophesying that it will render national boundaries meaningless. Whilst this may prove true in terms of its use and the dissemination of information, the same cannot be said for parties trying to seek to enforce their Intellectual Property ("IP") rights. If an IP right owner wishes to commence an action for infringement of his copyright or patent over the Internet, then the issue of which country's courts will hear the case, what part of the case they will hear, and what law they will apply, will remain at the forefront of his lawyer's mind.

In deciding where to commence an action, a potential claimant should consider: where he is most likely to win; where is least expensive; which country's courts give the most damages; where can he obtain legal aid; how easy is it to get a particular court's judgment enforced outside the country; and can he consolidate all his claims in the one court? England is an attractive forum in International IP cases: English courts can be very fast; English judgments are enforceable throughout the European Economic Area ("EEA") and in many other countries; English courts allow for the consolidation of claims under different laws; legal aid may be available; and a successful party can recover its costs.

Whilst this Chapter focuses primarily on actions before the English courts the principles discussed regarding jurisdiction and defendants domiciled within either a European Union ("EU") or European Free Trade Area ("EFTA") country (these two groupings of countries are collectively termed the EEA) could equally be applied to any EEA court or country.   However, in the context of a non-EEA domiciled defendant the relevant considerations could vary radically. French courts, for example, will accept jurisdiction against any non-EEA domiciled defendant if the claimant is French.

The first issue an international lawyer addresses when considering the Internet is whether it is a new form of communication, or a natural progression from existing methods of communication (i.e. the telephone, facsimile, television etc.). In terms of the conflicts of laws it is generally considered to be no different from the existing means of mass communication – it is essentially old wine in new bottles from a conflicts perspective. The conflict of law principles were developed in light of, and have been applied to, the press, the telephone, the facsimile and the television, and apply equally to this new form of communication. Information placed by a website provider for access over the Internet is sent by that person to others (potentially millions of others, simultaneously, in many different jurisdictions) just as a fax or letter or TV transmission is sent by its author, albeit the information passively awaits being accessed by the web users.[1] Nevertheless, the Internet makes information available simultaneously in every jurisdiction in the world and presents unique factual circumstances in which infringements of IP rights may be committed.

---

[1]   *See Shetland Times Limited v. Wills* ("The Times", 21 January 1997).

6.2   Territorial limitations on IP rights

There are two distinct forms of jurisdiction that are relevant in any case – "personal jurisdiction" and "subject matter jurisdiction".[2] The former is jurisdiction in the sense of amenability of the defendant to the court's writ.[3] The latter is jurisdiction in the sense of entertainment of disputes as to a particular subject matter.[4] Provisions which provide for "exorbitant" or "long arm" jurisdiction (such as Civil Procedure Rule ("CPR") 6.20(iii)) deal only with personal jurisdiction; they do not provide a court with jurisdiction over the subject matter of the action.[5] In most cases both personal and subject matter jurisdiction must be established if a court is to be able to hear and determine any dispute. This distinction becomes particularly relevant if a court is considering a statutory right.[6] If the claimant's right is statutory the courts resolve the issue of subject matter jurisdiction by interpreting the statutory provisions and/or by applying the relevant choice of law rule.[7] The ability to effect service of proceedings on a foreign defendant under a long arm service provision (such as CPR 6.20(iii)) will not conclusively establish the application of a statute of the forum to either the dispute or the foreign defendant.[8]

A court's subject matter jurisdiction, in cases in which the right or cause of action derives from the common law, is determined by the application of the relevant choice of law rule. However, in cases of a statutory right or cause of action this method must be subordinate to the terms of the legislation being characterised and the context, subject matter or object of the legislation.[9] If, for example, the statute provides that it applies only to acts of a person within the UK, then it can have no application to acts which take place outside the UK, notwithstanding the determination which the application of the applicable rule of private international law may generate.[10]

In cases dealing with statutory IP rights the court's subject matter jurisdiction is provided for expressly in the relevant legislation and the choice of law rules are therefore inapplicable in the determination of subject matter jurisdiction. The Patents Act 1977

---

2   *See MacKinnon v. Donaldson, Lufkin and Jenrette Securities Corp.* [1988] Ch.482,493; *Flaherty v. Girgis* (1987) 162 CLR 574 per Mason A.C.J., Wilson and Dawson J.J. at 598; *Mercedes-Benz AG v. Leiduck* [1996] 1 AC 284 (PC) per Lord Nicholls of Birkenhead at 305 (dissenting but not on this point).

3   Ibid.

4   Ibid.

5   Ibid.

6   *See* Peter Nygh: "Choice of Law Rules and Forum Shopping in Australia" (1995) 6 Public Law Review pp. 237, 241.

7   Stuart Dutson: "The Conflict of Laws and Statutes" (1997) 60 Modern Law Review 668.

8   *Holmes v. Bangladesh Biman Corporation* [1989] 1 AC 1112 per Lord Bridge of Harwich (Lords Griffiths, Ackner and Lowry agreeing) at 1135, semble *David Syme & Co. Ltd v. Grey* (1992) 115 ALR 247 per Gummow J. at 257-260, and cf. *Theophile v. Solicitor General* [1950] AC 186 per Lord Porter at 195.

9   *Arab Monetary Fund v. Hashim* (No. 9) (unreported, High Court of Justice Chancery Division, Chadwick J., 29.7.94, digested at "The Times" 11 October 1994 at 503) at 11-14; *Molnlycke AB v. Procter & Gamble Ltd* [1992] RPC 21 at 28; *Def Lepp Music v. Stuart-Brown* [1986] RPC 274. This will continue to be the law under the Private International Law (Miscellaneous Provisions) Act 1995 (UK).

10   *See Def Lepp Music v. Stuart-Brown* [1986] RPC 274.

Sections 60, 132(2)-(4); Copyright, Designs and Patents Act 1988 ("CDP") Sections 1, 2, 16; and Trade Marks Act 1994 Section 9(1) each provide in effect that the statute is limited in its operation to acts of infringement that take place within the UK.[11] Accordingly, an English court has subject matter jurisdiction to determine an action dealing with the infringement in England of an English statutory IP right, however, it cannot determine an action dealing with the infringement outside England of an English statutory IP right.[12]

In contrast, the tort of passing off is not territorially limited in this way. As a creature of the common law, its territorial scope is determined by the application of the appropriate choice of law rule in tort or delict.

6.3 Personal jurisdiction

A court must possess both personal and subject matter jurisdiction to determine any case. What follows is a discussion of the assumption of personal jurisdiction by an English court.

In the case of an action commenced in an English court against a defendant domiciled within the EEA, personal jurisdiction will be determined in accordance with the 1968 Brussels and 1989 Lugano Conventions (the "Conventions"),[13] which were brought into force in the UK by the Civil Jurisdiction and Judgments Act 1982 (UK) (as amended to incorporate the Lugano Convention by the Civil Jurisdiction and Judgments Act 1991 (UK)).[14] However, as against the defendants domiciled outside the EEA, subject to any agreements as to jurisdiction made between the parties,[15] personal jurisdiction is determined in accordance with the traditional English rules as to service out of the jurisdiction – Part 6 III of the CPRs.[16]

---

[11]   *See* further *Def Lepp Music & Others v. Stuart Brown & Others* [1986] RPC 273, *Molnlycke AB v. Procter & Gamble Ltd* (No. 4) [1992] RPC 21, and *Waterford Wedgwood plc v. David Nagili Ltd* [1998] FSR 92 at 102.

[12]   The statutory IP law applies throughout the UK. However, this article is solely concerned with actions commenced in English courts.

[13]   The provisions of the Conventions that are relevant to this article are identical.

[14]   The proposed EC Regulation on jurisdiction and the recognition and enforcement of judgments (com (1999) 348 final) is intended to update and replace the Brussels and Lugano Conventions. When finalised the Regulation will not apply in the first instance to the UK, Ireland and Denmark, however the UK and Ireland have indicated that they would opt-in to the Regulation. It remains to be seen whether the provisions of the Brussels and Lugano conventions will be amended to bring them into line with the Regulation after it has been finalised.

[15]   *See* Article 17 of the Brussels and Lugano Conventions.

[16]   Which replaced RSC (England) O.11. *See* Article 4 of the Brussels and Lugano Conventions. Note, however, that if an action has been commenced in one contracting state a court in another contracting state cannot duplicate those proceedings, albeit that the proceedings in both, or one only, of the states were commenced by the court(s) assuming jurisdiction pursuant to their own traditional jurisdictional rules rather than under the Conventions; *see* Article 21 of the *Conventions and Overseas Union Insurance v. New Hampshire Insurance* (Case C-351/89) [1991 – I] ECR 3317 (ECJ).

6.3.1 Proceedings regarding the infringement in England of English IP right committed by a foreigner

This kind of case raises no problems of subject matter jurisdiction.

Personal Jurisdiction must be addressed in terms of the Convention and the non-Convention States. Neither the Convention nor the non-Convention rules dealing with personal jurisdiction make any special provision for cases dealing with the infringement of IP rights. Accordingly, the general rules apply to infringement cases.

6.3.1.1 Defendant not domiciled in a Brussels/Lugano Convention country

Two issues will be relevant when a court considers jurisdiction under the traditional rules:

(a) whether the English court has the power to hear a case against the defendant and whether the court will decline jurisdiction or stay the proceedings. This second issue requires a consideration of the *forum non conveniens* doctrine. All leading private international law texts deal with this doctrine, and it is not IP specific. Accordingly, no consideration will be given to it here;

(b) the court's competence to hear a case against a particular defendant is wholly dependent on the service of a claim form on him. A claim form can be served on a defendant in three cases:

(i) he is present within the jurisdiction;

(ii) he submits to the jurisdiction of the English courts (RSC 0.10 r(1)5 which remains part of the CPR); and

(iii) the rules for service out of the jurisdiction (CPR Part 6 III – the "extraterritorial service provisions") can be satisfied.

The extraterritorial service provisions that may be relevant are CPR 6.20(2), (3) and (8).

CPR 6.20 (8) provides for extraterritorial service where a "claim is founded on a tort and the damage was sustained, or resulted from an act committed, within the jurisdiction".

Whether an action is "founded on a tort", and whether the requirements of CPR 6.20 (8) have been satisfied, is determined in accordance with the *lex fori*.[17]

In *The Electric Furness Company v. Selas Corporation of America*[18] the Court of Appeal considered that an action for infringement of a patent came within a similarly worded predecessor to CPR 6.20 (8). The law is the same in Australia.[19] Accordingly, CPR 6.20 (8) applies both to claims for the infringement of a statutory IP right and to the tort of passing off.

---

17   *Metall und Rohstoff A.G. v. Donaldson Lufkin & Jenrette Inc.* [1990] 1 QB 391 at 443 (CA), overruled in *Lonrho plc v. Fayed* [1992] 1 AC 448 but not on this point.

18   [1987] RPC 23 (CA) at 30-31 and semble *Unilever plc v. Gillett (UK) Ltd* [1989] RPC 83 (CA).

19   *Spotless Group v. Proplast* [1987] 10 IPR 668 and 670 and *Best Australia v. Aquagas Marketing* [1988] 83 ALR 217 at 220.

Prior to 1987 the English tort extra territorial service rule provided for a claim founded on a "tort committed within the jurisdiction". The new version of the rule was adopted in order to bring CPR 6.20 (8) into line with Article 5(3) of the Brussels Convention (which confers special jurisdiction on courts in matters relating to tort or delict) and the decision of the European Court of Justice in *Bier v. Mines de Potasse d'Alsace SA*.[20]

In *Metall und Rohstoff A.G. v. Donaldson Lufkin & Jenrette Inc.*[21] the Court of Appeal considered the identical predecessor to CPR 6.20 (8) in some detail and in so doing provided the only authoritative guidelines for the interpretation of it reported to date. The court made no reference to the pre-existing law on where a tort is committed in the context of the new tort extraterritorial service provision. The court held that it is not necessary that all the damage should have been sustained within the jurisdiction; it is enough if some significant damage has been sustained in England.[22] Nor is it necessary that all the acts have been committed within the jurisdiction;[23] the court must look at the tort alleged in a common-sense way and ask whether damage has resulted from substantial and efficacious acts committed by the putative defendant within the jurisdiction – whether or not other substantial and efficacious acts have been committed elsewhere.[24] In cases under IP statutes the act(s) will be the infringing act(s) identified in the statute (e.g. the unauthorised use of a patented product, or the copying or performance of copyright material), and in passing-off cases it will be the receipt of the defendant's misrepresentation(s) (e.g. that the defendant's business is related to the claimant's business) and the damage to the claimant's goodwill at the place where it exists.[25]

CPR 6.20 (2) provides for extraterritorial service where an injunction is sought ordering the defendant to do or refrain from doing anything within the jurisdiction (whether or not damages are also claimed in respect of a failure to do or the doing of that thing). This rule proved useful in *Re Burlands Trade Mark*[26] where the claimant obtained an injunction against a Scottish defendant in respect of infringements of its trade mark in England. Again, an infringing act must have taken place within England for this rule to be utilised.

CPR 6.20 (3) provides for extraterritorial service where the claim is brought against a person duly served within or out of the jurisdiction and a person out of the jurisdiction is a necessary or proper party thereto. The test applied to determine whether this rule is applicable is whether the party sought to be served could, if within the jurisdiction, have

---

20   (Case 21/76) [1976] ECR 1735. *See Metall und Rohstoff A.G. v. Donaldson Lufkin & Jenrette Inc.* [1990] 1 QB 391 at 437, *Societe Commerciale de Reassurance v. Eras International Ltd* [1992] 1 L1 LR 570 (CA) at 589.

21   [1990] 1 QB 391 (CA).

22   *Metall und Rohstoff A.G. v. Donaldson Lufkin & Jenrette Inc.* [1990] 1 QB 391 at 437 (CA).

23   This much is obvious on the wording of CPR 6.20 (8)); however, the court did then proceed to verbalise a test of sorts for when this portion of the rule is satisfied.

24   Ibid. at 437 (CA).

25   *See Mecklermedia Corporation v. DC Congress GmbH* [1998] Ch. 40.

26   (1889) 41 Ch D 542 where the claimant obtained an injunction against a Scottish defendant in respect of infringements of its trade mark in England.

been joined in the original action.[27] In *Washburn v. Cunard Steamship Company*[28] service was effected in reliance on this rule against the Irish owner of goods that infringed the claimant's patent after service had initially been effected on the Liverpool-based party who had imported the goods into England. There are decisions which state that the secondary defendant cannot be served under this extraterritorial service provision if the sole (as opposed to predominant) purpose of the action against the original defendant is to enable or facilitate jurisdiction against the secondary defendant.[29] These decisions were based on the express requirement that the proceedings be "properly brought" against the original defendant.[30] In England this has been replaced by a requirement that such an application be supported by an affidavit which includes a statement that there is a real issue between the claimant and the original defendant which the claimant may reasonably ask the court to try.[31] There is no guidance on whether this alteration affects the authority of past decisions; however, it appears that the end result will be the same under the new version of the rule.

A further method by which a defendant may be served under CPR Rule 6.20 is the "common design rule". If a claimant can establish that defendants have collaborated in a common design to infringe his IP right then the defendants will be liable as joint "tortfeasors".[32] If one of the defendants collaborating is outside England and the other is inside England then the foreigner can be served under CPR 6.20 (2), (3) and/or (8).[33] Accordingly, if an English resident party has committed acts within England which are alleged to have constituted primary infringements of a claimant's IP rights and those acts were committed in furtherance of a common design between it and an overseas party, such that the overseas party can be said to have procured or assisted the infringement, then the overseas party can be sued in England pursuant to CPR 6.20 (2), (3) and/or (8).

---

[27]   *Societe Commerciale de Reassurance v. Eras International Ltd* [1992] 1 L1LR. 570 (CA) at 592. cf. *Jan Poulsen & Co. v. Seaboard Shipping Co. Ltd* [1995] ILPr 698 at 702 (S.Ct.B.C).

[28]   (1889) 6 RPC 398.

[29]   *Coppin v. Tobler Brothers Canberra Marine Centre Pty Ltd* [1980] 1 NSWLR 183, *Rosler v. Hilbery* [1925] Ch 250, and *Multinational Gas Co. v. Multinational Gas Services Ltd* [1983] Ch 258 (CA). The position is the same in Canada: *Jan Poulsen & Co. v. Seaboard Shipping Co. Ltd* [1995] ILPr 698 at 702 (S.Ct.B.C.). However, the editors of Dicey and Morris favour the less stringent view of the minority in *Multinational Gas Co. v. Multinational Gas Services Ltd*: Collins (edn.) "Dicey and Morris on the Conflict of Laws" (1993) at 325.

[30]   See *Multinational Gas Co. v. Multinational Gas Services Ltd* [1983] Ch. 258 at 284-285 (CA).

[31]   CPR 6.20 (3)(b).

[32]   *Unilever plc v. Gillett (UK) Ltd* [1989] RPC 583 at 608 and *Uniliver plc v. Chefaro Proprietaries Ltd* [1994] FSR 135.

[33]   Ibid.

6.3.1.2   Defendant domiciled in a Brussels/Lugano Convention country

The primary rule provided for in the Conventions is that a defendant should be sued in his place of domicile.[34] "Domicile" is specially defined for the purposes of the Conventions and their implementing legislation.[35]

To determine whether a party is domiciled in the UK, an English court will apply the definition of domicile given in the 1982 Act. As regards individuals, domicile is equated with the state where:

(a) a person is resident; and

(b) the nature and circumstances of his residence indicate that he has a substantial connection with it (Section 41 of the Act).

An individual is presumed to have a substantial connection with a state if he has resided there for more than three months: Section 41(6). However, to determine whether an individual is domiciled in another Convention State, a court must apply the law of that state.[36]

As regards companies, the "seat" of the company or association is treated as its domicile.[37] The basic rule is that the seat is where:

(a) a corporation has its registered office or some other official address; or

(b) its central management and control is exercised.[38]

To determine which state, if it is not England, a company is domiciled in, the court will apply these same rules. However, a company cannot be regarded as having its seat in another Convention State if that state's laws would not so decide.[39] In these cases it appears that the company has no domicile.

However, subject to recent English, German and Dutch decisions, in IP cases Article 2 of the Conventions can prove to be particularly problematic. Because of the territorial nature of statutory IP rights it may only be possible to obtain subject matter jurisdiction in an English court in the jurisdiction in which the infringing act(s) took place. If this jurisdiction is not the defendant's domicile then Article 2 is rendered nugatory and a claimant may be forced to turn to the special jurisdiction provisions of the Conventions to identify a jurisdiction in which this concurrence of subject matter and personal jurisdiction occurs.

---

[34]   Article 2. Note that Article 16(4) of the Conventions does not apply to infringement actions: *Duijnstee v. Goderbauer* (Case 288/92) [1983] ECR 3663.

[35]   *See* Sections 41 to 46 of the 1982 Act.

[36]   Article 52 of the Conventions.

[37]   Section 42(1) of the 1982 Act.

[38]   Sections 42(2)-(6) of the 1982 Act.

[39]   Section 42(7) of the 1982 Act.

Article 5(3) of the Convention grants jurisdiction in matters relating to tort or delict to the court of "the place where the harmful event occurred". Disputes concerning the infringement of an intellectual property right are matters relating to tort, delict or quasi-delict.[40] This is in accordance with the treatment of actions for infringement of intellectual property rights in the law of the contracting states to the Brussels Convention – they are regarded as actions in tort or delict.

Article 5(3) is also applicable in a common design case.[41] It appears that Article 6 (discussed below) would also be available in a common design case.

It is not an improper use of Article 5(3) or the common design principle to obtain jurisdiction under Article 5(3) solely to recover documents in that party's possession. In *Molnlycke* the claimant joined the German defendant in the action with the particular aim of recovering documents relevant to the claims against other defendants in that case as well as to the claim against the German defendant.

The meaning of the phrase "the place where the harmful event occurred" (under Article 5(3)) has been considered by the European Court of Justice in three types of cases:[42]

(a) where the place of the event giving rise to the damage and the place where the damage occurs, being a single instance of damage, are not the same;[43]

(b) where the claimant has suffered indirect damage;[44] and

(c) where it is difficult to ascertain the place in which the damage occurred because the causal event gave rise to more than one instance of damage.[45]

In *Bier v. Mines de Potasse d'Alsace SA*[46] the court held that the place where the harmful event occurred under Article 5(3) encompassed both the place where the damage occurred and the place of the event giving rise to the damage.[47]

In *Dumez France and Tracoba SA v. Hessiche Landesbank*[48] the court pointed out that Article 5(3) supported the need for a close connecting factor between the dispute and the court hearing the case.[49] Consequently, the court held that the phrase "the place where the damage occurred" (as used in *Bier v. Mines de Potasse d'Alsace SA*) is the place where the tortuous conduct, which gave rise to the damage directly, produced its harmful effects

---

40   *Coin Controls Ltd v. Suzo International & Others* [1997] 3 All ER 45, and *Pearce v. Ove Arup Partnership Ltd & Others* [1997] Ch 293 at 4.

41   *Molnlycke AB & anor v. Procter & Gamble Ltd & Others.* (No. 4) [1992] RPC 21 (CA).

42   *See Shevill v. Presse Alliance SA* (Case C-68/93) [1995] 2 AC 18 (ECJ) per A.G. Darmon at 34.

43   *Bier v. Mines de Potasse d'Alsace SA* (Case 21/76) [1976] ECR 1735.

44   *Dumez France and Tracoba SA v. Hessiche Landesbank* (Case C-220/88) [1990] I ECR. 49.

45   *Shevill v. Presse Alliance SA* (Case C-68/93) [1995] 2 AC 18 (ECJ).

46   (Case 21/76) [1976] ECR 1735.

47   It is this interpretation of Article 5(3) which CPR 6.20 (8) patently attempts to, and does, replicate.

48   (Case C-220/88) [1990] 1ECR 49.

49   *See Shevill v. Presse Alliance SA* (Case C-68/93) [1995] 2 AC 18 (ECJ) per A.G. Darmon at 34.

upon the person or the property of the person who is the immediate victim of that event.[50] In *Marinari v. Lloyds Bank plc*[51] the court further clarified this point of law by stating that "the place where the harmful event occurred" could not be construed so extensively as to encompass any place where the adverse consequences of an event that had already caused actual damage elsewhere could be felt.[52] Consequently it did not include the place where financial loss resulting from initial damage suffered by the claimant in another state is sustained or felt by the claimant.[53]

In *Shevill v. Presse Alliance SA*[54] the court stated that where a causal event gives rise to more than one instance of damage the "place where the damage occurred" (as used in *Bier v. Mines de Potasse d'Alsace SA*) means all of the places in which damage arose. Therefore a claimant would be entitled to commence proceedings in a tort action before the courts of: the defendant's domicile, the place of the harmful event, and the places in which the damage arose. However, only the courts of the defendant's domicile and the place of the harmful event are competent in respect of all the damage. The courts within whose jurisdiction damage has arisen only have jurisdiction with respect to the damage which has arisen within their own jurisdiction. Furthermore, the court held that in determining whether it has jurisdiction *qua* court of the place where the damage occurred pursuant to Article 5(3) "the criteria (that the court must employ) for assessing whether the event in question is harmful and the evidence required of the existence and extent of the harm alleged by the victim ... are not governed by the Convention but by the substantive law determined by the national conflict of law rules of the court seized, provided that the effectiveness of the Convention is not thereby impaired".[55]

In the one case where the European Court of Justice has not yet considered Article 5(3) – a case in which there was more than one domicile where the event giving rise to the damage could have occurred – an English court has taken a different approach to that adopted in *Bier v. Mines de Potasse d'Alsace SA*. In *Minister Investments Ltd v. Hyundai Precision & Industry Co. Ltd*, J Steyn resorted to the English "where in substance the cause of action arises" test.[56] He stated that this approach was derived from the terms of Article 5(3), and that the decision in *Bier v. Mines de Potasse d'Alsace SA* was not to be treated as providing comprehensive guidance on that provision. In *Jakob Handte GmbH v. Traitements Mecano-chimiques des Surfaces*,[57] Advocate General Jacobs stated: "It is clear that Article 5(3) is intended to refer to any event which could give rise to liability in delict".[58]

---

[50]   *See Shevill v. Presse Alliance SA* (Case C-68/93) [1995] 2 AC 18 (ECJ) per A.G. Darmon at 36.

[51]   (Case C-364/93) [1996] QB 217 (ECJ).

[52]   Ibid. at paragraph [14].

[53]   Ibid. at paragraphs [15] and [21]. *See Kitechnology BV v. Unicor GmbH Plastmaschien* [1994] IL Pr 568 (English CA).

[54]   (Case C-68/93) [1995] 2 AC 18 (ECJ).

[55]   *Shevill* at 63-64.

[56]   [1988] 2 LILR 621.

[57]   (Case C-26/91) [1993] IL Pr 5.

[58]   *Jakob Handte GmbH* at 17 n.24.

Accordingly, in any case in which the owner of an IP right wishes to commence infringement proceedings and rely on Article 5(3) to establish the court's jurisdiction, he must carefully consider whether Article 5(3) is in fact appropriate in light of these decisions.

In so far as the tort of passing off is concerned, the damage is to the claimant's goodwill – the effect on his reputation.[59] The direct harmful effects are located wherever the claimant's goodwill is located and a claimant in a passing-off case has the option to commence his proceedings in that jurisdiction.

Article 6 of the Conventions provides that a person, who is one of a number of defendants, may be sued in the courts of the location where any one of them is domiciled. Article 6 is applied in the same circumstances as O.11 r.1(1)(c) – a party may be sued in England under this Article only if he could have been properly joined in the original action had he been within the jurisdiction.[60] In contrast to Article 5(3) it is improper to rely on Article 6 to sue a party in England merely to recover documents in that party's possession.[61]

Article 24 of the Conventions allows for a claimant to obtain interlocutory injunctions against infringements in the place(s) of infringement whether or not that country has jurisdiction under Articles 2, 5 or 6. This provision will prove most valuable in passing-off cases, where the concurrence of personal and subject matter jurisdiction can be obtained in respect of more than one jurisdiction.

6.3.1.3   Different defendants domiciled both in and outside a Brussels/Lugano Convention country

There appears to be no reason why a claimant cannot use the Conventions' jurisdictional rules within the EEA against, for example, an EEA domiciled importer in conjunction with the traditional rules (O.11) against a non-EEA domiciled manufacturer; an American or Japanese domiciled manufacturer can therefore be joined in the same action as an English or German domiciled importer.

6.3.2   Proceedings regarding the "infringement" abroad of an English IP right

6.3.2.1   Pre-Private International Law (Miscellaneous Provisions) Act 1995

English statutory IP rights are strictly territorial in their operation. English IP legislation will apply to infringements in England of IP rights conferred by English legislation and will not apply to acts of infringement outside England. However, these territorial limitations are subject to the scope of the common law tort of passing off and the practical effect of the common design principle (where an extraterritorial defendant has a common design with a party within the jurisdiction to infringe an English statutory IP right within England). The common design principle will facilitate an action being brought against a foreigner in the English courts. Exceptionally, a contributory act towards the eventual

---

[59]   *Mecklermedia Corporation v. DC Congress Gesellschaft* [1998] Ch. 40.

[60]   *Kalfelis v. Schroder, Munchmeyer, Hengst & Co.* (Case C-198/87) [1988] ECR 5565, and *Molnlycke AB & anor v. Procter & Gamble Ltd & Others* (No 4) [1992] RPC 21 (CA) at 27.

[61]   *Molnlycke AB & anor v. Procter & Gamble Ltd & Others* (No 4) [1992] RPC 21 (CA) at 27.

infringement of an English IP right may take place outside England.[62] This is a question of interpretation of the territorial application of the statute and is not a matter giving rise to any conflicts of law.

The common law tort of passing off is not subject to the same strict territorial limits as the statutory IP rights. Its territorial scope is determined by application of the choice of law rule in tort.[63] The English law of passing off applies to conduct in a foreign country which would have been actionable as passing off if it had occurred in England, and which is actionable in the country where the infringement occurred.[64] However, before a court will grant an injunction to restrain a passing off that occurs in a foreign country, the claimant must provide the court with evidence of actionability under foreign law.[65]

6.3.2.2 *Post-Private International Law (Miscellaneous Provisions) Act 1995*

The Post-Private International Law Act 1995 (the "PIL Act") abolishes the former *Phillips v. Eyre* double actionability choice of law rule in tort and provides as a general rule that the applicable law is the law of the country in which the events constituting the tort or delict in question occur.[66] Where elements of those events occur in different countries the applicable law is the law of the country in which the most significant element or elements of those events occur.[67] The Act also provides for an exception to these rules where it is substantially more appropriate for the applicable law to be the law of another country.[68]

Sections 10, 14(2) and 14(4) of the Act provide:

"Section 10 – the rules of the common law, in so far as they:

(i) require actionability under both the law of the forum and the law of another country for the purpose of determining whether a tort or delict is actionable; or

(ii) allow (as an exception from the rules falling within paragraph (a) above) for the law of a single country to be applied for the purpose of determining the issues, or any of the issues, arising in the case in question

are hereby abolished in so far as they apply to any claim in tort or delict (which is not a defamation-type claim).

---

[62] For example infringing acts with respect to material to be imported into the UK (Section 27(3) (CDP Act), "authorising" a breach of an English copyright: CDP Act Section 16(2) and *see ABKCO v. Music Collection International* [1995] EMLR 449 (CA).

[63] Stuart Dutson: "The Conflict of Laws and Statutes" (1997) 60 Modern Law Review 668 at 669.

[64] "Dicey & Morris on the Conflict of Laws" (12th edn) Rule 203, *Walker (John) & Sons Ltd v. Henry Ost & Co. Ltd* [1970] 1 WLR 917, and *Alfred Dunhill Ltd v. Sunoptic SA* [1979] FSR 337 (CA).

[65] *Alfred Dunhill Ltd v. Sunoptic SA* [1979] FSR 337 (CA) at 368 and 377, *Intercontex v. Schmidt* [1988] FSR 575 at 578, *Waterford Wedgwood plc v. David Nagli Ltd* [1998] FSR 92 at 107.

[66] Section 11(1) of the PIL Act.

[67] Section 11(2)(c) of the PIL Act.

[68] Section 12 of the PIL Act.

Section 14(2) – nothing in this Part affects any rules of law (including rules of private international law except those abolished by Section 10 above).

Section 14(4) – this Part has effect without prejudice to the operation of any rule of law which either has effect notwithstanding the rules of private international law applicable in the particular circumstances or modifies the rules of private international law that would otherwise be so applicable."

The result of the application of Sections 10, 14(2) and 14(4) on the pre-PIL Act position is that the law dealing with the infringement of English statutory IP rights overseas remains unchanged. Section 14(4) will preserve the position that English IP legislation will be territorially limited in its operation.

The English law of passing off or a similar foreign law will now be applied in accordance with the choice of law rule provided for in Section 11 of the Act.[69]

6.3.3   *Proceedings in England regarding the "infringement" of a foreign IP right*

6.3.3.1   Pre-Private International Law (Miscellaneous Provisions) Act 1995

Until 1997 actions for the infringement of foreign IP rights were "non-justiciable" before English courts[70] for these two reasons:

(a) an action for the infringement of a foreign IP right is a local (as distinct from a transitory) action. Accordingly the questions of the validity, title to and infringement of an IP right fall exclusively within the jurisdiction of the courts of the country by the laws under which the IP right was created;[71]

(b) an action for the infringement of a foreign IP right falls foul of the first limb of the choice of law rule in tort – it is not actionable in England.[72]

However, courts in other EEA countries are becoming more willing to assume jurisdiction in actions for infringement of foreign IP rights.[73] Moreover, Professor Cornish has suggested that English courts should entertain actions for the infringement of a foreign IP right where the other country is a member of the EEA because this is consistent with the principles embodied in the Brussels and Lugano Conventions.

---

[69]   *Waterford Wedgwood plc v. David Nagli Ltd* [1998] FSR at 107.

[70]   *Pearce v. Ove Arup Partnership Ltd & Others* [1997] Ch 293.

[71]   *Tyburn Productions v. Conan Doyle* [1991] Ch 75, *Plastus Kreativ v. Minnesota Mining* [1995] RPC 438 at 446-7, *LA Gear v. Gerald Whelan & Sons* [1991] FSR 670 at 674 and 676 and compare *James Burrough Distillers plc v. Speymalt Whisky Distributors Ltd* [1989] SLT 561. Grounds for the decision in Tyburn has been criticised in: North and Fawcett "Cheshire and North's Private International Law" 12th edn, 1992 at p.263; and Carter (1990) 61 BYIL 400.

[72]   *James Burrough Distillers plc v. Speymalt Whisky Distributors Ltd* [1989] SLT 561 and compare *Def Lepp Music & Others v. Stuart Brown & Others* [1986] RPC 273.

[73]   *See* Brinkhof "The Infringement of Foreign Patents" [1994] 8 EIPR 360.

In 1997, in the space of only six months, the English law dealing with the infringement of foreign IP rights was radically altered. Since then it has been the subject of much curial and extra-curial discussion in England and, it seems, in the Netherlands. In *Pearce v. Ove Arup Partnership Ltd*[74] Lloyd J decided that the 1968 Brussels Convention requires an English court to assume jurisdiction over the infringement of a foreign IP right if the defendant is domiciled in England. Lloyd J's decision was upheld by the Court of Appeal.[75] In *Coin Controls Ltd v. Suzo International (UK) Ltd*,[76] Laddie J followed *Pearce v. Ove Arup Partnership Ltd* and added a limit to that decision's compass. He concluded that the combined effect of Articles 16(4) and 19 is that where both validity and infringement of a registrable IP right were in issue, infringement is a principal issue, together with validity, which has to be determined in the court of the state in which it is registered. Laddie J also stated that if a claimant's virtually identical IP rights are being infringed both in England and in other Convention States, and the parties infringing the claimant's foreign IP rights in those states are not the same entity, he can bring consolidated proceedings against them in England pursuant to Article 6(1).

In *Fort Dodge Animal Health Ltd and Others v. Akzo Nobel NV and Another*[77] the English Court of Appeal approved Laddie J's judgment on the effect of Articles 16(4) and 19 but overruled Laddie J's judgment on Article 6(1). In *Fort Dodge* the court stated that cases in which different defendants are alleged to have infringed different country's patents can never produce irreconcilable judgments because they are actions relating to two different national rights, limited in territory to different states, and the ambit of them may be different because amendment is possible. It follows from the court's decision that Article 6(1) can never be used in such a case. The Dutch courts have interpreted Article 6(1) in a different way. In *Boston Scientific Ltd v. Palmaz and Others*,[78] the Hague Court of Appeal stated that, in cases where the defendant domiciled within the court's jurisdiction is the company within a group that is in charge of putting the infringing items onto the market and the alleged infringers are within the same group of companies, it would be prepared to allow Article 6(1) to be used to consolidate actions with respect to identical IP rights.[79]

Article 24 of the Brussels Convention provides that application may be made to the courts of a Contracting State for such provisional (including protective) measures as may be available under the law of the State even if, under the Convention, the courts of another Contracting State have jurisdiction as to the substance of the matter. In *Fort Dodge Animal Health Ltd and Others* the Court of Appeal decided that Article 16(4) produced the result

---

[74]   [1997] Ch. 293.

[75]   Unreported Roch LJ, Chadwick LJ, May LJ; 21 January 1999.

[76]   [1997] 3 All ER 45.

[77]   [1998] FSR 222, Court of Appeal.

[78]   Unreported, 23 April 1998, The Hague Court of Appeal.

[79]   Followed in *Chiton v. Roche* (23 December 1998) Hague District Court. Note, however, the Hague District Court decision in *Augustine Medical v. Mallinckrodt* (unreported, 15 July 1998) in which the court distinguished and was prepared to adopt a more liberal test in granting a cross-border injunction.

that the UK courts have exclusive jurisdiction over any dispute relating to the UK patent where its validity is challenged. Accordingly, provisional relief with respect to a UK patent whose validity has been challenged can only be granted by a UK court in aid of UK proceedings. This amounts to a determination that Article 24 is subject to Article 16.[80]

Accordingly, these 1997 High Court decisions have unearthed a limited liability in the English courts to accept jurisdiction and determine infringement actions in cases in which foreign IP laws must be applied. The result is that the potential may exist to consolidate – in one action in an English court in which jurisdiction has been obtained over at least one defendant pursuant to the Conventions – infringement actions brought under English and/or foreign IP laws against different defendants infringing different countries' IP laws. For example, an action can be imagined where a claimant sues in an English court an English domiciled defendant for infringement of English IP rights, an EEA domiciled defendant for breach of English and/or foreign IP rights, and a non-EEA domiciled defendant for breach of English IP rights. However, this potential to consolidate cross-border infringement claims is limited by: the effect of Articles 16(4) and 19, as explained in *Coin Controls Ltd* and *Fort Dodge Animal Health Ltd and Others*; the requirements in Article 6(1) and O.11 r.1(1)(c) that the English and foreign IP rights in the infringement actions in which the court is seized pursuant to those provisions be virtually identical (again as explained in *Coin Controls Ltd* and *Fort Dodge Animal Health Ltd and Others*; and, at least in cases in which the alternative forum is a non-Convention State,[81] the application of the doctrine of *forum non conveniens*.

The result of the limitations imposed by Articles 16(4) and 19 is that registered and unregistered IP rights may be subject to different regimes and this may result in a proliferation of proceedings.

For example, an action for passing off in England, an action for trade mark infringement in the country in which the mark is registered and an action for infringement of a European Patent Convention ("EPC") patent throughout Europe may require suits in all EPC countries. These limitations also mean that a defendant can – in cases in which jurisdiction was obtained pursuant to the Conventions and the IP right was registered, within the limits of the place where the suit was commenced and the place where the IP right is registered – "forum shop" by deciding whether to attach the validity of the IP right in its defence. Correspondingly, in cases in which jurisdiction can be obtained pursuant to the Conventions, a claimant can forum shop; he has the potential to commence proceedings in every jurisdiction in which his IP right is infringed.

Some English judges have expressed a willingness, if they thought that they did have jurisdiction, readily to invoke the doctrine of *forum non conveniens* in cases in which the claimant is claiming for infringement of a foreign IP right.[82] Under this doctrine an English court will have to weigh up the desirability of having all related infringement claims determined in one court against any unease that it has about applying a foreign country's IP law and any evidence that a foreign country is the appropriate forum for all (or only some) of the infringement actions. An action for infringement of a foreign IP right may

---

[80] *See* Stuart Dutson: "The Infringement of Foreign Intellectual Property Rights – a Restatement of the Terms of Engagement" (1998) 47 International and Comparative Law Quarterly 659.

[81] *See Re Harrods (Buenos Aires) Ltd* [1992] Ch 72 (CA).

[82] *See*, for example, *Plastus Kreativ AB v. Minnesota Mining and Manufacturing Co.* [1995] RPC 438 at 447.

well be ripe for the application of the *forum non conveniens* principle, particularly in cases in which the action for infringement of a foreign IP right is not combined with an action for infringement of an English IP right in England.

A practice that has been employed in defamation cases to great effect, but has been stifled in cases in which an injunction has been sought to restrain passing off outside the jurisdiction, is to plead actionability under the foreign law and then rely on the English law presumption that an unproved foreign law is identical to English law. In these cases the claimant has contended that if the defendant wishes to disprove its liability then it must go to the considerable, and many times prohibitive, expense of proving each of the foreign defamation laws which the claimant relies upon. The prospect of this potentially very expensive exercise is used as a tactic to force defendants to settle the action early. If the courts do not prevent a claimant employing this technique in an Internet IP infringement case then one can foresee cases in which a defendant is required to positively prove manifold foreign laws (due to the global reach of the Internet) and prove that it is not liable under each of those laws if it is to avoid liability. The expense involved in such an exercise may be enough to force many defendants to settle a case which they otherwise might have been able to defend successfully.

6.3.3.2   *Post-Private International Law (Miscellaneous Provisions) Act 1995*

Lloyd J's decision in *Pearce v. Ove Arup Partnership Ltd* applies equally in both Pre- and Post-Private International Law Act cases.[83] Accordingly, the conclusions reached above regarding the Pre-Private International Law Act apply equally here and what follows deals only with non-Convention cases (and possibly with Convention cases in which the relevant IP law comes from a non-Convention country).

The second reason that the courts have proffered for foreign IP rights not being justiciable in English courts – limb 1 of the rule in *Phillips v. Eyre* – has been extinguished. Section 11 of the Act allows for an English court to apply the law of the country in which the events constituting the tort occur.

However, the first reason is left unscathed by the Act. Accordingly, actions dealing with foreign IP rights in which the court is not seized of jurisdiction pursuant to the conventions remain non-justiciable before English courts.[84]

Another point that may prove significant is the law dealing with *forum non conveniens* as discussed above.

---

[83]   *See* the Court of Appeal's judgment on appeal in that case of 21 January 1999.

[84]   *Coin Controls Ltd v. Suzo International & Others* [1997] 3 All ER 45 and *Pearce v. Ove Arup Partnership Ltd & Others* [1997] 3 All ER 45. *LA Gear v. Gerald Whelan & Sons* [1991] FSR 670 at 674 and 676 and *Molnlycke AB v. Procter & Gamble Ltd* [1992] RPC 27 at 28.

6.4   **The relationship between the proposed replacement to the Brussels and Lugano Conventions and the proposed EC Directive on Electronic Commerce**

As noted above[85] there is currently a draft regulation before the EC which is intended to up-date and replace the Brussels and Lugano Conventions. The EC has also published the Amended Proposed EC Directive on Electronic Commerce (COM (1999) 427 Final) (the "Directive"). The Directive is intended, amongst other things, to ensure that an Information Society service provider is subject only to the regulatory laws of the Member State in which it is established (the "country of origin principle"). The Articles which attempt to achieve this are Articles 3(1) and 3(2). It is not clear how the Directive restricts itself only to regulatory laws, however, it appears that the Directive's "co-ordinated field" in Article 3(1) is the means by which this will be achieved. The co-ordinated field appears to be the requirements set out in the Directive.[86] The Directive and its attempts to create a "country of origin principle" extend almost exclusively to these regulatory matters; the Directive does not attempt manifestly to affect civil or commercial substantive law.[87]

A number of newspaper and World Wide Web news group articles have appeared decrying apparent tension between the Proposed Regulation and Directive and alleging that the Regulation will prevent the Directive's "country of origin" principle being realised. In the present author's opinion, talk of manifest tension between Regulation and Directive is unwarranted. First, the Regulation deals with personal jurisdiction while, in contrast, the Directive deals almost exclusively with what regulatory laws will be applied to a service provider domiciled within the EU (i.e. subject matter jurisdiction).[88] Second, while the Directive deals almost exclusively with regulatory laws the Regulation is only applicable to personal jurisdiction in respect of "civil and commercial matters".[89] Regulatory laws do not fall within this definition therefore the Regulation is largely inapplicable to personal jurisdiction in respect of matters arising under the Directive.[90] Moreover, in the present author's opinion the impact of the Regulation on personal jurisdiction in e-commerce cases will be minimal.[91]

---

[85]   *See* Section 6.3 personal jurisdiction footnote 14.

[86]   *See* Article 2 (g).

[87]   However, the Directive could have some effect on some relatively minor civil or commercial substantive laws; *see* Stuart Dutson: "Transnational E-commerce" (2000) 10(6) Computers and Law 25 at 25. Reprinted at (2000) 16 Computer Law and Security Report 105.

[88]   *See* further Stuart Dutson: "Transnational E-commerce" (2000) 10(6) Computers and Law 25 at 26-27.

[89]   *See* Article 1 of the Proposed Regulation.

[90]   *See* further Stuart Dutson: "Transnational E-commerce" (2000) 10(6) Computers and Law 25 at 25-26.

[91]   *See* further Stuart Dutson: "Transnational E-commerce" (2000) 10(6) Computers and Law 25 at 26-27.

6.5   Foreign infringers beyond the reach of the law

If a person with no presence in the UK uses the Internet to infringe English IP rights, what remedies can the injured party seek?

6.5.1   *Remedies in English law*

English statutory IP laws are territorial in their application. An infringer resident in a jurisdiction whose IP laws, courts system, or parochial judiciary offer no, or limited, protection to the foreign owner of an IP right (e.g. China) can infringe English IP rights and disseminate information on the Internet with impunity. An injured party's only recourse against the infringer in English law will be in an action in passing-off and an investigation into whether International IP conventions and treaties may be relevant. In these cases an English IP owner will be limited, subject to the availability of a passing-off action, to pursuing any persons who secondarily infringe his IP rights within the jurisdiction.

6.5.1.1   *Persons requesting/ordering information from the Internet*

The CPD Act 1988 defines the infringing act of "copying" to include the making of copies that are transient or are incidental to some other use of the work.[92] Because a receiving computer momentarily records the signals which it receives in order to display their content, it appears that the act of transmission is an act of copying. This act of copying is committed both by the person ordering the transmission[93] and by the person who supplies it from a data server, if the act takes place in England.[94] Of course, if the person receiving the infringing material on his computer screen then deals with that material, he will be liable for further acts of infringement of the English copyright such as copying (i.e. making a hard copy of an on-screen image or downloading it to a computer disk), issuing copies to the public, displaying the work in public, or broadcasting.

6.5.2   *Remedies in foreign law*

The injured party should consider whether he has any course of action under the infringer's country's laws.

6.5.3   *Remedies in US law*

The nature of the Internet is such that any acts that take place in one country are likely to have some impact in the US. The US rules dealing with when a US court assumes personal jurisdiction are more liberal than their English counterparts. Applying their long-arm statutes, US courts have assumed jurisdiction in cases in which a defendant's only contact with a State is over the Internet, (e.g. creating a website that can be accessed in the US State).[95] If the claimant is able to extend US IP laws to non-resident defendants and extend infringing acts outside the jurisdiction, as well as overcoming any *forum non conveniens* argument, then a claimant could pursue the foreign infringer through the US courts.

---

[92]   Section 17(6) of CDP Act 1988.

[93]   *See Bookmakers' Afternoon Greyhound Services Ltd v. Wilf Gilbert Ltd* [1994] FSR 723.

[94]   "Cornish Intellectual Property" 3rd edn., 1996 at paragraphs 13-56.

[95]   *Panavision International L.P. v. Toeppen*, [1996] WL 534-83 (C.D. Cal, 19 September 1996); *Inset Sys., Inc. v. Instruction Set, Inc.*, [1996] US Dist. LEXIS 7160 (D. Conn. 17 April 1996). *Contrast Bensusan Restaurant Corp. v. King* [1996] US Dist. LEXIS 13035 (S.D.N.Y. 9 September 1996).

6.5.4   *Enforcement*

However, the above discussion of the possible means of pursuing the foreign infringer presupposes that any judgment could be enforced. In these cases, being able to assume jurisdiction and obtain an award for damages or an injunction against future infringements must be considered. Whilst a foreign infringer may have assets within the EEA, the only course of action available against him may be in passing off and this may not be appropriate in all circumstances. Accordingly, there may be many cases in which an aggrieved IP owner will be powerless and frustrated under English law.

6.6   The liability we expose ourselves to in putting material on the Internet

6.6.1   *Possible exposure*

In putting material on the Internet we do not know who will access it, where they might be, or what laws may apply in that jurisdiction. A person may place material on to the Internet via a website in England without infringing an English IP right or constituting the tort of defamation but yet find himself liable for just that in a foreign jurisdiction or even before English courts if they decide to apply foreign IP laws.

The nature of the Internet is such that material placed onto the Internet in England can be transmitted and accessed throughout the world. Each of these jurisdictions will have their own IP and civil wrongs laws, and laws dealing with jurisdiction and the choice of law. Accordingly, a website provider in England should be aware that a foreign court could consider that it has jurisdiction over the English website provider where his site is accessed in that country. If the material on the site infringes that country's laws – either IP or more general laws dealing with civil wrongs – then he may be held liable in that foreign jurisdiction.

It appears that in some cases an action for infringement of a foreign IP right cannot be brought before an English court. Therefore, in these circumstances the English website provider may not be in danger of having infringement proceedings commenced against him in England. However, the potential does exist for a foreign claimant to commence an action in the English courts for infringement of the foreign IP law or any other relevant foreign tort alleging liability under the foreign law (i.e. the law that the English choice of law rule would designate as the applicable law). Foreign laws (apart from IP laws) that could be relevant include: laws dealing with negligent or fraudulent misrepresentation in which the liability criteria or the class of persons able to claim are more widely drawn than in English law; defamation laws that do not have the defences that are available in English law (Section 13 of PIL Act, and "Dicey and Morris" Rule 203(2)); or causes of action that have no counterpart in English law (e.g. intentional interference with business relations in New York law).

6.6.2   *Limiting access to a website*

One possible means of limiting or removing exposure to a particular jurisdiction would be to prevent persons in that jurisdiction gaining access to a website. It appears impossible at present to limit access to websites or to fence off particular jurisdictions to prevent users in those jurisdictions from accessing a website. The use of domain names such as ".com" removes any trace of nationality, and information can be routed through a non-excluded jurisdiction. In the absence of an effective limit, or a fencing-off mechanism, the website owner may seek to limit its exposure to tort claims by the use of disclaimers.

6.7   Conclusion

While the Internet is a medium that allows for communication on a previously undreamed of scale, the law treats it like any other modern method of communication. Accordingly, international disputes in which the Internet plays a part are dealt with utilising the usual conflict of laws principles.

English statutory IP rights are strictly territorial in their nature – an action for infringement only applies to infringing acts that occur within England. However, if the common design principle can be utilised, or an overseas act is merely preparatory to infringing acts in England, then an action for infringement may possibly be brought for what might appear to be *prima facie* a foreign infringement. The passage of the PIL Act does not alter the strictly territorial nature of these laws, but the new choice of law rule in the Act will apply to the common law tort of passing off.

Personal jurisdiction must be addressed in terms of Convention and non-Convention countries. In a non-Convention case, O.11 r.1(1)(b), (c) and (f) may be relevant. In a Convention case Articles 2, 5(3), 6 and 24 may be relevant. The Convention and non-Convention rules may be utilised concurrently in the one case against different defendants.

Recent English decisions have paved the way for English courts to apply foreign IP laws to the infringement of foreign IP rights in cases in which the court is seized of jurisdiction pursuant to the Conventions. In these cases, if one defendant can be sued pursuant to the Conventions' rules then the potential exists to consolidate claims against different defendants in one English action for the infringement of different IP rights. This ability to consolidate infringement actions is subject to Article 16(4), the requirements of Article 6(1) and O.11 r.1(1)(c), and the doctrine of *forum non conveniens*. However, in cases in which the court is seized of jurisdiction pursuant to the non-Convention rules, English courts will not be entitled to apply foreign IP laws.

In cases in which a foreign infringer is resident in a jurisdiction with lax IP laws, the injured party may be limited to pursuing secondary infringers of his IP rights within the jurisdiction.

A website provider must be aware that, even if his website does not infringe English IP laws, it may infringe the IP or other laws of a foreign country in whose jurisdiction the website can be accessed.

CHAPTER 7
DATA PROTECTION

Christopher Millard
Partner
Clifford Chance

7.1 Introduction

7.1.1 *Origins of data protection laws*

The jurisprudence of privacy has a fragmented history. Privacy, as a distinct legal concept, probably has its origins in an essay published in the Harvard Law Review in 1890. In "The Right to Privacy",[1] Samuel Warren and Louis Brandeis reviewed the long history of protection under the English common law for various individual liberties and private property and extrapolated a general "right to privacy". Ironically, more than a century later, the US still does not have a privacy law with general application to the private sector. Instead, it has a patchwork quilt of sector specific laws and regulations covering such diverse subject matter as consumer video rental records,[2] consumer financial services,[3] interception of electronic communications,[4] and the online privacy rights of children.[5]

Eighty years after Warren and Brandeis' seminal article, popular concerns about the implications of widespread use of computers in the public and private sectors led to the adoption of data protection laws in various European jurisdictions. The first was the German State of Hessen in 1970.[6] Since then more than 40 jurisdictions around the world have enacted data protection legislation intended to protect individuals' rights to privacy by restricting the manner in which information about them may be processed in the private sector.[7] A number of other jurisdictions have legislation regulating processing of personal data in the public sector.[8]

---

[1]   (1890), 4 Harvard Law Review, p. 193-220.

[2]   Video Privacy Protection Act of 1998, 18 U.S.C. § 2710 (1994).

[3]   For example, Fair Credit Reporting Act of 1970, 18 U.S.C. § 1681 (1988); the Fair Credit Billing Act of 1976, 15 U.S.C. §§ 1601, 1602, 1637, 1666 (1988); the Right to Financial Privacy Act of 1978, 12 U.S.C. §§ 3401-3422 (1994); Gramm-Leach-Bliley Financial Modernization Act of 1999, 15 U.S.C. §§ 6801-6810, 6821-6827.

[4]   Electronic Communications Privacy Act of 1986, § 2510 et seq.

[5]   Children's Online Privacy Protection Act of 1998, 15 U.S.C. §6501 et seq., Children's Online Privacy Protection Rule, 16 C.F.R. Part 312.

[6]   Hessisches Datenschutzgesetz (HDSG), 30 September 1970, Hess. GVOBL. I 1970, p. 625. The first national law was the 1973 Swedish Data Act, as amended in 1997.

[7]   For details of existing data protection laws, see Millard and Ford (eds.) "Data Protection Laws of the World" (London: Sweet & Maxwell, 1998).

[8]   For example, in the US, the Privacy Act of 1974, 5 U.S.C., §§ 552 et seq.

7.1.2   *Underlying principles*

Typically, in addition to restricting certain activities, data protection laws impose a number of positive obligations on controllers of data, such as an obligation to make a filing with a regulatory body and to allow individuals access to information held about them. At the heart of almost every law is a set of principles of good practice in relation to personal data.

In 1980 an Organisation for Economic Co-operation and Development ("OECD") group of experts on transborder data barriers and privacy protection formulated eight basic principles of data privacy.[9] With essentially self-explanatory titles, these principles are the:

(a) Collection Limitation Principle;

(b) Data Quality Principle;

(c) Purpose Specification Principle;

(d) Use Limitation Principle;

(e) Security Safeguards Principle;

(f) Openness Principle;

(g) Individual Participation Principle; and

(h) Accountability Principle.

This analysis has stood the test of time. For example, all of these elements can be found in the 1995 EU Data Protection Directive (the "Framework Directive").[10]

A key element of most data protection laws is regulation of the transfer of personal data to other jurisdictions for processing or use. Such restrictions are essentially an anti-avoidance measure. They are based on a concern that, just as money tends to gravitate towards tax havens, there may be a tendency for personal data to be processed in jurisdictions with the most lax, or no, data protection standards. As one Swedish official put it in 1979, "We do not really trust the Data Acts in other countries or…we understand that there are none at all. So we feel unprotected in those countries with our Data – like walking down Fifth Avenue in our underwear".[11]

7.1.3   *The impact of technology*

When data protection laws started to appear in the early 1970s there were relatively few computers in the world and, due to their enormous cost, most were in the public sector. Computers tended to operate on a stand-alone basis and typically were housed in purpose-designed secure facilities. Most processing took place on a "batch" or off-line basis. A government or other regulator that wished to supervise the automated processing of personal data had a good chance of knowing or finding out who was carrying out the processing.

---

[9]   OECD Guidelines for the Protection of Privacy and Transborder Flows of Personal Data, Recommendation by the Council of the OECD, adopted 23 September 1980, available at: http://www.oecd.org//dsti/sti/it/secur/prod/PRIV-EN.HTM#1.

[10]   Directive 95/46/EC of the European Parliament and of the Council of 24 October 1995 on the protection of individuals with regard to the processing of personal data and on the free movement of such data.

[11]   Hessisches Datenschutzgesetz (HDSG), 30 September 1970, Hess. GVOBL. I 1970, p. 625. The first national law was the 1973 Swedish Data Act.

Two developments have transformed that scenario. The first is the personal computer ("PC"), launched in 1981 and now increasingly pervasive in businesses and homes around the world. The second is the networking of computers and, in particular, the dramatic expansion of the Internet since the early 1990s. It is now impossible for governments or regulators to keep track of even a tiny fraction of the processing and international transfers of personal data that take place on a real-time basis, every minute of every day. A typical pocket computer today has more processing power and storage capacity than the largest mainframe of the 1970s. Connected to a communications device such as a cellular phone, a pocket computer can be used to send personal data to or retrieve such data from anywhere on the planet. In marked contrast to the early stand-alone computer systems, the Internet, as a vast network of networks, is a massively distributed processing environment.

Unfortunately, data protection concepts have moved on very little since the early 1970s. For example, the Framework Directive requires the EU Member States to impose restrictions on transfers of personal data to countries that lack "an adequate level of protection" for personal data.[12] Although the Framework Directive envisages various exceptions to this blanket export ban, there will be numerous instances where prior regulatory clearance should be obtained before a transfer is made. This is not credible in an environment where some 200 million people worldwide have Internet access and can transfer personal data to other Internet users by merely clicking on a "send" button in an email package.

7.1.4 Scope of this Chapter

This Chapter will provide a brief overview of the international aspects of data protection and of the relevant EU directives on data protection (in particular, the Framework Directive and the 1997 directive on data protection and telecommunications (the "Telecoms Data Protection Directive")).[13] It will then focus on the UK legislation implementing such directives. An attempt will be made to analyse the key requirements of the relevant UK legislation and their application to and likely impact on Internet-related activities.

7.2 The international context

7.2.1 International initiatives to harmonise data protection rules

7.2.1.1 Organisation for Economic Co-operation and Development Privacy Guidelines

The proliferation of national data protection laws has given rise to various transnational initiatives over the past three decades to limit the emergence of inconsistent national rules that might become obstacles to cross-border trade. In 1974, the OECD established an expert group, the Data Bank Panel, to study various aspects of computers and privacy.[14] A second expert group, established under the chairmanship of Mr Justice Kirby, chairman of the Australian Law Reform Commission, developed Guidelines on basic rules to facilitate harmonisation of national data protection laws and pre-empt unnecessary restrictions on

---

[12]   Framework Directive, Article 25(1).

[13]   Directive 97/66/EC of the European Parliament and of the Council of 15 December 1997 concerning the processing of personal data and the protection of privacy in the telecommunications sector.

[14]   In 1977 the Data Bank Panel organised a symposium in Vienna out of which came "Transborder Data Flows and the Protection of Privacy" (Paris: OECD, 1979).

transborder data flows. A Recommendation containing the Guidelines was adopted by the OECD Council and became applicable on 23 September 1980.[15] The Memorandum accompanying the OECD Guidelines contains a recommendation that Member Countries "take into account in their domestic legislation the principles concerning the protection of privacy and individual liberties set forth in the Guidelines ... [and that] ... Member countries endeavour to remove or avoid creating, in the name of privacy protection, unjustified obstacles to transborder flows of personal data".

The OECD Guidelines represent an attempt to balance the conflicting priorities of data protection and the free flow of information. The most fundamental limitation of the Guidelines is that they have no legal force. They are not embedded in any convention. Moreover, the open-textured nature of the Guidelines means that they can only serve as a loose framework for the harmonisation of national laws.

7.2.1.2   Council of Europe Convention

Unlike the OECD, which is essentially concerned with the economic development of its Member States, the Council of Europe has a broader political mandate. In 1968 the Parliamentary Assembly of the Council of Europe expressed concern over the adequacy of the European Convention on Human Rights in securing privacy protection in the context of information technology. As a response, the Committee of Ministers conducted a study and subsequently passed two Resolutions establishing data protection principles, one for the private sector,[16] the other for the public sector.[17] The Committee of experts that prepared the Resolutions called for the development of an international data protection agreement. After many drafts, the final text of the "Convention for the Protection of Individuals with regard to Automatic Processing of Personal Data"[18] was adopted by the Committee of Ministers and was opened for signature on 28 January 1981. The Convention came into force on 1 October 1985 after five states had ratified it. The UK ratified the Convention on 26 August 1987, with effect from 1 December 1987. At the time of writing, 20 states had ratified the Convention.[19]

The Convention deals with the automatic processing of any information relating to an identifiable individual. Ratifying states must place obligations on controllers of files to comply with various principles and to grant various rights to data subjects. In relation to transborder data flows, the Convention prohibits the imposition, on the grounds of privacy protection, of restrictions on the transfer of data from the territory of one Convention party to that of another. Two exceptions are permitted: one is where the first party gives special protection to a particular category of data and the second party does not; the other is where the data is to be re-exported to a non-Convention state.

---

[15]   OECD, "Transborder Data Flows and the Protection of Privacy" (Paris: OECD, 1981).

[16]   Resolution (73) 22.

[17]   Resolution (74) 29.

[18]   European Treaty Series, No. 108.

[19]   These were Austria, Belgium, Denmark, Finland, France, Germany, Greece, Hungary, Iceland, Ireland, Italy, Luxembourg, Netherlands, Norway, Portugal, Slovenia, Spain, Sweden, Switzerland and the UK.

7.2.1.3   EU data protection initiatives

In 1981, the same year that the Council of Europe's Convention was opened for signature, the European Commission recommended that the EC Member States that had not already done so should sign the Convention and seek to ratify it by the end of 1982.[20] The Commission indicated in its recommendation that it would engage in a compulsory harmonisation programme if Member States were too dilatory in ratifying the Council of Europe Convention. These exhortations had little effect. In July 1990, the Commission submitted to the Council of Ministers a series of proposals, including two draft Directives, intended to harmonise data protection regulation throughout the EC (as it then was). The first would deal in general terms with data protection and transborder data flows,[21] the second specifically with data protection aspects of public digital telecommunications networks.[22]

After five years of protracted debates in the European Parliament and European Council, a substantially revised version of the first proposal was finally adopted as the Framework Directive. It took a further two years before the adoption of the Telecoms Data Protection Directive. These Directives are the key European measures regulating data protection in the context of e-commerce. The deadline for the 15 EU Member States to implement both Directives was 24 October 1998. As of 1 February 2001, the Framework Directive had been implemented by all of the EU Member States except Belgium, France, Germany, Ireland, Luxembourg and the Netherlands. The Telecoms Data Protection Directive had been implemented by all of the EU Member States except Belgium,[23] France, Germany, Ireland and Luxembourg.

Detailed guidance on the application of the two Directives to online activities has been provided by the EU Data Protection Working Party (the "Working Party").[24] The views of the Working Party are strongly indicative of likely regulatory practice across the European Economic Area ("EEA"), as its members are the national data protection regulators of the EEA Member States. On 21 November 2000, the Working Party adopted a paper entitled:

---

[20]   Recommendation of the Commission No. 81/679.

[21]   Proposal for a Council Directive concerning the protection of individuals in relation to the processing of personal data (90/C 277/3).

[22]   Proposal for a Council Directive concerning the protection of personal data privacy in the context of public digital telecommunications networks, in particular the Integrated Services Digital Network ("ISDN") and Public Digital Mobile Networks (90/C/277/04).

[23]   A Belgian Royal Decree of 8 July 1999 implemented some of the provisions of the Telecoms Data Protection Directive.

[24]   The Working Party is established under Article 29 of the Framework Directive.

"Privacy on the Internet – An Integrated EU Approach to On-line Data Protection".[25] This paper brought together various opinions and documents relating to Internet issues that the Working Party had adopted between December 1997 and November 2000.[26] A detailed review of this paper is beyond the scope of this Chapter, but various aspects will be mentioned in connection with specific issues discussed below.

7.3 The UK Data Protection Act 1984

The Data Protection Act 1984 (the "DPA 1984"), which had been in force fully since 1987, was enacted to enable the UK to ratify the Council of Europe Convention.[27] The DPA 1984 has since been superseded by the Data Protection Act 1998 (the "DPA 1998") and hence this Chapter will deal primarily with the DPA 1998.

The DPA 1984 regulated the use of "personal data", which was defined as data relating to a living, identifiable individual.[28] In general terms, it imposed two broad types of obligation. First, most holders of personal data ("data users") were required to register with the Data Protection Registrar. This was largely a formality, although failure to register was a strict liability criminal offence. The registration had to specify matters such as the types of data to be held and the purposes for holding them, the categories of people to whom personal data were likely to be disclosed, and the countries to which international transfers of personal data were anticipated. Once a registration had been effected, data users were obliged to ensure that their operations remained within its scope.[29]

---

25   5063/00/EN/final, WP37.

26   Recommendation 3/97 on Anonymity on the Internet, adopted on 3 December 1997, 5022/97/EN/final, WP6; Opinion 1/98: Platform for Privacy Preferences ("P3P") and the Open Profiling Standard ("OPS") adopted on 16 June 1998, 5032/98/EN/final, WP11; Working Document: Processing of Personal Data on the Internet, adopted 23 February 1999, 5013/99/EN/final, WP16; Recommendation 1/99 on Invisible and Automatic Processing of Personal Data on the Internet Performed by Hardware and Software, adopted on 23 February 1999, 5093/99/EN/final; Recommendation 2/99 on the Respect of Privacy in the Context of Interception of Telecommunications, adopted on 3 May 1999, 5005/99/EN/final, WP18; Opinion 3/99 on Public Sector Data and the Protection of Personal Data, adopted on 3 May 1999, WP20; Recommendation 3/99 on the Preservation of Traffic Data by Internet Service Providers for Law Enforcement Purposes, adopted 7 September 1999, 5085/99/EN/final, WP25; Opinion 1/2000 on Certain Data Protection Aspects of Electronic Commerce, adopted on 3 February 2000, 5007/00/EN/final, WP28; Opinion 2/2000 concerning the General Review of the Telecommunications Legal Framework, adopted on 3 February 2000, 5009/00/EN/final, WP29; Opinion 5/2000 on the Use of Public Directories for Reverse or Multi-criteria Searching Services (reverse directories), adopted on 13 July 2000, 5058/00/EN/final, WP33; Opinion 7/2000 on the European Commission Proposal for a Directive of the European Parliament and the Council concerning the Processing of Personal Data and the Protection of Privacy in the Electronic Communications Sector of 12 July 2000 COM (2000) 385, adopted on 2 November 2000, 5042/00/EN/final, WP36.

27   *See* Section 7.2.1.2 above.

28   DPA 1984, Section 1(2).

29   DPA 1984, Part II.

Secondly, on an ongoing basis, data users had to comply with eight "Data Protection Principles" that set out the manner in which personal data may be collected, stored and processed.[30] These included: a requirement that personal data only be collected and processed fairly and lawfully, that they be accurate and up-to-date, that they not be excessive in relation to the purposes for which they were held, that they not be held for longer than was necessary for the purposes for which they were collected, and that appropriate security measures should be in place. Similar principles are to be found in the DPA 1998 and are discussed in Section 7.4.5 below. A significant loophole in the DPA 1984 was that breach of any of the Data Protection Principles had no direct consequences. Such a breach was not a criminal offence, nor did it give rise directly to any cause of action by an aggrieved data subject. For the Principles to bite, an "enforcement notice" must first have been served by the Data Protection Registrar requiring a data user to take specified steps to comply with one or more of the Principles.[31] Failure to comply with such a notice was a criminal offence.[32] Moreover, the Registrar could only serve an enforcement notice on a data user who had registered. The only action that could be brought against unregistered data users was prosecution for failure to register. This loophole has now been closed in the DPA 1998, which imposes on all data controllers an automatic obligation to comply with the Data Protection Principles, breach of which may have direct civil consequences.

7.4　　　The UK Data Protection Act 1998

7.4.1　　*Overview*

The DPA 1998 was enacted to implement the Framework Directive. As the Framework Directive and the DPA 1984 were both based on the 1981 Council of Europe Convention there are, not surprisingly, many similarities between the DPA 1984 and DPA 1998. Like the DPA 1984, the DPA 1998 is structured around a set of Data Protection Principles together with a registration system. There are, however, a number of key differences. The binding nature of the Principles under the DPA 1998 has already been mentioned. The other main changes introduced by the DPA 1998 included:

(a) a requirement of a legitimate justification for processing personal data with particular restrictions relating to "sensitive data";

(b) automatic restrictions on many transfers of data outside the EEA;

(c) new provisions relating to structured manual records;

(d) increased rights for data subjects; and

(e) increased powers for the regulator (who was renamed, initially, the Data Protection Commissioner and, subsequently, the Information Commissioner).

30　　DPA 1984, Schedule 1.

31　　DPA 1984, Section 10(1).

32　　DPA 1984, Section 10(9).

7.4.2 Legislative status

The DPA 1998 received the Royal Assent on 16 July 1998 and came into force on 1 March 2000. The Act provides for secondary legislation to be introduced in relation to some 34 different matters. Although the UK Government had intended to bring the DPA 1998 into force by the 24 October 1998 deadline set by the Framework Directive, it was clear by the time of Royal Assent that this would not be possible.

By failing to bring the new law into force by 24 October 1998, the UK Government was in breach of its obligations under the Framework Directive. As a result of the "direct effects" doctrine, it is possible that UK Government departments, public bodies, and state-owned or state-controlled businesses may, as emanations of the UK Government, have incurred liability to organisations or individuals who suffered loss or harm as a result of the Government's failure to comply with the Directive.[33] In addition, the 24 October 1998 deadline has remained important in relation to the availability of transitional relief.

7.4.3 Transitional provisions

The passage of the Framework Directive was contentious. One of the many political compromises was the inclusion of a broad-reaching transitional framework.[34] This is optional and will have different consequences in different Member States. In some, the existing data protection laws are in most respects already as restrictive, in some cases more restrictive, than the Framework Directive. It is unlikely that the transitional provisions will be of much significance in such jurisdictions. In the UK, however, the regulatory regime established under the DPA 1998 is significantly more restrictive than the rules under the DPA 1984. Consequently, the transitional provisions, which Parliament has chosen to take full advantage of, are of considerable significance.

Detailed rules for two transitional periods are set out in Schedule 8 to the DPA 1998. Broadly speaking, "eligible data", both automated and manual, are exempted from most of the new requirements for up to three years from 24 October 1998 (i.e. until 23 October 2001).[35] Personal data qualify as "eligible data" at any particular time only "if, and to the extent that, they are at that time subject to processing which was already under way immediately before 24 October 1998".[36] In the second transitional period (24 October 2001 to 23 October 2007) certain exemptions will continue for eligible manual data. It should be noted, however, that data subjects will have access rights during that period.[37]

There is some uncertainty as to the meaning of "if, and to the extent that, they are at that time subject to processing which was already underway". A strict reading might suggest that data could only qualify as "eligible data" if such data were in existence before 24 October 1998 and already being processed. This would mean that any new data added to

---

[33]   *Marleasing S.A v. La Comercial Internacional de Alimentation S.A.* Case C-106/89 [1992] 1 CMLR 305.

[34]   Framework Directive, Article 32.

[35]   DPA 1998, Schedule 8, Part II.

[36]   DPA 1998, Schedule 8, Part I, paragraph 1(1).

[37]   DPA 1998, Schedule 8, Part III.

existing systems after that date would automatically be outside the scope of the transitional relief. The view of the UK Government, however, is that the concept of "eligible data" should be interpreted broadly. In a written answer given in the House of Commons on 14 May 1998, Lord Williams of Mostyn, on behalf of the Government, stated regarding "processing already underway":

"The Government believe that this expression includes, among other things:

· amendments to existing data;

· the addition of personal data on existing data subjects;

· the addition of personal data on new data subjects;

· essential program and software changes to enable such processing to continue."[38]

This suggests that technical changes to software to effect, for example, millennium or Euro compliance would qualify as "essential program and software changes". On the other hand, a substantial change in the purpose for which data are processed or the addition of fundamentally different types of information would, presumably, constitute new processing operations to which the full requirements of the DPA 1998 will apply immediately.

While the Information Commissioner has not officially stated that she disagrees with the Government's flexible analysis of the transitional provisions, she has indicated informally that she will not accept that processing by an organisation was "already under way" by 24 October 1998 if that organisation was not appropriately registered in respect of such processing immediately before that date. For this reason, the 24 October 1998 deadline was significant.

7.4.4 *Key concepts*

7.4.4.1 *Data, personal data and data subject*

The DPA 1998 defines "data" extremely broadly as information which is, or is intended to be, processed electronically, or which forms, or is intended to form, part of a "relevant filing system".[39]

---

38 House of Commons, Hansard, 14 May 1998, Col WA128, http://www.parliament.the-stationery-office.co.uk.

39 DPA 1998, Section 1(1). A "relevant filing system" is a manually stored set of information that is "structured, either by reference to individuals or by reference to criteria relating to individuals, in such a way that specific information relating to a particular individual is readily accessible". In addition to automated data and information in relevant filing systems, "accessible records" (i.e. health, education and certain public records) also constitute data. DPA 1998, Section 68, and Schedules 11 and 12.

The definition of "personal data" is "data which relate to a living individual who can be identified –

(a) from those data, or

(b) from those data and other information which is in the possession of, or is likely to come into the possession of, the data controller".[40]

This appears to be a narrower concept than the definition of "personal data" in the Framework Directive, which merely requires the individual concerned to be identifiable "directly or indirectly". In that definition there is no presumption that all the elements necessary to identify an individual are, or are likely to come into, the possession of a particular data controller.

Under the DPA 1998, anonymous data will only be personal data in the hands of a data controller if that data controller has, or is likely to obtain, possession of any look-up table or other data necessary to match up anonymous records with particular individuals. In relation to the Internet, this distinction may be significant in various contexts. For example, a website operator may only be able to link data relating to a particular visit to a website to a dynamically allocated Internet Protocol ("IP") address and may have no way of discovering the identity of the visitor. Under the DPA 1998 such data would not be personal data. Under the Framework Directive, it is arguable that the data would be personal data if the individual concerned were identifiable "indirectly" from records held by his Internet Service Provider ("ISP").

A "data subject" is "an individual who is the subject of personal data".[41]

"Sensitive personal data" is defined in Section 7.4.5.1, below, in the context of the justifications for processing such data.

7.4.4.2   *Processing*

The definition of "processing" is also very broad. It covers "obtaining, recording, or holding … information or data or carrying out any operation or set of operations on the information or data…".[42] The full definition contains the following examples of activities that will constitute processing:

"(a)   organisation, adaptation or alteration of the information or data;

(b)   retrieval, consultation or use of the information or data;

(c)   disclosure of the information or data by transmission, dissemination or otherwise making available; or

(d)   alignment, combination, blocking, erasure or destruction of the information or data."

---

[40]   DPA 1998, Section 1(1). Unlike the DPA 1984, which excluded from the definition of "personal data" in relation to any individual "any indication of the intentions of the data user in respect of that individual", in the DPA 1998 the concept "includes any expression of opinion about the individual and any indication of the intentions of the data controller or any other person in respect of the individual".

[41]   DPA 1998, Section 1(1).

[42]   DPA 1998, Section 1(1).

It is difficult to imagine anything that could be done with data that would not constitute "processing". Needless to say, vast quantities of data are processed via the Internet by numerous "data controllers" and "data processors".

7.4.4.3   Data controller

A "data controller" is "a person who (either alone or jointly or in common with other persons) determines the purposes for which and the manner in which any personal data are, or are to be, processed".[43] It is important to identify the controller in relation to any particular processing activity, as it is that person who has primary responsibility for compliance with the DPA 1998. In addition to notification requirements (*see* Section 7.4.6.6, below), data controllers have an automatic statutory duty to comply with the Data Protection Principles.[44] Breach of the Principles may give rise to liability to any adversely affected individual, regardless of whether there is any regulatory intervention.[45]

The Internet is a massively interconnected community of some 200 million individuals and organisations. It is likely that there will be many instances of joint or co-control of personal data. In other cases, different individuals or organisations may control different aspects of a particular activity. By way of example, the "Recitals", or preamble, in the Framework Directive contain the observation that, in relation to a telecommunications or email service, "the controller in respect of the personal data contained in the message will normally be considered to be the person from whom the message originates, rather than the person offering the transmission services; whereas, nevertheless, those offering such services will normally be considered controllers in respect of the processing of the additional personal data necessary for the operation of the service". Thus, for data protection purposes, the sender of an email will normally be responsible for the message content, whereas one or more ISPs and telecommunication network operators will be responsible for traffic and billing data relating to transmission and storage of that message.

7.4.4.4   Data processor

In relation to personal data, a "data processor" is "any person (other than an employee of the data controller) who processes the data on behalf of the data controller".[46] The Internet is characterised by numerous arrangements that constitute processor/controller relationships. For example, ISPs process data on behalf of their customers and on behalf of other ISPs with which they have peering (i.e. interconnection) arrangements. Similarly, many data controllers outsource the hosting of their websites to data processors.

In some cases, the provider of a web hosting service may have sufficient direct control over the processing activities to make it a controller, or possibly joint or co-controller, of certain data. For example, a service provider may not merely host a site by providing connectivity but may also have a degree of autonomy in the way it provides additional services such as handling payments or conducting sophisticated traffic analyses.

---

[43]   DPA 1998, Section 1(1).

[44]   DPA 1998, Section 4(4).

[45]   DPA 1998, Section 13. As already noted, this is an important change from the DPA 1984 under which breach of the Data Protection Principles had no direct consequences.

[46]   DPA 1998, Section 1(1). Interestingly, the definition in the Framework Directive on which this is based does not exclude employees. Framework Directive, Article 2(e).

7.4.4.5   Application of the Data Protection Act 1998

The DPA 1998 only applies to data controllers in respect of particular data if the controller is either established in the UK and the data are processed in the context of that establishment, or the controller is established outside the EEA "but uses equipment in the UK for processing the data otherwise than for the purposes of transit through the United Kingdom".[47] A data controller who falls into the second category must nominate a representative in the UK in relation to its obligations under the DPA 1998.

This apparently straightforward statement of territorial scope is fraught with difficulty in the Internet and online services context. For one thing, due to the breadth of the establishment concept in the DPA 1998 it is possible that an ISP will be established in multiple states within the EEA.[48] Similarly, a commercial organisation may find that it is subject to multiple, and in certain respects inconsistent, national rules in relation to its internal cross-border intranet. Even where a data controller is not established in multiple EEA states, it may at least use equipment in multiple states. The Framework Directive makes it clear that "when the controller is established on the territory of several Member States, he must take the necessary measures to ensure that each of these establishments complies with the obligations laid down by the national law applicable...".[49]

The second problematic aspect of the territoriality provision is the exception for the processing of data using equipment in the UK which is merely "for the purposes of transit through the United Kingdom".[50] What if, for example, a website on a server in the US is "mirrored" by a UK-based ISP on a server in the UK to facilitate access to that site by UK-based customers of the ISP? Will the ISP in the UK become a data controller in relation to any personal data contained in that website? Will the ISP in the US be deemed to be a controller in the UK merely because an ISP in the UK has chosen to make a copy of the site (quite possibly without the site controller's knowledge)? What if a website on a server in the US plants a "cookie" on the PC of a UK-based visitor to the site and subsequently interrogates that cookie remotely each time the visitor returns to the site? Is the data controller in the US "using" equipment in the UK (i.e. the visitor's PC) to process data about that visitor? Given that "processing" includes "obtaining, recording or holding... information or data" such a construction is possible. This would, however, be an absurd result as the website operator in the US would presumably have to appoint the UK visitor as its representative for the purposes of compliance with the DPA 1998!

---

[47]   DPA 1998, Section 5(1).

[48]   Section 5(3) of the DPA 1998 provides that, in addition to UK individuals, companies and partnerships, "...any person who maintains in the United Kingdom – (i) an office, branch or agency through which he carries on any activity, or (ii) a regular practice..." will be treated as established in the UK.

[49]   Framework Directive, Article 4(1)(a).

[50]   DPA 1998, Section 5(1)(b).

7.4.5 *The Data Protection Principles*

7.4.5.1 *First Principle: fair and lawful processing*

The First Data Protection Principle provides that "personal data shall be processed fairly and lawfully...".[51] The interpretation provisions make it clear that personal data will not be considered to be processed "fairly" unless certain information is provided, or made readily available, to the individual concerned.[52] The information to be given to data subjects must include the identity of the data controller and any nominated representative, the purpose or purposes for which the data are intended to be processed, and "any further information which is necessary, having regard to the specific circumstances in which the data are or are to be processed, to enable processing in respect of the data subject to be fair".[53]

Where data are obtained directly from the data subject, the requisite information should normally be provided at, or be made available from, the time of data collection.[54] This is consistent with the approach taken by the Data Protection Registrar under the DPA 1984. In her 1998 Annual Report the Data Protection Registrar stated: "when information is input onto a form on a website it is immediately capable of being processed as personal data. Notifications of the uses and disclosures of the data should therefore be given at the beginning of the form, so that the individual can decide, on the basis of full information, whether or not to proceed with the transaction".[55] In any other case, the information should normally be provided at the time the data are first processed or first disclosed to a third party.[56] One way in which the requisite information might be provided to visitors to a website is via a privacy notice of some kind. On its own, however, such a notice may not be sufficient to discharge the information provision requirements. In this regard, the Working Party "strongly encourages the provision of information to the data subject directly on the screen or using information boxes ... at the point when data are collected without requiring the data subject to take any positive action to access this information, as Internet users do not always read the privacy policies of all the sites they visit when surfing from one to another".[57]

It is likely, in most instances, to be relatively easy to provide the requisite information via an email message or a notice on a web page. In any event, the information provision obligation only applies "so far as practicable". Moreover, in the case of data that are not obtained directly from the data subject, the obligation to provide information does not

---

[51]   DPA 1998, Schedule 1, Part 1, paragraph 1.

[52]   DPA 1998, Schedule 1, Part II, paragraph 2(1).

[53]   DPA 1998, Schedule 1, Part II, paragraph 2(3).

[54]   DPA 1998, Schedule 1, Part II, paragraph 2(2).

[55]   "The Fourteenth Annual Report of the Data Protection Registrar" (London: The Stationery Office, 1997) p. 60.

[56]   DPA 1998, Schedule 1, Part II, paragraph 2(2).

[57]   "Privacy on the Internet – An Integrated EU Approach to On-line Data Protection", 5063/00/EN/final, WP37, at 47.

apply where provision "would involve a disproportionate effort", nor where the data controller is required by law to record or disclose the data.[58] It should be noted, however, that a record must be kept of the reason for not providing information in reliance on the "disproportionate effort" exception.[59]

The Working Party has stressed the importance of providing information regarding secondary uses of personal data, that is, any use beyond the primary purpose or purposes of collection. In the view of the Working Party, consent as well as notice will be required in relation to secondary uses that are incompatible with the main purpose of collection. In the e-commerce context, the Working Party gives as examples of such incompatible secondary uses:

> "the communication of transactional data to third parties to allow them to establish buyer profiles for their advertising campaigns ... or the use of datamining tools to extract behaviour patterns from the list of names of websites visited by an Internet user."[60]

In addition to the information provision requirement, personal data must not be processed unless one of a number of conditions is satisfied. These are set out in Schedule 2 to the DPA 1998. In summary, processing is legitimate:

(a) if the data subject has given his consent;

(b) if it is necessary for the performance of a contract to which the data subject is a party (or for taking steps to enter into a contract);

(c) to comply with a legal obligation (other than contractual); or

(d) for certain public sector purposes.[61]

In addition, processing is justified if it is "necessary for the purposes of legitimate interests pursued by the data controller or by the third party or parties to whom the data are disclosed, except where the processing is unwarranted in any particular case by reason of prejudice to the rights and freedoms or legitimate interests of the data subject".[62] This so-called "balance of interests test" is well known in the data protection regulatory regimes of some civil law jurisdictions but is new to English data protection law. If interpreted broadly, it would justify many routine business data processing activities. However, until such a time as guidance has been provided in secondary legislation,[63] or has been published by the Information Commissioner, or the concept has been tested in the courts, it would not be prudent to rely heavily on this rather vague justification for processing data. If a data controller begins processing data in reliance on the balance of interests test and subsequently finds that the test has been failed, it may at that stage be very difficult to establish one of the other grounds for processing.

---

[58] DPA 1998, Schedule 1, Part II, paragraph 3.

[59] *See* The Data Protection (Conditions under Paragraph 3 of Part II of Schedule 1) Order 2000, SI 2000 No. 185.

[60] "Privacy on the Internet – An Integrated EU Approach to On-line Data Protection", 5063/00/EN/final, WP37, at 69.

[61] Broadly, these are that the processing is necessary for the administration of justice, in relation to any statutory or government function or other public function exercised in the public interest.

[62] DPA 1998, Schedule 2, paragraph 6(1).

[63] DPA 1998, Schedule 2, paragraph 6(2) provides that "[t]he Secretary of State may by order specify particular circumstances in which this condition is, or is not, to be taken as satisfied.

More stringent conditions apply to the processing of sensitive data. These are set out in Schedule 3 to the DPA 1998. The DPA 1998 defines "sensitive personal data" as "personal data consisting of information as to a data subject's racial or ethnic origin, political opinions, religious beliefs or other beliefs of a similar nature, membership of a trade union, physical or mental health or condition, sexual life, or commission or alleged commission or proceedings in relation to any offence".[64]

The processing of sensitive data will only be legitimate if:

(a) the data subject has given his "explicit consent";

(b) the processing is necessary in relation to an employment right or obligation;

(c) the processing is necessary to protect the vital interests of the data subject or another person in circumstances where consent is not obtainable;

(d) the processing is by a charitable body in relation to its members;

(e) the data subject has made the data public;

(f) the processing is necessary in relation to legal proceedings or advice; or

(g) the processing is for certain public sector purposes.

In addition, processing may be legitimate in the public or private sectors where it is carried out for:

(a) medical purposes by a health professional; or

(b) with appropriate safeguards, for ethnic monitoring purposes to promote or maintain equality.

In addition, the Secretary of State may, and is likely to, specify other circumstances in which sensitive data may be processed.

In the Internet context, some activities may relate overtly to sensitive data. In other cases, the association may be more subtle or uncertain. For example, does the hosting by an online service provider of a discussion or chat forum relating to a particular medical condition or treatment constitute processing of sensitive personal data? In that case the relevant question would be whether the data consisted of "information as to" the data subject's "physical or mental health or condition". The answer would depend on the facts. For example, information relating to the physical or mental health of a particular individual probably would be sensitive personal data, whereas comments posted by a surgeon in relation to a particular surgical procedure, without reference to any patient, probably would not be sensitive personal data. What if an airline or Internet travel agency collected data via a website relating to the dietary requirements of passengers? Again, whether that would constitute processing of sensitive personal data might depend on the precise facts. For example, a request for a vegetarian meal on a flight would probably not be sensitive personal data, whereas a request for a kosher or diabetic meal on a flight probably would be.

---

64   DPA 1998, Section 2.

7.4.5.2   *Second Principle: specified and lawful purposes*

The Second Data Protection Principle provides that "personal data shall be obtained only for one or more specified and lawful purposes, and shall not be further processed in any manner incompatible with that purpose or those purposes".[65] This is very similar to the Second Principle in the DPA 1984, which has tended to be interpreted narrowly as merely requiring that an appropriate registration, broadly equivalent to a notification under the DPA 1998, be in place and that there be no inherent illegality in the purpose for which data are processed. The interpretation of the Second Principle in the DPA 1998 states that the purpose or purposes for which data are obtained may be specified in a notice given to the data subject or in a notification to the Commissioner.[66] It will clearly be important for data controllers to anticipate the various purposes for which data are to be processed and explain these to data subjects in a manner consistent with any notification.

7.4.5.3   *Third Principle: adequacy, relevance and proportionality*

The Third Data Protection Principle provides that "personal data shall be adequate, relevant and not excessive in relation to the purpose or purposes for which they are processed".[67] This has important implications for data collection via the Internet. Many website operators require regular visitors, and in some cases also occasional surfers, to register before gaining access. Website operators should make it clear why any non-essential questions are being asked and whether a response is optional. For example, capturing an email address may be necessary for the provision of a particular service, whereas collecting information about gender, marital status, income and age may be irrelevant or excessive. Such data may, of course, assist a website operator in building profiles of visitors to the site for its own or third party marketing purposes. If, however, the declared and registered purpose of the processing does not extend to cover processing for that purpose such processing would probably be unfair, unspecified and excessive and thus in breach of the First, Second and Third Principles.

7.4.5.4   *Fourth Principle: accuracy and timeliness*

The Fourth Data Protection Principle provides that "personal data shall be accurate and, where necessary, kept up-to-date".[68] The interpretation provisions state that this Principle will not be contravened where data obtained from the data subject or a third party are inaccurate provided that "the data controller has taken reasonable steps to ensure the accuracy of the data" and the data record any view that the data subject may have expressed to the controller as to their accuracy. The reasonableness of any verification steps is to be judged in the light of the purposes for which the data were obtained or further processed.[69]

---

65   DPA 1998, Schedule 1, Part I, paragraph 2.

66   DPA 1998, Schedule 1, Part II, paragraph 5.

67   DPA 1998, Schedule 1, Part I, paragraph 3.

68   DPA 1998, Schedule 1, Part I, paragraph 4.

69   DPA 1998, Schedule 1, Part II, paragraph 7.

Application of this Principle to Internet-related activities is likely to prove problematic. The World Wide Web and the Usenet constitute a vast repository of information of highly variable accuracy and timeliness. For example, a recruitment consultant might use one or more Internet search engines to scour the web and the Usenet in order to build a dossier on a prospective candidate for employment. Material might well be retrieved that was either inaccurate or out of date. In such a case, the recruitment consultant should consider what steps should be taken to verify the data, especially in relation to any material that might be particularly prejudicial to the candidate concerned.

7.4.5.5   Fifth Principle: retention limitation

The Fifth Data Protection Principle provides that "personal data processed for any purpose or purposes shall not be kept for longer than is necessary for that purpose or those purposes."[70] Modern IT systems generally make compliance with this Principle counter-intuitive for many businesses. Mass storage media are now so inexpensive that it is often cheaper to retain all digital material indefinitely than to ascertain what should be destroyed on the grounds that it has served its purpose and is no longer relevant. Once again, the Usenet and the web are enormous, and rapidly expanding, repositories of information. Indefinite archiving of data is often the path of least resistance and organisations should consider whether it is necessary to develop, and implement, an information retention and destruction policy that applies to email archives and material on websites as well as to traditional documents.

7.4.5.6   Sixth Principle: data subject rights

The Sixth Data Protection Principle requires data controllers to process personal data "in accordance with the rights of data subjects under this Act."[71] An interpretation provision states that a person will only be regarded as contravening this Principle if he fails to provide access to data as required, fails to comply with a notice from a data subject requiring him to stop processing data for certain purposes, or fails to comply with the procedures relating to automated decision making.[72] This restrictive statement should, however, be read in conjunction with the general right which an individual has under Section 13 of the DPA 1998 to compensation where he has suffered damage as a result of contravention by a data controller of any of the requirements of the DPA 1998. The difference between these two provisions is that a breach of the Sixth Principle may trigger the service on the data controller by the Information Commissioner of an Enforcement Notice whereas breach of Section 13 may form the basis for a civil claim for compensation for damage and, possibly, distress.

7.4.5.7   Seventh Principle: security

The Seventh Data Protection Principle provides that "appropriate technical and organisational measures shall be taken against unauthorised or unlawful processing of personal data and against accidental loss or destruction of, or damage to, personal data".[73] Given the degree of public concern regarding the security, or otherwise, of communications and transactions via the Internet, this Principle needs to be considered carefully, notwithstanding that public concerns may be vastly overstated.

---

[70]   DPA 1998, Schedule 1, Part I, paragraph 5.

[71]   DPA 1998, Schedule1, Part I, paragraph 6.

[72]   DPA 1998, Schedule 1, Part II, paragraph 8. For details of these data subject rights, *see* Section 7.4.7.2, below.

[73]   DPA 1998, Schedule 1, Part I, paragraph 7.

The DPA 1998 contains some interpretation of this Principle from which a number of practical conclusions can be drawn. The first is that what constitutes "appropriate" security will vary widely depending on the circumstances. Relevant factors include the nature of the data to be protected, an assessment of the harm that might result from unauthorised or unlawful processing or accidental loss, destruction or damage, the state of technological development and the cost of any security measures.[74] This suggests, for example, that whereas publication on a website of information that is already in the public domain might require little or no security cover, the collection via email or the web of medical or other sensitive data might necessitate the adoption of rigorous security measures.

Secondly, data controllers are required to "take reasonable steps to ensure the reliability of any employees ... who have access to the personal data".[75] Again, the use of the word "reasonable" suggests different measures may be appropriate depending on the circumstances, ranging from minimal supervision to positive vetting.

Thirdly, where a data controller uses a data processor, the controller will automatically be in breach of the Seventh Principle unless both of the following criteria are satisfied:

(a) the processor provides "sufficient guarantees in respect of the technical and organisational security measures governing the processing to be carried out" and the controller takes "reasonable steps to ensure compliance with those measures";[76] and

(b) the processing is governed by a written contract requiring the processor to act only as instructed by the controller and to comply with security obligations equivalent to those imposed on the controller.[77]

In the Internet context, data controllers will need to ensure that they have appropriate, and properly documented, contractual arrangements in place with any ISPs or other third parties that process data on their behalf, for example by hosting websites. Moreover, even within a group of companies, it will be necessary to put written contracts in place to cover processing carried out by any group company on behalf of any other group company. This might be the case, for example, where a particular group has a service company that provides IT services to other members of the group. It will equally be necessary where any external service provider processes personal data on a regular or *ad hoc* basis. All existing outsourcing and service bureau arrangements should be reviewed with this in mind. Furthermore, since "processing" encompasses everything that may be done with data from initial collection by any means through to final destruction, the Seventh Principle may have an impact on a whole range of peripheral arrangements with suppliers and service providers. Examples might be a controller's arrangements with a marketing company that collects data on prospects and with a cleaning contractor that is responsible for removal and destruction of any data media (including paper).

---

[74]   DPA 1998, Schedule 1, Part II, paragraph 9.

[75]   DPA 1998, Schedule 1, Part II, paragraph 10.

[76]   DPA 1998, Schedule 1, Part II, paragraph 11.

[77]   DPA 1998, Schedule 1, Part II, paragraph 12.

7.4.5.8   Eighth Principle: international transfers

The Eighth Data Protection Principle ("Eighth Principle") provides that "personal data shall not be transferred to a country or territory outside the European Economic Area unless that country or territory ensures an adequate level of protection for the rights and freedoms of data subjects in relation to the processing of personal data".[78] On the face of it, the Eighth Principle appears to be incompatible with Internet architecture and typical e-commerce structures. The theoretical scope of the Eighth Principle and its likely practical impact will now be examined in some detail.

7.4.6   Transborder data flows in practice

7.4.6.1   What constitutes adequacy?

As already noted, the Eighth Principle prohibits transfers of data from the UK to a country outside the EEA that does not ensure "an adequate level of protection" for data subjects. One of the interpretation provisions relating to the Eighth Principle provides that adequacy depends on "all the circumstances of the case", including the nature of the data, the country or territory of origin and final destination of the data, the law in force and international obligations of those jurisdictions, the purposes and duration of the intended processing, "any relevant codes of conduct or other rules which are enforceable in that country or territory", and any security measures taken in the destination country or territory.[79]

This greatly complicates, though in so doing adds flexibility to, the Eighth Principle which refers only to the adequacy of the country or territory concerned. Factors relating to particular transfers must also be considered. Examples include the nature of the data, the purposes of processing and the security arrangements. As a result, a given country may be regarded as ensuring an adequate level of protection in relation to some transfers but not others. The Data Protection Commissioner has published guidance on such issues arising out of the subject of transborder data flows.[80]

In the Internet context, many website operators now post a privacy policy on their sites. Is such a policy, combined with appropriate practices and security arrangements, likely to be sufficient to achieve adequacy?   A definitive answer to this question will, of course, depend on "all the circumstances of the case". However, reliance on a policy to achieve adequacy may only be effective if the policy is in fact "enforceable" in the relevant country or territory. If a particular policy is backed by a contractual framework that gives directly enforceable rights to data subjects, such an arrangement might suffice. Alternatively, it might be possible to show that effective external policing and enforcement mechanisms exist in the country concerned. An example might be the processing of customer data in a highly regulated sector, such as banking.

---

78   DPA 1998, Schedule 1, Part I, paragraph 8.

79   DPA 1998, Schedule 1, Part II, paragraph 13.

80   "Legal Analysis and Suggested 'Good Practice Approach' to Assessing Adequacy" (dated July 1999), which can be found at http://wood.ccta.gov.uk/dpr/dpdoc.nsf.

7.4.6.2   *Automatic exceptions to the requirement for adequacy*

It is likely that there will be many situations in which it cannot be demonstrated that a destination country ensures an adequate level of protection. To overcome the Eighth Principle's prohibition on transfer in such cases it will be necessary to rely on one or more of the exemptions listed in Schedule 4 to the DPA 1998. There are nine exemptions: the first seven of which apply "automatically", in the sense that no prior regulatory approval is needed; the remaining two are not automatic and require the prior approval of the Information Commissioner.

Probably the most straightforward automatic exemption is that the data subject has consented to the transfer.[81] Although the Internet is perceived by some as a threat to privacy, it may in fact prove to be a particularly effective medium for obtaining data protection consents. An individual can be provided, by email or via a web page, with the requisite information to make an informed decision about an international transfer. The consent of that individual can then be captured via a return email or a "click-through" on a website.

The second and third automatic exceptions to the prohibition on transfer relate to contracts that a data controller might enter into with, or for the benefit of, a data subject, as well as preparatory steps in relation to such contracts.[82] Again, there may be many instances in the Internet context where one of these exemptions will justify the transfer of personal data to "inadequate" countries. Obvious examples would be the various transfers necessary to set up and complete an e-commerce transaction. These might include payment arrangements with credit card issuers and fulfilment arrangements with suppliers and shippers.

The remaining automatic exemptions are likely to be of much more limited relevance in the Internet context. The fourth covers transfers that are necessary for reasons of substantial public interest.[83] The fifth applies to transfers that are necessary in connection with legal proceedings, legal advice or for establishing, exercising or defending legal rights.[84] The sixth is available where the transfer is "necessary to protect the vital interests of the data subject",[85] and the seventh covers transfers of personal data from a public register.[86]

7.4.6.3   *Special exceptions to the requirement for adequacy*

This leaves the two non-automatic exemptions to the prohibition on transfers. These are the only other grounds on which personal data may lawfully be transferred to a non-EEA country that fails to ensure adequate protection for data subjects. The first covers transfers that are "made on terms of a kind approved by the Commissioner as ensuring adequate safeguards for the rights and freedoms of data subjects".[87] The second covers transfers that

---

[81]   DPA 1998, Schedule 4, paragraph 1.

[82]   DPA 1998, Schedule 4, paragraphs 2 and 3.

[83]   DPA 1998, Schedule 4, paragraph 4.

[84]   DPA 1998, Schedule 4, paragraph 5.

[85]   DPA 1998, Schedule 4, paragraph 6.

[86]   DPA 1998, Schedule 4, paragraph 7.

[87]   DPA 1998, Schedule 4, paragraph 8.

have been "authorised by the Commissioner as being made in such a manner as to ensure adequate safeguards for the rights and freedoms of data subjects".[88] As of 1 February 2001, the Commissioner had not approved any terms or authorised any transfers pursuant to these provisions.

Some important guidance on the adequacy requirement has been published by the Working Party.[89] So far, the Working Party seems determined to adopt a strict approach to assessing both adequacy and special exceptions to the prohibition on transfer to non-adequate countries. This is consistent with the Framework Directive, in which a discussion in the preamble regarding transborder data flows concludes with the simple statement that: "...in any event, transfers to third countries may be effected only in full compliance with the provisions adopted by the Member States pursuant to this Directive".[90]

Article 26 of the Framework Directive, on which these exemptions are based, provides that a Member State that grants any special authorisation must provide details to the European Commission and the other Member States. If a Member State or the Commission raises a valid objection to the authorisation, the Commission must "take appropriate measures" and the national regulator would be required to "take the necessary measures to comply with the Commission's decision".[91]

Article 31 of the Framework Directive has established a further committee comprising representatives of the Member States. The European Commission is required to submit to this committee drafts of any measures to be taken in relation to special international transfer authorisations. The committee may disagree with the Commission's approach resulting in suspension of the relevant "measures" and referral to the EU Council of Ministers, which may ultimately "take a different decision".[92]

7.4.6.4 Adequacy findings

The concept of "adequacy" is complex and may be more flexible than it appears at first sight. The European Commission has already made a "finding", binding on the Member States, that Hungary and Switzerland ensure an adequate level of protection; and a further "finding" that the US ensures an adequate level of protection for personal data transferred to US organisations that have signed up to the US Safe Harbor Principles published by the US Department of Commerce.[93] While entry into the Safe Harbor provides a means of

---

[88]   DPA 1998, Schedule 4, paragraph 9.

[89]   *See*, in particular, the Working Party's working document entitled: "Transfers of personal data to third countries – applying Articles 25 and 25 of the EU Data Protection Directive", adopted on 24 July 1998, 5025/98/final, WP12.

[90]   EU Directive, Recital 60.

[91]   Framework Directive, Article 26(3).

[92]   Framework Directive, Article 31.

[93]   These findings, made under article 25(6) of the Framework Directive, were made in the Commission Decision of 27 July 2000 pursuant to Directive 95/46/EC of the European Parliament and of the Council on the adequacy of the protection provided by the Safe Harbor Privacy Principles and related Frequently Asked Questions issued by the US Department of Commerce. Information about the Safe Harbor is available at: http://www.export.gov/safeharbor/.

overcoming restrictions on transfers of personal data from the EU to the US, take up has been slow.[94] This is perhaps because of concerns regarding potential civil and criminal risks to which Safe Harborites may be exposed in the US if they breach their Safe Harbor commitments.[95] Moreover, the Safe Harbor arrangements are of limited benefit to organisations operating globally via the Internet as the Safe Harbor only covers exports to the US. Further, country-specific, findings of adequacy are expected in the near future.

In addition to adequacy findings in relation to particular countries, the Framework Directive envisages that the European Commission may decide "that certain standard contractual clauses offer sufficient safeguards".[96] On 29 September 2000, the European Commission issued a preliminary draft of a decision in relation to standard clauses for transfers and invited comments.[97] An amended version of the draft decision was issued on 19 January 2001.[98] In due course, such standard clauses may provide a useful basis for justifying transfers of personal data from EU countries to countries anywhere in the world that do not provide an adequate level of protection for personal data.

7.4.6.5 Applicability of transborder data flow rules to the Internet

The transborder data flow rules in the Framework Directive and the DPA 1998 seem to be based on a presumption that international data traffic always follows precise and predictable routings. This assumption is fundamentally at odds with the way in which information is in fact conveyed via the Internet for at least two reasons. First, the Internet, which is a vast and dynamically configured network of networks, has a so-called "self-healing" architecture. Messages, or data representing information of any other kind, are split into "packets" which are sent via the most efficient routing at any given instant. A technical obstacle to the transmission of particular packets will be bypassed automatically and the packets concerned will be forwarded via a different route. Transfers are thus not predictable in geographical terms.

Secondly, because Internet email can be downloaded, and web pages can be viewed from anywhere on the planet where an individual or organisation has a connection to an ISP, the sender of a message or operator of a website has no effective control over where a particular message will be downloaded or web page viewed. Even where, for example, there are rigorous access controls on a particular website, even if the website operator can verify conclusively the identity of a particular visitor to that website it is difficult to see how the operator can be sure of the physical location of that visitor. Consequently it must be assumed that data contained in Internet email messages and web pages potentially may be transferred to any country in the world, without regard to the adequacy or otherwise of the local data protection safeguards, if any.

---

94 As of 1 February 2001, only 20 organisations had entered the Safe Harbor. The current list is available at: http://www.export.gov/safeharbor/shlis.nsf/WebPages/safe+harbor+list.

95 The standard to which Safe Harborites commit is not dissimilar to that established by the EU Framework Directive.

96 Framework Directive, Article 26(4).

97 Preliminary draft of a Commission decision under Article 26(4) of the Directive 95/46/EC on standard clauses for the transfer of personal data to third countries that do not provide an adequate level of protection for the processing of personal data, http://www.europa.eu.int/comm/internal_market/en/media/dataprot/news/callcom.htm.

98 Draft Commission Decision pursuant to Article 26(4) of the Directive 95/46/EC on Standard Contractual Clauses for the Transfer of Personal Data to Third Countries (Version of 19 January 2001), http://europa.eu.int/comm/internal_market/en/media/dataprot/news/clauses.htm.

Moreover, the sheer volume of personal data which is conveyed via the Internet and the vast number of data transfers make it inconceivable that even a significant minority of transfers can be regulated in any meaningful way under the cumbersome rules established by the Framework Directive and the DPA 1998. Given the limited resources available to the national data protection regulators in the EEA, it would not be surprising if regulatory scrutiny can only be exercised in relation to a tiny minority of international data transfers.

7.4.6.6   *Notification and preliminary assessment*

The registration system under the DPA 1984 has been replaced by a, broadly similar, notification system under the DPA 1998. Subject to various exemptions, under the DPA 1998 it is a strict liability offence for a data controller to process personal data without first making a notification to the Information Commissioner.[99] The DPA 1998 lists various "registrable particulars" that must be included in a notification, including the controller's name and address, or that of any nominated representative; a description of the personal data to be processed; the purposes for which the data are to be processed; the recipient(s) to whom the data may be disclosed; and details of countries outside the EEA to which the data may be transferred. In addition, a notification must specify "a general description of measures to be taken for the purpose of complying with the seventh data protection principle".[100] This last requirement, which relates to the controller's technical and organisational security environment, is a significant addition to the registration requirements under the DPA 1984. In the Internet context, controllers may have to describe, in broad terms, their firewall, anti-virus software and other data security arrangements. Detailed rules relating to notification arrangements, including precise procedures and fee requirements, have been established under secondary legislation.[101]

The Commissioner is required to make the register of notifications available to the public. The Commissioner publishes the register on the web, which is updated on a weekly basis, and it is possible for interested parties to search the register via the Data Protection Commissioner's website.[102] It is also possible for data controllers to make a notification online assisted by a notification self-assessment guide.[103]

A new procedure will apply to "assessable processing" – that is, processing that appears to the Secretary of State "to be particularly likely –

(a) to cause substantial damage or substantial distress to data subjects, or

(b) otherwise significantly to prejudice the rights and freedoms of data subjects".[104]

---

99   DPA 1998, Sections 17(1) and 21(1).

100   DPA 1998, Section 18(2).

101   SI 2000/188 Data Protection Register (Notification and Notification Fees) Regulations 2000.

102   The Data Protection has been made available at: http://www.dpr.gov.uk/search.html.

103   This can be found at: http://www.dpr.gov.uk/notify/4.html.

104   DPA 1998, Section 22(1).

If the Commissioner is of the opinion that a notification application describes assessable processing, within 28 days the Commissioner must give the data controller concerned a notice regarding the degree to which the processing is likely or unlikely to comply with the provisions of the DPA 1998.[105] It will be difficult to predict the likely impact of this procedure on Internet-related activities until more detailed rules have been promulgated in secondary legislation.

7.4.7 Data subject rights

7.4.7.1 Subject access

Data subjects are entitled to be informed as to whether a particular data controller holds personal data about them and, if so, to be provided "in an intelligible form" with the relevant personal data and any information which the controller has as to the sources of that data.[106] Data controllers are only obliged to give access to personal data if they have received a written request and payment of any fee they may choose to charge (up to a statutory maximum).[107] Moreover, a data controller may, in general, refuse to give access to data if it would be impossible to comply with an access request without disclosing information about another identifiable individual, unless that other person has consented to the disclosure. However, the controller must provide as much requested information as can be disclosed without identifying the other individual concerned.[108]

Responding in an appropriate manner to subject access requests may prove complex in the Internet context. For example, if a customer of an ISP were to ask the ISP to supply a copy of all information relating to that customer, the ISP might have to compile a comprehensive report based on all relevant historic and current data in its network management systems, billing systems, customer support databases, etc. If such systems had not been designed so as to provide ready access to such data "in an intelligible form", it might require a substantial effort to convert the data into such a form in order to comply with each subject access request. Similar issues might face a business that maintains extensive data archives containing detailed records of the use by its employees of Internet email and the web.

7.4.7.2 Objection to various types of processing

An individual may serve a written notice requiring a data controller to cease, or not begin, processing personal data about that individual on the ground that the processing "is causing, or is likely to cause, substantial damage or substantial distress to him or to another".[109]

---

[105] DPA 1998, Section 22(2) and (3).

[106] DPA 1998, Section 7(1).

[107] DPA 1998, Section 7(2). The statutory maximum is currently £10. The Data Protection (Subject Access) (Fees and Miscellaneous Provisions) Regulations 2000. SI 2000, No. 191.

[108] DPA 1998, Section 7(4) and (5). Section 8 contains additional rules in relation to subject access and further requirements will be added by secondary legislation.

[109] DPA 1998, Section 10. The notice may relate to all processing or processing for a specified purpose or in a specified manner.

Moreover, an individual may serve a written notice requiring a data controller to cease, or not begin, processing personal data about that individual for direct marketing purposes.[110] This means, for example, that an organisation that engages in direct marketing by email would be in breach of this provision if it continued to send marketing emails to an individual who had requested that no further emails be sent. In her 1997 Annual Report, the Information Commissioner stressed her support for privacy enhancing technologies ("PETS") and proposed the use of simple "privacy markers" to facilitate the suppression of email addresses of individuals who do not wish to receive unsolicited email or have their addresses passed on to third parties.[111] In her 1999 Annual Report the Information Commissioner again commended PETS as a mechanism for improving privacy protection. In this context she encouraged software providers to make PETS "as easy to use as possible to ensure that unsophisticated users are not put at a disadvantage and can play an important part in advancing the education of the average Internet user".[112]

The DPA 1998 also contains detailed rules in relation to "automated decision-taking". An individual may serve a written notice requiring a data controller to ensure that no decision is taken that "significantly affects" the individual based solely on the automated processing of data about that individual "for the purpose of evaluating matters relating to him such as, for example, his performance at work, his creditworthiness, his reliability or conduct".[113] Moreover, even if an individual has not served such a notice, the data controller must notify any individual about whom such a decision was made "as soon as reasonably practicable".[114] This rule is subject to certain qualifications and will not apply, for example, where the decision is taken in the course of entering into or performing a contract provided "steps have been taken to safeguard the legitimate interests of the data subject (e.g. by allowing him to make representations)".[115]

---

[110] DPA 1998, Section 11. The definition of "direct marketing" is "the communication (by whatever means) or any advertising or marketing material which is directed to particular individuals".

[111] Thus, "J.Smith+PRIV@XYZ.UK might indicate that J Smith does not want to receive unsolicited mail at this address, whereas J.Smith@XYZ.UK would contain no such indication.... The concept of a marker could allow for a variety of messages in addresses. For example, an address in the form +PRIV@... might indicate that an individual does not want any information sent to him. Alternatively he might use +PER@... to indicate that he does not want the address passed on to others, although he would not object to information from the site owner". "The Thirteenth Annual Report of the Data Protection Registrar" (London: The Stationery Office Limited, 1997), pages 52-53 and Appendix 14.

[112] 1999 Annual Report: p. 109. A similar enthusiasm for PETS has been expressed by the Working Party which devoted to this topic Chapter 9 of "Privacy on the Internet – An Integrated EU Approach to On-line Data Protection", 5063/00/EN/final, WP37.

[113] DPA 1998, Section 12(1).

[114] DPA 1998, Section 12(2).

[115] DPA 1998, Section 12(4) – (8). The individual then has 21 days to serve a notice requiring the controller to reconsider the decision or take a new decision on a different basis. The controller then has a further 21 days within which to respond in writing "specifying the steps he intends to take to comply with the data subject notice".

One of the attractions of e-commerce is that routine interactions with customers may be automated to the extent that an unmanned server may be used to handle certain transactions without any need for human intervention. This new rule relating to automated decision making may be of relevance where a particular individual is adversely affected by a web-based automated decision. An example might be where a web server rejects a request for the supply of goods or services because of a profile of a prospective purchaser that has been assembled and analysed automatically.

7.4.7.3   Compensation

As already mentioned, the DPA 1998 establishes a right of compensation for an individual who suffers damage as a result of any breach of the DPA 1998 by a data controller. In addition, an individual may also be entitled to compensation for distress if the individual has suffered damage or the relevant breach by the data controller relates to the processing of data for journalistic, artistic or literary purposes. In relation to a claim for compensation, a defence of "reasonable care" is available to a data controller.[116]

7.4.7.4   Rectification, blocking, erasure and destruction of data

An individual may apply for a court order requiring a data controller to rectify, block, erase or destroy data relating to that individual on the ground that the data is inaccurate. Where a court makes such an order, it may also order the data controller to inform third parties to which the data have been disclosed of the rectification, blocking, erasure or destruction. Such an additional order will, however, only be made where the court "considers it reasonably practicable". Similar orders, including third party notification requirements, may also be made where a court is satisfied that a data subject has suffered damage as a result of any breach of the DPA 1998 by a data controller.

In the Internet context, it may be impossible for a data controller to identify the third parties to whom data have been disclosed, for example where the data in question have been posted on a publicly accessible website or in a Usenet group. Moreover, the DPA 1998 states that, "in determining whether it is reasonably practicable to require such notification... the court shall have regard, in particular, to the number of persons who would have to be notified".[117]

7.4.7.5   Exemptions

Certain activities are exempted from various obligations imposed by the DPA 1998.[118] Many of the exemptions are solely or primarily of relevance to the processing of personal data in the public sector, for example those relating to national security, crime, taxation, health, education, social work, and regulatory activities. Specific exemptions that may be important in the private sector include those relating to research, history and statistics, confidential references given by the data controller, management forecasts, certain corporate finance activities, and legal professional privilege.

---

[116]   DPA 1998, Section 13.

[117]   DPA 1998, Section 14.

[118]   These are set out in Part IV and Schedule 7 of the DPA 1998, supplemented by secondary legislation, full details of which are available at: http://www.homeoffice.gov.uk/ccpd/dpsubleg.htm.

New, and somewhat controversial, exemptions are available in relation to processing personal data solely in connection with journalism, literature and art – the so-called "special purposes". Most of the provisions relating to data subject rights, including the right of access to data, the right to prevent processing in certain circumstances, and the right to rectification, blocking, erasure or destruction of data may be inapplicable in such cases. However, this broad exemption is only available where a data controller "reasonably believes that, having regard in particular to the special importance of the public interest in freedom of expression, publication would be in the public interest, and ... that compliance with that provision is incompatible with the special purposes".[119]

The Internet is used extensively as a medium for news and comment. Most conventional media organisations have a presence on the web and they are being joined by many others who are using the web as a medium for journalistic and other activities which, due to their literary or artistic nature, may fall within the "special purposes". Nevertheless, data controllers seeking to rely on the exemptions relating to the special purposes should do so with caution as they may be exposed to both intervention by the Data Protection Commissioner and compensation claims from individuals if they stray outside the narrow parameters of those exemptions.

7.4.8   Supervision and enforcement

7.4.8.1   The Information Commissioner

The DPA 1998 provides for the office of the Data Protection Registrar, established under the DPA 1984, to continue under the new name of the office of the Data Protection Commissioner.[120] As of 30 January 2001, the Office of the Data Protection Commissioner was renamed the Office of the Information Commissioner, to reflect her additional responsibilities in relation to the Freedom of Information Act. In many respects, the Commissioner has similar functions to those of the Registrar, but has additional powers and the opportunity to take a more proactive approach to police compliance by data controllers with the Data Protection Principles and other obligations imposed on them under the DPA 1998.

The Commissioner has various roles under the DPA 1998, including promoting compliance with the Act by data controllers, overseeing the notification system and "special purposes" exemptions, reporting to Parliament and representing the UK in relation to the Council of Europe Convention and the EU Directive.[121] Of her specific supervision and enforcement powers, it is likely that the most significant will be her powers to serve various notices on data controllers.

If the Commissioner "is satisfied that a data controller has contravened or is contravening any of the data protection principles", she can serve an enforcement notice requiring the data controller to take, or refrain from taking, specified steps, or to refrain from specified processing activities in relation to all or some personal data. Specifically, an enforcement notice may back up a data subject's right to have data rectified, blocked, erased or destroyed.[122] As they move increasingly into e-commerce, more and more businesses will

---

[119]   DPA 1998, Section 32.

[120]   DPA 1998, Section 6(1).

[121]   DPA 1998, Sections 51–54.

[122]   DPA 1998, Section 40.

become dependent on their ability to process personal data in particular ways. The threat of an enforcement notice is thus a potent one. Such a notice might force an organisation to modify radically the way in which it does business and, in an extreme case, might make it impossible for it to continue trading.

The second type of notice which the Commissioner may serve is an information notice, requiring a data controller to provide specified information relating to a request for an assessment to be made of a particular processing activity or of a data controller's compliance with the data protection principles.[123]

The Commissioner may also serve a third type of notice – a special information notice – to enable her to ascertain whether particular personal data are in fact being processed for the special journalistic, artistic or literary purposes. Moreover, if it appears to her that any personal data are not in fact being processed only for the special purposes she may make a "determination" to that effect.[124]

Failure to comply with an enforcement notice, an information notice or a special information notice is a criminal offence.[125]

7.4.8.2   *The Data Protection Tribunal*

The Data Protection Tribunal established under the DPA 1984 has also continued under the DPA 1998.[126] The principal role of the Tribunal is to hear and determine appeals brought by data controllers against notices served by the Commissioner.[127]

7.4.8.3   *The courts*

The DPA 1998 creates various criminal offences, including a strict liability offence of processing personal data without notification.[128] Failure to comply with a notice served by the Commissioner is an offence in relation to which it is a defence to have "exercised all due diligence to comply with the notice in question".[129] Offences under the Act are triable in either Magistrates' or Crown courts.

---

[123]   DPA 1998, Section 43.

[124]   DPA 1998, Sections 44 and 45.

[125]   DPA 1998, Section 47.

[126]   DPA 1998, Section 6(2).

[127]   DPA 1998, Section 28, 48 and Schedule 5, Part II.

[128]   DPA 1998, Section 2(1).

[129]   DPA 1998, Sections 47(1) and (3).

Data subjects have direct access to the civil courts for enforcement of rights under the Act. These include the right of access to personal data, the right to prevent processing likely to cause damage or distress, the right (by written notice) to prevent direct marketing, rights in relation to automated decision making, and the right to have personal data rectified, blocked, erased or destroyed. Data subjects may also take civil action for compensation for damage caused by any contravention of the requirements of the Act.[130]

There is also a right of appeal to the civil courts against decisions of the Data Protection Tribunal on a point of law.[131]

7.5   Communications-specific regulations

7.5.1   *Introduction*

The Telecoms Data Protection Directive regulates the processing of personal data in connection with the provision of publicly available services consisting wholly or partly in the transmission and routing of signals on public telecommunications networks.[132] The regime established by the Telecoms Data Protection Directive compliments the general regime under the Framework Directive.

The Telecoms Data Protection Directive is rooted in traditional telephony concepts and its precise application to Internet-related activities is uncertain. Some of the provisions of the Telecoms Data Protection Directive are intended to apply only to public network operators and suppliers of telecommunications services to the public. Some ISPs may also be network operators and, arguably, all ISPs provide "services [consisting] wholly or partly in the transmission and routing of signals on telecommunications networks".[133] Nevertheless, there are likely to be difficulties in applying to ISPs the detailed rules in the Telecommunications Directive relating to, for example, restrictions on collection and use of traffic and billing data, and the presentation of calling and connected line identification.

The provisions of the Telecoms Data Protection Directive that relate to direct marketing activities were implemented initially in the UK by means of the Telecommunications (Data Protection and Privacy) (Direct Marketing) Regulations 1998 (the "1998 Regulations").[134] The 1998 Regulations came into force on 1 May 1999 but on 1 March 2000 were revoked and superseded by the Telecommunications (Data Protection and Privacy) Regulations 1999 (the "1999 Regulations"). The 1999 Regulations implemented the entire Telecoms Data Protection Directive with the exception of Article 5. Article 5, which deals with monitoring and interception of communications, has since been implemented in the Regulation of Investigatory Powers Act 2000 (the "RIP Act") which came into force in October 2000 (*see*

---

130   DPA 1998, Sections 7–15.

131   DPA 1998, Section 49(6).

132   Telecoms Data Protection Directive, Articles 2(d) and 3(1).

133   Telcommunications Directive, Article 2(d).

134   SI 1998 No. 3170.

Section 7.5.4 below). The proposed Directive of the European Parliament and of the Council concerning the processing of personal data and the protection of privacy in the electronic communications sector ("Electronic Communications Privacy Directive")[135] would replace the Telecoms Data Protection Directive with the intention of clarifying and, to some extent widening, the application of privacy rules to online communications.

7.5.2 *1999 Regulations – direct marketing rules*

The terminology used in the 1999 Regulations suggests that they were drafted with conventional voice and fax calls in mind and it is not clear whether the restrictions on direct marketing activities apply also to email communications. Depending on the circumstances, email can be characterised as being analogous either to conventional mail, on the one hand, or to a voice or fax call, on the other. In many instances, an email message will be sent to the intended recipient's ISP where it will be stored until such a time as the recipient connects to the ISP to retrieve the message. Such an arrangement is rather like a conventional mail system using post office boxes and is certainly very different from a real-time phone or fax call. On the other hand, where the recipient has a real-time connection to the Internet a message may be received almost instantaneously. Indeed, a lengthy document can be delivered via email in such circumstances in a small fraction of the time it would take to deliver the same document via fax. It is possible that the sending of an email message in such circumstances might be regulated as an unsolicited direct marketing call. If that were the case, Regulation 22 would prohibit the sending to either business or individual recipients of unsolicited emails using an "automated calling system". A computer that is used to distribute a mass email mailing may constitute such a system as it may "make calls without human intervention". Even where an automated mailing system is not used, it may be a breach of Regulation 25 to send a marketing email to an individual subscriber who has either requested the particular sender not to send such messages or who is listed on a register of individuals who object to receiving unsolicited calls (the "TPS register"). An alternative, and probably better, interpretation of the 1999 Regulations is that the references to telephone numbers and the use of concepts such as "subscriber's line" and "unsolicited call" indicate that the 1999 Regulations are only intended to apply to conventional voice and fax calls.

The proposed Electronic Communications Privacy Directive would make it clear that unsolicited emails for the purposes of direct marketing are to be treated in the same way as such communications sent via phone or fax.[136]

---

135   Com (2000) 385 final, Brussels, 12 July 2000.

136   Proposed Electronic Communications Privacy Directive, Article 13(1).

7.5.3   *Interception of Communications Act 1985*

The Interception of Communications Act 1985 provides that "...a person who intentionally intercepts a communication in the course of its transmission by post or by means of a public telecommunication system shall be guilty of an offence...".[137] This is subject to various exceptions, notably that the interception has been authorised by a warrant issued by the Secretary of State or that the interceptor has reasonable grounds for believing that the sender or recipient of the message has consented to the interception. The only grounds for issuing a warrant are that it "...is necessary (a) in the interests of national security; (b) for the purpose of preventing or detecting serious crime; or (c) for the purpose of safeguarding the economic well-being of the United Kingdom".[138] The Secretary of State must consider whether the information that is sought could reasonably be acquired by other means.[139] With regard to its scope, it is clear that the Interception of Communications Act 1985 has no application to an interception that takes place outside a public network.[140]

The RIP Act repeals the Interception of Communications Act 1985 and replaces it with a much broader regime covering all types of communications via both public and private networks (*see* Section 7.5.4 below).

7.5.4   *Regulation of Investigatory Powers Act 2000*

The RIP Act was enacted on 28 July 2000 and most of its provisions had been brought into force by 24 October 2000.[141] The RIP Act has replaced the Interception of Communications Act 1985 and, among other matters regulates "Intrusive Investigative Techniques", empowering the police and other authorised persons to compel individuals or organisations to disclose information necessary to decipher encrypted messages. While these encryption-related provisions clearly have an impact on Internet privacy, a detailed discussion of those rules is beyond the scope of this Chapter.

---

[137]   Interception of Communications Act 1985, 5.1.

[138]   Interception of Communications Act 1985, Section 2(2). The economic well-being justification is only available in relation to "information relating to the acts or intentions of persons outside the British Islands." Id., Section 2(4).

[139]   Interception of Communications Act 1985, Section 2(3).

[140]   *See*, for example, *R v. Effick* [1994] Crim LR 832, 99; Cr App Rep 312, 158 in which the court held that interception by the police of telephone conversations on a cordless telephone was not subject to the Interception of Communications Act.

[141]   The Regulation of Investigatory Powers Act 2000 (Commencement No. 1 and Transitional Provisions) Order 2000. SI 2000 No.2543 (c.71).

With regard to interception of communications, Section 1(1) of the RIP Act makes it "an offence for a person intentionally and without lawful authority to intercept, at any place in the United Kingdom, any communication in the course of its transmission by means of:

(a) a public postal service; or

(b) a public telecommunication system".

A similar offence is created in relation to private telecommunication systems[142] with the exception that no offence would be committed if the interception either is made by a person with the right to control that system or is made with consent of the system controller.[143] The Explanatory Notes to the bill give examples of activities within this exception, such as: the use of a second handset in a house to monitor a call or routine recording of calls by a financial institution to provide evidence of transactions.[144] The Secretary of State is permitted to issue a warrant authorising or requiring the interception of communications in specified circumstances.

In addition to the criminal offences created by Sections 1(1) and 1(2), Section 1(3) has created a new tort of unlawful interception on a private network:

> "Any interception of a communication which is carried out at any place in the United Kingdom by, or with the express or implied consent of, a person having the right to control the operation or the use of a private telecommunication system shall be actionable at the suit or instance of the sender or recipient, or intended recipient, of the communication if it is without lawful authority and is either –
>
> (a) an interception of that communication in the course of its transmission by means of that private system; or
>
> (b) an interception of that communication in the course of its transmission, by means of a public telecommunication system, to or from apparatus comprised in that private telecommunication system."

Thus, a system controller who is protected from criminal liability under Section 1(2) may nevertheless face civil proceedings for breach of Section 1(3). As the Explanatory Notes to the RIP Act observe "where an employee believes that their employer has unlawfully intercepted a telephone conversation with a third party, either the employee or the third party may sue the employer".[145] This would also be the case in relation to an intercepted

---

142   RIP Act, Section 1(2).

143   RIP Act, Section 1(6).

144   Explanatory Notes to RIP Act bill paragraph 25.

145   Explanatory Notes to RIP Act, paragraph 21.

email message. However, the key issue will be whether the employer has "lawful authority" to intercept the communication. There are two main grounds on which lawful authority might be based. First, on the fact, or reasonable belief, that both the sender and the intended recipient of the communication in question have consented to the interception.[146] This may lead to employers inserting consent clauses in employee contracts and possibly also in customer or other individual third party contracts. There are likely, however, to be many situations where the consent of both parties to a communication cannot be obtained. This is likely, in particular, to be a problem in relation to senders of communication as an employer usually cannot predict who will send communications to its employees. As a result, considerable reliance will in practice have to be placed on an alternative ground for lawful authority, as set out in the "Telecommunications (Lawful Business Practice) (Interception of Communications) Regulations 2000" (the "Lawful Business Practice Regulations").[147]

The Lawful Business Practice Regulations authorise the interception of a communication if it is effected by or with the express or implied consent of the system controller (e.g. an employer) for specific purposes relating to monitoring, or keeping a record of, communications relevant to the system controller's business.[148] Communications are relevant if they are transactional, otherwise relate to the business or otherwise take place in the course of carrying on the business.[149] Qualifying business purposes include establishing the existence of facts, ascertaining compliance with regulatory or self-regulatory practices or procedures and ascertaining or demonstrating that standards have been achieved (e.g. quality control or training). In addition, such interception may be justified in the interests of national security, for crime prevention or detection purposes, for investigating or detecting unauthorised use and for purposes related to effective system operation.[150] Furthermore, the Lawful Business Practice Regulations authorise monitoring for the purpose of distinguishing business from non business-related communications.[151] In every case, however, the system controller must have made "all reasonable efforts" to

---

[146]   RIP Act, Section 3(1).

[147]   Statutory Instrument 2000 No. 2699, issued pursuant to Sections 4(2) and 4(3) of the RIP Act.

[148]   Lawful Business Practice Regulations, Regulation 3.

[149]   Lawful Business Practice Regulations, Regulation 2(b).

[150]   Lawful Business Practice Regulations, Regulation 3(1).

[151]   Lawful Business Practice Regulations, Regulation 3(1)(b). The Regulations also permit monitoring of "communications made to a confidential voice-telephony counselling or support service which is free of charge (other than the cost, if any, of making a telephone call) and operated in such a way that users may remain anonymous if they so choose". (Regulation 3(1)(c)).

inform every user of the system that communications may be intercepted.[152] Rather curiously, the Lawful Business Practice Regulations state that interception for business purposes is only authorised to the extent permitted by Article 5 of the Telecoms Data Protection Directive. This perhaps suggests that the Government anticipated a challenge to the pragmatic way that the power to override the confidentiality rule in that Article has been used.[153]

In addition to the uncertainty that the Lawful Business Practice Regulations have introduced, substantial concern and confusion has arisen from the publication by the Data Protection Commissioner of a "Draft Code of Practice on the Use of Personal Data in Employer/Employee Relationships" (the "Draft Code").[154] Probably the most controversial section of the Draft Code is that relating to employee monitoring in general, and monitoring of communications in particular.[155] This Section envisages that employers who wish to monitor the communications of their employees are constrained by various restrictions that go well beyond those established by the RIP Act and Lawful Business Practice Regulations. For example, the Draft Code recommends that, in relation to email, unless it is unavoidable traffic records only should be monitored, not email content; the "autonomy" as well as the privacy of recipients of emails should be respected; and employees should be provided with a means by which they can "effectively expunge from the system emails they receive or send".[156] This latter recommendation betrays a surprising lack of understanding of technical and commercial realities. Even if it were feasible from a technical perspective, to give employees the means to remove emails from an employer's systems, permanently and without trace, would appear to be a fraudster's charter. At the time of writing, a public consultation exercise was underway in relation to the Draft Code and it is to be hoped that some of its more impractical provisions will be modified.

7.6 Conclusion

Public awareness of, and anxiety relating to, online privacy issues appears to be growing. The importance of addressing such concerns seems to be recognised by legislators, regulators and businesses not only in the UK and throughout the EU but also in major economies that so far do not have omnibus data protection laws, most notably the US. It could be argued that the DPA 1998 and similar laws in other jurisdictions that implement the Framework Directive will facilitate the development of the Internet. It is indeed likely that e-commerce will not flourish to the full extent possible in the absence of a sufficient degree of public confidence in the legal protection of privacy and security. Unfortunately, however, the restrictive, cumbersome and inflexible nature of many of the specific rules in the Framework Directive and the DPA 1998 may, if enforced strictly, stifle online innovation. The costs of e-commerce may be raised significantly without there being much to show in terms of enhanced protection for consumers and other data subjects. Moreover,

---

[152] Lawful Business Practice Regulations, Regulation 3(2)(c).

[153] Lawful Business Practice Regulations, Regulation 3(3).

[154] http://www.dataprotection.gov.uk/ (Guidance & other publications/Codes of Practice).

[155] Draft Code, Section 6.

[156] Draft Code, Section 6.3.2.

certain requirements may turn out to be completely unworkable. In particular, the transborder data flow regime that EU Member States are required to implement may prove to be fundamentally incompatible with the "any-to-any" network architecture of the Internet. National data protection regulators, and the European Commission, may eventually have to concede that it is futile to try to superimpose virtual border controls, based on terrestrial jurisdictional boundaries, on data traffic and Internet-related activities in cyberspace.

Chapter 8
ADVERTISING

Rafi Azim-Khan
Partner
McDermott, Will & Emery

8.1   Introduction

Any business looking to advertise or promote its goods or services on the Internet needs to consider both the traditional laws and self regulatory rules that apply to such activity as well as the ever increasing raft of new "e" focused law and regulation that applies peculiarly to cyberspace. In addition, one also has to consider such rules that may exist not only in the "home" jurisdiction but also that of other countries to whom the advertising may be targeted or indeed merely accessible. This latter point is particularly relevant to B2C ventures as consumer law can often be deemed to apply by protective national courts, especially if consumers in that territory are deemed to have been targeted or have had trade concluded with. As this is a very complicated area and one which very much depends upon the facts and circumstances of each case, advertisers should simply note the need to seek advice on such international aspects in addition to compliance with home regulation. It is on the latter that this Chapter concentrates, namely the regulation of Internet advertising in the UK.

8.2   Principal rules governing advertising in the UK

8.2.1   Nature of the regulatory regime

The regime governing advertising in the UK is a blend of statute, civil law and a well developed self-regulatory regime. Statutory regulation exists in the form of, for example, the Trade Marks Act 1994 controls on comparative advertising use of others' marks, the Consumer Protection Act 1987 controls on misleading pricing information, the Trade Descriptions Act of 1968 controls on product descriptions and so on. In addition the Control of Misleading Advertisements Regulations 1988 and the Control of Misleading Advertisements (Comparative Advertisements) (Amendment) Regulations 2000, which came into force on 23 April 2000, deal directly with advertising. Other examples of statutes which are not specifically directed at advertising but which do impact on advertising, include the Data Protection Act 1998 (the "DPA 1998"), the Consumer Protection (Distance Selling) Regulations 2000 and the Financial Services and Markets Act 2000 (the "FSMA"), examined further below.

The Control of Misleading Advertisements Regulations 1988 and the Control of Misleading Advertisements (Comparative Advertisements) (Amendment) Regulations 2000 implement the Misleading Advertising Directive (84/450/EEC). The Regulations provide the Director General of Fair Trading (the "DGFT") with the power to seek an injunction to prevent specific misleading advertising and the activities of advertisers with a track record of producing misleading material.

---

* Based on the original Chapter of the first edition contributed by Peter Watts.

This is the "stick" to back up the self-regulatory regime discussed below although it is not often used. In practice the DGFT has only sought an injunction on the basis of the Regulations in a small number of cases of advertisers who have sought to take advantage of the unwary through grossly misleading material. A typical example is that of the co-ordinators of "home-work" schemes who promise low income and housebound people an apparent opportunity to earn substantial amounts of money through performing clerical tasks from their own homes. When, in fact, little or no remuneration follows.

The Regulations' direct relevance is to set the framework for the self-regulatory regime operated by the Committee for Advertising Practice ("CAP") and the Advertising Standards Authority ("ASA").

The CAP is a truly self regulatory body, its members being drawn from advertisers, promoters, agencies, media and associated professional organisations. It is CAP that draws up the Codes of Practice for advertising and for sales promotions.

The ASA is an independent body established to oversee the self-regulatory regime and to ensure that it maintains public confidence. The ASA is the industry "watchdog". Through its Secretariat it investigates complaints that the Codes have been breached and undertakes research into advertising practice. Once the Secretariat concludes an investigation, it reports to the ASA Council which provides an adjudication.

Aside from the ultimate sanction of referral to the DGFT as mentioned above, the common sanctions which can be imposed include a boycott by the relevant media to have an ad "pulled", or the withdrawal of financial incentives. In practice, the main downside for reputable businesses in transgressing the Codes is the adverse publicity which results from the widely publicised monthly reports of the Council's adjudication. These are, of course, now available internationally via the Internet.

In October 1999 the ASA unequivocally confirmed the application of the Codes to advertising and sales promotions on the Internet. This was given further support by the announcement on 24 November 1999 that the Internet Advertising Bureau, the body representing companies selling 90 per cent of online advertising, had agreed to observe the Codes and enforce the ASA's rulings against its members.

8.2.2   *The Advertising Code*

The main requirements of the Code are as follows:

(a) all advertising must be legal, decent (i.e. not likely to cause offence), honest (e.g. it should not seek to take advantage of the credulity of the audience) and truthful. These principles are the most well-known elements of the Code. They are also the most important in practice. The more detailed rules within the Code are not necessarily interpreted literally in the same way as a UK statute. Both the Code and those who apply it in practice are at pains to point out that it must at all times be interpreted to give effect to its spirit. These four principles are the most important embodiment of that spirit and as such they suffuse the entire Code;

(b) if advertising contains any claims which are capable of objective substantiation, the advertiser must always have material, in advance of making the claim, which would prove the relevant facts;

(c) advertising should always be clearly identifiable. In particular it should be possible always to distinguish advertising from editorial material. This may be a difficult rule to apply in practice as, in the context of the Internet, the advertiser himself may not always be sure what is the status of particular material;

(d) advertising must not unfairly attack or exploit the goodwill of others. In particular, any comparisons made must be fair. This approach to comparative advertising is similar to that taken in the EU Comparative Advertising Directive (97/55/EC) and the 2000 Regulations referred to above. It also reflects the principles of the Trade Marks Act 1994 which was specifically altered to enable fair "knocking copy" comparisons to be made.

What these rules mean in practice is that if an Internet advertiser wants to make claims which compare his product or service to that of a competitor, he must ensure that the basis for that comparison is fairly selected and explained. It will not be acceptable to state that one car is "better than" another simply because it has a higher top speed, particularly if the other car has better fuel consumption. On the other hand, in the same situation it may well be acceptable to describe the car as "faster" (and to use the competitor's trade mark in that comparison) provided it is clear that the comparison is so limited. It is important to note that comparative advertising is notoriously tricky and these requirements are important not only to avoid a potential code breach but also a potentially expensive suit from a competitor based on, for example, the Trade Marks Act 1994 or for malicious falsehood.

Amongst other things, this means that any factors which might affect the validity or application of the price need to be explained. This can be particularly important for those who use the Internet for their advertising. Many such retailers have no retail network and any sales are made directly by credit card or other form of electronic payment with the goods being transported by mail. In these circumstances it is essential that any elements of the price which will be affected by customer specific influences such as location are clearly spelt out.

Separately, there are rules which aim to protect the privacy of individuals. Although there is no specific requirement to get permission from every person portrayed in a campaign, the Code "urges" advertisers to do so. In practice, the attitude of the ASA will differ depending on whether the individual in question is a public figure or simply a private individual.

It is generally accepted that images of public figures may be used provided that there is no suggestion that the individual endorses the product or supports the campaign and the product is not inconsistent with the views of the personality involved. Advertisers should always remember that if they do advertise in a way which seeks to use the name or image of anyone with a public reputation, they also risk a claim that in doing so they are seeking to "pass themselves off" as being connected with that person. If this is established, the advertiser may well have to make a substantial payment to the figure involved. Also, it would be unwise to advertise an alcoholic product using the image of a public figure who was teetotal as such advertising may also give the figure a claim against the advertiser for defamation.

If the person in question is not already publicly known, the ASA will expect the advertiser to obtain consent to the use of their image or name, unless they are simply part of a crowd or other general outdoor shot.

Children benefit from particular protection under the Code. The ASA states that it will take account of the age and experience of children to whom advertisements are addressed and the context in which they are presented in assessing whether the content is acceptable. In the case of material on the Internet, it remains to be seen whether the presumption will be that, because access to websites is not generally restricted, all websites should be judged by reference to the standards applied to relatively young children or whether the intended target audience will be the determining factor, in the same way as there is, for example, a difference between the standards applied to children's comics and to the news sections of broadsheet newspapers or to material broadcast before and after the 9.00 p.m. "watershed".

The Code includes specific provisions dealing with distance selling activities. Together with other rules on this issue, these are dealt with in Section 8.7.6. There are also specific rules which deal with products, tobacco and so on.

8.2.3   *The Sales Promotion Code*

This Code, which regulates promotional activity such as on pack offers, prize draws and giveaways, should be read in conjunction with the Advertising Code and the same principles of legality, decency, honesty and truth must be complied with by promoters as well as any specific rules applicable (e.g. in the case of children or promotions involving products such as alcohol, cars or health and beauty products). In addition:

(a) all sales promotions should be prepared with a sense of responsibility to consumers and to society, and promoters should avoid causing unnecessary disappointment by reason, for example, of a failure to properly anticipate demand for promotional products;

(b) promoters and also any intermediaries and agencies, are responsible for ensuring compliance with the Code;

(c) specific rules apply to the compilation and use of lists containing information obtained from those who participate in promotions (*see* Sections 8.7.4 and 8.7.5);

(d) sales promotions should always specify:

    (i)   how to participate;

    (ii)   any restrictions applying to those people who are eligible to participate and whether permission is required from an adult/employer;

    (iii) closing dates;

    (iv) the full name and business address of the promoter;

    (v)   any conditions of entry, proof of purchase requirements or other costs of participation;

    (vi) any restrictions applying to and a clear description of what prizes or promotional products are;

    (vii) whether any cash or other alternatives are available;

    (viii)what the criteria are for judging entries and whether winners will have to participate in any future publicity.

(e) where they have to make a purchase in order to enter participants should be told (iii), (v) and (vi) before making a purchase;

(f) applications for promotional goods should generally be fulfilled within 30 days and prize winners should receive their prizes no more than six weeks after the end of the relevant promotion;

(g) special rules apply to promotions linked with charities and in such cases, promoters will also need to comply with the Charities Act 1992 and supplementary legislation; and

(h) in the case of promotions aimed at trade customers, promoters should ensure that prior agreement is obtained from employers where appropriate.

Certain forms of sales promotion also run both the commercial risk of over redemption and further legal risks due to unwittingly committing a criminal offence, for example, via bribery or lottery legislation (the latter examined in further detail at Section 8.3 below).

8.2.4 *Specific regimes in the UK for major consumer products*

8.2.4.1 *Banking, consumer credit and financial services*

There are a number of both statutory and self-regulatory controls on advertising in the financial services industry.

Banking rules essentially control activities relating to the acceptance of banking deposits. The Banking Act 1987 (Advertisement) Regulations 1988 set out general requirements for advertisements containing an invitation to make a deposit. The Financial Services Authority (the "FSA") is also given powers under Section 33 of the Banking Act 1987 to take action where it considers that any such advertisement, either issued or proposed to be issued, by an institution which is authorised to accept deposits (i.e. a bank) is misleading. Although the matter is not expressly dealt with in the rules the FSA has expressed the clear view that the rules extend to the Internet.

The Code of Conduct for the Advertising of Interest Bearing Accounts, published by the British Bankers Association, applies specifically to advertising of all interest bearing accounts maintained within the UK. It covers all press and broadcast advertisements, direct marketing, brochures, leaflets and automated telemachine displays. Again, good practice will require compliance with the Code.

Under the Code, advertisers must ensure that consumers are informed about the nature of any commitment which they may enter into as a result of such advertising and that the deposit taking institution is clearly identified in the advertisement.

The Banking Code of Practice was drawn up by the British Bankers Association, the Building Societies Association and the Association for Payment Clearing Services and applies to the relationship between banks and their personal customers. Whilst it is a voluntary code, most banks and building societies operating in the UK comply with its provisions.

The Code requires all advertising to comply with the British Codes of Advertising and Sales Promotion Practice and other relevant codes. It also requires all such institutions to ensure that advertising and promotional literature is fair and reasonable and does not contain misleading information, as well as to inform potential customers that all lending is subject to appraisal of their financial standing. Whilst the Internet is not specifically mentioned in the Code, by analogy with the ASA Codes it will apply. It will always be good practice to comply with the Code in relevant advertising on the Internet.

In relation to such advertisements appearing on the Internet, the general view is that it will be considered as having been issued in the UK if it is made available to or can be obtained by someone in the UK. Advertisers outside the UK should therefore be made aware that investment advertisements issued overseas may nevertheless be caught by the provisions of the Financial Services Act 1986 (the "FS Act") and the FSMA if they are specifically directed to potential customers in the UK.

Credit advertising is regulated under Part IV of the Consumer Credit Act 1974 (the "1974 Act"). Section 43 of the 1974 Act provides that such controls apply to:

> "Any advertisement, published for the purposes of a business carried on by the advertiser, indicating that he is willing:
>
> (a) to provide credit; or
>
> (b) to enter into an agreement for the bailment or (in Scotland) for the hiring of goods by him."

The Consumer Credit (Advertisements) Regulations 1989 prescribe the information which credit advertising must contain and require such information to be clear, easily legible and "shown together as a whole".

Section 189 of the 1974 Act defines an advertisement as including "every form of advertising, whether in a publication, by television or radio, or in any other way, and references to the publishing of advertisements shall be construed accordingly". The Local Authorities Co-ordinating Body on Food and Trading Standards ("LACOTS") which gives guidance to the local enforcement authorities is that credit advertisements appearing on the Internet will be subject to the provisions of the 1974 Act and the Regulations and this must be the only safe view.

Questions have been raised whether or not each "screen" of text should be treated as individual credit advertisements each carrying the required statutory information.

Helpfully, LACOTS have expressed the view that any consideration of compliance should be based on a reading of the document as a whole rather than on single screens of information. Provided therefore that the credit advertisement contains the required information and does not otherwise mislead or contravene the statutory controls, individual screens within the advertisement are not subject to additional requirements.

Section 57 of the FS Act controls "investment advertisements" which are those which contain an invitation or information likely to lead directly or indirectly to persons entering into or offering to enter into investment agreements". An "investment advertisement" may not be issued in the UK unless its contents have been approved by a person who is authorised for the purposes of the statute. There are a range of detailed criteria which an "authorised person" must apply in approving investment advertisements.

8.2.4.2 Insurance

There are detailed legal requirements for the advertising and offering of insurance policies in all media which are supplemented by a Code of Guidance produced by the Association of British Insurers (the "ABI"). The ABI has produced a "New Code of Guidance on Telephone Sales, Direct Marketing/Direct Mail and the Internet" which lays down specific guidelines in relation to the Internet. In essence, the Code envisages two different scenarios:

(a) where an Internet page carries only general product information or contact details for the insurer, detailed information need not be given as no policy can be directly taken up. An insurance intermediary, who must normally make his status clear, may do so either on the website or in the course of subsequent communication;

(b) if consumers could obtain insurance cover directly from the website, the full legal and general Code requirements will apply to the site and, in particular, a summary of cover (including main provisions and restrictions) and the name of the insurer should be clearly stated.

8.2.4.3 *Food*

The advertising of food is governed generally by the Food Safety Act 1990 (the "1990 Act") and the Food Labelling Regulations 1996 (the "1996 Regulations"). The 1990 Act prohibits the publication of an advertisement which falsely describes food or is likely to mislead consumers as to its true nature or quality. The 1996 Regulations regulate the use of more specific advertising claims (e.g. "low fat" or "rich in vitamin C") by requiring that such claims are only used where certain conditions relating to the food's formulation or nutrient content are met. LACOTS offers general advice on food advertising and produces regular guidance notes on the subject.

8.2.4.4 *Pharmaceuticals*

The advertising and promotion of medicines is regulated by the Medicines Act 1968 and supplementary legislation including the Medicines (Advertising) Regulations 1994 and the Medicines (Monitoring of Advertising) Regulations 1994. The 1968 Act prohibits the advertisement of medicines unless they are licensed by the Medicines Control Agency and any claims made about such products must conform with the terms of the licence.

8.2.4.5 *Tobacco, beauty*

The Broadcasting Act 1990 prohibits advertising of tabacco on television and radio. In addition to general requirements set out in the British Codes of Advertising and Sales Promotion ("BCASP"), the UK Government Department of Health, the Tobacco Manufacturers Association and the Imported Tobacco Products Advisory Council have drawn up a separate Cigarette Code. The Cigarette Code requires advertisers to obtain signed, dated and numbered certificates of clearance from the CAP before displaying or publishing advertisements for cigarettes or hand rolling tobacco and sets out specific rules for the content of such advertisements. There are also additional self-regulatory agreements which have been reached between Government Health Departments, the Department of National Heritage and the tobacco industry concerning advertising expenditure, media selection, health warnings, promotions and controls on sports sponsorship. Breaches of these agreements are dealt with by the Committee for Monitoring Agreements on Tobacco Advertising and Sponsorship ("COMATAS"). There are also specific rules restricting advertisers from advertising prescription-only medicines to the public and prohibiting them from addressing advertisements for medicines to children.

8.3   Competitions, prize draws and games

The nature of the Internet encourages advertising of an interactive nature.

Technically, the increasing complexity afforded by techniques such as Java-based programming means it is possible by downloading a single page of text to incorporate sophisticated games which can be played immediately. The availability of the return path enables the advertiser to run competitions which are interactive and involving in a way that traditional media could never achieve.

From an advertiser's perspective, the immediacy of the interaction offered by games and competitions encourages potential customers to remain with the advertiser's site. In addition, material which encourages interaction makes it more likely that the user will supply information about themselves and their purchasing habits to the advertiser (e.g. on a competition entry form).

Most countries have very specific rules which control the playing of games and competitions in a commercial setting. Generally, such rules were originally designed to safeguard consumers from exploitation in the same way as the regulation of gambling. However, they continue to have a significant impact on the freedom of promoters today.

In the UK the main statutory controls which are likely to be relevant are those under the Lotteries and Amusements Act 1976. That Act provides that all lotteries, with certain exceptions, are generally unlawful. Although not a defined statutory term the following meaning for the word "lottery" has developed under UK case law:

> "The distribution of prizes by chance where the persons taking part in the operation, or a substantial number of them, make a payment or consideration in return for obtaining their chance prize."[1]

There are a number of activities in connection with the operation or promotion of a lottery which will be an offence under the Lotteries and Amusements Act 1976 including:

(a) printing, selling, distributing or advertising the sale of lottery tickets;

(b) printing, publishing or distributing advertisements for lottery tickets or details of prize winners;

(c) receiving lottery tickets into the jurisdiction or sending lottery monies out of the jurisdiction;

(d) causing another person to do any of the above.

The same statute (Section 14) also makes prize competitions unlawful in cases where success does not depend to a substantial degree on the exercise of skill or where prizes are offered for forecasting the result of a future or past event.

In order to determine whether a particular promotional activity (such as prize draws, instant win scratchcard promotions or sweepstakes) will amount to a lottery three factors will need to be established:

---

[1]   *Imperial Tobacco Limited v. AG* [1980] 2WLR466.

(a) *distribution of prizes* – there are any number of ways in which this test might be satisfied and prizes could be either cash prizes or indeed anything else which could be said to be of some value;[2]

(b) *winner selection by chance* – where participants are required to exercise even a limited degree of skill or effort in order to win, there will not be a lottery. This need not be skill or effort of a particular kind and could be "any kind of skill or dexterity, whether bodily or mental, in which persons can compete" as long as the result depends partly on such skill or dexterity.[3] However, if there is only a minimal degree of skill and winning does not depend to a "substantial degree" on the exercise of skill then one may still be caught by virtue of the promotion still amounting to an unlawful competition under Section 14 of the Act;

(c) *contribution by participants* – provided that entry into a promotion is free then it will not be a lottery. A word of caution however, as case law has established that other forms of contribution or valuable consideration will be sufficient to fulfil the test, even where no monetary payment is made. This could therefore include the purchase of a product as a requirement of entry; a practical obligation on participants to buy something; inviting participants to telephone a premium telephone number. In promotions where participants may enter online by using a local rate telephone line, this could arguably amount to making a contribution for these purposes although this has not yet been tested by the courts.

8.4 Are websites advertising? – the blurred distinction

8.4.1 Importance of distinction

The ASA has confirmed that the Advertising and Sales Promotions Codes apply to advertising within websites. Whilst, however, such rules will clearly apply to paid for advertising on websites in the same way as they apply to traditional media formats, it is less clear to what extent every commercial website and its content might be treated as advertising.

Increasingly websites include additional "editorial" material which goes beyond a straightforward promotion of the products and services it is offering. The ASA specifically states that the Codes "are primarily concerned with advertisements and promotions and not with terms of business, products themselves or other contractual matters".

Therefore in order to determine the extent to which both statutory and self-regulatory rules will apply, advertisers will need to try to distinguish between what is "advertising" and what is simply "editorial" or other material which is not intended to be caught by the rules.

8.4.2 Traditional definitions

Traditionally, advertising has been seen to include any direct or indirect promotion of products by implied or direct, written, spoken or visual means. Press releases, public relations material, editorial communications, product packaging and labels are, however, specifically excluded from the ambit of the Codes (although may well still be covered by relevant statutory and civil law).

---

[2]   *DDP v. Bradfute and Associates Ltd* [1967] 2QB291.

[3]   *Scott v. DDP* [1914 2KB 868].

8.4.3   *Traditional distinctions maintained by industry regulation*

BCASP requires advertisers, publishers and owners of media to ensure that advertisements are designed and presented in such a way that can be easily distinguished from editorial.

For broadcast advertisements Rule 10.6 of the Code of Advertising Standards and Practice for Television Advertising (the "ITC Code") also provides that no undue prominence should be given in any programme to a commercial product or service, and branded products may not as a general rule be referred to by the brand name or shown in close up. A number of other provisions in the ITC Code set out the principle that a distinction should be drawn between advertising and sponsored credits. The Periodical Publishers Association has also published guidelines requiring "special advertising sections" and "sponsored editorial" to be differentiated in magazines.

8.4.4   *Blurring of distinction*

Traditional distinctions maintained by current industry regulation become harder to apply in the case of advertising on the Internet, more detail of which is given in Sections 8.5 and 8.6 of this Chapter. Traditional concepts of advertising have been expanded to include:

(a) editorial material supporting lifestyle marketing which the advertiser hopes its brand will be associated with;

(b) material published by an advertiser on its commercial website which has no direct connection with the products or services it is offering but which promote a particular brand image;

(c) electronic versions of products such as newspapers and magazines.

Of course, the Internet is not the only media where distinctions are becoming blurred. Similar issues are beginning to emerge as brand benefits are developed through a variety of channels. For example, the lifestyle magazines which supermarkets and banks distribute to customers are sometimes linked closely to loyalty benefits whilst in other cases the connection is less clear cut.

8.4.5   *ASA approach*

In assessing what is or is not Internet advertising, a number of factors are likely to affect the ASA's decision in each case including:

(a) whether a website is clearly aimed at selling or promoting products or services;

(b) whether lifestyle material which is closely related to the products it is supporting is likely to amount to advertising; and

(c) whether references to events or activities sponsored by the advertiser are also likely to increase the chances of it being advertised.

8.5 Webvertising, e- and i-Marketing

8.5.1 *Banner advertising*

The most common form of advertising on the Internet is, of course, banner advertising (an advertisement placed on a website, usually at the top, which can function as a hypertext link between the website on which the banner is advertised and the website for the product which is being advertised). The benefits of using banner advertising on Internet websites is that the advertiser can pre-select his audience by linking the banner advertisement by cookie or key word search. For example if a banner advert is being shown on an Internet search page, if the user enters a key word search for "car" the list of websites generated may be prefaced with a banner ad for car related products, whereas a search for the key word "music" will have a list of websites prefaced by a music related banner.

However, this method of audience targeting is not without risk. It has in fact been tested in the courts of California when in 1999 Playboy lost its case against the search engines Excite and Netscape when the court ruled that the portal sites did not violate Playboy's trade marks by selling the key words to other companies to enable them to buy the banner adverts to advertise their own, often competing, products for such key words. Note the distinction here from misuse of another's trade mark through metatags, which in many cases may well amount to trade mark infringement.

8.5.2 *Interactive advertising*

As the use of digital technology advances, the distinction between traditional broadcast and Internet advertising becomes increasingly blurred. By way of example, the UK's first nationwide interactive advertisement was screened on Sky Digital in March 2000. The advert for a cook-in sauce, allowed viewers to call up a menu of recipes and have the chance to order a redeemable voucher using their remote controls via an icon on their TV screens. The interactive advert followed interactive trials in Manchester for a shampoo which asked viewers to answer questions about their lifestyle and hair and provide contact details in return for a personalised hair diagnosis and free product samples.

Through interactive adverts brand owners can gather detailed personal information about viewers, their brand preferences and loyalties which can then be used to tailor products and target adverts more effectively. Viewers benefit from the interactive adverts with the opportunity to request more information, compare alternatives and, for example, be rewarded with free samples or vouchers.

There is already some anxiety over the amount, use and ownership of data that is captured through interactive adverts. It raises questions regarding how the Information Commissioner will view such data and whether interactive adverts will have to display a notice stipulating how the data will be used? Advertisers may arguably have to set up their back end operations to process customer requests that their details be removed from company databases. Current best practice must surely be to take a view on whether personal data is being processed and comply accordingly.

The introduction of interactive advertising also throws up a number of other regulatory issues. Broadcast advertising in the UK is regulated by the Independent Television Commission (the "ITC") and has traditionally been regulated on the basis of time. The present ITC Rules on the Amount and Scheduling of Advertising state that digital TV adverts should only take up nine minutes per hour and that all advertisements must be clearly distinguishable from programme content. This may cause difficulties in the near future. Cable companies such as NTL are developing services which would allow the Internet to be accessed from television screens. If a channel wished to run banner adverts during a television programme in the style of present Internet adverts, it might breach the ITC Codes with respect to duration and the distinction between advertisements and programme content. In addition, if a viewer was able to click on a particular product on screen and was taken to the product's website this would pose further problems regarding potential sponsorship and product placement restrictions. However, the ITC indicated in a Consultation Paper published on 29 February 2000 that the further the viewer is taken away from the original programme, the less the imposition of strict regulatory controls is appropriate.

The ITC's consultation indicated its current intention to apply a light touch regulatory approach to interactive services. The document is the first indication of what the ITC considers the more effective, and perhaps the only, method of exerting regulatory control over the provision of interactive services which rely on or originate from proprietary technology distinct from broadcasting and television.

8.5.3   *Virtual advertising*

For several years companies have been supplying software which allows computer generated images to be inserted or more strictly "synthesised" onto television broadcasts. However, it is now much clearer what advertisers wishing to utilise such software can and cannot do. The benefits are obvious, whether signs on hoardings at sports events or product placements in TV shows, either can be tailored to audiences in specific geographic regions. A bottle of beer strategically placed in a scene from a syndicated TV series could carry almost any label. Rights holders could sell the space over and over again. However, there are potential drawbacks, covering an entire football pitch with a sponsor's logo would be likely to detract from the event itself.

In April 1998, the ITC bolstered its Code of Programme Sponsorship with brief but precise guidance notes on electronic imaging systems or "virtual advertising" as it is now known. Significantly, at the beginning of this year FIFA, the international football governing body, introduced detailed regulations to be applied to the use of virtual advertising at football matches.

A regulatory line was drawn in the UK in the form of a guidance note issued in April 1998 (No. 1: Electronic Imaging Systems or "Virtual" Advertising) which supplements Rule 13.5 of the ITC Code of Programme Sponsorship. The ITC guidance note requires the use of electronic imaging systems to be made transparent to viewers, either at the beginning or end of a broadcast that uses such a system. Explanatory credits are required stating for example that "this broadcast uses electronic imaging to replace some of the actual advertising billboards at the sports arena with advertising aimed at the UK market". Whilst not overly subtle it is arguably an example of mid to light touch regulation.

However, when read in conjunction with the guidance notes Rule 13.2 of the ITC Code of Programme Sponsorship is perhaps unnecessarily restrictive. The basic rule is that visual or oral references to any advertising, signage or branding at an event must be limited to what can clearly be justified by the editorial needs of the programme itself. On top of that, virtual advertising cannot be used to place advertising additional to that which is at an event nor to place advertisements on unused billboards or other sites. Should the technology permit, moving imagery can only be used on "virtual" billboards that replace actual advertising billboards that are themselves animated, and the ITC may require external verification of this use, although there is no outright restriction on virtual advertising technology being used to replace advertising on moving objects.

Finally, broadcasters must not in any way be involved in selling virtual advertising to advertisers or their agents. For the time being, in the UK at least, virtual advertising is likely to be limited to fulfilling the role of cheaper perimeter or on-pitch advertising. And if you are wondering why no mention has been made of virtual product placement, this is because it doesn't even get off the blocks owing to the blanket prohibition on product placement in Rule 12.1.

8.6   Impact of international rules

8.6.1   *Worldwide accessibility*

As mentioned above, advertising appearing on the Internet may, very well, be accessed simultaneously by users of the Internet worldwide. This raises two major issues:

(a) compliance of such advertising should technically be considered from an international point of view in terms of the legal and self-regulatory regimes which apply in all relevant countries, certainly those countries to whom the advertising is directed or trade conducted with; and

(b) the site/advertising should be amended/constructed accordingly.

Despite the European Commission efforts there is still no real standardisation across Europe. Advertisers should therefore consider the practical steps that can be taken to limit their international exposure.

8.6.2   *The practical approach*

General issues relating to the international nature of the Internet are dealt with in Chapter 6 of this Guide. It is however possible to identify certain practical steps which advertisers on the Internet can follow in order to limit their exposure as far as possible:

(a) stating clearly on the advertisement that it relates to goods or services supplied in the UK or other named jurisdictions where the legal position is known;

(b) limiting applications for interactive sales promotions from or concluding trade with jurisdictions where the legal position is unknown. The rules concerning prize competitions, for example, are more stringent in a number of other European countries than in the UK;

(c) avoiding obvious high risks by ensuring that advertising material is as non-contentious as possible. If a "contentious" approach (e.g. one which makes comparisons with or criticises products or businesses operating in a particular jurisdiction) is essential to the advertiser's marketing strategy then copy should be cleared everywhere that is likely to be relevant;

(d) determining whether any foreign rights in trade marks or other intellectual property rights have been infringed and stating that the advertisement relates only to goods and services supplied in the UK and other specified countries where trade mark clearance has been obtained;

(e) adhering to special rules in most jurisdictions on advertising (e.g. international securities, consumer credit, food and drink rules, competitions and lotteries). The Securities and Investment Board has stated that, in its opinion, the FS Act (Section 57) could apply to a person who is outside the UK but who runs a UK website that includes an "investment advertisement";

(f) obtaining insurance cover to the extent it is available in light of the nature of the website.

Whilst these steps may go some way towards limiting potential exposure, ultimately advertisers should be made aware that advertising on the Internet will inevitably mean that they are advertising in countries all over the world and any one or more of those countries may decide to assert jurisdiction.

8.7   Other liability

8.7.1   *Intellectual property*

8.7.1.1   *Roles of intellectual property in advertising*

Any advertising campaign carried out on the Internet will involve the creation and exploitation of intellectual property rights. Whilst intellectual property issues are dealt with in further detail elsewhere in this Guide, those involved in advertising must bear in mind the very specific implications for them.

The intellectual property rights involved in advertising on the Internet will range from the copyright in a particular page of the website used for a limited period (which may not be of significant value) through to the very valuable trade mark and other rights which can underpin a brand image which is the major asset of a consumer business.

Because advertising by its nature can require that a business's most valuable intellectual property rights be displayed it is vital for advertisers to consider carefully the threats which it may pose to the sanctity of those intellectual property rights.

8.7.1.2   *Copyright infringement*

The use of any work which qualifies for protection under the Copyright, Designs and Patents Act 1988 (the "CDPA") should also be avoided. This could cover the use of extracts of text, music, logos and icons, photographs and film clips from third party sources some of which may well have not been "cleared" with the relevant copyright owner. A particular concern in relation to Internet websites is the potential for copyright infringement through hypertext links to third party websites, particularly "deep" linking (links which bypass the home page or are otherwise unclear as to origin).

8.7.1.3   *Ease of copying and piracy*

Advertising material posted on the Internet may also, potentially, be downloaded worldwide. Where downloaded it may be printed and used or even amended and posted back on the Internet. The ease with which material on the Internet can be tampered with makes it all the more important for advertisers to ensure that they take basic precautions with regard to intellectual property.

8.7.1.4   *What to say*

Whilst, under UK law, copyright protection arises automatically, establishing the requisite proof of authorship can be a problem. In other jurisdictions, the position will not be so clear. In addition, it is not yet entirely clear what rights a user has to download and print copyright material from the Internet. Advertisers should therefore always include a clear and prominent statement as to ownership of the material appearing on its website (including requisite copyright and trade mark notices), responsibility for its contents and permitted use.

8.7.1.5   *Trade mark infringement*

Advertisers should check to ensure that the website does not contain the registered trade marks of third parties which may well have been included without consent. The Trade Marks Act 1994 (the "TMA") introduced some wide ranging changes to UK trade mark law and essentially made it possible to apply for registration of any mark "capable of graphical representation". This means that apart from the obvious word marks and logos, advertising straplines, slogans, shapes, colours and even smells are theoretically registrable.

The TMA does provide by virtue of Section 10(6) for an exemption to trade mark infringement, where one simply uses a mark for the purposes of identification subject to particular tests as to honesty and avoiding taking unfair advantage of or causing detriment to the repute of the mark in question.

If a mark is not registered there may still be liability for any use of a "well known" mark under Section 56 of the TMA.

8.7.1.6   *Passing off*

The common law tort of passing off is primarily aimed at preventing one trader from making representations about his goods or services which damage the goodwill of another regardless of any intention or negligence. The claimant must prove three key factors to succeed in the passing off action, namely that the claimant's had reputation or goodwill which was mis-represented or portrayed by the defendant so as to cause confusion which led to the claimant's loss or damage. The key essence of a passing off action is confusion that is, that customers have been, or are likely to be, mislead into thinking that claimant's goods or services are a third party's or in some way connected to a third party.

Advertisers should check to ensure that there are no references to any third party companies or service providers in a way which may suggest a connection if no formal arrangements exist. Furthermore, again hypertext links, unless pre-agreed and clearly "flagged", can be a source of confusion.

8.7.2   *Pricing – Consumer Protection Act 1987*

It is a criminal offence, pursuant to Section 20 of the Consumer Protection Act 1987 (the "CPA"), to give price indications to consumers (i.e. B2C; not B2B) which are or become misleading and which relate to the price of any goods, service, accommodation or facility.

A "misleading" price is any price indication that the price is less than in fact it is; or that the price does not depend on facts when it does; or where an additional charge is in fact made.

Additionally, an offence will also be committed if one gives a price indication which subsequently becomes misleading after it has been given if some or all of those consumers might reasonably be expected to rely on the indication at a time after it has become misleading; and one fails to take all such steps as are reasonable to prevent those consumers from relying on the indication.

Other key areas which often prove problematic are, for example, hidden extras (VAT, packaging and transport), failing to update prices which become out-of-date, and not quoting VAT inclusive prices to consumers. Certain products, such as mobile phones, hi-fi upgrades and tracking devices are notoriously problematic due to the amount of options available and related on-going contracts.

Care should also be taken with any use of the words "free", "bonus" or "only" in any promotional copy. As a breach of the CPA is a criminal offence, it should be noted that not only do companies risk being fined on a corporate level, but also any "consenting or conniving" directors or managers, or any other persons in positions of responsibility, involved risk personal fines and/or imprisonment.

8.7.3   *Product descriptions – Trade Descriptions Act 1968*

It is a strict liability offence to apply a false trade description to any goods in the course of trade or business. Under the Act any person who, in the course of a trade or business, either applies a false trade description to any goods or supplies or offers to supply any goods to which a false trade description is applied shall be guilty of an offence. A trade description is an indication, direct or indirect, and by whatever means given of any of the following matters with respect to any goods or parts of goods, that is to say quantity, size or gauge; method of manufacture, production, processing or reconditioning; composition; fitness for purpose, strength, performance, behaviour, or accuracy.

There is a defence of "innocent publication" available to a person who can show that he is a person whose business it is to publish or arrange for the publication of advertisements and that he received the advertisement for publication in the ordinary, course of business and did not know and had no reason to suspect that its publication would amount to any offence under this Act. This defence is not available to the advertiser responsible for creating the problematic material, although a company which can show it exercised due diligence to avoid committing an offence may have a defence.

The Trade Descriptions Act is enforced by Trading Standards Officers through both the Magistrates' and Crown Courts. Penalties can include a fine and/or imprisonment for up to two years.

8.7.4   *Data protection*

8.7.4.1   *Current regime*

An interactive advertising medium encourages the capture of data and accordingly increases the risks to advertisers of breaching data protection law. In the UK, the DPA 1998 regulates the activities of those who collect, hold and/or process personal data (data controllers), about living individuals from which the individual can be identified (data subjects). In essence it imposes requirements on data controllers to notify the Information Commissioner and to comply with the eight data protection principles, that personal data is:

(a) fairly and lawfully processed;

(b) processed for limited purposes and not in any manner incompatible with those purposes;

(c) adequate, relevant and not excessive;

(d) accurate;

(e) not kept for longer than is necessary;

(f) processed in line with the data subject's rights;

(g) held securely;

(h) not transferred outside the European Economic Area ("EEA") to countries without adequate protection

The Fair Processing Code includes requirements that data subjects are made aware that their personal data is being collected and the purposes for which it will be used.

8.7.4.2   *Notification*

Registration under the Data Protection Act 1984 has been replaced under the DPA 1998 by notification. All data controllers (with the exception of some not-for-profit organisations; those processing personal data for personal, family or household affairs; and data controllers who only process personal data for the maintenance of a public register) will need to notify the Information Commissioner. Notification is more general than the old system of registration. Data controllers have only one entry in which they are required to give broad outlines of the purposes of their processing; the personal data processed; the recipients of the personal data processed; the places overseas to which the data are transferred (if any of these are outside the EEA this must be expressly stated) and the security measures in place to protect the data. The information provided in a notification is less specific than that given under the coded categorisation used for registration. Data controllers must update their notification and pay the notification fee annually. All notification information is made publicly available in a register.[4]

8.7.4.3   *Collection and use of data*

Whenever activities involve interaction with individuals over the Internet, it is likely that processing of personal data will occur and such information may be collected by advertisers in a number of different ways both with and without the knowledge of the person providing it.

---

[4]   *See* http://www.dataprotection.gov.uk.

For example:

(a) collecting information directly from Internet users (e.g. when participants in a competition are required to provide their name and address);

(b) collecting information indirectly (e.g. when email addresses are obtained from those responding to a collectively sent message or by means of cookies); and

(c) users inputting data both about themselves and others (e.g. by means of newsgroups, bulletin boards and other public discussion fora).

8.7.4.4   *Application of the rules to such activities*

Many advertisers who use, or are planning to make use of, the Internet for certain activities will already have collected personal data as a result of more traditional form of advertising and will therefore be registered. However, advertisers will need to identify any changes which need to be made to reflect Internet use, in particular the implications of the potential for disclosure and transfer of data overseas. The basic principle should be that whenever personal data is collected, the data controller should make the data subject aware of the collection and processing of the data and the data subject should consent to the same (when collecting sensitive personal data the data subject's explicit consent is mandatory). All data collection and processing should be for a legitimate purpose and the amount of information should be restricted to a minimum.

8.7.4.5   *Security*

The Act requires an advertiser to take steps to ensure appropriate security for the protection of personal data held by them. The Internet is an inherently insecure environment and the network itself cannot be relied upon to provide protection from unauthorised access to, or disclosure of, personal data. An advertiser will need to assess what is "appropriate", having regard to the state of the art, the nature of the data and the damage that may result from improper use or disclosure. Practical steps will need to be developed in order to ensure that, as far as possible, the security of personal data is maintained. These might include:

(a) ensuring the reliability of staff collating and processing personal data;

(b) making use of password protection or anonymous access to the Internet network; or

(c) vetting all those who process personal data and ensuring that any services are provided under a written contract.

The Information Commissioner's office has expressed the view that a notice should be displayed on websites, warning the user that the Internet is not a secure system and that any personal data transmitted in this way may be accessed by third parties. The current view is that a so-called "data protection statement" should be used on screen where information is being sought from data subjects. All such disclaimers should be clear and precise. For example:

> "The Internet is not a secure system and your privacy cannot be guaranteed. You should not continue if you do not want your details to be stored on our database or processed by us for billing, marketing and promotional purposes [or an adequate description of the proposed use] and used by us [or third parties] within [and outside] the European Economic Area."

8.7.4.6   *Data protection statements*

To fulfill their obligations to those who visit their sites, advertisers should make clear:

(a) who is collecting the information;

(b) what information is being obtained;

(c) the purposes for which that information will be used; and

(d) the identity of any third parties to whom the information might be disclosed.

In the case of sensitive personal data, for example data regarding the data subject's racial or ethnic origin; political opinions; religious or other beliefs; trade union membership; health; sex life; criminal proceedings or convictions, data protection statements will need to be more explicit and express consent of the data subject will need to be obtained.

8.7.4.7   *US data protection and the safe harbor principles*

The data protection "safe harbor" became operational in the US at the beginning of November 2000. The US Department of Commerce and the European Commission had to come up with a way of dealing with the prohibitive provisions in the EU Data Protection Directive (95/46) relating to the transfer of personal data outside the EEA. The need arose because the EU does not feel that the US sectoral approach based on a mix of legislation, regulation and self-regulation (with the emphasis on the latter) protects personal data sufficiently to meet the requirements under the Directive that personal data should only be transferred to a non-EEA country if that country provides an "adequate" level of protection for that data.

Organisations that eventually do decide to participate in the safe harbor, (for the first four months from launch only 12 had done so) will essentially be required to self-certify annually that they agree to adhere to the safe harbor's requirements which take the form of seven core principles. Those doing so will then appear on a publicly available list of self-certified organisations maintained by the Department of Commerce. To qualify for the safe harbor, an organisation can either join a self-regulatory privacy programme that adheres to the requirements or, alternatively, develop its own self-regulatory privacy policy that conforms to the safe harbor. Cross indemnities will be prerequisites for data importer and exporter and, in addition to indemnification, the exporter should insist on proof of self-certification. Where the importing company is self certified rather than part of a certified scheme, its details will feature on the Department of Commerce list.

Self-certifying means complying with the seven safe harbor principles. These are notice (to individuals that their data is being collected and the purposes for which it will be used); choice (for the individual to opt out of the data collection); onward transfer (transfers to third parties) (informing individuals as to who their information will be transferred); access (of individuals to personal information held about them); security (to protect personal information from loss, misuse and unauthorised access, disclosure, alteration and destruction); data integrity (ensuring that data is reliable for its intended use, accurate, complete, and current); enforcement of the safe harbor principles, (using readily available and affordable independent recourse mechanisms and procedures for verifying that the commitments companies make to adhere to the safe harbor principles have been implemented; and obligations to remedy problems arising out of a failure to comply with the principles. As well as an effective dispute resolution system, organisations participating in the safe harbor must ensure that the sanctions which dispute resolution bodies can apply are severe enough to ensure compliance with the safe harbor principles).

In case the private sector cannot look after itself, the Federal Trade Commission or (eventually) other appropriate industry regulators in the US have underlying enforcement powers. Under the Federal Trade Commission Act, a company's failure to abide by commitments to implement the safe harbor principles might be considered deceptive and actionable by the FTC which also has the power to grant injunctions and issue fines up to $12,000 per day. Persistent failure to comply with the safe harbor will mean expulsion from the scheme and the Department of Commerce will indicate on the public list those specific organisations that have been guilty of persistent failure.

The European Parliament, which took a critical stance on the new US arrangements, plans to review the effectiveness of the Safe Harbor Agreement in late 2001 to determine what additional steps need to be taken to clear the path for legitimate personal data flows from the EU to the US and it is suspected that the European Commission will be disinclined and the European Parliament dead against any European concessions on the regulation of cross-border data flows.

8.7.5 *Spam*

Direct marketing opportunities facilitated by the Internet are obviously an attraction for advertisers. "Spam" however is not so popular. Spamming is the sending of unsolicited email for the purposes of commercial advertising, either to user groups or individuals. It is increasingly viewed as annoying as junk mail and according to a European Commission study is costing Internet users worldwide an estimated €10 billion in Internet Service Provider ("ISP") and telephone charges to download. It can clog up an ISP's service and can result in costs being incurred by both end-user and service provider, whilst costing the sender little either in money or effort.

In response to the rapid growth of spam, the email marketing industry is working with Internet users towards systems of data collection and exchange based on the express permission of the user. Implementing legal protection against unsolicited email has either gone for an "opt-in" or an "opt-out" regime. With opt-out potential recipients of marketing emails are asked to give an express indication that they do not wish to receive unsolicited information. Under the stricter opt-in system, unsolicited email cannot be sent unless the recipient has made a formal request to receive such information. Austria, Denmark, Finland, Italy and Germany have all adopted the opt-in approach. The UK on the other hand could not make up its mind which system to adopt and has chosen to rely currently on the self-regulatory schemes that are in place to provide the necessary protection.

The UK therefore remains without any clear regulation of unsolicited email. The DTI leaves it to consumers to register with the E-mail Preference Scheme. However, the UK's approach is likely to prove academic in the light of the Commission's proposal to update the Telecommunications Data Protection Directive as part of the general re-organisation of legislation in the communications sector announced in July 2000. The proposal favours the opt-in approach, as from the industry viewpoint the more effective and viable method of data collection and from the point of view of the consumer the method most conducive to e-confidence.

8.7.5.1 *What initiatives are in place to tackle the problem of spamming?*

Industry self-regulatory initiatives, for example, Direct Marketing Association ("DMA") initiatives in the US and EU with Electronic Mail Preference Service ("e-MPS"). EU legislation, specifically the Distance Selling Directive 97/7/EC and the E-Commerce Directive.

8.7.5.2 *Arguments for opt-out/opt-in*

General interpretation is that Directive wording implies opt-out. Recent EU-based Telecommunications Data Protection Regulations in a number of implementing States use opt-out The Direct Marketing Association preference system e-MPS is based upon the opt-out principle. The reason for this choice is that opt-out is seen as placing less burdens on industry (i.e. those wishing to market directly).

If the opt-in option is to be used, although this places the costs burden on recipients and ISPs who carry the mail, it also means that there are more restrictive burdens on unscrupulous traders, and it may actively encourage e-commerce development through enhanced consumer confidence. Inclusion of a name in an opt-out list runs the risk of unscrupulous marketers actually targeting that individual (i.e. the precise opposite of the intended effect).

8.7.5.3 *What does the E-Commerce Directive propose?*

It requires that any unsolicited email be clearly identifiable as such as soon as it is received by the recipient. In addition, national governments shall ensure that users of this tool consult opt-out registers containing details of those persons who do not wish to be contacted in this manner before any communication is sent.

If the problem remains, however, what further measures might need to be taken?

Should the measures in the E-Commerce Directive not prove sufficiently effective, it is likely that further legislation will be brought forward. Possible measures include efforts to enforce service provider contracts to prevent the sending of unsolicited bulk email, prohibiting "spoofing" (misrepresentation of the origin of email) to aid the tracking of spammers and, if necessary, extending the EU Telecommunications Data Protection Directive (97/66) provisions to the use of email.

8.7.5.4 *What measures are ISP's taking, if any?*

There are frequently ISP Terms and Conditions prohibiting Spamming from/via the ISP portals and abusers can have their account terminated. Certain ISP's in the US have examined acquiring software which would filter out spamming to email addresses under their control.

8.7.5.5 *Have any initiatives arisen from the US?*

In the US, there is a similar conflict between an opt-out and opt-in approach. The conflict is primarily between those who wish to seek legislation to deal with the problem (various groups of Internet users and ISP's) and the trade association of those who use spamming as a business tool, the DMA which favours a system of self regulation. It seems likely that the former's approach will succeed, particularly as a series of bills are currently being considered by the US Congress which would seek to make spamming much more difficult.

In contrast the DMA argues that an approach where consumers can opt-out by registering at a website (www.e-mps.org) their preference not to receive unsolicited marketing email is the appropriate solution to this problem.

8.7.5.6 *So what is the position currently regarding spam?*

Legislators in the US and Europe are seeking to enact measures which will make it increasingly difficult to rely on unsolicited email as a marketing tool. However, best practice remains to consider your home country and target country rules and self-regulatory initiatives on spamming and comply with them. In most cases this means identifying the email as coming from the business in question and clearly regarding a promotional offer. Also checks should be made against your own opt-out lists as well as any national or international lists. In the event that laws on this point do come into effect on this point additional advice should be sought.

8.7.6 *Distance selling*

8.7.6.1 *The EU Directive and the UK Regulations*

The Internet is increasingly becoming recognised as a marketplace for goods and services as well as a medium for the exchange of information. In the context of consumer transactions for goods and services which are concluded over the Internet, practitioners will need to consider the impact of the Consumer Protection (Distance Selling) Regulations 2000 which implement EU Directive 97/7/EC on distance selling. The Regulations afford a number of safeguards to consumers in so-called distance contracts for goods and services where there is no simultaneous physical presence of both the supplier and the customer. The adoption of the Directive is a notable advance in the area of European wide rules applicable to web marketing activities.

8.7.6.2 *Transactions*

The Regulations cover the supply of goods and/or services to consumers and apply to all contracts save for certain exemptions for example, for property, financial services or auctions. Some of the Regulations will not apply to contracts relating to the deliveries of food or beverages, transport, accommodation, catering or leisure services provided on specific dates.

However, the position will not always be straightforward. Where a sale is made in the course of a telephone call in response to a newspaper advertisement inviting such calls, the Directive will apply. It is however unlikely to apply when a face-to-face contract follows up.

8.7.6.3 *Main provisions of the Directive*

Customers must be provided with certain information including:

(a) the name and address of the supplier;

(b) the main characteristics of the goods, their price and any additional delivery costs or other charges; and

(c) (in most cases) that they have at least seven working days to withdraw from the contract without penalty or cause.

This information must be clearly presented in writing before a distance contract is concluded although certain types of contract (including those for financial services) are excluded. Failure to provide such information before contracting will extend the seven day cooling-off period during which a consumer can cancel a contract without reasonable penalty, in the case of goods starting with the date of delivery, and for services seven days from the day on which the consumer agreed to go ahead with the contract. The cooling-off period only begins once all correct information has been provided to the consumer. If the consumer chooses to exercise his right to return the goods or cancel the services during the cooling-off period the consumer is not obliged to return the goods to the supplier, such obligation can only be addressed through careful drafting of terms and conditions.

In addition, suppliers must, in performing such contracts:

(a) fulfil orders within 30 days;

(b) provide consumers with a refund within 30 days if goods are unavailable or have been returned during the cooling-off period; and

(c) expressly reserve the right to substitute goods of equivalent quality and price in advance if they wish to do so.

The Regulations also ban the supply of unsolicited goods or services to consumers. Anyone found guilty of this offence may be fined up to £2,500. Where the supply of unsolicited goods or services is accompanied by a demand for payment, or threatening legal action, placing a consumer on a list of debtors or threatening or invoking a collection procedure, the fine is up to £5,000 per offence. It should be noted that it goes wider than the current provisions of the Unsolicited Goods and Services Act 1971, which covers only a limited number of services.

8.8   Structure of a site

8.8.1   *Implications of legal rules for design of sites*

Traditionally, regulations and codes of practice assume separate and distinct images and these rules may be difficult to apply to a medium where links between different images are seamless. Existing advertising copy should be checked once it has been reformatted for Internet use, to confirm that its presentation and content remains suitable in the context of a new medium. In traditional forms of advertising media, it may have been possible to segment markets for different products whereas advertising on the Internet is potentially accessible to all groups in society including adults and children, consumers and trade customers. Where previously, advertising may have complied with self-regulatory codes relating to specific market segments, it should now comply with all relevant rules. Advertisers should ensure that advertising material is clear as to who it is addressed to in order to avoid, as far as possible, any unwanted attention from foreign enforcement authorities.

8.8.2 *Health warnings*

Bearing in mind the substantial risks which can be involved in advertising on the Internet, all relevant health warnings should appear prominently in positions where they are most likely to be seen and read. There are, in addition, certain requirements under industry specific legislation, including the Consumer Credit Act 1974 and FS Act, which prescribe the way in which some health warnings must appear. Existing advertising material which has been reformatted for use on the Internet should be checked in its new format to ensure that it remains compliant.

8.8.3 *Exclusions and limits on liability*

Where products or services are offered directly within Internet advertising, the advertiser must consider the terms (particularly any limitations or exclusions of liability of the advertiser) which should apply to the supply of those items. Once the order has been placed by respondents to advertising it will be too late to seek to qualify the advertiser's responsibility or to impose additional requirements on the respondent (e.g. to make payment in a particular way).

8.8.4 *Data protection statements*

Individual screen formats should be reviewed to ensure that data protection statements appear in close proximity to the information being obtained and in a way so that it is not possible for the user to send the information without seeing these notices.

8.8.5 *Presentation*

Advertisers should be encouraged always to make "health warnings" as prominent as possible. In addition, in certain areas there will be additional statutory requirements concerning the form, content and placing of such statements.

It is unlikely to be practically or commercially acceptable to include the full text of every "health warning" and other editorial guidelines on every screen of text within a website. Use can be made of hypertext links whereby users are alerted to the existence of additional rules and given the opportunity to view them in full by means of the hypertext link. However, if this approach is followed the existence and nature of the link should be drawn to the attention of the user of a site at every possible opportunity. Advertisers should avoid actively discouraging users to read such warnings.

8.9 Using specialist agencies

8.9.1 *Contractual arrangements*

Businesses using the Internet as a medium for advertising their goods and services are likely to make use of one or more specialist agencies to develop and manage advertising on their behalf. These might include arrangements with design agencies, sales promotion houses, direct marketing and advertising agencies, as well as media buying houses.

In all cases, it is advisable that formal written contracts are in place between advertisers and the specialist agencies they use and that such contracts clearly define the scope of the work which the agency is expected to carry out, as well as allocating acceptable levels of risk between the parties. The Institute of Practitioners in Advertising (the "IPA") has published a model contract which serves as a useful checklist as to the types of issues which need to be covered in an advertising agency contract. However, in most cases a directly tailored contract should be drawn up, particularly to cover novel or specific issues typically present for an Internet campaign.

8.9.2　　Key terms

Either way, the principal matters to be covered in a contract for the creation of advertising on a website should cover at least the following:

(a) *the scope of work contracted for* – the basic distinction within the industry is between appointments for a specific project and for all encompassing retainer covering all requirements for a certain period. This will be important in that it will establish whether there is any element of exclusivity in the appointment;

(b) *the basis of remuneration* – the traditional commission-based approach (which is in decline in the advertising industry generally) is unlikely to be appropriate in this field;

(c) *the ownership of intellectual property rights* – clarification as to who will own intellectual property rights in material created by the agency and responsibility for obtaining any consents necessary to use material which incorporates intellectual property rights owned by third parties. It is vital for the advertiser to obtain all rights necessary to use work so that it cannot be held to ransom by the agency if it considers it important to change; and

(d) *allocating responsibility for ensuring the legality of the advertising content and compliance with self-regulatory codes* – this will to some extent depend on the relative expertise of the parties. Notwithstanding, the agreed responsibility allocation it may be more efficient for the advertiser itself to undertake compliance rather than pay for an agency who is new to a particular industry to do so. In the context of Internet advertising it will be important to establish the jurisdiction and scope of compliance work. In any event, agencies will be likely to resist any attempts to fix them with liability if the advertiser is to be responsible for campaign content or otherwise insists on a final say on the advertising.

Chapter 9
SELLING AT A DISTANCE

Margaret Jordan, Partner
Nieves La Casta, Professional Support Lawyer
Lovells Boesebeck Droste

9.1   The Distance Selling Directive – introduction

Directive 97/7/EC on the protection of consumers in respect of distance contracts[1] was adopted on 20 May 1997 after a long process that started with the adoption of a first proposal by the European Commission in April 1992 and followed a painstaking and complicated co-decision procedure, resulting in three readings by the European Parliament and the Council of Ministers.

According to Article 15 of the Directive, Member States had three years to implement the provisions of the Directive into national law, and the UK did so with the adoption of the Consumer Protection (Distance Selling) Regulations 2000 which entered into force on 31 October 2000[2] (the "Distance Selling Regulations"). The Department of Trade and Industry (the "DTI") consulted extensively before preparing the final version of the regulations and will shortly be placing guidance notes for businesses on its website.

The introduction of new technologies means that consumers can now obtain information about, and place orders for, goods and services available anywhere in the European Union. However, Member States have taken different or divergent measures to protect consumers in respect of distance selling. The purpose of Directive 97/7 is to guarantee the free movement of goods and services for private individuals and, in order to achieve this goal, the Directive introduces at community level a minimum set of common rules in the area of distance selling. This means that consumers will be able to have access to goods and services in another Member State on the same terms as the population of that state. It should however be stressed that, according to Article 14 of the Directive, Member States may introduce more stringent provisions to ensure a higher level of consumer protection, including a ban on the marketing of certain goods or services, particularly medicinal products, within their territory, by means of distance selling, provided that the more stringent provisions are compatible with the provisions of the EC Treaty.

9.2   Scope of application

According to Article 2, the Directive applies to "any contract concerning goods or services concluded between a supplier and a consumer under an organised distance sales or service scheme run by the supplier, who, for the purpose of the contract, makes exclusive use of one or more means of distance communication up to and including the moment at which

---

[1]   OJ L 144/19 of 4 June 1997.

[2]   SI 2000 No. 2334.

the contract is concluded". A "consumer" is defined as any natural person who is acting for purposes which are outside his trade, business or profession. It is clear from these definitions that the Directive does not apply to business-to-business contracts or to one-off distance contracts or to contracts not entered into in the context of an organised distance-selling scheme.

The same article defines "means of distance communication" as any means which, without the simultaneous physical presence of the supplier and the consumer, may be used for the conclusion of a contract between those parties. Annex I of the Directive provides a non-exhaustive list of "means of communication", namely:

(a) unaddressed printed matter;

(b) addressed printed matter;

(c) standard letter;

(d) press advertising with order form;

(e) catalogue;

(f) telephone with human intervention;

(g) telephone without human intervention (automatic calling machine, audiotext);

(h) radio;

(i) videophone (telephone with screen);

(j) videotex (microcomputer and television screen) with keyboard or touch screen;

(k) email;

(l) facsimile machine;

(m) television (teleshopping).

This Directive was finalised in 1997, slightly before the e-commerce boom, but it is clear that it covers commerce through the Internet.

In Article 3 the Directive exempts certain types of contracts from the application of its provisions, namely contracts:

(a) in relation to financial services. A non-exhaustive list of these is given in Annex II of the Directive and includes investment services, banking services, insurance and reinsurance operations, and operations relating to dealings in futures and options (*see* Section 9.4 below);

(b) concluded by means of automatic vending machines or automated commercial premises;

(c) concluded with telecommunications operators through the use of public payphones;

(d) concluded for the construction and sale of immovable property or relating to other immovable property rights, except for rental;

(e) concluded at an auction.

Furthermore, some of the most important provisions of the Directive, such as the provisions on information, written confirmation, right of withdrawal and time limits, do not apply to certain contracts, such as the contracts for the supply of foodstuffs, beverages or other goods intended for everyday consumption supplied to the home of the consumer, his residence or his workplace by regular roundsmen or to contracts for the provisions of accommodation, transport, catering or leisure services where the contract is concluded to provide these services on a specific date or within a specific period. This makes practical sense given that the products may, for example, have a limited shelf life, which would make the right of withdrawal impossible (*see* Section 9.3.3 below).

9.3   Main provisions of the Directive

9.3.1   *Information*

One of the main features of the Directive, established in Article 4, is the requirement that the supplier must provide extensive information to the consumer prior to a contract being concluded. This information has to be provided "in good time" prior to the conclusion of the distance contract and "in a clear and comprehensible manner". The supplier must also ensure that the information is provided with due regard to the principles of good faith. Moreover, in the case of telephone communications, the identity of the supplier and the commercial purpose of the call shall be made explicitly clear at the beginning of the conversation.

In particular, Article 4 requires the following information to be provided:

(a) the identity of the supplier and, in the case of contracts requiring payment in advance, his address;

(b) the main characteristics of the goods or services;

(c) the price of the goods or services including all taxes;

(d) delivery costs, where appropriate;

(e) the arrangements for payment, delivery or performance;

(f) the existence of a right of withdrawal;

(g) the cost of using the means of distance communication, where it is calculated other than at the basic rate;

(h) the period for which the offer or the price remains valid;

(i) where appropriate, the minimum duration of the contract in the case of contracts for the supply of products or services to be performed permanently or recurrently.

9.3.2   *Written confirmation*

Most of the information required by Article 4 must, according to Article 5 of the Directive, be received in a "durable medium available and accessible" to the consumer in good time during the performance of the contract, and at least by the time of delivery, unless the information has already been given to the consumer in an appropriate durable medium available or accessible to him. The Directive does not define what a "durable medium" is, so there is bound to be some debate as to whether for instance, an email communication constitutes a durable medium in all the jurisdictions for these purposes or if written details are to be sent along with the goods or sent by more traditional means.

The DTI takes the view that fax and email are durable media in the sense that it is open to the consumer to retain the information, which is not of course the case with information provided verbally. According to the DTI, what current or future means of communication will meet this test is ultimately a question of community law.[3]

In any event, the confirmation must contain:

(a) written information on how to exercise the right of withdrawal (*see* Section 9.3.3 below);

(b) the address of the place of business of the supplier (to which the consumer may address any complaints);

(c) information on after sales service and any guarantees;

(d) details of how to cancel the contract, where it is of unspecified duration or a duration exceeding one year.

9.3.3 *Right of withdrawal*

Consumers are further protected by Article 6, which confers on consumers a mandatory right of withdrawal from the contract within a period of seven working days, without any penalty and without giving any reason. This is the so-called "cooling-off" period and is the most important aspect of consumer protection contained in the Directive. Recital 14 of the Directive explains that the reason for creating this right of withdrawal is the fact that the consumer is not able actually to see the product or ascertain the nature of the service provided before concluding the contract.

When the right of withdrawal is exercised:

(a) the supplier shall be obliged to reimburse the sums paid by the consumer and the only charge that may be made to the consumer is the direct cost of returning the goods;

(b) the reimbursement must be carried out as soon as possible and in any case within 30 days (Article 6(2)).

The seven-day cooling-off period is calculated:

(a) in the case of goods, from the day of receipt by the consumer where the obligations laid down in Article 5 have been fulfilled;

(b) in the case of services, from the day of conclusion of the contract or, if Article 5 is complied with after the conclusion of the contract, from that date, provided that it is within three months after the completion of the contract.

If the supplier fails to supply the information as required by Article 5, then the period within which the right of withdrawal can be exercised shall be three months instead of seven days. The calculation of the three-month period shall begin:

(a) in the case of goods from the day of receipt by the consumer;

(b) in the case of services, from the day of conclusion of the contract.

---

[3]   DTI press release P/2000/707 of 27 October 2000.

However, if the information referred to in Article 5 is supplied within this three-month period, the seven-day cooling-off period shall begin as from that moment (Article 6(1)).

According to the Distance Selling Regulations there is no prescribed form of notice of withdrawal (or cancellation as it is referred to in the Regulations). Anything that indicates the intention of the consumer to cancel the contract is sufficient. However, it must be in writing or in another durable medium accessible or available to the supplier. In giving notice, the consumer may use the address, facsimile number or email address last known to him (Regulation 10). Where a notice of cancellation is given, this notice shall also have the effect of cancelling any related credit arrangement (Regulation 15).

The consumer has a duty to retain possession of the goods and to take reasonable care of them until they are collected, provided that the supplier notifies the consumer of when they are to be collected, within 21 days of cancellation. Alternatively the consumer may return the goods at his own expense. If a term requiring the consumer to return the goods on cancellation has been included in the contract the consumer is under a duty to take reasonable care of them for six months (Regulation 17).

It should be stressed that the right to cancel is in addition to other rights and applies regardless of the state of the goods and whether the supplier has complied with the contract. If the consumer has a right to reject the goods under the contract, for example because they do not comply with the description or because they are delivered late, the supplier may not charge for the recovery of the goods. Similarly, if the term requiring the consumer to return the goods is unfair under the Unfair Terms in Consumer Contracts Regulations 1999 (and hence unenforceable), no charge may be made for the return of the goods. This might arise, for example, if statements in advertising suggest that the goods can be returned free of charge or if the description of the goods was insufficient (Regulation14).

Unless the parties have agreed otherwise, the right of withdrawal cannot be exercised in respect of contracts (Article 6(3) of Directive and Regulation 13):

(a) for the provision of services if performance has begun, with the consumer's agreement, before the end of the cancellation period. Implied agreement may be sufficient;

(b) for the supply of goods or services the price of which is dependent on fluctuations in the financial market which cannot be controlled by the supplier;

(c) for the supply of goods made to the consumer's specifications or clearly personalised or which, by reason of their nature, cannot be returned or are liable to deteriorate or expire rapidly;

(d) for the supply of audio or video recordings or computer software which were unsealed by the consumer;

(e) for the supply of newspapers, periodicals and magazines;

(f) for gaming and lottery services.

9.3.4 *Performance of the contract*

According to Article 7, the supplier must execute the contract within 30 days of the contract's conclusion. The parties can agree to a longer or a shorter time period for performance.

If the supplier fails to deliver because of the unavailability of goods or services, the consumer is entitled to a refund within 30 days of the specified or agreed performance date. Nevertheless, Member States may lay down that the supplier may provide the consumer with goods or services of equivalent quality and price provided that this possibility was provided for prior to the conclusion of the contract or in the contract. The consumer shall be informed of this possibility in a clear and comprehensible manner. The cost of returning the goods following exercise of the right of withdrawal shall, in this case, be borne by the supplier, and the consumer must be informed of this.

9.3.5   Enforcement

Article 11(1) of the Directive requires the Member States to ensure compliance with the Directive in the interests of consumers. Therefore the consequences of non-compliance will turn on the type and extent of any sanctions imposed by national legislation.

In order to reinforce the protection provided to consumers, the Directive imposes an obligation for Member States to include provisions whereby public bodies or their representatives, consumer organisations having a legitimate interest in protecting consumers or professional organisations having a legitimate interest in acting, may take action before the courts or before the competent administrative bodies (Article 11(2) of the Directive).

Member States may stipulate that the burden of proof concerning the existence of prior information, written confirmation, compliance with time limits or consumer consent, can be placed on the supplier (Article 11(3) of the Directive), the reason being that in the use of new technologies, the consumer is not in control of the means of communications used (Recital 22 of the Directive).

In the UK any term in a contract which is inconsistent with a provision in the Regulations for protection of the consumer is void (Regulation 25).

The Distance Selling Regulations are enforced by the Director General of Fair Trading and by the weights and measures authorities. They have a duty to consider complaints made to them about breaches of the Regulations and may apply to court for injunctions to enforce the Regulations. Suppliers may be asked to give undertakings in order to avoid injunctions being applied for. The Director General of Fair Trading will publish details of undertakings given and orders made under the Regulations, including the names of the relevant suppliers (Regulations 26 to 29).

Member States shall take the measures needed to ensure that suppliers and operators of means of communication, where they are able to do so, cease practices which do not comply with measures adopted pursuant to this Directive.

Furthermore, Member States may provide for voluntary supervision by self-regulatory bodies of compliance with the provisions of the Directive and recourse to such bodies for the settlement of disputes to be added to the means which Member State must provide to ensure compliance with the directive.[4]

---

[4]   This paragraph reflects the so-called e-confidence strategy of the European Commission, that is trying to encourage alternative dispute resolutions ("ADRs"). A big step in this direction is the proposal to set up a European Extra-Judicial Network ("EEJ-Net"), the aim being to have recourse to courts only as a last resort.

9.3.6   *Waiver*

It is worth noting that under Article 12 of the Directive, a consumer may not waive the rights conferred on him as a result of the transposition of the Directive into Member States' law. Also, the Article provides that a consumer does not loose the protection granted by the Directive by virtue of the choice of law of a non-EU country as the law applicable to the contract, as long as the contract has close connection with the territory of one or more Member States. In other words, a supplier cannot seek to circumvent the Directive by stating in an advertisement or contract that the law of a non-Member State is the applicable law of the contract (*see* also Regulation 25(5)). Quite how effective this would be will depend on the choice of jurisdiction clause and choice of law made. For instance, the claimed applicable law of a non-Member State might provide that it is to take precedence over any other law, including EU law.

9.3.7   *Other provisions*

Other provisions of the Directive and the Distance Selling Regulations that are of interest are as follows:

(a) *Restriction on the use of certain means of distance communication* – in accordance with Article 10 of the Directive the consumer's prior consent is required for the use of automated calling systems and unsolicited faxes (i.e. for unsolicited commercial communications from business to consumers by phone, fax or email, the consumer must "opt-in"). All other means of distance communication can only be used where there is no clear objection of the consumer (i.e. the consumer needs to "opt-out"). The Distance Selling Regulations do not specifically implement Article 10 of the Directive. In the case of phone and fax, implementation has already been made by means of the Telecommunications (Data Protection and Privacy) Regulations 1999. For mail and email the DTI considers that the self-regulatory schemes that are currently in place provide the necessary protection. Legislation is already in place covering the abuse of personal data – and the majority of email addresses may fall within this definition. There are a number of schemes which allow consumers to register their wish not to receive unsolicited marketing materials or calls.

(b) *Payment by card* – appropriate measures must exist to allow consumers to request cancellation of a payment where fraudulent use has been made of his payment card in connection with a distance contract and, in the event of fraudulent use, to be re-credited with the sums paid or have them returned (Article 8 and Regulation 21). These new rules also amend the Consumer Credit Act so that the consumer can no longer be made liable to pay the first £50 when his credit or debit card is used fraudulently.

(c) *Inertia selling* – Member States shall take the measures necessary to prohibit the supply of goods or services to a consumer, which have not been ordered by the consumer beforehand, where such supply involves a demand for payment. Member States must also exempt the consumer from the provision of any consideration in cases of unsolicited supply, the absence of a response not constituting consent (Article 9). In the UK, the Distance Selling Regulations replace parts of the Unsolicited Goods and Services Act 1971 so that the rules on unsolicited goods sent for non-business use are tightened. Under the Regulations the goods become an unconditional gift to the recipient immediately on receipt. The following actions are offences, if committed in relation to unsolicited goods or services supplied other than for business purposes, unless there is reasonable cause to believe that there was a right to payment (e.g. because it was believed that the recipient requested the goods or services):

(i) demanding payment, or asserting a right to payment;

(ii) threatening legal proceedings to obtain payment;

(iii) putting the recipient on a list of defaulters or debtors or threatening to do so;

(iv) invoking any other collection procedure or threatening to do so (Regulations 22 to 24).

(d) *The languages used for distance contracts are a matter for the Member States (Recital 8 of the Directive)* – this may cause problems in assessing exactly what businesses must do in order to comply with the Directive. It would be wise for the supplier to provide the information required by the Directive in the languages of the Member States to which it is targeting its sales; no easy task when marketing on the Internet.

9.4 The proposed Directive on Distance Marketing of Financial Services – introduction

Although it was the Commission's wish that financial services should be included in the Distance Selling Directive, after a great deal of argument within the Council, the proposal was dropped and financial services were excluded from its scope of application. Accordingly, Article 3 of Directive 97/7 specified that it shall not apply to financial services and its Annex II established a non-exhaustive list of such services (*see* Section 9.2).

However, shortly after the Distance Selling Directive was adopted, and in order to rectify this legal omission, the Commission launched a consultation process on whether or not there was a need for a Distance Selling Directive for the financial services sector and, not surprisingly, this resulted in the Commission concluding that such a directive was desirable.

In the Summer of 1997, not one but two drafts of the Directive were circulating informally. They had been produced by two different Directorates General at the European Commission and took diametrically different approaches to regulation.

At that time, it appeared to many spectators that the Commission was divided on the question of whether or not there should be such legislation and, if so, what it should say.

Subsequently, in November 1997 a single revised (but still unofficial) draft emerged, which appeared to have the sanction of both warring factions. It had a number of similarities with the General Distance Selling Directive, but had two provisions in it specific to the financial services industry and contained suggestions such as introducing objective dispute/complaint procedures (to the extent that banks did not already have them) which was pretty unlikely in the UK, given the requirements, at least for the retail end of the market, for complaint procedures to be provided and publicised under the Banking Code of Practice (Revised Edition 1998, effective from 31 March 1999).

The November 1997 document metamorphosed into the "official" draft that was finally adopted by the Commission on 14 October 1998[5] and received its first reading in the European Parliament on 5 May 1999.[6] The Commission then adopted an Amended Proposal on 23 July 1999, taking account of a number of the amendments suggested by the European Parliament.[7]

The Commission's "Action Plan for the Financial Markets" issued in May 1999, indicated that the Commission at that time hoped to see political agreement on this initiative before the end of 1999, with adoption in the year 2000. The draft text itself provides that Member States are required to bring into force the laws, regulations and administrative provisions necessary to comply with the Directive by 30 June 2002, at the latest. In the Financial Services, Priorities and Progress Third Report, adopted on 8 November 2000, this proposal is considered by the Commission as a priority and the Commission still expected a political agreement and adoption of the Directive by the end of 2000.[8] The proposal was last examined in the Internal Market Council that took place on 12 March 2001.

The aim of the proposal is to ensure a high level of protection for consumers of retail financial services marketed by telephone, by electronic means such as the Internet or by mail, so as to encourage consumer confidence in such services and provide financial service suppliers with a clearly defined legal framework valid for distance selling throughout the Internal market without hindrance. The proposal takes into account the specific nature of these services. The rules are intended to complement, not replace, existing rules applying to financial services and rules concerning privacy and data protection will not be affected.

The proposal follows the same structure as the Distance Selling Directive but, unlike that Directive, this Proposal is based on a "maximum harmonisation" approach with the intention that rules in this area should be totally harmonised throughout the EU. Member States, therefore, cannot adopt stricter rules. Certain Member States – in particular France and Finland – are opposed to this approach, as it will not allow them to impose stricter standards than the minimum rules set out in the Directive.

9.5 Scope of application

Article 1(1) of the Amended Proposal lays down the general objective of the Directive, which is to approximate the laws, regulations and administrative provisions of the Member States concerning the distance marketing of consumer financial services. The Proposal is specifically designed only to regulate the method of selling financial services and its provisions in no way regulate the contents of such services.

Article 1(2) specifies that, in the case of contracts for financial services comprising successive operations or a series of separate operations performed over time, the provisions of the Directive shall apply only to the first operation, irrespective of whether those operations are deemed by national law to form part of a single contract or individual separate contracts. The explanatory memorandum of the original Proposal clarifies the

---

5   COM (1998) 468 final, OJ C385/10, 11 December 1998.

6   OJ C279/197, 1 October 1999.

7   COM (1999) 385 final, OJ No C177E /21, 27 June 2000.

8   COM(2000)692/2 Final.

meaning of this paragraph. A financial service involving a series of successive operations or a series of separate operations may give rise to different legal interpretations depending on the law of the Member State. To ensure the Directive does not unnecessarily impinge on national law, it will only apply to the first operation. Thus, for example, opening a bank account at a distance constitutes a contract to which the rules of the Directive would apply. However, subsequent operations by consumers in connection with this account (transfers, cash withdrawals, etc.) would constitute operations in the performance of this contract, so they would not be subject to the Directive.

Article 2 of the Amended Proposal establishes the definitions. "Distance contract" means any contract concerning financial services concluded between a supplier and a consumer under an organised distance sales or service-provision scheme run by the supplier, who, for the purpose of that contract, makes exclusive use of means of distance communication up to and including the time at which the contract is concluded. This definition, as well as the definitions of "consumer", "supplier" and "means of communication" are the same as in Directive 97/7. The Proposal does not include, however, an exhaustive list of the means concerned and it opts for a flexible and technologically neutral definition, which can be adapted to future technical developments.

The most important notion is that of "financial services", which refers to any banking, insurance, investment or payment service. This definition is very broad in order to ensure that all financial services liable to be offered to consumers are covered. An annex with an indicative list of financial services which formed part of the original proposal has been removed in order to avoid misunderstandings. A new definition was also introduced in the Amended Proposal, namely "real estate credit" in order to respond to the need expressed by the European Parliament to establish particular provisions for this type of credit. "Real estate credit" means any credit, irrespective of any surety or bond attached thereto, mainly intended to permit the acquisition or maintenance of property rights in a site or a building to be constructed or under construction, or the renovation or improvement of a building.

Finally, Article 2 contains, in contrast to the silence of Directive 97/7, a definition of "durable medium" (*see* Section 9.6.2).

9.6 Main provisions of the Directive

9.6.1 Information

As in the general Distance Selling Directive, the consumer must receive certain information prior to the conclusion of the contract, the idea being to draw up a list of information items which have added value in the context of a distance contract for the supply of financial services. This list is in line with existing rules in the sectoral directives (concerning non-life insurance, life insurance, OCITS, prospectuses and investment). Accordingly, Article 3 of the Directive provides that, in good time before conclusion of the contract, consumers shall be provided with information concerning:

(a) the identity and address of the supplier and the identity and address of the representative of the supplier in the consumer's country of residence whom he can consult where necessary, if such a representative exists;

(b) a description of the main characteristics of the financial service;

(c) the total price of the financial service, including all taxes;

(d) the arrangements for payment, delivery or performance of the contract;

(e) the period for which the offer or the price remains valid;

(f) when the price is liable to vary between the time the information is provided and the time the contract is concluded, an indication of this possibility and particulars allowing the consumer to verify the price at the time of conclusion of the contract;

(g) the cost of using the means of distance communication, where it is calculated other than at the basic rate;

(h) the existence and duration of a right of withdrawal and the conditions and procedures governing its exercise;

(i) the absence of a right of withdrawal for certain financial services;

(j) the amount to be paid or the amount used for calculating the price to be paid by the consumer if he exercises his right of withdrawal;

(k) where appropriate, the minimum duration of the contract, in the case of financial services to be performed permanently or recurrently;

(l) information on cancelling the contract;

(m) the law applicable to the contract, when there is a contractual clause which makes it possible to choose a law other than that of the consumer's place of residence;

(n) the court having jurisdiction in the event of a dispute, when there is a clause concerning the choice of jurisdiction vesting competence in a court other than that of the consumer's place of residence in the event of a dispute; this provision is without prejudice to the 1968 Brussels Convention on Jurisdiction and Enforcement of Judgments in Civil and Commercial Matters;[9]

(o) reference to the supervisory authority on whom the supplier depends, when it is subject to supervision; and

(p) out-of-court complaint and redress procedures.

Some exceptions are provided in paragraph 2 concerning the need to provide certain items of information for certain financial services covered by sectoral directives.

As in the Distance Selling Directive, the commercial purpose must be clearly apparent and the information must be provided "in a clear and comprehensible manner" and must comply with the principles of fairness in commercial transactions and the protection of persons who are legally incapable pursuant to national law.

---

[9] On the 30 November 2000, the Justice and Home Affairs Council of Ministers reached a political agreement on the Proposal for a Regulation replacing the Brussels Convention. The Regulation will ensure the protection of the consumers by allowing them to bring disputes before the courts of their country of residence. However, regarding consumer protection in commercial transactions operated through the Internet, the Council and the Commission, in a Declaration, have stipulated that this right will only be applicable when a good and in due form contract has been concluded. The fact that an Internet site is accessible, the language or the currency used in the site is not enough for the Regulation being applicable. A contract must have been concluded.

9.6.2   *Communication of the contractual terms and conditions and of the prior information*

The contractual terms and conditions and the information provided in Article 3, must be communicated in writing or in a durable medium before conclusion of the contract or immediately after conclusion of the contract, if the consumer did not already have the information at the moment of conclusion of the contract (Article 3a of the Amended Proposal). These two eventualities also determine the moment when the withdrawal period referred to in Article 4 begins to run.

According to Article 2, paragraph (f), "durable medium" means any instrument enabling the consumer to store information addressed personally and specifically to him and which is mainly contained on floppy disks, CD-ROMs, and the hard drive of the consumer's computer on which email is stored. The explanatory memorandum of the original Proposal makes clear that it must be possible to get the information without any particular action being required on the consumer's part, and more specifically the consumer must not be required to store the data on his own initiative. Floppy disks or CD-ROMs must be sent to the consumer but the data may also be transmitted by the supplier via email.

The choice of medium is determined by joint agreement between the parties.

9.6.3   *Right of withdrawal*

Article 4 of the Amended Proposal establishes a general right of withdrawal from the contract, determines the moment when the withdrawal period starts to run and establishes a series of exceptions to this principle.

Paragraph 1 provides that Member States shall provide that consumers have a right of withdrawal within 14 to 30 days, depending on the nature of the financial services concerned, without having to indicate grounds and without penalty.

The UK position on Article 4, appears to be that this provision does not reflect a harmonised approach. The UK would like to see it amended to make all short-term contracts subject to a 14 day cooling-off period, while longer-term contracts (such as those for insurance and pensions) would be subject to a 30-day period.

The period within which the right of withdrawal may be exercised is calculated as follows:

(a) when the contractual terms and conditions and the information referred to in Article 3(1) have been provided to the consumer prior to conclusion of the contract, from the date of conclusion of the contract;

(b) when the contract has been concluded at the express request of the consumer before the contractual terms and conditions and the information referred to in Article 3(1) have been communicated to him, from the date of receipt of these particulars or the last of such particulars.

The principle of mutual recognition would then apply, so when the supplier respects the withdrawal period provided for by the Member State in which he is established, he is not required to respect a different withdrawal period in the Member State in which the consumer resides.

This Article provides for certain exceptions to the general right of withdrawal:

(a) financial services in respect of which exercise of the right of withdrawal might lead to a risk of speculation (foreign exchange services or the reception, transmission and/or execution of orders related to, and services in respect of or related to money market instruments, transferable securities, OCITS and other collective investment schemes, financial futures and options, and exchange and interest rate instruments whose price depends on fluctuations in the financial market outside the supplier's control);

(b) non-life insurance for a period of less than two months (e.g. holiday insurance);

(c) contracts whose performance has been entirely completed before the consumer exercises the right of withdrawal.

Although a general exclusion of all forms of credit would not be desirable, in order to address the concerns expressed by the European Parliament and the Council, the Amended Proposal contains a specific regime as regards the right of withdrawal for real estate credit. Member States may provide that the consumer may not rely on the right of withdrawal when:

(a) with his consent, the amount borrowed has been transferred to the seller of the property or to his representative;

(b) when a notarial act relating to the real estate credit to which he is party has been validly and regularly recorded (it should be stressed that in most cases when a notary has to be present for the contract to be concluded, the act will be recorded in the presence of the parties, and so the contract will not be a distance contract within the meaning of the definition of Article 2).

However, in the case of credit funded by bonds secured against real estate, Member States may provide that the consumer shall not benefit from the right of withdrawal.

Article 4(2) refers to unfair inducement and establishes that, without prejudice to the right of withdrawal, when a consumer has been unfairly induced by the supplier to conclude the contract, this contract may be annulled, with all the attendant legal consequences in terms of the law applicable to the contract, without prejudice to the consumer's right to seek compensation for the harm he has suffered under national law. When suppliers communicate objective information to the consumer on prices of financial services that depend on market fluctuations, this shall not be considered as an unfair inducement. The "unfair inducement" rule may require sellers to demonstrate that they have adequate control procedures in place.

As regards the form of notice of withdrawal, the consumer shall exercise his right of withdrawal in writing or in a durable medium available or accessible to the supplier. The other legal effects and conditions of withdrawal shall be governed by the law applicable to the contract.

According to Article 5 of the Amended Proposal when the consumer exercises his right of withdrawal he may be required to pay either:

(a) a lump sum corresponding to the price of the financial service effectively provided by the supplier before exercise of the right of withdrawal, independently of the moment of withdrawal; or

(b) when the cost of the financial service effectively provided by the supplier depends on the time at which the right of withdrawal is exercised, an amount enabling the consumer to calculate the price to be paid on a pro rata basis for the period between the day on which the contact was concluded and the day on which he exercises his right of withdrawal.

The amount payable may not be such that it could be construed as a penalty.

It is important to note that the information on the price to be paid in case of withdrawal is part of the information to be provided in conformity with Article 3(1). Accordingly, unless the supplier can prove that the consumer was duly informed about the price, he cannot require the consumer to pay any amount if the consumer exercises his right of withdrawal.

Finally, without any undue delay and in any event within the 30-day period, the supplier should return to the consumer any sums he has received from the consumer on conclusion of the distance contract, except for the sums referred to above.

On the other hand when the consumer exercises his right of withdrawal, he shall return to the supplier any original contract document bearing the supplier's signature communicated to him on conclusion of the contract, with a view to preventing possible fraud. The return of the documents is limited to original documents since these are the only ones liable to be binding. Such requirement cannot be extended to copies, the reproductions of such copies being uncontrollable, or to advertising material (Article 8a).

9.6.4   *Performance of the contract*

Article 5 (1) of the Amended Proposal provides that the supplier may not start to perform the contract before expiry of the time limit for the exercise of the right of withdrawal, without the consumer's express consent.

Article 8 concerns the unavailability of the service contracted for. Without prejudice to the rules of civil law of the Member States pertaining to the non-performance of contracts, if the financial service, which is the subject of the contract, is partly or totally unavailable, the supplier shall inform the consumer of this. If the financial service is totally unavailable, the supplier shall, within 30 days, reimburse any sums paid by the consumer, and, if the financial service is only partly available, the contract may only be performed with the express consent of the consumer and the supplier. Failing this express agreement, the supplier shall within 30 days, return to the consumer any sums he may have paid. Where the service is only partly performed, the supplier shall return to the consumer all sums relating to the part of the service that has not been performed, within 30 days. The obligation of the consumer to return original documents established in Article 8a applies also in this case.

9.6.5   *Enforcement*

Article 12(1) of the Amended Proposal deals with the adequate and effective complaints and redress procedures which must be put in place for the settlement of disputes between consumers and suppliers. Member States may use existing procedures, including courts and administrative actions but under paragraph 2, these procedures must also enable public bodies, consumer organisations and professional organisations to take action with a view to enforcing the provisions of the Directive.

Pursuant to paragraph 4, Member States must adopt the necessary measures to ensure that operators and suppliers of means of distance communication, when they are in a position to do so, terminate practices which infringe the provisions adopted under the Directive (e.g. it is possible to disconnect a telephone line but not to isolate a class of letters out of all letters received by the postal services). The same obligation is also enshrined in Directive 97/7/EC in respect of the distance selling of all other products and services. The obligation on operators and suppliers of means of communication must result from a court decision, an administrative order or an order issued by a monitoring authority, and addressed to them.

Article 12a is devoted to out-of-court remedies and establishes that Member States shall encourage bodies established with a view to the out-of-court settlement of disputes to co-operate in the resolution of cross border disputes. The Explanatory Memorandum indicates that one potential area of co-operation concerns the consumer's freedom to seek redress from the out-of-court dispute settlement body in his country of residence, which would then contact its opposite number in the supplier's state, so that the consumer himself does not have to institute proceedings in another Member State.

The burden of proof of compliance with the obligation to inform consumers as well as the consumer's consent to conclude the contract and, where appropriate, its performance lies with the supplier (Article 13). The point is that it is up to the party which is familiar with the selling technique to demonstrate that it has fulfilled its obligations. Furthermore, any contractual term or condition providing that the burden of proof regarding compliance by the supplier with its obligations under the Directive should lie with the consumer, shall be an unfair term within the meaning of Council Directive 93/13/EC on Unfair Terms in Consumer Contracts.[10]

9.6.6   *Waiver*

Article 11(1) of the Amended Proposal establishes that consumers may not waive the rights vested in them by the Directive and paragraph 3 of the same Article adds that consumers may not be deprived of the protection granted by the Directive where the law governing the contract is that of a third country if the consumer is resident on the territory of a Member State and the contract has a close link with the Community. As with the similar provision in Directive 97/7, it is doubtful how effective this will be (*see* Section 9.3.6).

9.6.7   *Other provisions*

As in Directive 97/7, there are some other interesting provisions such as:

(a) *Restriction of the use of certain means of communications* – as in Directive 97/7, the use by a supplier of automatic calling machines and fax machines requires the consumer's prior consent. As regards the other means of communication, Member States are free to choose between a system providing that the consumer must first indicate his consent or a system in which he has to indicate in advance that he does not wish to be contacted. In the case of telephone communications, the identity of the supplier and the commercial purpose of the call shall be made explicitly clear at the beginning of any conversation with the consumer. Member States shall provide for appropriate penalties in the event of the supplier's failure to comply with these particular provisions and they may provide notably that the consumer may cancel the contract at any time, free of charge and without penalties (Article 10 of the Amended Proposal).

---

[10]   OJ L 95/29, 21 April 1993.

(b) *Payment by card* – the same rules in Directive 97/7 apply (Article 8a) (*see* Section 9.3.7).

(c) *Inertia selling* – the purpose of Article 9 of the Proposal is to prohibit the distance supply of financial services without the consumer's prior consent and enshrines the principle that the consumer's silence may not be construed in such cases as constituting consent to the conclusion of the contract. This Article in no way prohibits the tacit renewal of contracts concluded with the validly expressed consent of the consumer. Article 9 establishes that Member States shall take the necessary measures to prohibit the supply of financial services to a consumer without a prior request on his part, when this supply includes a request for immediate or deferred payment; and exempt the consumer from any obligation in the event of unsolicited supplies, the absence of a reply not constituting consent.

9.7 The future

The Amended Proposal was adopted in July 1999 but Member States have failed to make significant progress.

In the Internal Market Council of 7 December 1999, with a view to moving forward, the Council decided that the Commission should prepare an inventory of national provisions currently in force, focusing on information requirements in the area of financial services. This is to be based on information provided by the Member States. It was hoped that this inventory would enable the Council to consider each Member State's requirements, in order to reach a common position. The aim is to agree a text that satisfies Member States' consumer protection concerns, is based on the maximum harmonisation approach and avoids distortion of competition between service providers due to differences between national regulations.

The Commission sent out a questionnaire to the Member States in early January 2000, requesting details of their national provisions. It has now finalised its report based on the responses received and expects to issue this to the Council. The French Presidency which lasted until the end of 2000, had a strong national interest in the adoption of legislation in this area, which they believed would give impetus to the creation of a single EC capital market. On 4 July 2000, they issued the following statement:

> "In line with the conclusions of the Lisbon European Council, the French Presidency will work to secure political agreement on the proposal for a Directive on the distance selling of financial services, the aim being to keep up with developments in electronic commerce in this field by guaranteeing consumers a high level of protection."

In the Internal Market Council which took place on 30 November 2000, the French Presidency presented a paper on the state of negotiations but no further progress was achieved towards the adoption of the Proposal.

Member States took note of the fact that consistency with other legislation, such as the E-commerce Directive[11] or the UCITS Directive,[12] should be ensured. In this sense, the Council underlined that the Ecofin Council of 17 October 2000, when reaching agreement on the content of the UCITS Directive, made the following statement on the relation between the UCITS Directive and that on e-commerce:

> "The Council and the Commission recognise the opportunities and challenges presented by e-commerce in the field of financial services and the importance of developing, expeditiously, a clear and coherent policy for the whole financial sector, including UCITS sold on-line. That policy will be outlined in the Commission's forthcoming communication on e-commerce and financial services, which will enable all interested parties to contribute to defining the optimum way to proceed. The Commission will present a communication around the end of the year so that it can be taken into account with a view to the 1 March 2001 date."

In its Financial Services Priorities and Progress Third Report, adopted on 8 November 2000,[13] the Commission set the date for the issue of this Communication as the beginning of 2001, and the Communication on e-commerce and financial services was adopted on 9 February 2001.

The Internal Market Council that took place on 12 March 2001 under the Swedish Presidency did not adopt the common position on the proposal as expected, but a clear majority of the Member States committed themselves to reaching a political agreement by June 2001 at the latest, subject to resolving certain outstanding issues. These concern a transitional approach to full harmonisation in this field, (on the basis of the Commission's February 2001 Communication on e-commerce and financial services) and the inclusion in the text of the proposal of satisfactory provisions concerning applicable law and jurisdiction.

---

[11]   Directive 2000/31/EC of the European Parliament and of the Council of 8 June 2000 on certain legal aspects of information society services, in particular e-commerce, in the Internal Market ("Directive on e-commerce"), OJ L 178/1 of 17 July 2000.

[12]   Amended proposal for a Directive of the European Parliament and of the Council amending Directive 85/611/EEC on the co-ordination of laws, regulations and administrative provisions relating to undertakings for collective investment in transferable securities ("UCITS") , OJ C 311E/302 of 31 October 2000.

[13]   *See* above footnote 8.

Chapter 10
PAYMENT SYSTEMS ON THE INTERNET

Robert Caplehorn
Senior Counsel
Bolero International Limited

10.1   Introduction

For electronic commerce ("e-commerce") to realise its full potential, it is recognised that trusted payment systems must be available over the Internet. The purpose of this Chapter is to explore the main initiatives developed in this area to date and to analyse the legal and regulatory issues which relate to them.

The new electronic methods of retail payment that are currently being implemented in a number of markets include multi-purpose prepaid cards (sometimes known as "electronic purses" or "stored value cards") and prepaid or stored-value payment systems for executing payments over the Internet. In this Chapter these initiatives are generically referred to as "electronic money ("e-money")" or "electronic cash ("e-cash")", although a precise definition of either of these terms is difficult in view of the diversity of initiatives available and the variety of the features which they offer. In addition, more traditional forms of payment such as the credit and debit cards are being adapted for use on the Internet and these are proving to be the most popular payment vehicles since e-money has been very slow to penetrate the marketplace.

Payment systems encompass small-value fund transfer systems used by consumers as well as large-value inter-bank fund transfer systems underpinning national and international money and capital markets. Payment systems are made up of several components covering money, liabilities expressed as monetary liabilities, and systems and procedures for transferring and recording ownership of these liabilities. The scope of this Chapter is limited to retail payment systems. It should be recognised that, in view of the novelty of many of these initiatives, the application of existing laws and regulatory structures is to a large extent uncertain and the variety of systems available means that the application of the law is unlikely to be uniform. Also, with the exception of credit and debit cards, the payment systems described in this Chapter are at an early stage in terms of market penetration and, at the time of writing, it is by no means clear as to which of them will prove to be the most suitable for use across the Internet or which will survive even in the medium term in what is proving to be an intensely competitive marketplace. Indeed, since the first edition of this Guide was published in mid–1999, it may be the case that certain product offerings featured in this Chapter have ceased to be operational. Similarly, the approach to be adopted by the relevant regulatory authorities is only just emerging and varies from country to country.

10.2   Electronic methods of retail payment

10.2.1   *Credit cards*

Under the traditional scheme model, the cardholder is issued with a plastic payment card pursuant to a contract with the card issuer – a financial institution, which is a member of the payment scheme (which may be either domestic or international), whose brand appears on the card. The nature of the contract is, by definition, one for credit under which the cardholder is normally billed periodically and incurs an obligation to repay a proportion of the debt during each period. The contract is usually governed by the consumer credit laws of the country in which the card is issued (e.g. the Consumer Credit Act 1974 in the UK). The contract permits the cardholder to purchase goods and/or services from any retailer which displays the payment scheme brand at the point of sale. The retailer, in turn, is entitled to accept cards bearing the brand under the terms of a contract (usually known as an acquirer contract) with a member of the payment scheme which may, or may not, be the same member which issued the relevant card. Under the acquirer contract, the retailer is usually entitled to deposit the amounts of all transactions accepted at the point of sale in a nominated bank account. The acquiring member (which is some form of regulated financial institution) then seeks settlement for transactions effected with the issuing members as appropriate who will, in turn, debit the accounts of the cardholders. All members of the scheme are contractually bound to operate the scheme in accordance with the scheme rules which may require settlement via a specific network operated by the scheme.

The structure described above applies equally to transactions on the Internet as it does to transactions on the physical high street.

Currently, credit card transactions over the Internet take place in a similar way to telephone transactions, with the cardholder communicating his card number to the retailer on-line. This has given rise to significant security issues leading to a requirement for the development of a secure on-line protocol enabling the cardholder to present his card information securely, and for the retailer to be able to validate that information and obtain the necessary authorisation for the transaction to proceed. Such a protocol, known as Secure Electronic Transactions ("SET"), has been developed by the international payment scheme associations involving the encryption of the card number during transmission. Further details are provided below. A diagram of how credit and debit cards function, both within SET and generally, is given in Figure 1. At the time of writing, SET has not been widely introduced, largely (it is said) because of the implementation costs involved and the ability of credit card acquirers to pass on liability for fraud to retailers under the terms of their contract to accept credit card payments.

As fraud levels relating to card use continue to rise, both on the Internet and in the high street, there is more pressure on financial institutions to adopt more robust methods of reducing fraud risk. One approach under consideration in the UK is to adopt PIN entry at the point of sale.

10.2.2   *Debit cards*

The distinction between a credit card and a debit card lies in the underlying account relationship which the cardholder has with the issuing financial institution. A credit card is linked to a credit account held with the issuing institution; a debit card is linked to a current or savings account held with the issuer. In other respects, the structure outlined for credit cards will apply both in the physical and virtual marketplaces. The underlying account relationship essentially determines the application of the legal and regulatory regime governing the relationship, most notably the fact that the Consumer Credit Act 1974 governs credit cards but has only limited application to debit cards.

10.2.3   *Monneta prepaid e-cash*

This is described as a cash-equivalent e-payment method for Internet shopping. Consumers maintain a prepaid account with a bank. The operational process is as follows:

(a) the consumer requests the issue of an amount of e-cash;

(b) the e-cash software in the consumers personal computer ("PC") sends a request to the bank over a secure channel;

(c) the bank approves the request;

(d) the bank creates the e-cash;

(e) the bank sends the e-cash to the consumer;

(f) the consumer receives the e-cash and is ready to spend it;

(g) the e-retailer accepts the e-cash payment and sends confirmation to the consumer; and

(h) the e-retailer obtains redemption from the bank.

10.2.4   *Cybercash*

Cybercash provide electronic "wallet" software which is loaded onto the cardholder's PC. The software passes encrypted payment information between the cardholder and the retailer. The cardholder is issued with a wallet ID which is registered with Cybercash and one or more of his cards are then linked to the wallet by entering relevant credit card processing information. In order to effect a transaction, the wallet encrypts the credit card data and invoice with the key assigned to the wallet ID which is then sent to the retailer whose own software (issued by Cybercash) requests authorisation and then digitally signs and encrypts the payment information with the key issued by Cybercash. At no stage does the retailer see the card number. The Cybercash server, via the Internet, decrypts the message and checks the invoice. The credit card data and the retailer's request for payment are then re-encrypted and sent to the acquirer bank which processes the information in the normal way.

10.2.5   *Cybercash "coins"*

This is a form of e-money designed to be held on PCs for use on the Internet. The user loads "coins" from a bank or credit card account which are held on his PC. The funds in respect of the "coins" are then transferred to a bank account which acts as a pooled account held in the name of Cybercash as agent for the users. All transactions are on-line and go through a central database maintained by Cybercash. All information transferred over the Internet is encrypted and cannot be accessed by Cybercash, although Cybercash maintains an encrypted archive copy of each transaction.

In order to effect a transaction, the user clicks on the item to be purchased and this activates the Cybercash wallet, transfers the coins to the retailer, updates the user's balance and effects delivery of the product or service to the user over the Internet. Users can deposit "coins" in their bank accounts by using the service and can make purchases across national borders by using "coins" denominated in foreign currencies. Once used, however, the "coins" cannot be spent again. A diagram showing how this works is given in Figure 2.

10.2.6 Digicash

This is another system designed specifically for use on the Internet. The user purchases "coins" from his bank. The PC then generates a set of random serial numbers representing specific amounts or denominations which are then encrypted and transmitted to the bank for validation. The user's bank debits the user's account and credits an Digicash liability account on its own books. The "coins" are stored on the user's PC waiting to be spent.

In order to effect payment, the user transfers the "coin" to the retailer or other user. The retailer's software then automatically sends the "coin" to the issuing bank. The bank then verifies the "coin" (by using the unique serial number associated with it) to the retailer before the retailer decides to accept it as payment. This process is known as "blind verification" in that the bank is able to verify the authenticity of the "coin" without identifying the user. This offers the user a certain level of privacy. From the retailer's perspective, the "coin" appears to have come from the bank. Once spent, the "coins" cannot be reused. A diagram showing how Digicash works is set out in Figure 3.

10.2.7 VisaCash

VisaCash has been developed primarily to effect e-cash transactions in the physical marketplace. Although the generic name, VisaCash, is used, the system makes use of a variety of technologies and thus the features vary from implementation to implementation. It is not therefore a globally, inter-operable system. Smart cards (which may be disposable or reloadable) are loaded with electronic value units via specially adapted ATMs and value is then transferred to the retailer at the point of sale in return for goods or services. Payment transaction data is then collected and transferred to a central archive for the purposes of clearing between the participating banks. It is not known whether this system will be adapted for use on the Internet. The system is fully accounted in that each use of the card at the point of sale is routed back to a central archive maintained by Visa and is cleared back to an account maintained by the customer with the issuing bank. At the merchant level, each use of the card needs to be separately uploaded to the acquiring bank. The involvement of more than one bank in such a system gives rise to the need for a clearing and settlement system (the central archive) for the processing of each transaction. These factors have a strong bearing on the cost of each transaction and may render them uneconomical for very low value transactions such as so-called micro transactions on the Internet. At the time of writing, VisaCash is still in pilot phase. According to the Visa website, it has been trialled in 11 countries worldwide in a total of 3.7 million transactions.

10.2.8 Proton

Proton has been developed primarily for use in the physical marketplace and is understood to operate in a similar way to Visa. It is understood that a system of truncating transaction data at either the merchant or acquiring bank level is used in order to reduce the need to centrally clear every transaction and thereby reduce costs. Again, it is not known whether this system will be adapted for use on the Internet.

10.2.9   *Mondex*

Mondex has been designed to provide a smart card based e-cash solution for both the physical and virtual marketplaces. From the outset it has been modelled on the way in which traditional physical cash operates. Electronic value units denominated in the currency of a particular country are loaded from a bank account onto a smart card via adapted ATMs, PCs and telephones designed to accept smart cards and then are transferred to the retailer at the point of sale in return for goods and/or services. The value accumulates in the smart card held in the retailer's terminal and is transferred to the retailer's bank account, usually at the end of the working day. Value can also be transferred to other cardholders by means of an electronic wallet or via the telephone. Cards are able to hold five currencies simultaneously and the system is globally inter-operable. An originator is formed for each currency in which Mondex value is denominated. The originator has ultimate responsibility for the creation, issue and redemption of all Mondex value denominated in that currency. It is envisaged that Mondex will operate in the same way in the virtual marketplace as it does in the physical marketplace; the Internet effectively representing a conduit for value transfer. The security resides in the microchip held in the smart card and is not therefore as vulnerable to the usual perceived Internet security risks provided secure hardware is used at the other end of the transaction. An important distinction between Mondex, on the one hand, and Digicash and Cybercash, on the other, is that Mondex value can be transferred off line as many times as the parties wish (subject to certain operational constraints), whereas the "coins" issued by the other two must be redeemed as soon as they are spent. Mondex value can accordingly be transferred from cardholder to cardholder by using an electronic wallet or via a telephone or PC.

An important distinction between Mondex and VisaCash and Proton is that Mondex does not require a clearing and settlement system. This is because once the electronic value has left the banking system, it can be used at the point of sale and for transactions between cardholders without creating a separately identifiable accounting record on each occasion. Value is uploaded to the acquiring bank on an aggregated basis and may be re-circulated or redeemed with the originator. This reduces individual transaction costs to a negligible amount and thus renders the system economically viable for micro payments across the Internet and in the high street. A diagram depicting the operation of Mondex is given in Figure 4.

10.2.10   *Multi-function smart cards*

A few words ought also be said about multi-function smart cards which are now available. These are based on a multi-application operating system which allows applications other than e-cash to co-reside on the card. This would encompass such financial services as credit and debit cards as well as other, non-financial applications such as mass transit ticketing, loyalty schemes and access to secure buildings. Mondex has its own initiative in this area, known as Multos.

10.2.11   *Web based loyalty schemes*

Loyalty schemes are developing on the Internet. One in particular, "beenz.com" holds itself out as the Internet's "currency". Loyalty points are collected by on-line shoppers who subscribe to beenz.com, by making purchases from participating e-retailers. Points can be collected simply by making a visit to particular websites. The points are held in an account maintained for the customer by beenz.com and are redeemable at other participating e-retailer websites in return for goods and/or services. Beenz.com make their money from the difference between the price at which they issue beenz to participating retailers and the price at which they redeem them. The fact that beenz are collected from a variety of sources and are redeemable in return for a wide range of goods and services gives it at least the appearance of cash. The question arises therefore as to whether beenz.com could be an Electronic Money Institution ("EMI") within the meaning of the new EU Directive (*see* Section 10.10.3 below). It is understood, however, that beenz are not redeemable from the issuer for cash.

10.3   Legal and regulatory issues relating to credit and debit cards

As we have seen, the systems themselves function in very similar ways but the application of the law will depend essentially on the underlying contract with the financial institution which issued the card. This application of the law will not differ materially whether the card is used in the physical or virtual marketplace.

10.3.1   Credit cards

An agreement for the issue of a credit card to a consumer will normally be regulated by the Consumer Credit Act 1974. This Act provides consumer protection in a number of ways.

(a) The issuer of the card (usually a financial institution) needs to be licensed to carry on consumer credit business by the Director General of Fair Trading (*see* Section 21 of the Consumer Credit Act 1974). A licence will only be issued to such persons who satisfy the Director that it is a fit and proper person to undertake such a business (*see* Section 25 of the Consumer Credit Act 1974) and the licence can be revoked by the Director under procedures laid out in the Act in the event that matters come to his attention which indicate otherwise. The cardholder thus has the comfort of knowing that there is a statutory regime in place which regulates the business within which the card is issued. Indeed, the Office of Fair Trading has been active in offering advice to consumers on pitfalls related to Internet shopping.

(b) The general rule set out in the Act is that the customer will not be liable to the creditor for any loss arising from any use of the credit facility by an unauthorised person not acting (or to be treated as acting) as the cardholder's agent (*see* Section 83 of the Consumer Credit Act 1974). However, the card itself will be a credit token (*see* Section 14 of the Consumer Credit Act 1974) and the liability of the cardholder in the circumstances where it is used by an unauthorised person cannot exceed £50 (*see* Section 84 of the Consumer Credit Act 1974). The £50 limit may be less than this under the terms and conditions governing the issue of the card but, in the event that any such term purported to set the limit above £50, the provision would be void (*see* Section 173 of the Consumer Credit Act 1974). In an Internet situation, the perceived risk is, of course, that the card details may be intercepted during transmission across the Internet and used to create bogus transactions. This is dealt with in more detail below particularly with regard to the new Consumer Protection (Distance Selling) Regulations 2000 which came into effect on 31 October 2000 and required an amendment to Section 84 of the Consumer Credit Act to remove the £50 customer liability provision in relation to a transaction covered by the Regulations (which would include Internet transactions). Prior to the introduction of these Regulations, many credit card issuers had begun to offer customers a guarantee against losses incurred by reason of Internet fraud. This was in response to the much publicised risk of transacting payments across the Internet which has threatened to undermine the development of B2C e-commerce.

(c) The credit agreement itself and the procedures covering its making are subject to strict procedures and documentation requirements set out in the Consumer Credit Act 1974 and regulations made under it which are designed to ensure that the potential cardholder is fully aware of the nature of the agreement, that his statutory rights are drawn to his attention, and that he has a short cooling-off period within which to change his mind (*see* Sections 60 to 69 of the Consumer Credit Act 1974).

(d) The cardholder will not be liable for any misuse of the card prior to its receipt and acceptance by him (*see* Section 66 of the Consumer Credit Act 1974).

(e) Perhaps the most significant provision in the Act in terms of cardholder protection is that contained in Section 75 which effectively provides that the creditor will be jointly and severally liable with the retailer for any breach of contract or misrepresentation by the retailer in relation to the transaction financed by the creditor. The transaction itself must be for a sum of at least £100 but not more than £30,000. There is some debate as to whether this provision applies where the retailer is based outside the UK or where the card issuer does not also have the acquirer contract with the retailer. However, the provision could provide significant protection where goods or services are ordered via the Internet but are not delivered, are not of reasonable quality, or for some other reason are not in accordance with the cardholder contract. It would offer no protection in the case of so-called micro transactions on the Internet since these, by definition, would be below the £100 limit.

It should be noted that, where the credit limit in relation to the card exceeds the financial limitations set out in the Act (currently £25,000)(*see* Section 8 of the Consumer Credit Act 1974) or where the credit agreement provides for the full amount of the credit used to be paid off in one instalment (i.e. a charge card), then the protection afforded by the Act will not apply (Consumer Credit (Exempt Agreements) Order 1989 S.I. (No. 869) made under Section 16).

10.3.2   *Debit cards*

Most of the credit card provisions given above do not apply to debit cards as normally there is no grant of credit. However, credit would be deemed to have been granted for the purposes of Section 14 of the Consumer Credit Act 1974 and debit cards are therefore treated as credit tokens (*see* Section 14 (3) of the Consumer Credit Act 1974). Secondly, where an overdraft is granted in respect of the account to which the debit card is linked, the card would be used to access the overdraft and a debit card could be considered to be a credit token for that reason. It is not within the scope of this Chapter to analyse these provisions in further detail.

A debit card would normally be linked to either a current account or savings account held with either a bank or a building society. As such, the issuer of the token would either be an institution authorised to take deposits under the banking or the building societies legislation. The cardholder therefore has the comfort of knowing that the business in relation to which the card was issued is a regulated business.

The Banking Code, which is a voluntary code of practice, is followed by banks and building societies in their relations with personal customers. It sets standards of good banking practice to be followed as a minimum by all banks and building societies which subscribe to it. There are a number of provisions in the Code which are relevant to the issue of debit cards. These relate mainly to the issue of lost and stolen cards. Some of the key provisions are set out below:

(a) the cardholder will not be expected to bear any losses incurred where a card is misused prior to delivery to the cardholder;

(b) if a card is misused following delivery but before the loss or theft has been reported to the bank or building society, the cardholder's liability will be limited to £50 except where the bank or building society can prove that the cardholder had acted fraudulently or with gross negligence, in which case the customer will be liable for all losses.

The reference to £50 limit of liability must now be read subject to the Consumer Protection (Distance Selling) Regulations 2000 (*see* Section 10.3.4 below).

10.3.3 *The nature of payment by credit or debit card*

When effecting a transaction by credit or debit card, the cardholder is effectively giving an instruction to his bank (or other financial institution) to debit the account to which the card is linked. The instruction is given via the retailer who will submit the transaction details to its acquiring bank which will then submit the details for processing in accordance with the rules of the particular payment scheme. The card issuing bank will settle with the acquiring bank and debit the cardholder's account.

The courts have held (*re Chargecard Services Limited* (1987) Ch 150) that, in relation to a chargecard scheme for the purchase of petrol, the payment was effective from the point at which the cardholder signs the voucher at the point of sale. The reasoning was based on the fact that, as the garage had no obvious means of tracing the customer, the parties must have intended that the payment would be complete at the point of sale. Consequently, the petrol station had no recourse to the cardholder when, due to insolvency, it could not obtain value from the chargecard company. Although the court specifically held that each method of payment must be judged on its own merits, there seems to be no reason why the same logic would not apply to credit and debit card schemes in general.

In the case of transactions over the Internet, the signing of a voucher is clearly not relevant although it is submitted that the courts would probably view the transaction as complete at the point at which the cardholder irrevocably consents to the transaction. This should be apparent from the series of messages which appear on screen as part of the protocol to effect the transaction.

Credit and debit card transactions over the Internet give rise to the following risks from the cardholder's perspective:

(a) the risk that the card details will be intercepted and used to conduct fraudulent transactions for which the cardholder will eventually be invoiced; and

(b) the risk that the virtual merchant (who could be anywhere in the world) will not honour the transaction and fail to send the goods or services to which the transaction relates.

It is important to examine the extent to which these risks are currently addressed by existing statutory protection (e.g. *see* Section 10.3.4).

The issue of merchants failing to deliver goods and/or services pursuant to a credit card transaction over the Internet may well fall within Section 75 of the Consumer Credit Act, thus affording the cardholder a high level of protection (*see* above). However, in practice there may be certain limitations on the degree of protection afforded:

(a) the protection only covers transactions where the purchase price for the goods or services is at least £100 (and not more than £30,000) and thus micro transactions would be excluded;

(b) the issue arises as to where the contract is concluded in a situation (as will often be the case) where the merchant is based in a different country. If the contract were deemed to have been concluded outside the UK, then there is an argument to the effect that the protection of Section 75 should not apply. This is not, however, thought to be the view of the Office of Fair Trading whose function it is to enforce large parts of the Act;

(c) where (as is also likely to be the case) the card issuing bank and the merchant's bank (the acquiring bank) are not the same, there is also an argument that the protection of Section 75 should not apply. Section 75, it is argued, envisages a tri-partite arrangement between the borrower (the cardholder), the lender (the issuer) and the seller or supplier of goods or services. It does not envisage a four party arrangement involving, in addition, the acquiring bank.

The consumer is thus reasonably well protected under the current law. The question, however, arises as to which of the acquirer, the issuer or the scheme company (e.g. Visa or MasterCard) should bear the risk in the event of fraudulently used credit/debit card details. This is effectively governed by the operating regulations and the acquirer contract which apply to the payment scheme in question and, amongst many other things, will set out the rules governing the allocation of liability in the various scenarios which can arise. A consideration of these is beyond the scope of this Chapter; much will depend on the extent to which the issuer, the retailer or the acquirer may have failed to observe the operational risk management requirements of the system. In practice, it tends to be the retailer who bears the liability by reason of provisions as to risk and liability which appear in the acquirer contract. This means retailers are often charged back in a situation where they have previously obtained authorisation prior to processing the payment transaction.

The major international payment card schemes, MasterCard and Visa have developed SET to standardise the on-line payment process and to deal with the perceived risks of disclosing credit card details over the Internet. The protocol involves a number of stages:

(a) the buyer indicates his wish to make a purchase;

(b) the merchant's system generates an invoice which it sends to the buyer;

(c) the buyer selects a card (MasterCard or Visa) for payment; the card needs to be SET compatible;

(d) the buyer's software requests both the merchant encryption public key and the one it uses to interface with the acquirer bank;

(e) the merchant's software generates a response including a unique transaction identifier and certificates for both the public keys. Certificates represent independently-verified certifications that the public keys belong to the merchant and acquirer respectively;

(f) the buyer's software verifies the payment gateways;

(g) the buyer's software generates an Order Information ("OI") message and a Purchase Instruction ("PI") message (each separately encrypted) and sends them to the merchant. The OI is seen by the merchant and contains the transaction identifier, brand of card and transaction date. The merchant does not see the card number. The PI is seen by the acquirer and contains the card number, transaction amount and description of the order;

(h) the OI and PI are sent to the merchant;

(i) the merchant checks for any tampering;

(j) assuming no tampering, the merchant's software requests authorisation for the payment; the request to the acquirer includes the transaction identifier, the PI and the merchant's certificate authority with their public key;

(k) the payment gateway decrypts the message and checks for tampering;

(l) the payment gateway requests authorisation from the buyer's bank (the issuing bank); the usual bank channels are used;

(m) the issuing bank approves or refuses the authorisation;

(n) the payment gateway generates an authorisation response (if appropriate);

(o) the payment gateway sends the authorisation response back to the merchant's software;

(p) the merchant's software decrypts the authorisation, checks and stores it;

(q) if the transaction is approved, the merchant software generates a message informing the buyer accordingly and confirming the goods or services will be delivered;

(r) the merchant's software then generates a capture request message to send to the payment gateway.

SET offers greater security by the use of strong cryptography and independently-verified certificates, and the merchant does not see the card number. The risk of card details being intercepted and used to generate fraudulent transactions is reduced. However, largely due to cost reasons, SET has not been as widely implemented as was originally anticipated.

10.3.4   *EC Directive on Distance Selling*

The Consumer Protection (Contracts Concluded by Means of Distance Communications) Regulations 2000 incorporate the provisions of this Directive into English law and generally provide for important consumer protection in respect of contracts concluded at a distance, which, by definition, would include contracts made over the Internet. The Directive, in its preamble, explicitly recognises that the introduction of new technologies is increasing the number of ways for consumers to obtain offers and place orders. The Regulations provide, *inter alia*, for a cooling-off period during which the consumer may withdraw from the contract without penalty and without reason. The only charge for which the consumer will be liable will be the direct cost of returning the goods.

The Regulations also provide that card issuers must now refund all money debited to a consumer's account as a result of fraudulent or dishonest use of a payment card. Consumers in a distance selling environment are also no longer liable for the first £50 of any fraudulent transaction and the Consumer Credit Act 1974 (Section 84) has been amended accordingly. It is considered by many that these provisions should instill greater confidence in shopping on the Internet.

10.3.5 *Application service providers*

The development of Internet shopping has lead to the development of a number of application service providers who offer secure services to on-line retailers wishing to accept payments by credit or debit cards. Typically, in return for a service fee, the retailer will be able to route all payment requirements via the service provider's secure website. The customer simply clicks on a hypertext link on the retailers website which takes him to the service provider's site where payment details are taken and remitted to the acquiring bank. The service provider takes responsibility for collecting and transmitting the payment card data in a secure environment thus reducing the risk of interception of the data and the fraud which could arise as a consequence. Some examples of on-line companies offering this type of service are worldpay.com, earthport.com and bibit.com. The on-line retailer benefits from the increased security since, in a fraudulent transaction, it is usually the retailer who ends up bearing the loss.

10.4 The legal nature of e-cash

The innovative nature of the products described above inevitably means that there is a lack of specific legislation applying to them. How far it will become necessary in the future to introduce legislation covering these products, only time will tell. Presently they represent an example of the current failure of the law to accommodate the evolution of e-commerce. What is required is an analysis of the existing principles to establish how the existing legislation affects the position.

10.4.1 *Money*

Many of the products are described as "cash" or "money" but how far do they represent money in the legal sense of the word and is this material in any event? The definition of money depends on the context in which it is used but generally includes cash in the form of bank notes and coins. It is not clear whether it is limited to legal tender which would not include e-cash (*see* Section 10.4.2 below).

There is case law (*Moss v. Hancock* (1899) 2 QB 111) which puts forward a wider definition of money which could encompass certain e-cash systems if and when they become generally accepted methods of payment. The case describes money as "that which passes freely from hand to hand throughout the community in final discharge of debts and full payment for commodities, being accepted equally without reference to the character or credit of the person who offers it and without the intention of the person who receives it to consume it or apply it to any other person other than in turn to tender it to others in discharge of debts or payment for commodities".

This sets out a number of criteria. The issue of final discharge and full payment are dealt with below. It seems clear that what is essential is the ability, once the money is received, to tender it to third parties; this effectively rules out Cybercash and Digicash from being correctly classified as cash since the "coins" used in those systems must be redeemed on receipt. Mondex clearly satisfies this requirement in view of the person-to-person payment facility under which the electronic value is accepted entirely off-line without any request for authorisation from a participating bank. VisaCash and Proton, if used on the Internet, would partially satisfy the requirement in that the stored value could be used to pay a variety of merchants but not other individuals, thus placing a limitation on the free circulation of the electronic value. The need to obtain authorisation/verification in certain systems from a central archive or the issuing institution would not satisfy the definition in that the value or "coins" would not be accepted without reference to the character or credit of the person tendering it. This would certainly rule out such systems as Digicash since each transaction involves prior authorisation from the issuing bank before the transaction is accepted and the goods or services despatched.

10.4.2 *Legal tender*

It has already been mentioned that e-cash is not legal tender. Bank notes and coins derive their status as legal tender from the Currency and Bank Notes Act 1954. The practical significance of this is limited to the fact that a person to whom a debt is owed cannot be obliged to accept electronic value as payment. This is subject to any agreement between the payor and the payee to the contrary and, in the usual course of events, it would be apparent from the conduct of the parties, as it would usually be evidenced by the display of a payment scheme logo on the computer screen that the payee was holding himself out to accept a particular form of e-cash as a payment method to discharge the debt in question.

The use of e-cash has not increased in line with the predictions made a few years ago despite the rapid growth of e-commerce during the same period. Whilst these products are in their infancy and represent a tiny proportion of the total cash in circulation the issue does not arise. If we ever do reach the stage where they represent a substantial proportion of the money supply, the issue becomes one for society as a whole which could lead to pressure for e-cash to be issued by, or under the auspices of, central government. If this occurs, it may seem appropriate to afford e-cash (or certain forms of it) the status of legal tender.

10.4.3 *Finality of payment*

The issue here is whether payment by e-cash represents a conditional or unconditional form of payment. Payment with legal tender for goods or services, or the discharge of a debt constitutes an absolute form of payment in that the payment is not conditional on the performance by a third party of an obligation. Payment by cheque, on the other hand, in the absence of a bank guarantee, constitutes a conditional form of payment in that the payee will have full recourse to the payer in the event that the cheque is not honoured by the bank upon which it is drawn. In the case of credit or charge cards, there is case law to the effect that the payment obligation is discharged at the point at which the payer signs the sales voucher; it is the merchant who is at risk if payment is not forthcoming from the credit or charge card issuer (*Re Charge Card Services*). It is ultimately a question of the parties' intentions.

As far as e-cash schemes are concerned, it is a case of looking at each one on its merits. There are features of the Mondex system, for example, which indicate that it would not be the intention of the parties that payment with Mondex value could be anything other than an absolute payment method. These are:

(a) the off-line nature of Mondex whereby there is no built in functionality to request authorisation; and

(b) the fact that value is actually transferred from card to card, be it a transaction in the physical or the virtual world.

Digicash, on the other hand, always requires a bank verification prior to the acceptance of the coins by the merchant and thus is clearly conditional on authorisation being forthcoming. Presumably, however, once the verification is forthcoming, the transaction would be without recourse to the user.

10.5   Deposit taking

In the UK, it is an offence for any institution to carry on a deposit-taking business without being authorised by the Financial Services Authority (the "FSA"). A deposit is defined in terms of it being a sum of money which is paid on terms under which it will be repaid, with or without interest or premium, either on demand or at a time, or in circumstances agreed by the parties. The essence of a deposit, therefore, is the undertaking to redeem.

The acceptance of e-cash on the basis that the sum in question will be credited to some form of account in the name of the payer is clearly a deposit-taking activity. More difficult is the question of whether electronic value held by the consumer or a merchant represents a deposit in the sense that it can be redeemed in return for legal tender or a credit to some form of account held with the redeeming institution. All e-cash systems involve the payment of money to the issuer in return for electronic value or "coins" held (or recorded on the card or PC), thus leaving an outstanding claim against the issuer. As the loading of the value is intended for spending rather than redemption, it would seem odd if it were classified as deposit taking.

This issue effectively determines whether an issuer of e-cash would fall within the supervisory jurisdiction of the FSA as the regulatory authority for banking in the UK.

E-cash issued by authorised banking institutions would, however, be regulated by the FSA as part of its general responsibility to regulate banking institutions. It is thus a highly significant point since it determines whether the new business of e-cash can be carried on only by those institutions already regulated by the FSA or whether new players whose business interests are closely aligned to the development of the Internet (such as telecommunications companies and software houses) may provide services in this area. The issue is now effectively resolved in the European Union by the introduction of Directive 2000/46/EC on the taking up, pursuit of and prudential supervision of the business of EMIs.

Again, the issue needs to be determined by reference to the features and contractual structure of each of the e-cash systems. In the case of Cybercash "coins", the "coins" are transferred to the customer's PC in return for a debit to the account held with the bank and the crediting of a pooled account held by Cybercash which acts as the float. If the consumer has a contractual right to redeem the "coins" against either the bank or the pooled account operated by Cybercash, then the "coins" may be interpreted as a deposit. If there is no right of redemption and all the consumer can do is spend the coins with an Internet merchant, there is no question of the "coins" amounting to a deposit. The fact that each transaction is separately routed through a central archive (something which would also be a feature of VisaCash and Proton if used on the Internet) would be a factor pointing towards classification of the "coins" as a deposit, since every use of the "coins" would be separately and identifiably debited to the issuing bank.

Although there is a clear right of redemption against the issuer, the structure of Mondex would tend to indicate that value held on the card could not appropriately be regarded as a deposit. The undertaking to the issuer's customer is not simply to redeem the amount loaded onto the card but to redeem such amount as the customer may be holding from time to time and, by reason of the person-to-person payment facility, this sum could be greater or lesser than the original sum loaded on to the card.

The position may be different in the case of those e-cash systems which do not permit person-to-person payments and operate on a fully-accounted basis with all transactions separately identifiable and individually settled. In that situation, the cardholder's claim against the issuing bank could never exceed the amount issued to him, and each use of the card would be separately and identifiably routed back to the issuer via the settlement system.

It may be possible to classify the issue and redemption of electronic value as a purchase and sale of the value which would take it outside the realm of deposit taking altogether. Much will depend on the structure of the terms and the conditions upon which the e-cash service is issued.

One major consequence of the outcome of this debate is the extent to which, if at all, the deposit protection scheme established by the Banking Act 1987 applies to e-cash products. This scheme is designed to protect depositors against bank insolvency and thereby provide a measure of confidence in the banking system. The outcome may mean that some products benefit from the protection of the scheme, thus securing a competitive advantage over those which do not. From a policy perspective, it could be argued that deposit protection schemes exist to protect savers, not spenders and that value stored on a card or PC is intended for spending and therefore should not attract protection.

In the US, the General Counsel of the Federal Deposit Insurance Corporation (the "FDIC") has published an opinion which divides e-cash products into:

(a) *bank primary* – where the bank holds the funds underlying the value directly; and

(b) *bank secondary* – where the funds are held by an (issuer) third party.

Bank primary products are then sub divided into:

(i) those where the funds are kept in a customer account; and

(ii) those where the funds are centrally pooled; and

bank secondary products are divided into:

(i) those where the bank purchases the value from a third party and then sells it on to customers; and

(ii) where the bank acts as a conduit between the issuer and the customers. The opinion concludes that the bank primary (customer account type) appeared to be an insured deposit whilst none of the other types of product gave rise to insurability.

No firm conclusions can be drawn in relation to the deposit issue. Each system must be assessed in relation to the contractual framework within which it operates.

One corollary of the deposit-taking debate is that if the value on the card or in the PC represents a deposit, then it would follow that the card or computer itself would effectively represent some form of account pass book and, presumably, a "bankers book" for the purposes of the Bankers Books Evidence Act 1979.

10.6 Investment

Although the application of the investment regulatory powers of the FSA with regard to e-cash appears far fetched, it should be noted that it is quite possible that markets could develop in the exchange of electronic value under which values would fluctuate depending on the strength of the issuing institution. Customers are likely to have more faith in e-cash issued by reputable financial or other major institutions than by unknown organisations, so one may trade at a discount against another, thus making them appear more like an investment.

10.7 Application of commercial law principles

10.7.1 *Chose in action*

A chose in action is property in an intangible. A good example is a debt which represents a claim for money owed by one person to another. Insofar as e-cash represents a right of redemption against the issuer to whom the holder has given consideration in return for the issue to him of e-cash, it is a chose in action. As commerce developed over the centuries, it became increasingly common to identify choses in action with documents which evidenced their existence and this has been reflected in the development of the law (most notably, for current purposes, the Bills of Exchange Act 1882). Bank notes are covered by the Act in that they are classed as Promissory Notes and benefit from the Act's protection. Now, with the development of information technology, there is a strong tendency for dematerialisation (in areas such as securities trading) of which e-cash is one example.

10.7.2 *Negotiability*

The doctrine of negotiability is an essential feature of monetary systems in that it generates confidence in the instruments which evidence the claim. The principles of the doctrine are that the instrument is transferable without the necessity for any formalities and that the holder of an instrument can pass a better title in the instrument that he had. If, for example, A steals a banknote from B and passes it to C who takes it in good faith and for value, C will have good title to the bank note as against B. Bank notes and bills of exchange are afforded negotiable status by reason of the Bills of Exchange Act but this Act is precluded from applying to any form of "instrument" which is represented by electronic data. The Act clearly requires such instruments to be "in writing". Negotiability is only relevant to those forms of e-cash, particularly Mondex, which can be passed from person-to-person as it is only with such systems that value is intended to circulate in the same way as bank notes and coins. The absence of negotiability does, to some extent, place e-cash at a disadvantage in that it may, in theory at least, have a bearing on the level of confidence generated in e-cash. It might be possible for these forms of payment to become accepted over time at common law as a form of bearer negotiable instrument by reason of commercial practice. There are examples of this (certificates of deposit is one) but none as yet in the field of computerised intangibles.

The Uniform Electronic Transactions Act 2000 (the "UETA") in the US makes provision for an electronic "transferable record" which gives the holder the same rights and defences that would apply to the holder of a paper bill. At the time of writing, the UETA has been adopted in 23 US states. It remains to be seen whether similar legislation will be adopted in the UK and the rest of Europe.

10.7.3 Sale of Goods Act and Supply of Goods and Services Act

The implied terms under this legislation covering, for example, fitness for purpose and satisfactory quality in the case of a sale of cards and other equipment, and use of reasonable care and skill in the case of the supply of computer software, would apply to the supply of e-cash products and would give the user some measure of protection. If, for example, a smart card containing value were faulty and the consumer lost e-cash as a result, there could be a claim against the seller or issuer of the card.

10.8 The criminal law

Reference has been made elsewhere in this Chapter to the failure to date of the current law to accommodate the development of e-cash and other electronic developments. The purpose of this Section is to examine the ways in which the criminal law may be inadequate to protect the participants in these schemes against fraud and fraud-related crime. In particular, the issue arises as to offences which may occur if fraudsters hack into e-cash systems and create forged value units.

In the past, in such cases as *R v. Gold* (1984) 1WLR962, the courts have made it clear that they will not "shoe-horn" a particular activity into the definition of a particular offence simply to keep pace with technological advances. When technology has advanced beyond the ambit of the criminal law, they take the view that it is for Parliament to remedy the situation. The situations set out below are likely, therefore, to give rise to the need for legislative change in the fullness of time.

10.8.1 Forgery and counterfeiting

The forgery of instruments is covered by the Forgery and Counterfeiting Act 1981. This creates a number of offences:

(a) making a false instrument (*see* Section 1 of the Forgery and Counterfeiting Act 1981);

(b) copying an instrument known, or believed, to be false (*see* Section 2 of the Forgery and Counterfeiting Act 1981);

(c) using an instrument or copying an instrument known, or believed, to be false (*see* Sections 3 and 4 of the Forgery and Counterfeiting Act 1981); and

(d) possessing certain types of instrument known, or believed, to be false either with or without intent to use them.

An instrument is defined to mean not only any document but also any disc, tape, sound track or other device on, or in, which information is recorded or stored by mechanical, electronic or other means. This would clearly include a smart card or PC storing electronic value. An instrument will be false if it tells a lie about itself but this has been interpreted as meaning that the document will not be false if it is in fact what it says it is but contains untrue statements. This is likely to be the situation where forged e-cash is created and held on a smart card or PC which is genuine. The problem would be exacerbated when the card or computer mixes forged value with genuine value. This would preclude the application of any of the offences listed above. Indeed, the forgery of value itself is unlikely to be regarded as an instrument by reason of the lack of tangibility. The sections in the Act dealing with counterfeiting relate only to the counterfeiting of notes and coins, and therefore have no application to the creation of false e-cash.

It is not clear whether electronic records can ever be truly unique in the sense that a paper record can be unique. No matter how good a counterfeit paper document, it is always possible (though often very difficult) to distinguish it from the original. That is not the case with electronic records of which perfect copies can be made. It would not therefore be possible to distinguish the counterfeit from the original and obtain evidence of forgery. Hence the need for specific anti-hacking legislation.

10.8.2 *Computer misuse*

The Computer Misuse Act 1990 creates three offences related to hacking into computer systems. These are:

(a) the unauthorised access to computer material (*see* Section 1 of the Computer Misuse Act 1990);

(b) the unauthorised access to computer material with intent to commit or facilitate commission of further offences (*see* Section 2 of the Computer Misuse Act 1990); and

(c) the unauthorised modification of computer material (*see* Section 3 of the Computer Misuse Act 1990).

The Act does not define computer. Although, technically, the microchip held on a smart card is a computer, the courts are likely to have difficulty with this notion by reason of the large number of everyday objects that now contain microchips (e.g. motor cars and washing machines) which would be inadvertently brought within the scope of the Act. Where electronic value is held on a PC, however, surely there can be no doubt that accessing the computer and interfering with the data contained in it, such to make the amount of value units held on the computer appear greater than is actually the case, would amount to an offence under Section 3 if not all three of the offences laid down by the Act. It would certainly seem odd if the effects of the Act were to protect electronic value held on a PC but not that held on a smart card.

10.9 Data protection and privacy

UK law on data protection is set out in the Data Protection Act 1998, which reflects the principles of the Data Protection Directive of the European Union. The Act applies to the holding of computerised personal data about individuals and lays down a number of principles relating to such data. These place obligations on the data holder in respect of such matters as the fair procurement of personal data, using it only for the purposes for which it was collected and keeping it secure. Many e-cash systems are described as offering privacy, although none can offer an absolute level of privacy. Digicash, for example, provides privacy to the extent that the issuing bank does not know which consumer is using the coins issued at the point of sale. This is because the consumer generates the serial number of the coin and this is not seen by the bank either at the time of issue of the coin or at redemption (*see* Figure 2). Mondex cards are issued with a personal identification number ("PID") which is captured by the purse with which it interfaces (together with a short transaction narrative) on a 10 transaction roll-over basis (i.e. it is not captured permanently but temporarily). The card issuing bank can match the customer's personal details with the PID but a merchant or other individual with whose card the customer's card interfaces cannot. Data held on the card may or may not, therefore, constitute personal data depending on the additional information held by the recipient (holder) of the data and whether it can be matched to the customer. It is quite likely that the ability of e-cash issuers to accommodate privacy principles will have a strong bearing on their acceptance by customers in the market. It may be possible to achieve anonymity for cards issued which are not linked to an account. If these are purchased for cash and there is no registration system, a high level of privacy would be afforded.

A recent development announced on the Internet is Internet cash (internetcash.com) which involves the purchase at physical retail outlets in the US of pre-paid smart cards loaded with e-cash. These are available in denominations up to $100 and may be used as a private way to make on-line purchases. No information is requested about the purchaser, so the cards are truly anonymous. The cards are particularly targeted at the youth market.

10.10 Regulatory attitudes and policy towards e-cash

In most countries, consideration of the regulatory issues to which e-cash gives rise has been driven mainly by the central banks and those regulatory organisations which have responsibility for regulating financial institutions.

In view of the global nature of payment systems, the Internet and the development of current initiatives, it was recognised at an early stage that consideration of the extent to which commonality exists in the views of regulators in different countries was desirable. This resulted in a number of reports and published opinions on the subject by such bodies as the Group of Ten (the central banks of the major economies), the European Monetary Institute and the European Central Bank. The latter covered only prepaid cards, although its conclusions may equally apply to software-based systems.

Regulatory policy in this area may be said to broadly cover the following objectives:

(a) *systemic risk* – there is clearly a need to limit the extent to which e-cash may give rise to systemic and other risks which could threaten the stability of financial markets or undermine confidence in the payment system;

(b) *supervision* – the issue arises as to which body (if any) should supervise e-cash issuance, the scope and nature of any such supervision, and the entry criteria which should apply;

(c) *consumer protection* – to ensure that consumers are adequately protected from fraud and unfair practices, financial loss in the event of insolvency etc. or any unwarranted intrusion into their personal privacy whilst, at the same time, encouraging the development of effective and low-cost, convenient payment systems for consumers and businesses;

(d) *monetary policy* – there is a need to ensure that the central bank and governments are able to conduct monetary policy effectively; and

(e) *law enforcement* – the need to ensure that law enforcement authorities (particularly in such areas as money laundering and tax) are not hindered in their need to prevent and detect the movement of funds associated with criminal activity.

Before considering each one of these regulatory objectives in turn, it is necessary to consider two fundamental points.

First, in most countries and for many years, the issue of money has been the exclusive preserve of the government. In the UK, this has been the case since the middle of 19th century. A fundamental point to address therefore is whether the issue of e-cash by private sector organisations is lawful at all. The Bank of England's monopoly on the issue of bank notes was given to it by the Bank Charter Act 1844. Section 11 of the Act provides that it shall not be lawful for any banker to "draw, accept, make, or issue, in England or Wales, any Bill of Exchange or Promissory Note or Engagement for the Payment of Money payable to Bearer on Demand...".

As indicated above, it is clear that e-cash cannot be classed as a bill of exchange or promissory note, as both these types of instrument must be in writing. The concept of an "engagement" would seem to suggest some form of promise or undertaking which e-cash does not of itself involve. It seems clear therefore that the issue of e-cash does not infringe the Bank of England's note-issuing monopoly.

Secondly, the consideration by regulators has always concentrated on those systems which are cash-like in their application and effect. Therefore, regulators have not been concerned about single-purpose payment systems such as telephones or mass transit payment cards where stored value is issued to a consumer who may use it to purchase goods or services from the issuer.

10.10.1 Systemic risk

The issue of e-cash creates a liability on the issuer's balance sheet. The issuer will at some stage (depending on the features of the system) be called upon to redeem the electronic units either from another issuer, a merchant or the customer to whom it issued the units in the first place. There may be a risk of issuers having to bear the risk of fraud in the event that they need to redeem counterfeit electronic value units or where the float which is created by the issue of the value units is not invested in such a way to ensure that it maintains the value of the e-cash in circulation. The liability created could threaten the solvency of the issuing institution which could, in turn, threaten the solvency of other organisations by means of the so-called domino effect. It is generally recognised, however, that the current size of the existing systems would not give rise to any issues of this nature. However, it is this type of issue which does give rise to arguments that the issue of e-cash should be restricted to banks which are subject to capital adequacy and liquidity requirements, thereby mitigating against risks of this nature.

10.10.2 Supervision

In Europe, the European Monetary Institute issued an influential report in 1994 which analysed the implications of prepaid cards for central banks and concluded that the balances on multi-purpose prepaid cards represented funding which, in economic terms, was equivalent to deposit-taking. Therefore, in order to ensure (as far as possible) the soundness of the issuer of electronic purses, the report recommended that only credit institutions (i.e. banks or their equivalent) should be allowed to issue them. This view has subsequently been reviewed and EU policy is now reflected in Directive 2000/46/EC on the taking up, pursuit of and prudential supervision of EMIs (*see* Section 10.10.3). In the US and Canada, for example, the stated policy is to maintain a watching brief on the development of current initiatives and to keep an open mind on whether organisations other than banks should be permitted to issue electronic purses.

It has been mentioned already that e-cash is unlikely to constitute deposit taking which would preclude the regulation of issuers as deposit takers by the FSA. Some form of supervision may, however, generate confidence in e-cash systems, although the full range of regulatory requirements which currently apply to banking organisations (e.g. solvency requirements and liquidity rules) may not be appropriate to organisations involved solely in the issue of e-cash. In the absence of clear laws to the effect that a regulatory body is responsible for supervision in this area – either through some form of licensing or by imposing minimum entry criteria – then it is open to any organisation to issue e-cash which (in theory at least) increases the possibility of users being at risk from fraud or financial cost.

10.10.3 *Directive 2000/46/EC Electronic Money Institutions*

The main provisions of the Directive are summarised below:

(a) The Directive introduces a separate prudential supervisory regime for EMI which are defined as undertakings issuing means of payment in the form of e-money. The competent authority (the FSA in the UK) has the responsibility for the prudential management of EMIs. The Directive recognises that the business of issuing e-money does not constitute deposit taking and accordingly not all of the regulatory requirements applying to banks should apply to EMIs.

(b) EMIs are required to have initial capital of not less than €1 million which should not fall below that amount. There are requirements for the EMI to have own funds to a level exceeding the total value of electronic money liabilities outstanding. This is to ensure that the EMI should always be able to meet its redemption obligations. Restrictions on the quality of investments which can be made by an EMI also apply and there are restrictions on the types of institutions in which EMIs may hold an interest.

(c) The activities of an EMI, other than the issue of e-money are restricted to ancillary functions related to e-cash and other payment methods (excluding the granting of credit). They may also be involved in the storing of data on the electronic device which facilitates their involvement in multi-function smart cards which could store a range of other services (e.g. loyalty points). This ensures that an EMI will not be exposed to liability from other commercial activities that may have a bearing on being able to meet their e-cash redemption obligations.

(d) There are requirements in the Directive for the EMI to operate sound prudential management, administration, accounting procedures and adequate internal control mechanisms.

(e) E-money is defined in the Directive as meaning monetary value as represented by a claim on the issuer which is:

   (i) stored on an electronic device,

   (ii) is issued on receipt of funds of an amount not less than the monetary value issued; and

   (iii) accepted as a means of payment by undertakings other than the issuer.

(f) The Directive requires that the bearer of e-money has the right to request redemption at par value and that any conditions relating to redemption must be in the contract between the issuer and the bearer. The contract may stipulate a minimum redemption threshold for redemption which must not exceed €10.

10.10.4   *Consumer protection*

It is recognised that e-cash is potentially of great benefit to consumers and such systems should be encouraged, provided they give rise to an acceptable level of risk. The potential benefits include convenience, flexibility, speed and a reduction in costs. The potential risks to consumers are as follows:

(a) *Insolvency of the issuer* – if the organisation against which the consumer's claim in respect of e-money held by him exists becomes insolvent, the consumer, in the ordinary course of events, is an unsecured creditor and is unlikely to receive back from the liquidator a large proportion of the value held on his card, or PC. This exposure may be reduced in the event that the value is deemed to be a deposit, thus attracting the protection of the deposit-protection scheme. The risk may also be reduced by a requirement to the effect that the issuer must be a single purpose entity, as this would reduce the potential number of creditors in the event of insolvency. Mondex seeks to address the risk by providing for all funds (the float) in respect of which electronic value is issued to be held with a separate entity – the originator. Cardholders' funds should be protected in the event of the insolvency of the card issuing institution, against which the cardholders' claims would usually lie.

(b) *Improper use of customer information* – some concern has been expressed about the extent to which new payment systems may give rise to greater opportunities for the collection of additional personal data about consumers and the extent to which this might be open to abuse. Physical cash is perceived to be anonymous whereas this is not necessarily the case with e-cash (*see* Section 10.9).

(c) *Lost or stolen cards or value* – There is a need to distinguish between loss of value held on a smart card or PC which issuers are unlikely to accept responsibility for, and unlawful access to a customer's account where the customer's liability should be limited as it is with other forms of payment card. These principles are now reflected in the Code of Banking Practice which states: "You should treat your electronic purse like cash in a wallet. You will lose any money left in the electronic purse at the time it is lost or stolen, in just the same way as if you lost your wallet. However, if your electronic purse is credited by unauthorised withdrawals from your account before you tell us of its loss, theft or misuse, your liability for such amounts will be limited to a maximum of £50, unless you have acted fraudulently or with gross negligence". This was clearly written to cover card-based systems as opposed to computer-based ones; future editions of the Code may therefore require revision. As with the provision of the Code relating to debit cards, the liability provision now needs to be read in the light of the Consumer Protection (Distance Selling) Regulations 2000 (*see* Section 10.3.4).

10.11 Monetary policy

Governments currently control the issue of their own currencies. To the extent that physical money is replaced by its electronic equivalent, it will not be controlled by central government but by the private sector. This could potentially impact on the ability of central government to control the money supply. To the extent that e-cash is issued without being fully backed by currency, there would be an increase in the money supply. If the float generated by the issue of e-cash is invested in a speculative manner, this could also potentially increase the money supply. Where e-cash issuers are regulated institutions currently supervised by the FSA, these issues can be addressed as part of the usual prudential management relationship that exists between them. This will, of course, not be the case where e-cash is issued by organisations outside the regulated environment.

10.12 Law enforcement

10.12.1 Money laundering

The main thrust of discussions in this area focuses on money laundering. This may be broadly defined as the means by which money generated by illegal activity may be converted into apparently legitimate funds. Money laundering is seen as a major area of concern by governments globally, with billions of dollars annually flowing into the international economy from illicit trades such as drug trafficking. The laws passed to address this issue – The Money Laundering Regulations 1993 – have tended to assume that criminals need to move funds through the financial system, primarily through banks, in order to conceal and benefit from the proceeds of their crimes efficiently. A similar approach has been taken in other countries. To the extent that new forms of payment could potentially give rise to the ability to conveniently hold large amounts of value outside the banking system, this assumption could be open to question and thus impact the efficacy of existing law. The questions which arise in relation to money laundering are:

(a) can the current laws be complied with?; and

(b) does e-cash give rise to opportunities for money laundering beyond those which currently exist?

The Money Laundering Regulations 1993, which enshrine the principles of the European Directive on the subject, stipulate that the financial institution must:

(a) know its customer;

(b) maintain adequate records; and

(c) report suspicious transactions.

It is submitted that it is perfectly feasible for financial institutions to comply with these principles when issuing and redeeming e-cash. A bank can insist on the same account opening procedures as it would for any other account relationship. The requirements to report and maintain records apply only at the point at which the value enters the system; the usual procedures can apply to identify and report suspicious transactions. Indeed, there are strong arguments to suggest that the reporting obligation would be fulfilled more efficiently if suspicious transactions were identified electronically rather than manually. Law enforcement authorities are on record as accepting that they are often unable to cope with the volume of paper-based transactions reported to them. It should be noted that the Regulations apply only to financial institutions and do not, therefore, apply to non-financial institutions entering the market; this may give law enforcement agencies some cause for concern.

One accepts that if e-cash systems were configured in such a way to facilitate large sums of money being transferred globally and held outside the banking system, then a convenient vehicle for organised crime would have been created. However, the product features and operational controls which apply to the current initiatives should prevent this from being a major issue in practice. Digicash and Cybercoin do not permit the value to be spent more than once and so it has to be repatriated to the issuer after each use. If the issuer is a bank, then the regulations will apply at that point. The operational limits which apply to Mondex cards ensure that:

(a) cosumer cards may only hold a maximum of a few hundred pounds;

(b) large volumes of person-to-person activity cause the card to switch off, requiring a visit to the issuer for the card to be reset; and

(c) higher-value merchant cards are configured so that they can only pay value into a bank account at which point the Regulations apply.

It is submitted that such controls effectively constrain any perceived risk within manageable proportions.

10.12.2   *Tax*

Taxation authorities have also expressed concern about payments on the Internet. The concern centres on the structure of indirect taxation systems (such as VAT) which rely on an obligation on the supplier of goods or services to collect the tax on behalf of the tax man. In a world where there is a greatly increased level of cross border sales, the supplier is much more likely to be outside the jurisdiction and thus beyond the control of the tax authorities. This has led to concern about the ability of payment systems to transmit large sums across borders and to suggestions that banks and payment system operators should be responsible for collection.

10.13   Future regulation

The Chapter makes reference to several legislative initiatives having a bearing on Internet payment systems. As regards Internet communications generally, the UK Government, in common with governments all over the world, are keen to facilitate electronic means of communication and to remove obstacles. Most of the initiatives covered by this Chapter depend on some form of digital or electronic signature and the Electronic Communications Act 2000 (which incorporates the requirements of the EU Directive on Electronic Signatures) was passed in July 2000. The Act provides for the legal recognition of electronic signatures and their admissibility as evidence in court proceedings. It also lays down a framework for removing legal obstacles to electronic communications.

Despite the attention given in this Chapter to the difficulty of applying current legislation and legal principles in relation to e-cash developments, and to the issues raised by regulators, it is generally regarded as premature to introduce specific detailed regulation. The variety of initiatives, the fact that it is not clear which ones will survive in the longer term, the sheer pace of commercial and technical development at the present time, and the lack of empirical experience of how these products really work are all factors supporting the view that detailed regulation at the time of writing would be premature. It could well add to costs and stultify developments. Regulations proposed to date by countries all over the world have tended to concentrate on the extent to which, and the terms on which, non-banks should be allowed to enter the business. Clearly, however, there is a need for regulators and law enforcers to maintain and develop close links with the industry with a view to monitoring developments and deepening their understanding. It is important that products are developed and maintained by responsible institutions which will gain the public's confidence and much could also be achieved through "voluntary self regulation" via payment scheme operating rules and regulations.

Figure 1 Credit Cards/SET

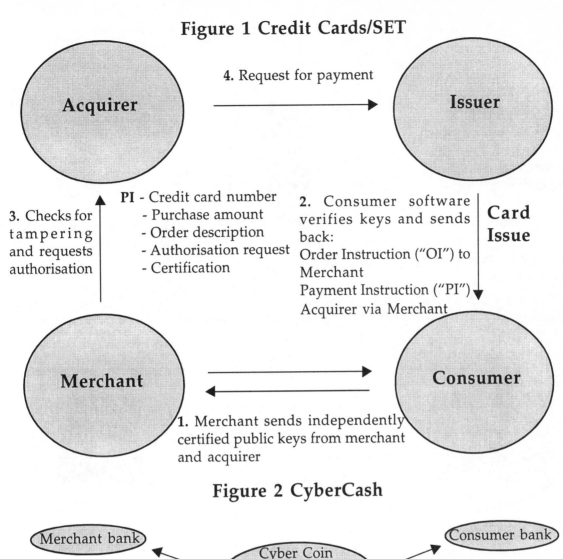

4. Request for payment

Acquirer → **Issuer**

3. Checks for tampering and requests authorisation

PI - Credit card number
- Purchase amount
- Order description
- Authorisation request
- Certification

2. Consumer software verifies keys and sends back:
Order Instruction ("OI") to Merchant
Payment Instruction ("PI") Acquirer via Merchant

Card Issue

Merchant → **Consumer**

1. Merchant sends independently certified public keys from merchant and acquirer

Figure 2 CyberCash

Merchant bank

Consumer bank

Cyber Coin merchant bank holding float

Fund transfers are made using proprietary banking network.

Cyber coin and red accounts are **Settled**.

1. Consumer & merchant **download** Cybercash wallet & cash register, and "bind" them to an existing credit or debit account.

4. Merchant cash register sends payment **instruction** to server which checks available funds, credits & debits shadow accounts & sends confirmation.

Cyber coin merchant using

2. Consumer purchases **"coins"** using bound account; value is then recorded in Cybercash server & wallet.

Shadow accounts at cyber cash server

3. Consumer **"sends coins"** (payment instruction)

Goods merchant

Consumer

5. Merchant dispatches goods.

Figure 3 Digicash

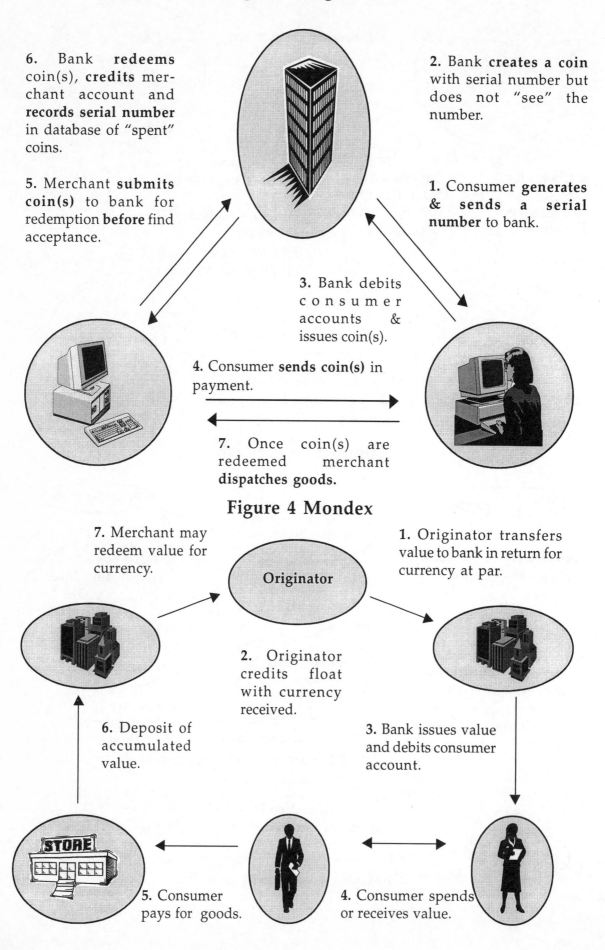

6. Bank **redeems** coin(s), **credits** merchant account and **records serial number** in database of "spent" coins.

5. Merchant **submits coin(s)** to bank for redemption **before** find acceptance.

2. Bank **creates a coin** with serial number but does not "see" the number.

1. Consumer **generates & sends a serial number** to bank.

3. Bank debits consumer accounts & issues coin(s).

4. Consumer **sends coin(s)** in payment.

7. Once coin(s) are redeemed merchant **dispatches goods.**

Figure 4 Mondex

7. Merchant may redeem value for currency.

Originator

1. Originator transfers value to bank in return for currency at par.

2. Originator credits float with currency received.

3. Bank issues value and debits consumer account.

6. Deposit of accumulated value.

STORE

5. Consumer pays for goods.

4. Consumer spends or receives value.

Chapter 11
ELECTRONIC SIGNATURES

Christopher Kuner
Attorney at Law
Morrison & Foerster LLP (Brussels)

11.1   Introduction

Security concerns have become one of the major stumbling blocks to the development of the Internet. These concerns relate not only to confidentiality, but also to authenticity and integrity. For example, proving that communications over the Internet were actually sent from the person from whom they purport to originate, and that they have not been changed since they were sent, are both very real security concerns, and problems that can be solved through the use of the proper electronic authentication technologies.

A number of authentication technologies have been developed to overcome these problems, the best-known of which are so-called "digital signatures". This Chapter will focus largely on digital signatures, which are perhaps the most technically sophisticated and effective method of ensuring authenticity and integrity over open networks, and have also been the focus of most electronic authentication legislation around the world. However, readers should remember that there are a number of other authentication technologies which to some extent compete with digital signatures, and to some extent complement them; such technologies will be discussed in this Chapter as appropriate. Moreover, authentication legislation is increasingly focusing on "electronic signatures" as a broader, more generic concept than just digital signatures.

11.1.1   Technical background

As stated above, there are many authentication technologies presently being used or under development. It is not possible here to give the technical background of each of them, rather, this description will focus largely on so-called "digital signatures", while mentioning other technologies when relevant.

Digital signatures are based on a highly complex mathematical procedure. While it is certainly not necessary for businessmen or lawyers to know all the details of this procedure, the more they know about the technical side of digital signatures, the more they will be able to understand the legal framework for using them.

In order to impart the technical basics of digital signatures, the description given here will be kept fairly simple and concise.

11.1.2   Cryptographic basics

Cryptography is the science of rendering a secret message unintelligible to third parties. It is important to separate two functions for which cryptography can be used, namely:

(a) confidentiality (i.e. keeping the substance of a message secret); and

(b) authenticity and integrity (i.e. ensuring the authenticity of the sender of a message and that the message has not been altered since it was sent).

This distinction is very important for legal and regulatory purposes, since confidentiality involves a number of difficult and contentious law enforcement issues which authenticity and integrity do not. Therefore, this Chapter will not deal with the use of cryptography for confidentiality. Readers should, however, be aware that some cryptographic techniques can be used for both purposes, so it is not always possible to separate these two issues as neatly as one would like.

11.1.3 Symmetric and asymmetric cryptography

The concept of digital signatures is based on asymmetric cryptography. Until its development cryptographic techniques had all been symmetric – that is, the same key was used to both encrypt and decrypt a message. Asymmetric cryptography was largely developed by Dr Martin Hellmann and Dr Whitfield Diffie in California in the mid-1970s (though recent information suggests that its basics may actually have been discovered by various government intelligence services in the 1960s). Diffie and Hellmann made the revolutionary innovation of providing separate keys for both encryption and decryption.

This innovation was important, since open networks do not provide a secure channel for the exchange of keys – that is, when two parties who already know each other and who are communicating over a secure channel wish to share a secret, it is at least theoretically possible for them to do so confidentially. However, when both parties do not know each other, or are communicating over an open network such as the Internet, in which it is relatively easy to intercept, read and even change data such as email, they will not be able to share private information, such as a key, and be sure that it has not been intercepted by an unauthorised third party.

Diffie and Hellmann's technique of asymmetric cryptography gets around these problems by allowing the use of separate keys for encryption and decryption. While it uses highly sophisticated mathematics, the technique is elegantly simple. Each user (that is, recipient and sender) generates his own key pair, the so-called "private key" and "public key", on his computer. The "keys" are actually long strings of prime numbers. The idea of asymmetric cryptography is that the private key must be kept strictly confidential and should be known only to the user, while the public key may be shared with the world without compromising security.

The data that is to be "signed" must be created in digital form. A mathematical value called a "hash value" is then created by the computer, which is in effect a "fingerprint" of the message. If the data is changed, the hash value will no longer correspond to it, so an error message will be generated. The signer then encrypts the hash value with his private key. This creates a digital signature which is unique both to the data unit and to the private key used, and is appended to the data to be sent. After the data is sent and received over the Internet, the recipient uses the sender's public key to regenerate the hash value and the digital signature. It is then compared to the digital signature appended to the message. If the result is identical, then the recipient can be sure that the data was indeed sent by the alleged sender, and that it has not been altered since it was sent.

Other types of authentication methods may be used instead of, or in combination with, digital signatures. For example, biometrics (authentication systems based on a physical characteristic of the user, such as a fingerprint or a retina scan) may be used as a kind of special password to access a user's private key. Likewise, so-called "signature dynamics" technology may authenticate a user based on the way he signs a document with a special electronic pen.

11.1.4 *Requirements for secure use of electronic signatures*

Even when the mathematical procedures for generating and using electronic signatures may themselves be nearly 100 per cent secure (as is the case with digital signatures), the security of electronic signatures (including digital signatures) is not automatic, but depends on several important conditions being met:

(a) first of all, secure procedures to create and verify signatures must be used. The use of insecure procedures, such as in the generation of random numbers, can result in signatures which are not completely secure, so that the authenticity and integrity of the data cannot be ensured with complete certainty. It is also vital that the signature formula or algorithm used has been thoroughly tested and found to be secure; the most popular such digital signature algorithm at present is the RSA algorithm, which was developed by Drs Ronald Rivest, Adi Shamir and Leonard Adelman at MIT in the 1970s;

(b) secondly (and this is particularly true with regard to digital signatures), it is absolutely essential that users keep their private key truly private – that is, it must never be shared or copied. This means, in practice, that the private key will either be stored on a smart card, or in the user's Personal Computer ("PC") in a secure software environment. It is for this reason that the storage of keys, variously known as "key recovery" or "key escrow", and which is often advocated by law enforcement authorities in the context of cryptography for confidentiality, is completely out of place in the context of signature keys. Whilst storage of a confidentiality key may be useful in some narrowly-defined situations (e.g. storing encryption keys used for corporate communications in case the employee in charge of encrypting the company's communications dies), there should never be a need to store signature keys. If a signature key is lost or cannot be accessed, the key owner can simply generate new keys, publish its new public key, and resign and resend the data. Thus, storage of signature keys is unnecessary and can introduce grave security risks by allowing anyone with access to the stored signature key to sign documents as if he were the key owner;

(c) thirdly, it is necessary for the recipient of a message signed with a digital signature to verify that the public key of the sender used by the recipient to regenerate the hash value and the digital signature actually belongs to the sender – that is, the sender must make his public key known to the world, and recipients of his digitally-signed messages must be able to verify that the public key, and thus the message itself, actually came from the sender. There are different methods for ensuring this, but by far the most popular is through the use of a "public key infrastructure" ("PKI") – that is, a structure of so-called "certification authorities" ("CAs") which are entities that certify that a public key actually belongs to the person who purports to use it. There are a number of companies already offering CA services, and it is expected that the number will increase significantly in the next few years.

(d) and finally, it is essential to remember that the security of an electronic signature depends not only on the security components of the signature itself (such as the key length, or algorithm used to generate the signature), but on the entire security environment in which the signature is used. Thus, for example, the use of highly-secure signature keys will not matter if the software environment in which the signature is generated is plagued by viruses. Security is thus a complex and never-ending process, rather than a static result to be achieved by using a particular component.

11.1.5   *Uses and applications of electronic signatures*

In considering the regulation of electronic signatures, it is always important to keep in mind the uses to which they may be put. As electronic signatures are, in the end, merely the result of a mathematical process, it is very difficult to consider their regulation in a vacuum.

Many people often forget that electronic signatures are nothing new, but have been used for years in various contexts. For example, millions of people everyday enter passwords (which is a type of electronic signature) in automatic bank teller machines. However, digital signatures are generally believed to be the most important variety of electronic signature technology, since they can ensure secure authentication over open networks (e.g., the Internet).

Nevertheless, digital signatures are not yet used as widely as one might expect. Part of the present difficulty in the wide deployment of digital signatures relates to the technological means for implementing their use. At the present time, it is much easier and more cost-effective to deploy digital signatures in a software environment; whilst a hardware environment, involving the use of smart cards, offers extra security, it is overly expensive, and the hardware infrastructure is lacking. Moreover, up to now there has not been a set of standardised products for digital and electronic signatures which would allow consumers to use them transparently and without extra effort; however, this situation is expected to change rapidly. Use of digital signatures in consumer transactions is already possible through the integration of "appropriate certificate functionality" in the main Internet browsers (Microsoft Internet Explorer and Netscape Communicator). Another problem has been the lack of a fully-developed and widely-available public key infrastructure. On the other hand, the business community, in particular financial institutions, already use digital signatures widely for money transfers, and plans are underway to deploy them much more widely in other areas as well. Time will tell whether digital signatures fulfill their enormous promise, or whether other, less costly and complex signature technologies fulfill many of the roles that have so far been foretold for digital signatures.

11.2   Legal aspects of electronic signatures

Discussing the legal aspects of electronic signatures is made more difficult by the fact that there is no general agreement as to the meaning of the terminology involved. For example, the term "digital signature" is generally used synonymously with asymmetric cryptography, but is sometimes understood to include other electronic authentication techniques as well, for example simple signature techniques such as scanning in a handwritten signature, or more complex technologies such as biometrics. It is thus important to be clear about definitions.

While the legal situation of electronic signatures is obviously dependent to a great extent on the law of the particular jurisdiction involved, a number of legal issues tend to be common to most jurisdictions, including in particular the following:

(a) *definition of a "signature"* – many jurisdictions have signature requirements that have traditionally required pen on paper (e.g. Germany). Uncertainty often arises when determining whether such requirements can be satisfied by electronic technologies, such as digital signatures. Common law legal systems tend to be more lenient as to what is considered a "signature" than do codified law systems;

(b) *liability issues* – there is considerable disagreement as to what extent existing liability rules apply to electronic signatures, and whether new liability rules are necessary for them. This disagreement finds expression in the welter of new electronic signature laws, some of which contain liability provisions, and others which do not;

(c) *international recognition* – since communication networks, whether closed like a corporate intranet or open like the Internet, are inherently global and borderless, it is essential that the legal frameworks allow electronic certificates and signatures to be recognised across national borders. National legal systems are presently inconsistent on this issue, and few of the new electronic signature laws contain explicit provisions on international recognition;

(d) *incorporation by reference* – some jurisdictions (particularly many codified law systems) do not recognise the common-law concept of "incorporation by reference", whereby a document referred to in another document may be deemed to be incorporated into it. This is a significant issue in regard to electronic signatures, since many firms offering digital signature products and services make use of incorporation by reference in their products. For instance, a certification authority's "Certification Practice Statement" ("CPS"), which sets out its standard terms and conditions of business, may be incorporated by reference electronically into its certificates; and

(e) *consumer protection issues* – because electronic signatures are a new and unfamiliar technology for most people (although, as described above, they are not really new), their ever-increasing use involves a number of consumer protection issues. For instance, the question arises as to what degree of care the holder of a private key should be obligated to exercise in keeping it secret, and who should be liable if it is misused. Privacy issues (e.g. allowing users to sign digitally using pseudonyms) are also likely to become increasingly important.

Legal rules relating to electronic signatures are in a state of flux, so readers should always inform themselves about the particular legal situation in force at a particular time. The discussion in this Chapter reflects the legal situation in December 2000.

11.2.1 *National legal systems*

It is impossible to give here a comprehensive survey of the legal situation in all jurisdictions around the world, rather, a representative sample will be discussed. Further materials, and materials concerning countries not discussed here, can be found at the websites listed in Table 1.

11.2.1.1   The UK

It is instructive to examine the situation under UK law before implementation of the EU Directive. UK law has contained over a dozen statutory definitions of "signature", and it was always unclear to what extent they could be extended to signatures in digital form. All but a couple of these statutory definitions did not refer explicitly to electronic documents. Case law has tended to be rather lenient in allowing a wide variety of signature methods (e.g. *Goodman v. J. Eban Ltd.*, [1954] 1 QB 550, [1954] All ER 763, [1954] 2 WLR 581, Court of Appeal). However, court decisions have tended to define a signature as a "mark" on a document, which is obviously difficult to extend to digital information. Moreover, in some instances legislation requires a "personal" signature, which requires handwriting, and courts have often enforced this requirement strictly. However, parties have always been free under English law to use electronic signatures, to the extent that legislation does not require a "personal signature" or a signature on a written document.

The UK Government made a number of specific proposals for a legal framework for digital signatures even before the EU Directive was finalized. For instance, in March 1997, the Government published a public consultation paper entitled "Licensing of Trusted Third Parties for the Provision of Encryption Services" (the so-called "TTP proposal"). The main points of the TTP proposal were as follows:

(a) CAs and other providers of public key certification services ("TTPs") to the general public would require a licence. However, a user in the UK would be free to choose their own TTP, and there would be exceptions to the licensing requirement for intra-company TTPs or similar closed user groups;

(b) the definition of encryption services was very broad and covered almost any service using cryptography, such as key generation, key management, key storage and the use of digital signatures; and

(c) the Government stated that it "had no intention" of accessing private keys used for only integrity functions, but would require deposit of keys used for confidentiality.

The government then rethought its policy, and in April 1998 published a revised "Secure Electronic Commerce Statement". Under the new policy, there would be no mandatory licensing requirement (even for confidentiality), but a voluntary licensing scheme would be introduced, under which key recovery would be mandatory for encryption services (i.e. for confidentiality), but not for digital signatures.

After a great deal of debate, on 25 July 2000 the Electronic Communications Act 2000, which implements the EU Directive (*see* below), came into force. The Act retreats from the government's earlier plans to introduce a key recovery scheme, and also leaves open the question of how a voluntary accreditation scheme for electronic signature products and services should be structured. Article 7 of the Act provides that "In any legal proceedings (a) an electronic signature incorporated into or logically associated with a particular electronic communication or particular electronic data, and (b) the certification by any person of such a signature, shall each be admissible in evidence in relation to any question as to the authenticity of the communication or data or as to the integrity of the communication or data", thus removing legal impediments to the use of electronic signatures. The structure of a possible voluntary accreditation scheme is presently under discussion.

11.2.1.2   *The US*

Traditionally, there has been no "law of electronic signatures" in the US; rather, electronic signatures generally fall under contract law, which is within the jurisdiction of the 50 states. Each state has its own legal principles which govern the use of electronic signatures, and which can vary greatly. Beyond that, there are general principles of contract law which tend not to vary much from state-to-state. Basically, any mark which indicates a person's intent to agree can constitute a signature in most US legal systems; however, there are some specific legal difficulties relating to the use of electronic signatures. For instance, the common law Statute of Frauds, which is still in force in most US jurisdictions, requires that contracts for a sum greater than $500 be in writing, which presents obvious difficulties.

By far the largest number of US legislative developments in the area of digital signatures have been at state level. Beginning with the Utah Digital Signature Law in 1995, nearly all states have passed digital signature laws. The laws vary greatly, from more regulatory approaches (such as the Utah law), to more minimalist laws (like that of Texas), to mixed approaches (the best example of which is the Illinois Electronic Commerce Security Act). To deal with the myriad of state digital signature laws, an expert group drafted a model law called the "Uniform Electronic Transactions Act" (the "UETA"), which was approved in July 1999, and is available for adoption by state legislatures (there is no requirement that UETA be adopted). The most important provisions of UETA concern the attribution of electronic signatures, the time when messages are deemed sent or received, mistakes in electronic contracting, admissibility of electronic records as evidence, electronic documents of title or promissory notes not secured by real property, and the manner in which paper processes will be converted to electronic processes by state governments. At the time this Chapter was completed, approximately 20 US states had adopted UETA.

Notwithstanding UETA, the variety of legislative approaches to digital signature regulation in the US led to calls for federal legislation to produce a unified legal framework. These calls were met by passage of the federal "Electronic Signatures in Global and National Commerce Act" (the "E-Sign Act"), which went into effect on 1 October 2000. While on the one hand creating enhanced legal certainty in some areas, the E-Sign Act also raises some important questions, in particular concerning its interaction with UETA.

The Act provides generally that for any transaction in or affecting interstate commerce, a signature, contract or other record, including formal notices and disclosures, in connection with that transaction shall not be denied legal effect simply because it is in electronic form. This broad language creates a federal principle of legal equivalency between paper and electronic methods of forming and authenticating contracts and other documents. It should be noted that the E-Sign Act does not require any party to a transaction to accept an electronic document or signature, and does not prevent any party from contesting the authenticity of an electronic writing or the reliability of the technology on which such a writing is based. In short, the statute puts electronic records and signatures in the same – but no better – legal position than their paper equivalents.

Exceptions to the general rule of the statute also are significant. The three principal categories of exceptions are:

(a) consumer consent requirements;

(b) exceptions based on state law; and

(c) specific exclusions for some types of records and transactions.

The consumer consent requirements apply to any record that is required by law or regulation to be provided or made available to a consumer in writing. Where such a requirement applies, it will be satisfied by an electronic record only if the consumer is provided with certain statutorily mandated disclosures, affirmatively consents to the use of an electronic record, and has not withdrawn that consent.

The legislation also permits the states to limit the application of the Act in several ways. Notably, a state may modify, limit or supersede its provisions: (a) through adoption of UETA; or (b) by specifying alternative procedures and requirements establishing the effect or enforceability of electronic contracts, agreements or records. In order to limit the states' discretion in this area, the Act also provides that non-UETA state laws affecting matters covered by the statute may not discriminate for or against particular technologies and must be consistent with the Act. These provisions will result in a period of inevitable uncertainty as to which provisions of existing state laws governing electronic signatures and records will be deemed to be preempted and which will remain effective.

The E-Sign Act includes provisions designed to promote the international legal interoperability of electronic signatures and certificates. In particular, it provides that "the Secretary of Commerce shall take all actions necessary in a manner consistent with such principles to eliminate or reduce, to the maximum extent possible, the impediments to commerce in electronic signatures, for the purpose of facilitating the development of interstate and foreign commerce (Section 301(a)(1)).

Besides the E-Sign Act, there are other pieces of federal legislation with direct relevance for digital signatures. For instance, on 20 March 1997 the US Food and Drug Administration promulgated "Rules on Electronic Records and Electronic Signatures" (21 CFR Part 11) which allow for the electronic filing of drug applications and the like.

11.2.1.3   Germany

The German Digital Signature Law, which took effect on 1 July 1997, was the first comprehensive digital signature law at federal level in Europe (and one of the first in the world). The German legislation, which comprises the Digital Signature Law, the Digital Signature Ordinance and Technical Catalogues, established a voluntary technical standard which enjoys enhanced evidentiary presumptions in court. At least originally, the German Government intended the statutory digital signature standard to become a de facto standard which would be widely used for all applications. However, the fact that the standard is set at such a high security level (elements for generation and storage of private keys are, for example, required to attain an ITSEC level of "E4 high", and thus virtually require the use of smart cards) has resulted in criticism from abroad, and lack of broad commercial acceptance in Germany. Thus, it is likely that the German digital signature standard will find broadest acceptance in applications requiring a particularly high degree of security (e.g. for financial transactions or communications in the legal system). The present German legislation does not presently contain any mention of liability or written-form requirements, as it was decided that further consideration is required.

At the time this Chapter was completed, the German legislation was in the process of being amended to implement the EU Directive. As substantial changes to the law will likely be necessary, the legal situation there may change in the near future.

11.2.2   *International organisations*

The Internet is itself borderless, and it is impossible to know in advance which route data transmitted over the Internet will use to arrive at the recipient. It is precisely this uncertainty and the increased security risks it brings which motivated the development of electronic signatures.

The development of international legal instruments dealing with electronic signatures is very recent, simply because they only began to penetrate the public consciousness in the mid-1990s. It was at this time that both users and governments began to realise that the borderless nature of electronic signatures would give rise to a myriad of legal and jurisdictional conflicts if international legal solutions were not devised to govern their use.

The following is an overview of some of the most prominent such international efforts to regulate electronic signatures, and it is by no means complete. Indeed, it seems that nearly every international organisation is working on the topic of electronic signatures. In fact, some countries are beginning to use digital signatures in signing agreements under international law; on 9 June 1998 Canada, Singapore, and the US State of Pennsylvania signed the first international treaty by digital means (concerning the establishment of a worldwide computer network for students).

11.2.2.1   *European Union*

The "Directive 1999/93/EC of the European Parliament and of the Council of 13 December 1999 on a Community Framework for Electronic Signatures" (the"Directive") is designed to create minimum legal standards for the use of electronic signatures across the EU Member States, and to create a common market for electronic signature products and services. The Directive is to be implemented into national law by all EU Member States no later than 19 July 2001.

The wide scope of the Directive is immediately clear when one looks at the title: rather than speaking of "digital signatures", the Directive refers to "a common framework for electronic signatures". In this regard, the European Commission took the stance that, while asymmetric cryptography may presently be the most promising technology for electronic authentication, other technologies are likely to develop, and the European regulatory framework should be flexible enough to encompass all electronic authentication technologies. In the introductory Section to the Directive, the Commission emphasises the necessity of ensuring a free internal market for electronic signatures and signature services, thus basing its jurisdiction on internal market principles.

The Directive provides that "Member States shall not make the provision of certification services subject to prior authorisation" (Article 3(1)), while empowering the Member States to "maintain voluntary accreditation schemes aiming at enhanced levels of certification service provision" (Article 3(2)). However, voluntary accreditation schemes must be "objective, transparent, proportionate, and non-discriminatory"; these are important terms deriving from EU law relating to the internal market. The Directive does provide that the Member States may "make the use of electronic signatures in the public sector subject to possible additional requirements" (Article 3(7)), though these requirements must also be "objective, transparent, proportionate, and non-discriminatory".

The Directive differentiates between so-called "qualified" certificates (those that meet the requirements set forth in Annex I and are provided by a service provider meeting the requirements of Annex II), and unqualified certificates. Such qualified certificates are both subject to particular legal requirements (e.g. those relating to liability in Article 6), and enjoy certain evidentiary presumptions (Article 5(1)).

The Directive provides for the free circulation of, and non-discrimination against, electronic signature services within the EU. In particular, "Member States may not restrict the provision of certification-services originating in another Member State in the fields covered by this Directive" (Article 4(1)), and are obliged to allow such services to "circulate freely in the internal market" (Article 4(2)). Member States are also not allowed to discriminate against electronic signatures or deny them legal effect on the grounds that they are not based upon a qualified certificate or upon a certificate issued by an accredited certification service provider (Article 5(2)).

The Directive contains minimum liability standards for electronic signature services. These provisions (Article 6) state in particular that issuers of qualified certificates are liable for certain information to persons reasonably relying on such certificates, such as the accuracy of information in the certificate (Article 6(1)), though other provisions specifically allow certification service providers to indicate liability limits in their certificates (Article 6(3)).

The problem of the written form is particularly thorny because of differences in civil law among the various EU Member States. For instance, while UK law is fairly liberal as to what constitutes a signature, German statutory signature requirements can only be fulfilled by pen on paper, and cannot be derogated from by the parties involved. Some of the Member States were quite concerned about overriding well-established written signature requirements as mandated by Article 5(1), which obliges them to ensure that electronic signatures "satisfy the legal requirements of a signature in relation to data in electronic form in the same manner as a hand-written signature satisfies those requirements in relation to paper-based data". The Directive attempts to meet these concerns by explicitly stating that it "does not cover other aspects related to conclusion and validity of contracts or other legal obligations where there are requirements as regard form prescribed by national or Community law" (Article 1), though the interaction between these two provisions is not entirely clear.

Article 7 of the Directive allows three methods for recognition of non-EU certificates, namely:

(a) the certification service provider obtaining accreditation within the EU;

(b) having a certification service provider within the EU which complies with certain minimum security requirements guarantee the certificate as its own; or

(c) recognition of the certificate under appropriate international treaties between the EU and non-EU countries.

Certification service providers are required to comply with EU data protection law, such as the Data Protection Directive, and to allow the use of pseudonyms (Article 8). Finally, the Directive provides for the establishment of an "Electronic Signature Committee", composed of representatives of the Member States, which will set generally-recognised standards for electronic signature products and requirements for certification service providers under Annex II. The Member States are empowered to set up voluntary accreditation regimes for certificate products and services. The Commission is charged with reviewing the operation of the Directive and reporting to the European Parliament and Council on its effects no later than 1 January 2003.

A closer examination of the Directive gives rise to a number of questions concerning its scope, application and implementation:

One such area is that of closed user groups. Contrary to earlier predictions, many observers now feel that digital signatures will be most widely used in closed user groups, whose members stand in a pre-existing legal relationship to each other, based, for example, on contract or employment law. Examples of such groups are credit card systems and corporate intranets. In such a closed system there is no need for government regulation of digital signatures, since the parties' liabilities and responsibilities are already sufficiently described by their existing legal relationship.

The Directive makes it clear that "a regulatory framework is not needed for electronic signatures exclusively used within systems which are based on voluntary agreements under private law between a specified number of participants", such as, presumably, authentication systems used in corporate networks (*see* Introductory Section, Paragraph 16 of the Directive). Thus, some of the provisions of the Directive (such as the liability provisions of Article 6) are explicitly limited to certificates offered "to the public", that is, to "open" systems. However, it is doubtful whether the Member States, in implementing the Directive, will pay much attention to the distinction between "open" and "closed" systems, and whether they will not, instead, simply apply implementing legislation to all certificates, whether offered to the public or not.

Another question relates to the liability provisions. For example, under Article 6(a), certification service providers ("CSPs") (a more generic term for certification authority) are liable for the accuracy of all information in a qualified certificate, while the same article goes on to state that liability does not attach if the CSP "proves that he has not acted negligently". This will likely lead CSPs to maximise the amount of information they request from customers in order to maximise their chance of showing that any incorrect information came from the applicant, which may conflict with their duty to minimise the collection of personal data (Article 8(2)).

There are also uncertainties relating to the definition of "signatory". In many countries with codified law systems, only a naturalised person may give a signature; this restriction does not however exist in many countries whose legal systems are based on common law. The distinction between naturalised and legal persons has had an effect on digital signature legislation; for instance, under the present German Digital Signature Law, a digital signature may only be given by a naturalised person. Since legal entities also need to be able to sign documents, German law introduces the concept of an "attribute certificate", which may contain information about the capacity of the person signing (though some feel that this is a somewhat unwieldy solution in practice). The Commission has indicated that the Directive allows both naturalised persons and legal entities to be a signatory.

In the end, the Directive is unlikely to produce a fully-harmonised legal framework for electronic signatures; indeed, it was the Commission's declared intention to create a "laboratory" of competing systems within Europe (all within certain boundaries, of course). While this conception has much to recommend it in terms of encouraging regulatory competition, it also carries the danger of producing a legal patchwork of regulation which does not interact efficiently. There are already signs that Member States are using the considerable leeway granted them under the Directive to create regulatory frameworks which protect domestic service providers and thus come close to violating the spirit, if not the letter, of the Directive. It is to be hoped that such protectionist initiatives will be overcome so that electronic signatures can be used across Europe in a legally-seamless way, as the Directive intends.

11.2.2.2   *International Chamber of Commerce*

In early 1998, the International Chamber of Commerce (the "ICC") adopted the "GUIDEC" (General Usage for International Digitally Ensured Commerce). The GUIDEC is a set of international guidelines for electronic authentication (though the drafters use the term "ensure" rather than the term "authentication", because of the latter's disparate meanings in different legal systems), and is intended to serve both as a set of standard terms and conditions for the use of digital signatures which parties can incorporate into their contracts (much like the ICC's Uniform Customs and Practices for Documentary Credits), and as a guide for legislators in drafting digital signature laws. Because of the ICC's global focus, particular care was taken in making the GUIDEC compatible with both common law and civil law systems. The GUIDEC is based predominantly on asymmetric cryptography, but will be updated periodically to keep pace with new technologies and legal developments. An updated version of GUIDEC is presently being drafted.

11.2.2.3   *UNCITRAL*

The "Working Group on Electronic Commerce" of the United Nations Commission on International Trade Law (the "UNCITRAL") has developed draft "Uniform Rules for Electronic Signatures", which were finalised in September 2000 (the draft Uniform Rules still have to be approved by the full UNCITRAL Commission). The draft Uniform Rules are high-level rules which are designed to provide guidance for States drafting their own electronic authentication legislation.

Table I

Useful Internet Sites

SITE	URL
Digital Signature Law Survey (including links to legal sources worldwide)	http://rechten.kub.nl/simone/ds-lawsu.htm
EU Commission Electronic Signatures Law Site	http://europa.eu.int/comm/internal_market/en/media/sign/index.htm
German Digital Signature Legislation	www.iukdg.de www.kuner.com
GUIDEC	http://www.iccwbo.org/home/guidec/guidec.asp
UNCITRAL Uniform Rules on Electronic Signatures	http://www.uncitral.org/
UK Electronic Communications Act 2000	http://www.uk-legislation.hmso.gov.uk/acts/acts2000/20000007.htm
US Federal "E-Sign" Act	http://frwebgate.access.gpo.gov/cgi-bin/getdoc.cgi?dbname=106_cong_public_laws&docid=f:publ229.106.pdf
An Analysis of International Electronic and Digital Signature Implementation Initiatives	http://www.ilpf.org/digsig/analysis_IEDSII.htm

Chapter 12
CONTENT LIABILITY AND ISPs

Karen Mason
Senior Manager (Solicitor)
Andersen Legal Garretts

12.1   Introduction

Despite a reasonable amount of new legislation having been introduced in the Internet arena over the past year or so in the UK and Europe, the question of liability for content carried over the Internet remains in many cases unclear, particularly when considering the role of Internet Service Providers ("ISPs").

This Chapter does not deal with the position of the ISP where it is the originator of material. (In this case the ISP would be liable in the same way as any other originator of material.) Rather, this Chapter deals with the questions as to the liability of ISPs which arises where the ISP has not originated the material in question, but either:

(a) the ISP is simply passing the material to or from its own customers; or

(b) material is traversing the ISP's systems between third parties which are in no way connected with the ISP.

The situation is further complicated by the fact that ISPs exist in many different forms. The liabilities of the traditional ISP, a provider simply of access to the Internet, are likely to be slightly different from those of the Online Service Provider ("OSP") which provides a selection of content which may be either originated by the OSP or chosen for presentation to its users from the vast amount of information available throughout the Internet. As an OSP has more control than an ISP over the content it provides, it is likely that it will be under a greater duty to regulate that content.

Arguably, the degree of liability should reduce for organisations involved in the provision of other Internet services, for example, managed services (where the management of servers is fully outsourced, sometimes even to the extent that the management company owns the servers in addition to managing them on behalf of clients, also known as web hosting) and facilities management (i.e. housing and servicing servers owned by others).

Although different measures may be considered by a court in assessing responsibility and/or culpability in any particular case, the same legal principles will apply in determining liability. This Chapter therefore concentrates on the role of the traditional ISP, identifying principles which can be applied to the other service providers.

ISPs could potentially be liable for third party content transmitted through newsgroups, file transfer protocol, Internet relay chat, World Wide Web and email. These are outlined in Chapter 1.

12.2   Areas of potential liability

The main areas of potential liability for ISPs are obscenity and indecency, defamation, infringement of copyright and trade marks, and misuse of data. These are outlined in turn below, along with the possible penalties, and some considerations on minimising risk.

12.3   Obscenity and indecency

Liability for obscenity and indecency is covered, not by any of the new Internet laws, but by several older areas of legislation. Most of these were enacted before the Internet existed and, although they apply, many would argue that they are not appropriate to the new environment. It is worth noting that most are yet to be tested in court in the current context.

The relevant laws are the Obscene Publications Acts 1959 and 1964, Protection of Children Act 1978, Criminal Justice Act 1988, Sexual Offences (Conspiracy to Incitement) Act 1996, Indecent Displays (Control) Act 1981, Video Controls Act 1984 and Telecommunications Act 1984.

12.3.1   *The Obscene Publications Acts 1959 and 1964 (as amended by the Criminal Justice and Public Order Act 1994)*

12.3.1.1   *Definition of obscenity*

Section 1(1) of the 1959 Act states that an article "shall be deemed to be obscene if its effect... is such as to tend to deprave and corrupt persons who are likely, having regard to all relevant circumstances, to read, see or hear the matter contained or embodied in it".

Although the word "article", at the time the Act was drafted, would have been intended to cover books and films, there is no reason why this Act should not extend to refer to material disseminated electronically, and in particular via the Internet. The case of *R v. Fellows and Arnold* [1997] held that computer disks and material held on servers for access via the Internet constitute "articles" for these purposes.

12.3.1.2   *The offence*

Under this legislation, an offence is committed by any person who "publishes an obscene article". Mere possession of such an article does not amount to an offence. However, possession of an obscene article for publication for gain is an offence. The question of "publication for gain" is an open one, it being unclear whether "gain" must be specifically related to the offending article, or whether it is sufficient for the ISP to be profiting generally from the various services it offers, in order for the offence to apply. The cautious view must be that any gain (whether via payment direct from customers or, in the case of the "free" ISPs, gain from advertising revenue) would make the ISP liable for this offence.

ISPs have, historically, argued that there is no offence under this legislation, since they are not involved in *publication* of any such article. However, the *Fellows and Arnold* case held that where one of the defendants had hosted obscene material on his employer's computer, this was sufficient to amount to publication under the 1959 Act. The publication argument has also been tested to some extent in the field of libel law (*Godfrey v. Demon Internet* (*see* Section 12.5.1 below)). It should also be noted that the Criminal Justice and Public Order Act 1994 amends the Act to define "publication" to include transmission of electronic data.

12.3.1.3 Defences

An ISP could in most cases rely on the defence of "innocent publication", provided that the ISP did not examine the material and had no reasonable cause to suspect that it was obscene. (*See* also Section 12.4 below.)

12.3.1.4 Corporate liability

Although an ISP could be charged with this offence, the Act does not make directors of the company liable.

12.3.2 Protection of Children Act 1978

12.3.2.1 The offence

The Protection of Children Act 1978 makes it an offence to distribute or show indecent photographs or pseudo-photographs of a child (defined as anyone appearing to be under the age of 16), or to possess indecent photographs or pseudo-photographs of a child with a view to their being distributed or shown. The inclusion of "possession" as an offence makes redundant the arguments surrounding "publication" which have served to cloud the application of the obscene publications legislation (*see* Section 12.3.1.2 above).

The question of what constitutes "indecency" is subject to the decision of the courts using "the recognised standard of propriety" (*R v. Stamford* [1972]). The term "pseudo-photograph" is intended to cover digitally manipulated images. Section 7(4)(b) of the Act makes clear that the term "photograph" includes data stored on a computer disk or by other electronic means which is capable of conversion into a photograph. This clearly covers the situation where material is held on an ISP's server which, when accessed via the Internet, displays on the user's screen an indecent image of a child.

12.3.2.2 Defences

ISPs may rely on two possible defences:

(a) that they did not know of or see the image and had no reasonable knowledge that the image was indecent; or

(b) that the image was not requested and was not kept for an unreasonable length of time.

Interestingly, under this Act, there is also a defence available to an ISP if it can show that it had a "legitimate reason" for showing, distributing or possessing such material. At the time of writing, there appears to be no case law on what might be a "legitimate reason". However, it is quite possible that if an ISP retained such material in order to assist a police investigation it may be able to rely on this defence. (*See* Section 12.4 for further comment on retention for these purposes.)

12.3.2.3 Personal liability

The seriousness of this offence cannot be sufficiently stressed. The Protection of Children Act 1978 makes clear reference to the liability of directors, managers, secretaries or other officers who, in addition to consent or connivance, can be culpable simply for "neglect". Maximum sentences of up to three years' imprisonment may be imposed, and/or unlimited fines.

12.3.3 Criminal Justice Act 1988

12.3.3.1 The offence

Section 160 of the Criminal Justice Act 1988 makes it an offence to possess indecent photographs or pseudo-photographs of children, whether or not for distribution to others. It is generally accepted that if an ISP has such an image on its servers, it is in possession of it. For this reason, the argument as to whether an ISP *publishes* (*see* Section 12.3.1.2) is redundant where child pornography is concerned.

12.3.3.2 Defences

The defences are similar to those under the Obscene Publications Acts 1959 and 1964 and the Protection of Children Act 1978 (*see* above), that is, that the ISP had not seen the material and did not know and had no cause to suspect it to be indecent.

12.3.3.3 Personal liability

Cases under the Criminal Justice Act 1988 can only be heard in the Magistrates' Court and therefore lesser sentences apply. Nevertheless, this could mean a prison sentence of up to six months, and/or a fine of up to £5,000.

12.3.4 Sexual Offences (Conspiracy to Incitement) Act 1996

This legislation makes it an offence to incite or conspire in the seeking of illicit sexual encounters abroad by British subjects. Section 3 of the Act states that "any act of incitement by means of a message (however communicated) is to be treated as done in England and Wales if that message is sent or received in England and Wales". So far the law is untested but ISPs should be aware that there is a slight possibility of liability as a accessory under this Act.

12.3.5 Indecent Displays (Control) Act 1981

This Act makes it an offence to display indecent material in public. If the material can only be viewed on payment of a fee it is then not classified as "on public display". However, it will be classified as a public display, despite payment, if persons under the age of 18 are admitted. It should be noted that, like the Protection of Children Act 1978 (*see* Section 12.3.2 above), this Act is concerned with "indecency", which covers more material than "obscenity".

The rules as to personal liability under this Act are the same as those for the Protection of Children Act 1978, set out at Section 12.3.2 above.

Under Section 1(1) of the Act, the person guilty of the offence is the one "causing or permitting the display to be made". Although there have been no cases to date of ISPs being charged under this Act they are undoubtedly potentially vulnerable. Provision by ISPs of effective rating and filtering software may assist in reducing culpability under this Act in that, it can be argued, attempts were thereby made to prevent viewing by those under the age of 18.

12.3.6   *Video Recordings Act 1984*

12.3.6.1   *The offence*

Under Section 9 of this Act a person is guilty of an offence if he "supplies" a video without a British Board of Film Classification ("BBFC") certificate. Video recordings are defined as "any series of visual images (with or without sound) (a) produced electronically by the use of information contained on an disc or magnetic tape, and (b) shown as a moving picture". Depending on the technology used, many of the moving images seen on the web or downloaded over the Internet may be classified as "video recordings" under this Act.

ISPs facilitate viewing of such images and, in so doing, are involved in their "supply". It seems unlikely that this legislation would be used to attach liability to ISPs and, at the time of writing, no prosecutions have been brought. However, as it becomes more and more common for users to watch films using the Internet, and if the originators or true suppliers of such films cannot be traced, the potential liability for ISPs may be used as a tool to prevent distribution of unwanted video material.

12.3.6.2   *Defences*

Some types of video (e.g. those designed to educate or those concerned with sport or religion) are exempt from the provisions of this Act.

If a video is not exempt, there is still no liability if the *supply* was exempt, that is, it was neither:

(a) a supply for reward; nor

(b) a supply in the course or furtherance of a business.

However, it is unlikely that an ISP could rely on this defence.

12.3.6.3   *Penalties*

This offence is notable in that the Act was amended by Section 88 of the Criminal Justice and Public Order Act 1994 to make it punishable by up to two years imprisonment and subject to a maximum fine of £20,000. The relatively high fine is intended to counter the large profits from the illegal distribution of videos. Arguably these should not apply to ISPs. However, whether this intention would be considered in practice is open to question. Directors, managers, secretaries and other officers may be personally liable.

12.3.7   *Telecommunications Act 1984*

This Act makes it an offence to transmit "a message or other matter that is grossly offensive or of an indecent, obscene or menacing character" over a public telecommunications network. Arguably the Act applies to material transmitted over the Internet, in so far as it is accessed using the public telecommunications system.

However, unlike the other legislation discussed, this Act is clearly intended to apply to the originator of the material, not to the distributor. ISPs and their officers should not, therefore, be caught by this Act.

12.4 **Practical protection from criminal liability for obscenity and indecency - the Internet Watch Foundation**

It was concern about child pornography on the Internet, and liability of ISPs under the Protection of Children Act 1978 in particular, which led to the Internet Watch Foundation (the "IWF") being set up in September 1996. This organisation works closely with ISPs, law enforcement agencies and the government to investigate material which may contravene the Protection of Children Act 1978 and other legislation, notifying ISPs and the police of material which may then be removed by ISPs from their systems and traced by the police.

Material which causes concern may be notified to the IWF by members of the public, the police, or by ISPs themselves. The obvious practical advantage of the IWF is that ISPs can delegate the onerous responsibility of checking such content themselves to an agency with staff trained specifically in this area. In addition, ISPs avoid the difficult situation in which they check material themselves, decide that it does not contravene the legislation, do not, therefore, remove it and the material is later found to be obscene or indecent. In this event, the defences under the relevant legislation would not be available as the ISP would clearly have been aware of the material and its nature. An honest belief that the material was legal would not constitute a defence in these circumstances.

12.5 **Defamation**

12.5.1 *Introduction*

The recent high profile case of *Laurence Godfrey v. Demon Internet Limited* [1999] has put defamation at the forefront of concerns for ISPs. The traditional fears regarding defamation (i.e. that juries tend to award punitive damages, unquantifiable in advance and out of line with the actual damage suffered by the complainant) were somewhat allayed in the *Godfrey* case in that it was agreed by the parties that the trial should be by judge alone, and the judgement in an interlocutory hearing stated that the damages would be likely to be limited.

It should be borne in mind that the case never reached full trial, having been settled on confidential terms before the trial was due to take place. As a result it gives limited assistance in clarifying the operation of the Defamation Act 1996. In particular, it gives no assistance in determining what constitutes actionable notice, or whether action can be taken by an ISP against someone notifying material which is eventually found not to be defamatory.

ISPs are placed in a difficult position in that, although it is possible for them to reserve to themselves the contractual right to remove their customers' material on receipt of notice alleging that it is defamatory, this is likely to be off-putting to customers, particularly those with significant business operations on the Internet where losses in these circumstances could be substantial.

12.5.2 *Practical protection - defamation policy*

It is now generally accepted that ISPs are not in a position to proactively monitor emails, usenet, or web content and that liability will only arise where ISPs have been notified of defamatory material or have become aware of it for other reasons.

ISPs would be well advised to publicise their policy on defamatory material, stating that they do not monitor content provided via their service and specifying how notice of any defamatory material should be provided and what steps will be taken on its receipt. It seems reasonable that, on receiving notice of defamation, ISPs should be entitled to request an indemnity from the notifier, similar to the kind of cross-undertaking in damages required when an injunction is sought. (*See* Chapter 4 Section 4.3 for more information on defamation.)

12.6 Copyright infringement

The whole area of copyright on the Internet is covered in detail in Chapter 3. Particularly relevant to the liability of ISPs are Sections 3.4.10 (providing the means for making infringing copies), 3.5 (linking), 3.6.1.1 (which deals with infringing copies under the Berne Amendment Treaty), and 3.6.7 (which points out that ISP liability has, to a large extent, been separated from the current EC copyright proposal, and will be added to the other issues - defamation privacy, pornography, etc. - which will be covered by the e-commerce directive).

The Copyright Directive states in broad terms that, for the purposes of copyright legislation, any kind of copy is a copy (and therefore potentially infringes copyright legislation) however and wherever it exists, whether that be on screen, on servers or in transit (Article 2). The Copyright Directive goes on to provide some protection for ISPs and telecommunications companies, however, in that it makes it mandatory for Member States to introduce an exception for technical copies whilst in transit, such that these copies will not infringe the relevant copyright legislation.

Similar consideration arise for ISPs in the treatment of material alleged to be infringing copyright, as arise in the treatment of material alleged to be defamatory, and similar principles should be applied in order to gain some protection.

12.7 Trade marks and domain names

The issue of trade marks and domain names is covered in detail in Chapter 4 Sections 4.9 to 4.11. Fortunately for the ISP, although it may be approached to assist in resolving a trade mark dispute, it is not usually liable for third party trade mark infringements, even where the alleged infringers are its customers. Nevertheless, it is helpful to include a contractual term requiring that customers comply with relevant trade mark legislation.

12.8 Data protection

ISPs are required to comply with data protection legislation in the same way as any other person. Chapter 7 covers this subject along with the Interception of Communications Act 1985 (*see* Section 7.5.3) and the recent Regulation of Investigatory Powers Act 2000 (see Section 7.5.4). The latter has particular relevance for ISPs.

Chapter 13
TAX IMPLICATIONS OF THE INTERNET

Philip Gershuny
Partner
Lovells

13.1   Introduction

The growth of electronic commerce ("e-commerce") has resulted in both national governments and international bodies re-examining their tax systems and formulating new policy, on how to maintain the integrity of their revenue in the context of radically new ways of doing business. In November 1999, the UK Inland Revenue and HM Customs and Excise published a paper: "Electronic Commerce: The UK's Taxation Agenda".[1] That paper sets out their approach to e-commerce and the ways in which they foresee the UK's tax system being applied and developed to meet the challenges posed by e-commerce.

The UK's approach is closely integrated with the proposals emerging from international bodies, led by the Organisation for Economic-Co-Operation and Development (the "OECD"), for a common international approach to the taxation of e-commerce. A major OECD Ministerial Conference took place in Ottawa in October 1998,[2] since then work has been progressing through the OECD to establish an international consensus on the achievement of the objectives identified.

In June 2000, the European Commission issued a proposed directive[3] for the reform of the EU-wide Value Added Tax regime, to change the current VAT rules on the supply of services by electronic means. Those proposals require unanimous agreement of EU Member States and will therefore take some time to be agreed and implemented. The taxation of e-commerce is therefore in a fluid, developing state.

The purpose of this Chapter is to analyse the current state of UK tax law as it relates to transactions carried out on the Internet, to indicate how the tax issues raised by transactions on the Internet are likely to be dealt with by the UK Revenue authorities and to consider the international issues arising from taxation of transactions on the Internet.

Before going into detail, however, it is worth considering why transactions on the Internet raise novel tax issues for the UK and other fiscal authorities around the world.

---

[1]   "Electronic Commerce: The UK's Taxation Agenda", 26 November 1999, www.inlandrevenue.gov.uk/e-commerce/ecom3.htm.

[2]   *See* OECD News Release, 13 October 1998 "Ottawa Conference on Electronic Commerce" and linked documents – www.oecd.org/daf/fa/e_com/e_com.htm.

[3]   European Commission Press Release IP/00/583, 6 June 2000.

The UK's system for taxing business profit (income tax and corporation tax) relies on the ability to answer two key questions:

(a) where is an individual, a group of individuals, or corporate entity "resident" for tax purposes?; and

(b) what (and where) is the source of specific income or profits which are potentially within the scope of taxation?

From the indirect tax point of view (VAT, customs duties) the key issues are a mixture of similar questions:

(a) where are the supplier and the customers "established"?;

(b) where does the supply take place?

and of categorisation questions:

(a) what is the nature of the supply?;

(b) is it a supply of goods or of services?; and

(c) if services, what kind of services?

From the compliance point of view, once the answers to these questions have been established, the system then relies on a mixture of:

(a) the taxable persons complying with their obligations to file returns and pay the appropriate taxes;

(b) third party intermediaries (banks, credit suppliers) within their jurisdiction reporting transactions to the revenue authorities, enabling them to identify non-compliance with primary reporting obligations; and

(c) the taxpayers (or their assets) being susceptible to the enforcement procedures available to the tax authorities.

In the direct tax field, (income tax, corporation tax) transactions on the Internet throw up new issues of how to apply the existing tax structure. The grey areas, discussed below, are, however, no more extensive than those generated by many other new kinds of business. The primary problem is that the structure is designed effectively to tax relatively static, local operations, carried out in only one country. It begins to show flaws when dealing with a business whose personnel are mobile, which does not require substantial localised assets, and which has a wide range of possible locations at which to base itself. In applying direct taxation to e-commerce activity, the main problems facing the UK and other countries are how to ensure compliance with the existing systems, rather than how to adapt the basic principles of these systems.

In contrast, in the field of consumption taxes, the major issue is how effectively to modify the VAT system to implement the principle which was agreed in the Ottawa conference in 1998: "the place of taxation of services supplied by electronic means should, in principle, be the place of consumption". Since "services" for this purpose is anything other than physical goods, the increased flow of digitised products across national borders makes the establishment of an effective mechanism to impose and collect tax no easy task. This is particularly the case where the consumer is a private individual.

The process in which the UK Revenue authorities are engaged, of attempting to establish common approaches to the open questions, is driven by a desire to ensure that the UK Treasury collects its "fair share" of the potential taxation generated by profits and turnover arising from Internet transactions. In seeking to achieve that objective, they have concluded that it is not necessary, "at this stage, to make any major changes to existing tax legislation and regulations, or to introduce new taxes". At the same time, "some changes may become necessary to existing domestic rules, to ensure that they continue to work effectively".[4]

The guiding principles which the UK and the OECD have concluded should apply to the taxation of international commerce are:

(a) *"neutrality* – taxation of electronic commerce should seek to be technology neutral, so that no particular form of commerce is advantaged or disadvantaged;

(b) *certainty and transparency* – the rules for the taxation of electronic commerce should be clear and simple, so that businesses can anticipate, so far as possible, the tax consequences of the transactions they enter into;

(c) *effectiveness* – the tax rules should not result in either double or unintentional non-taxation, and risks from increased evasion and avoidance should be kept to a minimum. The overriding aim should be that the right amount of tax is paid at the right time and in the right country. And the rules will need to be sufficiently flexible to continue to achieve this as technology develops; and

(d) *efficiency* – the tax rules should be efficient, keeping the compliance costs of business and the administration costs of government to the minimum compatible with effective tax administration. Measures to counter evasion or avoidance should be proportionate to the risks which they seek to address."[5]

Accordingly, it is clear that the UK proposes, at least for the time being, to continue to fit the taxation of Internet transactions within the current tax system, with only minor changes, while being guided by the principles set out above in formulating any necessary changes to the system.

The exception to this approach is that the UK will need, along with the other EU Member States, to modify its VAT regime to impose tax on services supplied by electronic means where the place of consumption of those services is the UK, or another Member State.

The following three sections of this Chapter analyse how the current UK tax system applies to:

(a) the seller of goods and services over the Internet;

(b) the buyer of those goods and services; and

(c) the operator of an Internet server address.

---

4   "Electronic Commerce: The UK's Taxation Agenda", (paragraph 2.10) – *see* footnote 1.

5   Ibid – (Box 2.3).

13.2   **Position of the seller or supplier of goods and services**

13.2.1   *Direct taxes*

The UK applies two basic rules to determine whether it has the right to tax business profits arising from a transaction and, if so, how much profit should be taxed. The UK charges individuals and companies which are resident in the UK to tax on their worldwide trading profits, with credit for foreign taxation of that profit. The UK also charges non-resident individuals and companies to tax on their UK source profits, derived from carrying on a trade within the UK. The seller of goods and services over the Internet may accordingly be liable to UK income or corporation tax on either of these bases.

13.2.2   *Residence as a basis for direct taxation*

In principle, establishing the place of residence of a seller of goods or services on the Internet raises no new issues. For individuals, residence is based on physical presence in the UK. The nature of e-commerce may make it easier for individual entrepreneurs to establish residence in jurisdictions with favourable tax systems, but this will not necessarily result in their avoiding UK direct taxation on sales in the UK.

If the seller is a company, it will be treated as a resident in the UK if either:

(a) it is incorporated in the UK; or

(b) its central management and control is exercised in the UK – traditionally this results in a company being resident where the board of the company meets, however, developments in telecommunications and the peripatetic tendencies of managers of companies have made this test more difficult to apply;

unless, in either case, it is treated as resident outside the UK under the residence "tie-break" rule in an applicable double taxation agreement. This will attribute residence to the company in the jurisdiction where its "effective management" is carried on and will (where it applies) automatically displace UK residence under either of the above tests.

13.2.3   *Source as a basis for taxation – trading in the UK*

A foreign resident is only assessable on profits from a trade if that trade is exercised in the UK.[6] Trading activities are subject to tax if they amount to carrying on a trade in the UK but are not subject to tax if they amount to carrying on a trade with the UK.[7]

Although many of the cases on this distinction focus on whether the relevant sale contract was made in the UK or elsewhere, in the context of Internet transactions, where the answer to this question is relatively easy to arrange, the courts are unlikely to give much weight to whether the sale contract was "made" in the UK or not. The test which they are likely to apply is that approved by the House of Lords in *Firestone Tyre & Rubber Co v. Llewellyn:*[8]

---

[6]   Income and Corporation Taxes Act 1988, Section 18, Schedule D(a)(iii).

[7]   The distinction has been explored in a number of cases – *see* for example *Grainger & Son v. Gough* [1896] A.C. 325, at pp 335-336.

[8]   (1957) 37 TC 111, at p. 142.

"Where do the operations take place from which the profits in substance arise?"

A non-UK resident seller of goods or services on the Internet is unlikely to expose itself to UK direct taxation on profits from its sales into the UK unless a significant amount of business activity (in addition to the mere location of a website or server in the UK) – in terms of the involvement of people in organising and conducting the business – takes place in the UK. Resolution of this issue will depend to a large extent on the nature of the business activity undertaken, and the extent to which it is carried out in the UK.

Further, there are additional hurdles which the UK Inland Revenue needs to surmount before being entitled to impose direct taxation on a non-resident seller.

First, a non-resident company is only liable to UK corporation tax if it carries on a trade in the UK through a branch or agency.[9] If it carries on a trade in the UK, but does not do so through a branch or agency, it is in principle liable to basic rate income tax although, in the absence of a branch or agency in the UK, enforcement of the liability is not straightforward. What constitutes a "branch or agency" for this purpose and the extent (if any) to which the concept of a "permanent establishment", discussed below, differs from a branch or agency is not always clear, but the case of *IRC v. Brackett*[10] indicates a substantial overlap between the two.

Secondly, if the seller is resident for tax purposes in a country with which the UK has a double tax treaty (the UK has treaties with over 100 countries, covering most of the world other than the tax havens) it will not normally be liable to UK direct tax (whether income tax or corporation tax) unless it has a "permanent establishment" in the UK, and the profits sought to be taxed derive from the operation of that "permanent establishment".

The issue of what constitutes a "permanent establishment" in the context of sales through the Internet is one which has generated considerable discussion, particularly in relation to whether a website or server located in the UK, is capable of constituting a "permanent establishment" of a non-resident seller, thereby exposing that seller to UK taxation on the profits derived from sales into the UK, through that website or server.

The definition of "permanent establishment" in the UK's double tax treaties is based on an OECD Model, but it is not identical in all the UK's treaties. That definition typically focuses on the existence of some physical presence of the non-resident concerned in the UK, a branch, office, factory, etc. It normally includes agents acting in the UK on behalf of the non-resident, unless they are independent agents acting in the ordinary course of their business. It normally excludes (among other things) the use of facilities solely for the purpose of storage, display or delivery of goods or merchandise belonging to the non-resident.

A press release of 11 April 2000 sets out the UK Inland Revenue's approach to this issue:

> "In the UK, we take the view that a website of itself is not a permanent establishment. And we take the view that a server is insufficient of itself to constitute a permanent establishment of a business that is conducting e-commerce through a website on the server. We take that view regardless of whether the server is owned, rented or otherwise at the disposal of the business."

---

9   Income and Corporation Taxes Act 1988; Section 11(1).

10   (1986) STC 521.

That approach contrasts with the conclusions of the OECD Committee on Fiscal Affairs. That committee adopted, on 22 December 2000, a "clarification"[11] of the application of the "permanent establishment" definition in the OECD Model Tax Convention. That document, while having no direct legal force in the UK, is likely to form the basis of broad future international consensus on the approach to this issue. It supports the UK view that a website located on a server in a particular country does not create a "permanent establishment" in that country. It diverges from the UK approach, however, in concluding that a server is capable of establishing a "permanent establishment" of the enterprise which operates that server. It goes on to point out, however, that where the server is owned and operated by an independent Internet Service Provider ("ISP"), the server is unlikely to constitute a "permanent establishment" of the business whose goods or services are sold via a website on that server, since the server, to the extent that it constitutes a "permanent establishment", will be an establishment of the ISP, rather than of its customer.

In contrast to the UK's position and that of the OECD Committee on this issue, Spain and Portugal apparently take the view that a website alone could be treated as a "permanent establishment". It would follow that businesses selling goods and services into the Iberian Peninsular through websites located on servers there could be treated as having a "permanent establishment" there, even where the servers are owned and operated by independent ISPs.

Further direct tax issues inevitably arise for the non-resident seller of goods and services on the Internet, if it is carrying on a trade in the UK through a "permanent establishment". If so, how much of the profit which it generates is attributable to that "permanent establishment", and how much of its overall expenditure is it entitled to deduct against those profits? These questions are discussed in more detail in Section 13.6 below. Neither is unique to e-commerce, but both the UK and the OECD are working on the subject of attribution of profits to "permanent establishments" through the "arm's length" principle, and further elucidation of their views is expected.

The seller into the UK of services involving an element of intellectual property will also be concerned with whether its UK customer will be required to withhold UK tax from any part of its charges. This topic is dealt with in Section 13.4 below.

13.3   Position of the seller or supplier of goods and services – VAT

As with direct taxation, the UK Revenue authorities consider that no fundamental changes are needed to the UK VAT system to accommodate the complexities of e-commerce, at least in the first two of the three categories of transaction to which the VAT system applies:

(a) supplies of physical goods to both business and private consumers;

(b) business to business supplies of services; and

(c) business to private consumer supplies of services and of "digitised" products.

Implicit in this view is confidence in the ability to distinguish between "goods" and "services" in the context of e-commerce, since the VAT consequences may be materially different. In many cases, this will not be difficult, but the ability to supply "digitised" products by electronic means when the non-digitised product (e.g. a book or CD) would

---

[11]   Clarification on the Application of the "Permanent Establishment" Definition in "Electronic Commerce" 22 December 2000 – www.oecd.org/faf/fa/first-en.htm.

constitute "goods" for these purposes has provoked some debate about the appropriate classification. It appears to be generally accepted that "digitised" products, supplied by electronic means, should be treated, for VAT and Customs Duties purposes, as services rather than goods.[12]

Computer software, not including any element of audio or video recording, is recognised as involving an element of goods (the carrier medium – if there is one) and services (the data and/or the instructions). In the case of "normalised" or off-the-shelf products, the VAT treatment depends on whether these two items are separately priced; if not, the software is treated as a supply of goods whereas with separate pricing there is a supply of both goods and services. With "specific" or "bespoke" software the carrier medium element is generally ignored with the result that the software is treated as a single supply of services.

Where there is no physical carrier medium (i.e. when the software is downloaded in digitised form) the supply will be treated as a supply of services, as discussed above. Audio and video packages are regarded (if supplied in the form of a physical carrier medium) as goods. Where they are supplied in digitised form, they will also be treated as a supply of services.

Against that background, the VAT position on the supply of goods and services via the Internet can be summarised as follows.

13.3.1   *Supplies of goods*

Where the supply is of physical goods (whether to businesses or private consumers) the seller will be normally liable to account for UK VAT on the supply if the goods are treated as supplied in the UK. For this purpose, goods are treated as supplied in the UK if they are in the UK and the supply does not involve their removal from the UK. However, there are numerous qualifications to this proposition. The principal issue for a non-UK business selling goods into the UK through the Internet will be whether, under these rules, it will be treated as supplying goods in the UK in the course of a business, so as to make it liable to register for VAT purposes, and to account to HM Customs and Excise for VAT on the resulting turnover. It will also be concerned with whether VAT is payable on importation of goods into the UK and, if so, who is liable to pay the VAT. In the context of the sale of goods, those issues are, however, no different in principle from selling by non-electronic means (e.g. by mail order).

13.3.2   *Supplies of services to businesses*

Again, the UK does not consider that any major modification of the existing VAT regime is necessary. In contrast to the basic rule in relation to the supply of goods, where the supply is a supply of services (and anything done for a consideration which is not a supply of goods is treated as a supply of services)[13] the crucial questions for the seller are:

---

12   "Electronic Commerce: The UK's Taxation Agenda" (*see* footnote 1), Box 6.1.

13   Value Added Tax Act 1994 – Section 5(2)(b).

(a) where are the services deemed to take place?;

(b) where is the seller established?;

(c) where is the customer established?;

(d) is the customer using the services for a business?

The question of whether a seller is established[14] in the UK for VAT purposes is different from the issues of whether it is resident in the UK or has a "permanent establishment" in the UK for direct tax purposes. The answer is determined under UK legislation by establishing where the seller has its business establishment. If it has more than one, it will be treated as established, (or "belonging") in the UK if its UK business establishment is the one most directly concerned with the supply of the services in question. However, the UK legislative formulation of this principle is arguably inconsistent with recent European Court of Justice decisions, under which the answer is to be found by applying the following principles:

(a) the primary place of taxation is the place where the supplier has established his business which may be the registered office of a company or may be the headquarters or principal place where the business is carried on;

(b) if the place where the business is established does not give a rational result for VAT purposes in that the place of taxation does not coincide with the place at which the service is supplied to the consumer, the place of taxation will be the fixed establishment of the business from which the service is supplied;

(c) if there is no fixed establishment, then the place of taxation must be the place where the supplier has established his business even if that produces an irrational result for VAT purposes;

(d) a place can only be regarded as a fixed establishment if it is of a certain minimum size and both the human and technical resources necessary for the provision of the services are permanently present;

(e) only if there is no place where the supplier has established his business and no fixed establishment is the place of taxation regarded as being the place where the supplier has his permanent address or usually resides; and

(f) in deciding whether or not a supplier has a fixed establishment, it is possible to regard a legally independent entity as a fixed establishment where it merely acts as an auxiliary organ of its parent or principal.

Certain services under the EU-wide system are treated[15] as supplied where they are received (as opposed to where the supplier is established). They include:

---

[14] The UK legislation uses the word "belongs" rather than "established". The latter is the word used in the Sixth VAT Directive, with which UK and other EU countries' legislation is required to comply, and is accordingly used throughout this Chapter.

[15] Under Article 9(2)(e) of the Sixth VAT Directive (and Schedule 5 to the Value Added Tax Act 1994).

(a) transfers and assignments of copyrights, patents, licences, trademarks and other similar rights;

(b) advertising services;

(c) services of consultants, engineers, consultancy bureaux, lawyers, accountants and other similar services; data processing and provision of information (but excluding services relating to land);

(d) banking, financial and insurance/reinsurance services;

(e) telecommunications services (but subject to special rules, discussed below); and

(f) arranging for the provision of any of the above services.

Other services are treated as supplied where they are physically carried out, which in the case of services delivered electronically can be difficult to determine. Such services include:

(a) education and training;

(b) entertainment and culture; and

(c) scientific services.

Further, services connected with property (such as services of architects, estate agents and lawyers) are treated as supplied where the property is situated.

Finally, telecommunications services (including certain Internet services) are supplied where the effective "use and enjoyment" of the service takes place, subject to exceptions which are discussed in more detail in Section 13.5.2 below.

The starting point for determining the incidence of UK VAT on a particular supply of services, and whether the seller is required to register for VAT purposes, is to establish where the supply takes place. If supplies are made in the UK, and exceed the registration threshold, the supplier is required to register and account for UK VAT on these supplies. If they are made in another Member State of the EU, the supplier will be required to register and account for VAT in that Member State.

If the services provided are within the categories set out above which are treated for VAT purposes as supplied where they are received, an EU customer using them for business purposes will be required to account for VAT at its local rate on the supply, under the "reverse charge" mechanism (*see* Section 13.4.2). Where the EU customer is using them for non-business purposes, the charges made (by an UK supplier) will incur UK VAT.

Where the supplier is established outside the UK, but in another EU Member State, it will be liable to register and account for VAT in the country in which it is established on supplies to non-business customers in the UK. In relation to supplies to business customers in the UK, it will not be liable to account for VAT locally, but its UK business customers are required to operate the reverse charge mechanism (*see* Section 13.4.2) under which they account for UK VAT on the supply to HM Customs and Excise.

If the supplier is established outside the EU altogether, it is not liable to register or account for UK VAT on sales to UK customers (unless the services concerned are telecommunications services, discussed in more detail in Section 13.5.2). However, UK business customers are required to operate the reverse charge mechanism (*see* Section 13.4.2) on supplies of services from outside the EU which are treated as taking place in the UK.

13.3.3   *Supplies of services to "private" consumers*

It is this category of transaction which gives rise to the most difficult VAT issues. In principle, provided that the supplier is established outside the EU and the service is not treated as taking place in the UK, there is no question of the seller currently being required to register and account for VAT in the UK (or any other EU country), on its turnover of sales into the UK. Nor is there any question of the private consumer, being required to operate the reverse charge procedure. The UK is working, with the EU, on the implementation of a number of general principles as a foundation for further action. One of those principles is that "the place of taxation of services supplied by electronic means should, in principle, be the place of consumption". How to impose (and enforce) an obligation to account for VAT on sellers located outside the EU, or on private consumers when services are provided electronically direct to the consumer's Personal Computer ("PC") without any physical goods moving across national boundaries, is a challenge with which the UK and the remainder of the EU are currently grappling.

This problem is not new. The place of supply of telecommunications services for VAT purposes was changed in 1997, in order to protect the UK's (and other EU Member States') VAT revenues in respect of telecommunication services provided from outside the EU. The solution adopted was to require the non-EU suppliers to account for VAT on supplies of telecommunications services to private consumers in the EU. The effect is described in more detail below (*see* Section 13.5.2), in relation to the treatment of ISPs. However, where the supplier belongs outside the EU and the service is provided direct to a private consumer, collecting VAT on the supply is likely to prove extremely difficult.

In June 2000 the European Commission published a Draft Directive with proposed changes to the common EU VAT system applicable to certain services supplied by electronic means.[16] The principal reason for the Directive is to impose VAT on the delivery from outside the EU of digitised services to individual customers within the EU. The proposed Directive would apply to the following kinds of services, when supplied by electronic means:

(a) cultural, artistic, sporting, scientific, educational, entertainment or similar activities, including the activities of the organisers of such activities, and where appropriate the supply of ancillary services including all forms of broadcasting and other sound and images released and delivered by electronic means;

(b) software;

(c) data-processing, including computer services (such as web-hosting, web-design or similar services); and

(d) supplying of information.

Under the proposals, supply of these services would be taxed where they are consumed. As a result, suppliers established outside the EU would be required to register in at least one EU Member State and account for VAT (at that state's VAT rate) on its supplies of services to private customers in the EU, subject to a *de minimis floor*. Although the original intention was that EU Member States should give effect to the proposed Directive by 1 January 2001, that target has not been achieved. Adoption of the proposals requires

---

[16]   European Commission Press Release IP/00/583.

unanimity between Member States, which is a notoriously lengthy process to achieve. The proposals are designed to create a level playing field as between EU suppliers of the services affected, and supplies from outside the EU, but as originally proposed, they would introduce further distortions, in that non-EU suppliers would have an incentive to register in the Member State with the lowest VAT rate, depriving other Member States of VAT revenues. Resolution of these issues is likely to take some time to achieve. Even assuming that a new Directive is agreed and implemented, a major enforcement problem will still arise for EU tax authorities.

13.4   UK tax position of the buyer of services over the Internet

The UK tax issues of primary relevance to the UK buyer of goods and services over the Internet are:

(a) is there any UK tax withholding requirement on payments for electronic transactions?;

(b) will the buyer have to account for VAT on services supplied to it over the Internet under the "reverse charge" procedure; and

(c) what is the customs duty and VAT position on goods imported into the UK?

13.4.1   *Withholding taxes*

UK law imposes an obligation[17] on a person paying royalties, or other periodic payments, in respect of some copyright material, where the "usual place of abode" of the owner of the copyright is outside the UK, to deduct income tax at the basic rate from the payment and account for the tax to the Inland Revenue. Relevant copyright material for this purpose excludes "cinematographic film" and video recordings, and (unless separately exploited) the sound-track of such films or recordings.

Payments made for other copyright material supplied via the Internet are in principle subject to this withholding obligation, to the extent that royalties or other periodic payments are made. Payments for software licences are potentially within its scope. A one-off payment for the down-loading and use, by a single user, of copyright material would not be treated as involving the payment of "royalties". However, if a separate charge is made for the right to use or to sub-license relevant copyright material, a UK buyer may be under an obligation to withhold tax from the payment. This obligation may be displaced by one of the UK's double tax treaties, if the copyright owner is resident in a treaty country, and the treaty removes the obligation, but if reliance is placed on a double tax treaty to remove the obligation, the buyer is required to obtain prior consent of the Inland Revenue to make the payment free of withholding tax.[18]

The UK law in this area is in a state of flux. In November 2000, the Inland Revenue published the fourth in a series of consultative documents on the taxation of intellectual property,[19] but provided no clarification of its own views on the circumstances in which payment for material protected by intellectual property rights fell within the scope of the royalty withholding requirement. It did, however, announce its intention to abolish all withholding obligations for payments made by companies to other companies within the scope of UK corporation tax, as from 1 April 2001.

---

17   Income and Corporation Taxes Act 1988 – Section 536.

18   Double Taxation Relief (Taxes on Income) (General) Regulations: SI 1970/488; Regulation 2.

19   "Reform of the Taxation of Intellectual Property: The Next Stage – 8 November 2000" at www.inlandrevenue.gov.uk.

In its paper: "Electronic Commerce: The UK's Taxation Agenda"[20] the Revenue acknowledges the need for an international consensus on the scope of royalty withholding requirements and the circumstances in which they should, and should not, arise. In February 2001, the OECD Technical Advisory Group ("TAG") on treaty characterisation of e-commerce payments released its final report[21] setting out its conclusions on no less than 28 categories of e-commerce transactions. The paper analyses the extent to which payments made in the course of these transactions should be treated as constituting royalty payments, for the purposes of double-tax treaties based on the OECD model. That report is subject to review by the OECD Committee on Fiscal Affairs. Even when it is adopted by the OECD, it will have no direct legal force as far as UK domestic law withholding requirements are concerned. However, in view of the importance placed by the UK Revenue on international consensus in this area, it is likely that it will have a strong influence on Inland Revenue policy and practice.

13.4.2 *VAT on goods and services supplied*

To the extent that the supply of goods or services via, or over, the Internet attracts UK VAT, the VAT will represent simply an additional cost of the purchase to a private consumer and to a business consumer which makes exclusively exempt supplies for VAT purposes.

Where, however, the buyer is itself VAT registered, it will be entitled to obtain credit for (or a refund of) any UK VAT charged on supplies made to it for the purposes of its business, to the extent that the supplies made to it are attributable to the buyer's own taxable supplies.

Where no UK VAT is charged, but the supply is a supply of services treated as taking place in the UK[22] the UK business buyer will be required to operate the reverse charge procedure,[23] under which it is effectively required to charge itself for the relevant services, and to account to HM Customs and Excise for VAT on the consideration which it pays. For a fully taxable business, this represents a compliance issue, rather than a tax cost, since it is entitled to use the resulting VAT as an input credit against the VAT which it charges on its own supplies. For a partially exempt business, however, the "reverse charge" represents a real cost.

13.4.3 *Customs duties and VAT on the importation of goods*

Customs duties are chargeable only on the importation of "goods". The discussion in relation to the distinction between goods and services (*see* Section 13.3), in the context of Internet transactions, also applies for customs duty purposes.

The UK has confirmed[24] that, in line with the World Trade Organisation Declaration on Global E-commerce, goods ordered and supplied electronically will continue to be treated as services, and as such, will be free of import duties. Physical goods ordered

---

[20]   *See* footnote 1.

[21]   *See* www.oecd.org/daf/fa/e_com/e_c2_TREATY_CHAR_Eng.pdf.

[22]   *See* footnote 15.

[23]   Under Value Added Tax Act 1994, Section 8.

[24]   "Electronic Commerce: UK Taxation Policy", paragraph 32, HM Customs and Excise News Release 25/98.

electronically, but delivered physically from outside the EU will continue to attract the rate of duty applicable to those goods. It has also confirmed that no additional import duties will be introduced relating to electronic transmissions.

So far as VAT on the importation of goods into the UK is concerned, there are no special rules which apply to goods which are the medium for delivery of digitised material, or which may simply have been purchased over the Internet. A discussion of the general rules which apply here is outside the scope of this Chapter. Broadly, the moment when customs duty is due on the goods is the time of importation for VAT purposes. This can trigger a charge to VAT and the identity of the party liable to account for the tax will depend on the terms of the sale contract.

13.5 The tax position of the Internet service provider

13.5.1 Direct tax

The UK direct tax issues which arise for an ISP relate to both:

(a) the potential UK taxation of its own profits; and

(b) the potential for the UK Revenue to assess it for tax on the profits generated by its non-resident customers, on trading activities carried on by them in the UK.

In relation to its own profits and income, the tax position will again depend firstly on whether it is UK resident or not, under the principles summarised above. If so, it will be liable to UK income or corporation tax on its worldwide profits, with credit for foreign taxes on these profits.

If it is not resident in the UK under those principles, it will again be necessary to determine whether it is nevertheless carrying on a trade in the UK and, if it is resident in a country with which the UK has a double tax treaty, whether it is doing so through a "permanent establishment" in the UK. If so, then it will be liable to UK direct taxation on the profits attributable to that trading activity.

As discussed above, the issue of whether a trade is being carried on in the UK is determined by an analysis of the business in question, seeking the answer to the question: where do the operations take place, from which the profits in substance arise?[25]

The location in the UK of material hardware owned or leased by the ISP will be one of the factors taken into account in arriving at the answer to that question, as will the conclusion of contracts in the UK, as with the seller of goods and services over the Internet. Ultimately, however, the question is likely to be answered by an analysis of where the people whose activities together generate the profits in question conduct those activities. If a significant contribution to those activities is made by people based in, or regularly travelling to, the UK, then it is likely to be found that the non-resident ISP is nevertheless carrying on a trade in the UK, exposing the profits of that trade to UK direct taxation.

---

[25] See *Firestone Tyre & Rubber Co v. Llewellyn* (1957) 37 TC 111, at p.142.

If the ISP is resident in a country with which the UK has a double-tax treaty, it will then be necessary to establish whether it has a "permanent establishment" in the UK. The comments made above about the application of the "permanent establishment" test to sellers of goods and services over the Internet also apply to ISPs. If their presence in the UK is limited to the ownership or use of a server or other hardware, it seems unlikely that this will, under the Inland Revenue's current approach to this issue, discussed above (*see* Section 13.2.3), result in their having one. If on the other hand they establish an office or other base from which their personnel, or personnel of their agents (other than independent agents), conduct business, then unless the activities carried out fall exclusively into the categories of activity which are excluded from the definition of "permanent establishment" in the relevant treaty, they will be found to have one. However, the OECD Committee on Fiscal Affairs takes the position that "human intervention is not a requirement for the existence of a 'permanent establishment'", and that a server located in a particular country can, without more, constitute a "permanent establishment". The views of that Committee are not binding on the UK Revenue, but reflect a broad international consensus on this point.

An ISP which is within the scope of UK direct taxation on its own profits will also need to structure its relationship within its non-resident customers so as to avoid creating a situation in which the ISP will be assessable to UK direct taxation on the profits generated by those customers, as their agent. The UK mechanisms for charging non-residents to direct taxation on their profits from trading in the UK include the ability to assess those non-residents in the name of their UK representative.[26] However, provided that the ISP, to the extent that it acts as the agent of a non-resident customer, does not act as agent in relation to those transactions in the course of carrying on a regular agency for the non-resident customer, it will not be liable to UK taxation on the profits of its customers under this principle.[27]

13.5.2 *The position of the Internet service provider – indirect tax*

As discussed above, (*see* Section 13.3.2), the UK VAT position in relation to the services provided by an ISP depends on the categorisation, for VAT purposes, of the service provided.

Most importantly, in this context, "telecommunications services" are treated in a special way, as a result of the rise in the provision of telecommunication services from outside the EU, and the resulting loss of VAT revenue to Member States. "Telecommunications services" are defined for this purpose as meaning:

> "Services relating to the transmission, emission or reception of signals, writing, images and sounds or information of any nature by wire, radio, optical or other electromagnetic systems, including the transfer or assignment of the right to use capacity for such transmission, emission or reception."

---

[26]   Finance Act 1995, Sections 126–129.

[27]   Ibid; Section 127(1)(a).

This definition includes access to the Internet. Where the services provided by an ISP consist exclusively of "telecommunications services" within this definition, then the VAT position will be as follows:

(a) *ISP established[28] in the UK*

(i) if the ISP is established in the UK, under the principles discussed above in Section 13.3.2, and the customer is also established in the UK, then the ISP will be required to account for UK VAT, unless the services are "used and enjoyed" outside the EU;

(ii) if the ISP is established in the UK and the services are provided to a business customer in a different EU Member State, the services are treated as received in that Member State, and outside the scope of UK VAT;

(iii) if the ISP is established in the UK and the services are provided to a non-business customer in a different EU Member State, the services are treated as supplied in the UK, and the ISP will be required to account for UK VAT, unless the services are "used and enjoyed" outside the EU;

(iv) if the ISP is established in the UK, and the customer is established outside the EU, the services are outside the scope of UK VAT, unless they are "used and enjoyed" in the UK.

(b) *ISP established in another Member State*

(i) if the ISP is established in another EU Member State and the customer is established in the UK and receives the services for business purposes, the services are, unless "used and enjoyed" outside the EU, within the scope of UK VAT, and the customer accounts for VAT through the reverse charge mechanism;

(ii) if the ISP is established in another Member State, but the customer is established in the UK and receives the services for non-business purposes, the services are supplied in the Member State where the ISP is established and outside the scope of UK VAT;

(iii) if the ISP is established in another Member State, and the customer is also established in another Member State, the services will be outside the scope of UK VAT;

(iv) if the ISP is established in another Member State and the customer is established outside the EU, the services are supplied outside the EU, and outside the scope of UK and EU VAT, unless they are "used and enjoyed" in the UK, in which case the ISP is liable to account for UK VAT, (unless the customer provides a UK registration number and itself accounts for VAT through the "reverse charge" mechanism).

(c) *ISP established outside the EU*

(i) if the ISP is established outside the EU, and the customer is established in the UK and receives the services for business purposes, then the services are treated as received in the UK, and the customer must account for VAT using the reverse charge mechanism, unless they are "used and enjoyed" outside the EU, in which case they are outside the scope of UK (and EU) VAT;

---

28   *See* footnote 14.

(ii) if the ISP is established outside the EU, and the customer is established in the UK and receives the services for non-business purposes, then the services are outside the scope of UK (and EU) VAT, unless the services are "used and enjoyed" in the UK, in which case the ISP must register and account for UK VAT (unless its supplies are below the registration threshold);

(iii) if the ISP is established outside the EU, and the customer is established in another Member State and receives the services for business purposes, then the services are outside the scope of UK VAT;

(iv) if the ISP is established outside the EU, and the customer is established in another Member State and receives the services for non-business purposes, the services are treated as supplied in the provider's country, and outside the scope of UK (and EU) VAT, unless they are "used and enjoyed" in the UK, in which case the ISP must register and account for UK VAT (subject to the registration threshold); and

(v) if the ISP is established outside the EU, and the customer is also established outside the EU, then the services are outside the scope of UK (and EU) VAT, unless they are "used and enjoyed" in the UK, in which case the ISP must register (subject to the threshold) and account for UK VAT, unless the customer provides a UK registration number and accounts for UK VAT by applying the reverse charge.

This system, poses a number of difficult issues for ISPs, particularly those located outside the EU. They must first be able to identify which of the charges they make are for services which fall into the category of "telecommunications services" within the above definition, then identify where their customer is established for VAT purposes and, if different, where it is going to "use and enjoy" the services provided. Finally, they must determine whether the services supplied are to be used for business, or non-business purposes. The answer to these questions determines whether they are required to register for VAT purposes in the UK (or in other EU Member States) and to account to the appropriate authorities for VAT on their relevant turnover.

This regime for telecommunications services does not apply to charges made for the content of a transmission, as opposed to access to the transmission services, so that, for example, charges made for whether information transmitted by fax or via the Internet would be treated as a supply of information, dealt with under the principles discussed in Section 13.3.2 above, not as a service of transmission. Where composite services are not separately charged for, it may be necessary to apportion the charge for VAT purposes and to apply the relevant principles to each component separately, unless one of the components is "incidental" or integral to a supply of the other component.

Services other than telecommunications services supplied by ISPs are dealt with, for VAT purposes, as described in Section 13.3 above.

13.6 International issues arising from Internet taxation

As the preceding discussion of the UK tax position has shown, e-commerce raises a number of difficult issues in the application of existing domestic tax principles. The focus of the continuing efforts on the part of the EU, the OECD, and others to establish common approaches in the international community to the resolution of those issues is driven by two main considerations:

(a)   the desire to avoid double taxation of the fruits of e-commerce; and

(b)   the desire (on the part of the Revenue authorities) to establish mechanisms under which they collect their "fair share" of the resulting profits and turnover.

From the point of view of the avoidance of double taxation, the primary international mechanism is the network of double taxation treaties, most of which are merely bilateral, between the main tax raising authorities in the world. That network is not global. The UK, which has the largest number of double tax treaties in the world, has treaties with just over 100 countries. Most countries have many fewer treaties. Additionally, they operate primarily in the field of direct taxation, leaving taxes on consumption unaffected.

The treaty network is individually negotiated, but most treaties are closely based on the OECD Model. That model, so far as it relates to business transactions, gives primary taxing rights to the country where the relevant business is resident for the purposes of the treaty. Where a business which is resident in one country also carries on business in another country, through a "permanent establishment", the country in which that "permanent establishment" is located has the right to tax the profits derived from the operations of the "permanent establishment". Double taxation of those profits is avoided by the country where the business is resident, either exempting the foreign "permanent establishment" profits from its own taxation system, or (as does the UK) giving credit for the foreign taxation against its own taxation charge.

The key direct tax questions posed for any business operating internationally are therefore:

(a)   where is it resident (both for the purposes of domestic laws, and for the purposes of double-tax treaties relevant to its operations)?;

(b)   is it exposed to direct taxation in other countries as a result of their domestic laws imposing taxes on business carried on in those countries?;

(c)   if it is resident in a country which has double tax treaties with those other countries (or some of them), does it have a "permanent establishment" in them for the purposes of the relevant treaty?; and

(d)   if so, what proportion of its profits is attributable to operations outside the country in which it is resident?

As noted above, attempts are being made, internationally through the OECD, to clarify the scope of the concept of "permanent establishment" in the context of e-commerce. Transactions on the Internet raise, for the reasons discussed in the UK context, a number of difficult issues in answering the first three of these questions. Perhaps the most difficult, however, is the fourth.

The common approach, under the OECD model treaty-based network, is the application of the "arms length" principle. In the words of the current model treaty:

> "there shall ... be attributed to [the permanent establishment] the profits which it might be expected to make if it were a distinct and separate enterprise engaged in the same or similar activities under the same or similar conditions, and dealing wholly independently with the enterprise of which it is a permanent establishment."[29]

---

29   OECD Model Treaty (1 June 1998); Article 7.2.

Accordingly, to apply this test, it is first necessary to identify a "permanent establishment" of the business in question, to assume that it is independent of the remainder of the business, and to determine what profit it would make from its activities it if were to charge for them, on an arm's length basis.

The business models on which this system has developed have tended in the past to be static, traditional businesses typified by a "trunk" organisation, located in a particular country, with "branch" operations outside that country advancing its business by local sales, after-care and other similar operations. These can be, and in many cases are, supplied by third parties, the cost and profit margins of which are familiar to taxing authorities, and can be used in applying the "arm's length" test.

E-commerce poses, however, particular difficulties in the application of this test, since it is quite possible to fragment the "trunk" operation between a number of different countries, and it may therefore be very difficult to arrive (in the absence of arm's length comparatives) at an apportionment of the overall profit generated by a business between the various countries laying claim to a part of those profits which is acceptable to all of them and which avoids double taxation. Dispute resolution in this context relies heavily on each of the interested tax authorities reaching "mutual agreement" on the appropriate apportionment and, even in its application to more traditional kinds of business, the process of arriving at that agreement is notoriously lengthy and arduous.

Clarification of the application of the "arm's length" principle to e-commerce in the context of international operation of the OECD-based double tax treaty network is firmly on the agenda of the OECD.

In the meantime, the possibility exists in the UK and in a number of other developed tax systems of entering into a negotiated advance pricing agreement with the appropriate tax authorities. An agreement of this kind has the merit of establishing certainty of treatment with at least one of those authorities.

In the indirect tax field, in the absence of an international network of double tax treaties, the scope for double taxation is materially increased. The principle established at the Ottawa conference that "consumption taxes should be levied in the country where consumption takes place, and that for the purposes of those taxes the supply of digitised products should not be treated as a supply of goods"[30] evidences a consensus, at least among the 29 Member States of the OECD (including the UK) as to how, in principle, double taxation should be avoided, but the practical application of that principle in individual countries (and in sub-divisions of those countries) will require considerable further consultation and negotiation on the part of business and taxing authorities worldwide.

---

[30]   OECD News Release 13 October 1998; "Ottawa Conference on Electronic Commerce".

Chapter 14
FINANCIAL SERVICES REGULATION

Martin Hollobone
Director
Emer Cashin
Manager, New Media Regulatory Team
KPMG

14.1   Introduction

Rapid technological growth is radically reshaping the financial services industry. There is a significant shift from the traditional in-house, standalone operating systems to the current trend for web-based, externally linked systems. For the financial services industry cutting edge technologies have become more reliable and affordable and so more common place. The industry is set to embrace the new links to the Internet currently being developed, such as digital TV and WAP[1] telephones. Internet based offerings are now an important part of the market and the Internet may in the future become the core delivery channel for many financial services products.

Legislation and regulation will be important in shaping future use of the Internet. Many legislators world wide have responded to the technological changes by developing legislation which aims to permit or encourage the growth of e-commerce. In the UK, Parliament has recently passed the Electronic Communications Act 2000 (the "EC Act"). Of particular importance to Internet users, the EC Act provides for the recognition of electronic signatures by the courts and processes under which such signatures are communicated, generated and verified. The EC Act establishes an approvals scheme for businesses and other organisations providing cryptography services, for example electronic signature services. The EC Act also provides powers to remove restrictions in existing laws on the use of electronic communication and storage in place of paper.

Regulators world wide have responded to the growth of the Internet by developing guidance on carrying on financial business on the Internet. There is currently no global regulator but there is a global securities policy-making body, IOSCO.[2] Its members include the major national securities regulators and it aims to promote co-operation between the regulators and so promote high standards of market regulation world wide.

This Chapter will focus on the impact of UK financial services legislation and regulation on the Internet. However, given the borderless nature of the Internet other jurisdictions are also discussed.

---

[1]   Wireless application protocol ("WAP").

[2]   The International Organisation of Securities Commissions ("IOSCO").

14.2 UK regulation

14.2.1 The Financial Services Act 1986

The current UK framework for regulating financial services (including Internet business) is the Financial Services Act 1986 (the "FS Act"). It was drafted in an era when business activities were more easily regulated within national borders and only aims to regulate financial services business carried on in the UK.

The cornerstone of the FS Act is Section 3 which prescribes that no person shall carry on "investment business" in the UK unless he is an "authorised person" or an "exempted person".

A person usually becomes authorised under the FS Act by becoming a member of a self-regulating organisation ("SRO") or obtaining authorisation from a recognised professional body ("RPB"). A few firms have obtained authorisation directly from the Financial Services Authority (the "FSA") (although the FSA now discourages direct applications for authorisation). The FS Act also deems as authorised persons certain insurers, friendly societies and operators and trustees of recognised collective investment schemes. A list of authorised persons is available on the FSA's Central Register which is accessible via the FSA's website.

The principal "exempted persons" under the FS Act include the Bank of England, recognised investment exchanges, recognised clearing houses, the Society of Lloyd's and Lloyd's underwriters, listed wholesale money market institutions, appointed representatives[3] and CRESTCo.[4]

14.2.2 Sanctions

Anyone failing to comply with Section 3, that is, carrying on investment business in the UK without being an authorised or exempt person not only commits a criminal offence[5] but will also find that his investment agreements are unenforceable against the other party (unless the court directs otherwise). The other party would also be able to recover any money or property transferred under the investment agreement and receive compensation for any resulting loss he has suffered.

14.2.3 The Secretary of State for Trade and Industry and HM Treasury

The powers of regulation under the FS Act primarily rest with the Secretary of State for Trade and Industry and HM Treasury.[6] Most of these powers have been transferred to the FSA known under the FS Act as the "designated agency".[7]

---

[3] Authorised persons under Section 44 of the FS Act.

[4] The operator of CREST (the electronic settlement system) in respect of non-clearing activities.

[5] Section 4 of the FS Act provides that a breach of Section 3 carries a maximum penalty of two years in prison and a fine. There is a defence under Section 4(2) that all reasonable precautions were taken and all due diligence was exercised to avoid breaching Section 3.

[6] Originally powers under the FS Act were given to the Secretary of State for Trade and Industry but were later transferred, to a great extent, to HM Treasury.

[7] Under Section 114 of the FS Act.

14.2.4   *The new regime*

A major reform of financial services regulation in the UK is currently under way. New primary legislation, the Financial Services and Markets Act 2000 (the "FSMA") was introduced into Parliament in June 1999 and it received Royal Assent in the following June. The FSMA introduced a single financial services regulatory regime covering most sectors of the industry (including insurance, banking and investment firms). Under the new regime there is a single statutory regulator with a single set of functions and powers. The new legislation also replaces financial services regulation currently found in a number of statutes.[8]

The corner stone to FSMA is Section 19 which prescribes that no person shall carry on a "regulated activity" in the UK unless he is an "authorised person" or an "exempted person". Under the FSMA this is referred to as the general prohibition. Regulated activities caught by the FSMA are set out in Schedule 2 of the Act and in secondary legislation.[9]

The sanctions under the new regime are similar to those operating under the current regime. A person contravening the general prohibition not only commits a criminal offence but will also find that his investment agreements are unenforceable against the other party (unless the court directs otherwise). The other party will also be able to recover any money or property transferred under the investment agreement and receive compensation for any resulting loss he has suffered.

14.3   The regulators

14.3.1   *The Financial Services Authority*

The FSA, formerly known as the Securities and Investments Board (the "SIB"),[10] oversees the regulatory regime created under the FS Act and is accountable to both the Secretary of State and the Office of Fair Trading for its actions. The FSA recognises and de-recognises the SROs and RPBs and has powers to prosecute and take enforcement action against persons that carry on unauthorised investment business and issue unauthorised investment advertisements.[11]

14.3.2   *The self-regulating organisations*

The FS Act establishes different tiers of regulations and under the FSA there are a number of SROs: the Securities and Futures Authority (the "SFA"), the Personal Investment Authority (the "PIA") and the Investment Management Regulatory Organisation (the "IMRO"). The SROs regulate different types of investment business (although there is some overlap) and so have different types of firms as members. The SFA regulates stockbrokers, securities houses, banks, derivatives brokers and clearing firms. Fund managers are generally regulated by IMRO. While independent intermediaries and the marketing of personal pension and insurance products are regulated by the PIA.

---

8   The Insurance Companies Act 1982, the Building Societies Act 1986, the Financial Services Act 1986, the Banking Act 1987 and the Friendly Societies Act 1992.

9   The FSMA (Regulated Activities) Order 2001.

10   The SIB was renamed the FSA in October 1997.

11   Some of these powers are exercised concurrently with the Secretary of State.

The SROs must themselves meet requirements under the FS Act: broadly they must have rules and practices to ensure that their members will be honest, competent and solvent and fit and proper to carry on investment business.[12] Membership of an SRO gives a person authorised status under the FS Act and it allows firms to carry on any type of investment business within the scope of their membership.

14.3.3 Recognised professional bodies

Certain professional bodies (e.g. the Law Society and the Institute of Chartered Accountants in England and Wales) that have obtained recognition under the FS Act can regulate incidental investment business carried on by their members.

14.3.4 The new regime

Under FSMA the tiers of regulation are stripped away and replaced by a single regulator: the FSA (which will acquire the regulatory powers currently resting with the SROs and other regulators).

This will be achieved when the relevant sections of the FSMA comes into force (which is likely to be mid to end 2001). The FSA's new powers will include:

(a) supervision of Lloyd's insurance market;

(b) direct authorisation of professional bodies in the conduct of investment business;

(c) powers to levy fines on regulated and unregulated firms;

(d) responsibility for recognising overseas exchanges in the UK (currently resting with HM Treasury);

(e) powers to prosecute firms for failing to have systems and controls in place to prevent money laundering and insider dealing offenses; and

(f) promoting public understanding of the financial system.

14.4 Investment business on the Internet

The Internet is a medium (like letters, faxes and phone calls) and so the provisions of the FS Act need to be taken into account when using it to carry on investment business or for issuing an investment advertisement in the UK.

Anyone providing or marketing financial services on the Internet should satisfy themselves as to whether they are carrying on investment business that falls within the FS Act. Broadly, if they are not an authorised person (e.g. a member of an SRO) or an exempt person under the FS Act, or permitted to carrying on investment activities by the Investment Services Regulations[13] they risk committing a criminal offence. In addition, restrictions apply to the marketing of financial services in the UK which are discussed below.

---

[12]   The FS Act Schedule 2.

[13]   A European firm is entitled to carry on certain types of investment business in the UK by virtue of the Investment Services Regulations which implement the Investment Services Directive.

14.4.1 What are "investments"?

Section 1(1) of the FS Act defines "investments" as any asset, right or interest falling within any paragraph of Part I to Schedule 1 to the FS Act. The FS Act has been amended to implement the Investment Services Directive ("ISD") (*see* Section 14.6.1 below) which extended the definition of investments. Investments include:

(a) shares[14] (paragraph 1);

(b) debentures[15] (paragraph 2) (e.g. bonds and other debt instruments);

(c) government and public securities (paragraph 3);

(d) instruments entitling to shares and securities (paragraph 4) (e.g. warrants to subscribe to shares);

(e) certificates representing securities (paragraph 5) (e.g. depositary receipts);

(f) units in collective investment schemes (paragraph 6) (e.g. units in a unit trust or shares in an open-ended investment company);

(g) options (paragraph 7);

(h) futures (paragraph 8);

(i) contracts for differences (paragraph 9) (e.g. swaps);

(j) long-term insurance contracts (paragraph 10);

(k) rights and interests in investments (paragraph 12).

14.4.2 The new regime

Investments under the new regime are expected to include those regulated under the current regime and a few banking and insurance additions. All the investments within the scope of the new regime are set out in a statutory instrument.[16] In addition to the FS Act investments, FSMA is expected to regulate:

(a) deposits;

(b) Lloyd's syndicate capacity and syndicate membership;

(c) general insurance contracts;

(d) funeral plan contracts;

(e) regulated mortgage contracts;

(f) rights under a stakeholder pension scheme.

---

[14] The ISD extended the definition of investments to include shares in UK industrial and provident societies (e.g. building societies).

[15] The ISD extended the definition of investments to include bills of exchange accepted by a banker.

[16] The FSMA (Regulated Activities) Order 2001.

14.4.3   *What is investment business?*

The FS Act defines "investment business"[17] as the business of engaging in one or more of the activities falling within the paragraphs in Part II of Schedule 1 to the FS Act and which are not excluded by Part III of that Schedule. The definition includes the word "business" and this suggests that the use of the Internet for non-business purposes, (e.g. for educational or recreational purposes) falls outside the scope of the FS Act.

14.4.4   *Investment activities (Part II of Schedule 1 to the Financial Services Act 1986)*

The activities constituting investment business are briefly discussed below. Clearly [all] these activities could in practice be carried out over the Internet although there is no Internet specific investment activity.

Dealing in investments (paragraph 12) – buying, selling, subscribing for or underwriting investments or offering or agreeing to do so, either as principle or agent. This paragraph will catch dealing carried out over the Internet including activities such as share dealing services where shares can be purchased on the Internet.

Arranging deals in investments (paragraph 13) – making, or offering or agreeing to make: (a) arrangements with the view to another person buying, selling, subscribing for or underwriting a particular investment; or (b) arranging with a view to a person who participates in the arrangements buying, selling, subscribing for or underwriting investments.

Part (b) of this paragraph tends to catch investment deals arranged (e.g. where parties are introduced) on the Internet. In certain circumstances, websites containing text about particular shares together with hypertext links to other websites where the shares can in fact be bought or sold can fall within paragraph 13. Also a firm providing a website for a market maker to post prices for investors information and to receive orders from investors will be likely to be seen as arranging deals where such arrangements are entered into by way of business and the purpose of the arrangements are for people to buy/sell shares.

Custody of Investments (paragraph 13A) – safeguarding and administering or arranging for the safeguarding and administration of assets belonging to another which consist of or include investments.

Managing investments (paragraph 14) – managing, or offering or agreeing to manage, assets belonging to another person which include investments, or which may include investments at the discretion of the manager.

Investment advice (paragraph 15) – giving, or offering or agreeing to give, investors or potential investors advice on the merits of their purchasing, selling, subscribing for or underwriting an investment, or exercising any right conferred by an investment to acquire, dispose of, underwrite or convert an investment.

---

[17]   Section 1(2).

Paragraph 15 is likely to catch websites that provide recommendations and encouragement to investors to buy or sell specific investments. Also, software configured to instruct users to buy or sell investment also is likely to be caught by this paragraph as the *MarketWizard* case[18] demonstrates. Call centres, linked to websites, providing customer services may also be caught by this paragraph if they are giving advice on the merits of an investment rather than dispensing pure information or providing technical ("IT") customer support services.

Collective investment schemes (paragraph 16) – establishing, operating or winding up a collective investment scheme (e.g. acting as a trustee of a unit trust scheme or as a depository or sole director of an open-ended investment company).

Sending dematerialised instructions (paragraph 16A) – broadly, sending electronic instructions relating to an investment on behalf of another person using a computer-based system, (e.g. CREST) or offering or agreeing to do so.

14.4.5 *Excluded investment activities (Part III of Schedule 1 to the Financial Services Act 1986)*

The investment activities under the current regime are briefly discussed below. Clearly these activities could in practice be carried out over the Internet although there is no Internet specific excluded investment activity.

Implementation of the ISD has also resulted in amendments to the excluded investment activities set out in the FS Act. Broadly, as a result of the amendments, core investment services under the ISD (*see* Table A at the end of this Chapter) provided to third parties on a professional basis by UK firms ("ISD investment firms") are not treated as excluded activities under paragraphs 17–19 and 21 of Schedule 1 of the FS Act. Excluded activities included:

Dealing as principal (paragraph 17) – dealings in certain investments including shares, debentures, government and public securities, warrants and unit trusts by a person acting as principal, unless the person is, broadly, a market maker or dealer in investments or regularly solicits the public to deal in those investments.

Group activities (paragraph 18) – certain investment activities, for example, dealing or arranging deals, managing investments or giving investment advice if the activity is carried on by and with companies in the same group.

Sale of goods and supply of services (paragraph 19) – certain transactions ancillary to the sale of goods and supply of services to customers where the supplier's main business is to supply goods and services and not to engage in activities in Part II of Schedule 1 to the FS Act.

Sale of a private company (paragraph 21) – dealing and arranging deals for the sale or purchase of a private company. Also any advice given in connection with the sale or purchase if, broadly, the shares involved carry 75 per cent or more of the voting rights.

---

[18]   [1998] 2 BCLC 282 – where the courts in effect deemed that it was possible for software to be configured so that it was giving investment advice with implications for those selling such software.

Advice given or arrangements made in the course of a profession or non-investment business (paragraph 24) – certain advice given or arrangements made in the course of carrying on a profession or non-investment business and which is, or are, a necessary part of such advice or service.

Advice given in newspapers (paragraph 25) – advice given in a newspaper, journal, magazine or other periodical publication, if the principal purpose of the publication, taken as a whole and including advertisements contained in it, is not to lead persons to invest in any particular investment.

A publication can apply for a certificate under paragraph 25 from the FSA which provides confirmation that the exclusion applies to that publication. Questions can arise here as to whether a website is a "periodical publication" for the purpose of the exclusion and indeed what can constitute the boundary of the publication (e.g. does it include material to which the sites links?).

Advice given in television, sound or teletext services (paragraph 25A) – advice given in any programme included, or made for inclusion in any television broadcasting service (within the meaning of Part I of the Broadcasting Act 1990) or other television programme service, any sound broadcasting service or licensable sound programme service, or any teletext service.

In respect of paragraph 25A there are interesting technological convergence issues. What for instance is the position where access to the Internet is provided through a "broadcast service"? Is such investment advice given over the Internet but contained within such a service deemed to fall within these exclusions? This is an area which at the time of writing is still an open question.

14.4.6   *The new regime – regulated activities and exclusions*

Under the new regime the "regulated activities" that fall within the scope of FSMA and the related exclusions are set out in a statutory instrument (which is currently in draft form). The draft order includes many of the activities regulated and excluded under the current regime and there are additions.

Changes from the current regime include clarification that "generic" advice does not constitute investment advice and that purely administrative arrangements (e.g. preparing legal documentation) does not constitute arranging deals in investments. Also "offering" to provide an investment service will not be a regulated activity. The regulated activities, followed by the relevant exclusions under the new regime are set out below:

(a) accepting deposits (BA):[19]

   (i)   sums paid by certain persons (derives from BA 87 S4 & Schedule 2);

   (ii)   sums received by solicitors (derives from BA 87 (Exempt Transactions (Regulations) 1997);

   (iii) sums received on terms involving the issue of debt securities (derives from BA 87 (Exempt Transactions (Regulations) 1997);

(b) effecting and carrying out insurance contracts (ICA):[20]

---

[19]   "BA" indicates derives from the Banking Act 1987.

[20]   "ICA" indicates derives from the Insurance Companies Act 1982.

    (i)   break down insurance;

    (ii) fidelity bonds etc. incidental to non-insurance business;

(c) dealing in investments as principal (FS Act):

    (i)   absence of holding out etc. (derives from FS Act Schedule 1, paragraph 17);

    (ii) dealing in contractually based investments;

    (iii) acceptance of instruments creating and acknowledging indebtedness (derives from FS Act Schedule 1, paragraph 12, Notes 1 and 2);

    (iv) issued by a company of its own shares etc.;

    (v) hedging (derives from permitted persons regime in FS Act Schedule 1, paragraph 23);

    (vi) other exclusions (trustees;[21] sale of goods and supply of services;[22] groups and joint enterprises;[23] sale of body corporate;[24] employee share schemes[25] and overseas persons);[26]

(d) dealing in investments as agent (FS Act):

    (i)   deals with or through authorised persons;

    (ii) other exclusions (sale of goods and supply of services; groups and joint enterprises; sale of body corporate; employee share schemes and overseas persons);

(e) arranging deals in investments (FS Act):

    (i)   arranging not causing a deal;

    (ii) arranging transactions to which the arranger is party;

    (iii) arranging deals with or through authorised persons;

    (iv) arranging transactions in connection with lending on the security of insurance policies;

    (v) arranging the acceptance of debentures in connection with loans;

    (vi) provision of finance;

    (vii) introducing (derives from FS Act Schedule 1, paragraph 13, Note 6);

    (viii)arranging for the issue of shares etc.;

    (ix) international securities self-regulating organisations (derives FS Act Schedule 1, paragraph 25B);

---

[21]   Derives from FSA Schedule 1, paragraph 22.

[22]   Derives from FSA Schedule 1, paragraph 19.

[23]   Derives from FSA Schedule 1, paragraph 18.

[24]   Derives from FSA Schedule 1, paragraph 21.

[25]   Derives from FSA Schedule 1, paragraph 20.

[26]   Derives from FSA Schedule 1, paragraphs 26 and 27.

     (x) other exclusions (trustees; profession or non-investment business; sale of goods and supply of services; groups and joint enterprises; sale of body corporate; employee share schemes and overseas persons);

(f) managing investments (FS Act):

     (ii) attorneys;

     (iii) other exclusions (trustees; sale of goods and supply of services and groups and joint enterprises);

(g) safeguarding and administering investments (FS Act):

     (i) acceptance of responsibility by third party;

     (ii) introductions to qualifying custodians;

     (iii) activities not constituting administration;

     (iv) safeguarding and administration of non-publicly traded shares;

     (v) other exclusions (trustees; profession or non-investment business; sale of goods and supply of services; groups and joint enterprises; and employee share schemes);

(h) sending dematerialised instructions (FS Act):

     (i) instructions on behalf of participating issuers;

     (ii) instructions on behalf of settlement bank;

     (iii) instructions in connection with takeover offers;

     (iv) instructions in the course of providing a network;

     (v) other exclusions (trustees and groups and joint enterprises);

(i) establishing etc. a collective investment scheme (FS Act);

(j) advising on investments (FS Act):

     (i) advice given in newspapers etc.[27] (derives from FS Act Schedule 1, paragraphs 25 and 25A);

     (ii) other exclusions (trustees; profession or non-investment business;[28] sale of goods and supply of services; groups and joint enterprises; sale of body corporate and overseas persons);

(k) advice on syndicate participation at Lloyd's (LA);[29]

(l) Lloyd's managing agents (LA);

(m) arranging deals in contracts of insurance written at Lloyd's (LA);

(n) funeral plan contracts;

(o) regulated mortgage contracts;

(p) agreeing to carry on certain regulated activities (FS Act).

---

[27]   Includes the giving of advice in a website.

[28]   Derives from FSA Schedule 1, paragraph 24.

[29]   LA indicates derives from the Lloyd's Act 1982.

14.4.7   *Future scope of Financial Services and Markets Act 2000*

The Government intends to keep under review potential changes to the scope of regulated activities caught FSMA. In particular, it intends to consider credit unions and long-term health care insurance.

14.4.8   *The regulators approach to the Internet*

The regulators, recognising the growing use of the Internet are aiming to develop appropriate regulatory standards covering electronic investment business. They are also endeavouring to identify and stop unauthorised investment business and fraudsters.

The FSA has produced an Internet questionnaire which has now become an integral part of the SFA's application procedure. In brief, the questionnaire covers strategy, project management, customer information, business information, systems security, IT recovery procedures, control procedures and systems documentation.

The SFA has issued guidance to its member firms on the Internet and e-commerce.[30] Generally, the regulators expect firms to apply the existing regulatory principles and rules to business carried out on the Internet. For example, firms are required to organise and control their affairs in a responsible manner.[31] Firms must apply this principle to the organisation and control of their Internet websites (as well as any investment business conducted via such a website). Firms are expected to monitor and ensure that their bulletin boards and chat rooms are being used appropriately by their customers and that an appropriate level of security is applied to their website and Internet business.

Certain guidance specifically cover Internet business. For example, the SFA allows firms to send contract and confirmation notes electronically.[32] Customers may also access contract notes via the firm's website[33] but firms must ensure that they monitor and apply an appropriate level of security to the website and that the client has accessed his contract note or confirmation within five business days of it being placed on the website.[34]

The SFA also encourages firms to engage in dialogue with it in respect of their proposed Internet activity,[35] for example, when they are setting up a website, starting new Internet business or making a major change to their website which affects theirs regulated business. Contacting the regulator can be useful as it should limit the risk of a firm's website inadvertently breaching regulations.

---

[30]   SFA Board Notices 416 and 543.

[31]   FSA Principle 9 (Internal Organisation).

[32]   SFA Conduct of Business Rule 5-34(6).

[33]   SFA Board Notice 543.

[34]   Where a private customer has not accessed his contract note/confirmation within five business days of it being placed on the website, he must be sent the contract note/confirmation in either hard copy or electronically (SFA Board Notice 543).

[35]   FSA Principle 10 (Relations with Regulators).

The FSA's conduct of business rules for the new regime[36] specifically provide guidance on the Internet and other electronic media. The FSA's stated aim is to ensure that consumers are as protected in their dealing with firms via electronic means (as they are when using more traditional media) but that FSAs' requirements do not stand in the way of innovation and competition.

14.5 The global dimension of the Internet

14.5.1 *Does the Financial Services Act 1986 apply?*

Given the borderless nature of the Internet it is important to consider the territorial implications of the FS Act. The FS Act does not apply to activities carried on outside the UK (although the scope of the SRO rules do apply to non-UK investment business carried on by member firms). It applies to investment activities (including offering and agreeing) carried on in the UK either from a permanent place of business in the UK maintained by the firm, or that caught by Part II of Schedule 1 to the FS Act and not excluded by Parts III and IV of that Schedule.

However, in the Internet world the question of where a business is being carried on is possibly the most fraught. Consequently, investment services offered over the Internet to persons in the UK are likely to be caught by the FS Act (unless the overseas persons exclusions apply).

14.5.2 *A permanent place of business in the UK*

A permanent place of business suggests a physical location in a particular jurisdiction, for example an office, but the nature of the Internet is borderless. A server or a web site that is maintained by the person carrying on investment business in the UK is likely to be caught by the FS Act. Generally, the location of the server and website is less important than the location of the individuals controlling the business activities. Consequently, investment services offered over the Internet to persons in the UK are likely to be caught by the FS Act (unless the overseas persons exclusions apply).

14.5.3 *Exclusions for overseas persons (Part IV of Schedule 1 to the Financial Services Act 1986)*

There are two excluded activities for persons without a permanent place of business in the UK (i.e. overseas persons) under the FS Act:

(a) *transactions with or through authorised or exempted persons (paragraph 26)* – under this paragraph a person could enter into deals in investments or arrange deals with a UK person, if the deals or arrangements are made with or through a person who is authorised[37] or exempt under the FS Act. A transaction is entered into through a person if he acts as agent or arranges for it to be entered into by another person as principal or agent;[38]

---

[36]   FSA Policy Statement – Conduct of Business Sourcebook.

[37]   This will include European investment firms carrying on home regulated investment business in the UK under the Investment Services Regulations.

[38]   FSA Schedule 1, paragraph 29.

A person based outside the UK (without a permanent place of business in the UK) can use the Internet to deal or arrange deals in investments with or through an authorised person (e.g. a bank or securities house that is a member of SFA) and not require authorisation under the FS Act. The overseas person could link with UK investors through an authorised person website.

(b) *unsolicited or legitimately solicited transactions (paragraph 27)* – under this paragraph certain investment activities are excluded from regulation under the FS Act if they are unsolicited by the overseas person or if they have been solicited without breaching the cold calling and investment advertisement requirements of the FS Act. These are discussed below.

14.6 Europe

The European Parliament has implemented many directives that relate to financial services business carried on in Europe. A brief outline of important European directives that impact on the provision of financial services on the Internet are set out below.

14.6.1 *The Investment Services Directive*[39]

The ISD implements[40] the Treaty of Rome's basic freedoms: freedom of establishment and freedom to provide services. It established for non-bank investment firms[41] a "single passport" regime allowing, subject to certain notification requirements, firms authorised in one Member State to do business in another Member State. This could be either through branches or on a cross-border basis, for example, on the Internet. Broadly, once authorised in its home state (i.e. the Member State where the firm has its head and registered office),[42] a firm may provide core investment services and other non-core services covered by the ISD throughout the European Economic Area ("EEA") (i.e. into the host state). The single passport applies to services including broking, dealing, portfolio management and underwriting[43] and so covers similar but not the same investment activities as the FS Act.

14.6.2 *The Second Banking Co-ordination Directive*[44]

A similar single passport regime applies to banks and other credit institutions under the Second Banking Co-ordination Directive (the "2BCD"). The activities covered by the single passport under 2BCD include accepting deposits, lending, financial leasing, money transmission services, trading for own account or for a customer in certain investments,[45] money broking, fund management and safe-custody services.

---

[39] 93/22/EEC, as amended. The ISD was implemented into UK legislation by the Investment Services Regulations 1995 (SI 1995/3275).

[40] In relation to the provision of financial services.

[41] Investment firm means a legal person whose regular business is providing core investment services (set out in Table A at the end of this Chapter) for third parties on a professional basis.

[42] If it is a legal person.

[43] *See* Table A at the end of this Chapter.

[44] 89/646/EEC, as amended.

[45] For example, money market instruments, foreign exchange, financial futures and options and transferable securities.

14.6.3   *UCITS*

The UCITS Directive established a similar single passport regime for collective investment undertakings (e.g. unit trusts or SICAVS). Broadly, the regime covers funds managed by qualified fund managers in a diverse range of assets according to defined risk criteria (currently "transferable securities"). There is currently a proposal to extend the investment powers of UCITS to permit a wider range of funds including money market funds and funds investing in bank deposits.[46]

14.6.4   *Third Life Directive*

The Third Life Directive completes the single market in the insurance sector. Likewise it introduced a single passport regime for insurance firms. As with the other directives it introduced a regime which allows insurance firms, subject to notification requirements, to carry on their business anywhere in the EEA.

14.6.5   *Electronic Commerce Directive*

The Electronic Commerce Directive establishes a legal framework for European e-commerce. It defines a firm's place of establishment as the place where it pursues its economic activity irrespective of where websites or servers are situated. It obliges Member States to remove any prohibition or restriction on the use of electronic contracts. Additionally, it aims to ensure legal security by imposing certain information requirements for the formation of electronic contracts. The Directive also establishes an exemption from liability for intermediaries where their role is passive and they act as a "mere conduit" of information from third parties, and limits service providers' liability from other intermediary activities such as the storage of information.

14.6.6   *Electronic Signatures Directive*

The Electronic Signatures Directive provides for the recognition and authentication of electronic signatures. It prevents Member States denying the legal effect of a signature in electronic form. It has recently been implemented into English law by the passing of the EC Act.

14.6.7   *Distance Marketing Directive*

The Distance Marketing Directive relating to financial services is still a proposal. It is doubtful whether it will be adopted before Summer 2001. It covers financial services contracts concluded at a distance and so will impact on such contracts concluded on the Internet. It requires that customers are given pre-contractual information and that contractual terms are provided in a durable medium. A durable medium suggests that displaying terms on a website will not be sufficient to comply with the Directive; contractual terms will also need to be sent to the customer, for example by email, on paper or via a CD ROM. The Directive also gives the customer a right to withdraw from the contract without penalty within a prescribed timescale (generally 14 days but for life assurance 30 days).

---

[46]   UCITS II.

14.7   US

14.7.1   The US Securities and Exchange Commission

The US has extra-territorial securities laws that protect US persons beyond the shores of America. Key US securities laws include the Securities Act 1933, the Securities Exchange Act 1934 and the Investment Company Act of 1940.

The Securities and Exchange Commission (the "SEC") is a key securities regulator in the US. Its primary aim is investor protection. It accomplishes this through corporate disclosures, investor education and enforcement of its regulations. It also develops securities regulations and guidance, including regulations relating to the use of the Internet by the financial services industry. A recent example of published guidance covers website content and the liability of securities issuers for information on third party websites accessed via a hyperlink. It also operates an Internet enforcement programme. SEC staff working within the programme surf the Internet in search of potential securities frauds.

The SEC and its Commissioners also publish papers on issues concerning the future development of securities law. In a recent speech[47] an SEC Commissioner suggested that fundamental principles of US securities law need to be re-examined as a result of the Internet. The Commissioner suggested the following issues need to be considered:

(a) what is a broker-dealer or what makes financial portals different from broker-dealers and should portals be included in tomorrow's regulatory scheme?;

(b) in times of Internet publication and newsletter what is an investment adviser?; and

(c) with technology providing additional trading places and competition what is tomorrow's market and how should competition and innovation be promoted there?

The SEC also operates an Electronic Data Gathering, Analysis and Retrieval System ("EDGARS") which performs automated collection and validation of submissions by companies who are legally required to file forms with the SEC. EDGAR also provides access over the Internet to certain information filed by companies.

14.7.2   International Organisation of Securities Commissions

The International Organisation of Securities Commissions ("IOSCO") is a global securities law policy-making body. Its members include all the major securities regulators (e.g. the FSA and the SEC). Regularly, its members gather to discuss issues of importance to securities regulators such as the impact of the Internet on securities regulation, and the need to develop cooperative enforcement initiatives.

IOSCO members have resolved to cooperate to promote high standards of market regulation and to exchange information. They have also agreed to cooperate on international securities transactions surveillance. For example, on 28 March 2000 certain IOSCO members[48] conducted an International Internet Surf Day, aimed at increasing

---

[47]   Commissioner Laura S. Unger speech dated 28 July 2000.

[48]   21 securities and futures regulators from 18 countries around the world co-ordinated their efforts to identify securities and futures fraud on the Internet. Regulators concentrated on fraudulent solicitation of investors, manipulation, the circulation of false or misleading information and insider trading.

investor protection and market confidence. The authorities also regularly work together to share information and technical expertise in detecting, deterring and investigating securities and futures fraud on the Internet.

14.8　　Investment advertisement on the Internet

Promotion of investments or investment services on the Internet aimed at persons in the UK is regulated by Section 57 of the FS Act. This Section provides that no person, other than an authorised person, shall issue or cause to be issued an investment advertisement in the UK unless its contents have been approved by an authorised person or a specific exemption applies. Anyone failing to comply with Section 57 commits a criminal offence punishable on conviction (on indictment) by up to two years imprisonment, or a fine, or both.

14.8.1　　*What is an investment advertisement?*

An investment advertisement is defined in Section 57 of the FS Act as:

> "any advertisement inviting persons to enter or offer to enter into an investment agreement or to exercise any right conferred by an investment to acquire, dispose of, underwrite or convert an investment or containing information calculated to lead directly or indirectly to persons doing so."

The definition of an investment advertisement will catch material containing information calculated (e.g. likely) to lead directly or indirectly to persons entering into investment agreements. An investment agreement is any agreement, the making or performance of which by either party, constitutes an activity which falls within any paragraph of Part II of Schedule 1 of the FS Act. The definition of advertisement under the FS Act[49] is widely drawn, including every form of advertising, so including advertising on the Internet.

14.8.2　　*Issuing an advertisement outside the UK*

The FS Act provides[50] that an advertisement issued outside the UK will be treated as issued in the UK if it is directed to, or made available to, UK persons. If an advertisement can be pulled up on a computer screen in the UK then that advertisement may be regarded as having been issued in the UK. This does not apply to advertisements issued in a newspaper, magazine or other periodic publication which are principally circulated outside the UK, or in a sound or television broadcast transmitted principally for reception outside the UK.

Consequently, persons advertising financial services from websites located outside the UK, because of the nature of the Internet are making the advertisements available to UK persons and so issuing them in the UK. Unless specific exemptions apply such advertisements must be issued or approved by UK authorised persons.

---

[49]　Section 207(2).

[50]　Section 207(3).

Clearly those providing websites on which such material has been posted could be seen to be "issuing or causing the issue" of that material and will need to ensure that if the material is an "investment advertisement", that it has been approved by an authorised person (under the FS Act). Such action will provide a defense where any offence has been committed (*see* below).

14.8.3   *The regulators approach to advertising on the Internet*

In response to concern expressed by overseas firms the FSA issued guidance[51] relating to the need for UK approval for advertising material issued on the Internet. The FSA stated that its primary concern in this area was investor protection. The FSA will first consider if the advertising is caught by Section 57. If it is, the FSA will consider the extent to which it is directed at persons in the UK. Factors the FSA will take into account, before taking any enforcement action include the degree to which positive steps have been taken to avoid material being made available or received by persons in the UK. These steps could include pre-registration, password protection, and whether the site contains disclaimers and warnings that the services are only available in certain countries and whether the warnings or disclaimers could be viewed by visitors to the site in the same browser format as the rest of the site.

The guidance also highlights the risk that by placing material on the Internet it may amount to conducting investment business in the UK by providing investment advice to, or investment services for, UK investors. This will be a matter of fact. The exclusions for overseas persons, discussed above, may be available, but will depend on the circumstances of each case.

14.8.4   *Approval of investment advertisements*

If a person, for example, a site provider is not authorised under the FS Act and wants to issue an investment advertisement he must get the advertisement approved by an authorised person. The authorised person will be responsible to its SRO (or the FSA if directly authorised) and will need to ensure that the rules of the SRO are complied with when it approves the advertisement. For example, the advertisement must be fair and not misleading and include suitable risk warnings. The advertisement will also need to indicate that it has been approved by an authorised person.

There is a defence available to a person who in the ordinary course of business, other than investment business, issues an advertisement to the order of another person. He must show that he had reasonable grounds to believe that the person who gave the order was authorised under the FS Act, that the contents had been approved by an authorised person or that the advertisement was permitted by exemption.

14.8.5   *Exceptions to Section 57 of the Financial Services Act 1986*

Section 58 sets out exceptions from the advertising restrictions of Section 57. In particular, Section 57 does not apply to advertisements issued by the UK Government and Bank of England. In addition there are specific exceptions set out in secondary legislation made under Section 58 which are summarised below.

---

51   FSA Guidance Release February 1998.

14.8.6   *Financial Services Act 1986 (Investment Advertisements) (Exemptions) Order 1996*

Article 3 exempts investment advertisements issued by bodies corporate (other than an open-ended investment company) to persons who are reasonably believed to be creditors or members, or persons who are entitled to certain other shares, bonds or investments issued by that body corporate or another body corporate within its group, provided that the advertisement is not an investment advertisement for any other body corporate.

A company should, therefore, be able to use the Internet to send an email to its shareholders or even possibly to allow access to a site for the purposes of downloading permitted information by such persons. Care must be taken to ensure that no other person can gain access which would cause loss of the exemption.

Article 4 exempts investment advertisements containing certain permitted information issued by a body corporate (other than an open-ended investment company) if it or its holding company has issued relevant securities (i.e. shares which are traded or dealt in on certain EEA markets or other approved securities markets) and advertisements containing or accompanied by the whole or part of a body corporate's accounts or director's report prepared in accordance with the accounting requirements of the UK or the equivalent requirements of an EEA State.

Companies can, subject to satisfying the conditions of the exemption, place certain information about themselves on a website. It will be necessary to check whether this is restricted in relation to any other jurisdiction outside the UK.

Article 5 exempts investment advertisements relating to bearer securities issued by a body corporate (other than an open-ended investment company). This exempts certain communications addressed to holders of bearer securities such as bearer bonds. The Internet might present an effective method of communication but it is important that the material is addressed to the relevant holder.

Article 6 exempts investment advertisements issued in connection with employees' share schemes. This is more likely to be relevant to a communication to employees (and certain categories of close relatives) by email through a network or on an intranet.

Articles 7 and 8 exempt investment advertisements issued within groups of bodies corporate and advertisements between participants or potential participants in a joint enterprise. This is also more likely to be relevant to email over a network or on an intranet.

Articles 9 exempts investment advertisements in connection with the sale of goods and supply of services. Therefore, certain transactions may be promoted and effected through the Internet by suppliers whose main business is to supply goods or services and not to engage in activities regulated by the FS Act, even if they include an investment business element.

Article 10 exempts certain investment advertisements by persons without a permanent place of business in the UK with certain persons with which is has previously dealt or has advised abroad. This may be more relevant to email and may be of use to overseas persons.

Article 11 exempts advertisements issued to persons sufficiently expert to understand the risk involved. This important exemption allows a person who is not authorised under the FS Act to issue an advertisement to certain categories of recipient including larger bodies corporate, unincorporated associations and trusts. The exemption does not extend to private individuals. Broadly speaking a body corporate must have at least 20 members and called-up share capital or net assets of not less than £500,000; or be part of a group which includes a body corporate with called-up share capital or net assets of not less than £5 million, an unincorporated association must have net assets of not less than £5 million and a trust must have assets (before deducting liabilities) of not less than £10 million. This may be relevant to certain email communications and sites which have strict pre-registration requirement prior to access.

Article 12 exempts advertisements with respect to shares or debentures in a "private company" relating to persons who might reasonably be regarded as having an existing and common interest with each other and with the company in the affairs of the company and what is to be done with the proceeds of the offer.

Article 13 exempts certain advertisements by trustees or personal representatives.

Article 14 exempts certain advertisements by operators of FSA-recognised collective investment schemes.

Article 15 exempts certain advertisements relating to publications and programmes which contain advice to which paragraph 15 of Schedule 1 to the FS Act does not apply by virtue of paragraph 25 or 25A of that Schedule.

Article 16 exempts advertisements issued by certain securities markets.

Article 17 exempts advertisements issued by certain property management companies.

Article 18 exempts advertisements issued in respect of the Parliamentary Commissioner for Administration.

14.8.7 *Financial Services Act 1986 (Investment Advertisements) (Exemptions) (No. 2) Order 1995*

Article 3 exempts certain advertisements for the purpose of raising share or debenture capital in a company for the purpose of promoting or encouraging industrial or commercial activity or enterprise in the UK.

Article 4 exempts advertisements for takeovers of private companies. There are detailed requirements before this exemption can apply and detailed document requirements. The Internet probably does not satisfy them.

Article 5 exempts advertisements for the sale of body corporate. This is limited to certain defined groups of persons.

Article 6 exempts dealing in the course of non-investment business. This exemption can apply if a person holds a permission under paragraph 25 of Schedule 1 to the FS Act exempting him from "investment business".

Article 7 exempts certain advertisements issued by a person who is not an authorised person and who is not unlawfully carrying on investment business in the UK if that advertisement is issued to particular kinds of person such as those whose business is to arrange the placing of advertisements.

Articles 8 to 10 exempt certain advertisements directed at informing or influencing persons of a particular kind, such as a government, local authority or public authority and certain persons involved in investment business.

Article 11 exempts certain advertisements required or permitted to be published by exchange or market rules. This allows a body corporate which has securities traded or dealt in on the markets listed in the Exemption Order, to publish information which is required or permitted by the rules relevant to that market. For example, certain announcements of results or acquisitions could be placed on that company's website.

Article 12 exempts certain advertisements by certain exchanges or markets. This exemption is relevant to financial markets themselves.

Article 13 exempts advertisements by industrial and provident societies relating to investments issued, or to be issued by it.

Article 14 exempts certain advertisements relating to public offers of securities. This allows the publication of prospectuses for unlisted securities in accordance with the Public Offer of Securities Regulations 1995 ("POS") and, certain information relating to such a prospectus or equivalent information for prescribed EEA markets.

Article 15 exempts advertisements required or authorised under enactments. This allows a communication if required or authorised by any enactment. It is unlikely that it has any particular application to the Internet.

14.9 Unsolicited calls

Section 56 of the FS Act prohibits any person from entering into an investment agreement in the course of, or in consequence of, an "unsolicited call" made on persons in the UK or from the UK on a person elsewhere, except so far as permitted by regulations. An "unsolicited call" means a personal or oral communication made without express invitation.

There is no criminal sanction for contravening Section 56 of the FS Act but compensation can be ordered by the court. Also, investment agreements entered into as a result of an unsolicited call are generally unenforceable against the customer. Clearly it is possible for emails to constitute unsolicited calls in that they can be seen to be personal communications. Overseas firms in particular are prone to fall foul of this provision, which in turn, can make the overseas persons exclusion (*see* above) unavailable.

14.10 The new regime – financial promotion

The current distinction between investment advertising and cold calling will disappear under the new regime. The FSMA aims to create a single media-neutral regime, broadly, prohibiting unauthorised persons from promoting financial services. However, the overseas persons exemptions will still be available. There will be little change from the current marketing restrictions relating to deposits and general insurance but there will be some changes to the marketing restrictions that apply to investment business.

The financial promotion framework is set out in Section 21 of FSMA. It provides that "A person must not, in the course of business, communicate an invitation or inducement to engage in investment activity" unless he is authorised, or the communication has been approved by an authorised person. Anyone failing to comply with Section 21 commits a criminal offence punishable on conviction (on indictment) by up to two years imprisonment, or a fine, or both.

A key change under the FSMA is that the new regime only applies to communications which are invitations or inducements (and not, as under the current regime, to advertisements including those which may indirectly lead to a person entering into an investment agreement). The new regime also only applies to promotions made in the course of business. The new regime covers all forms of communication, including "real time communication", both solicited and unsolicited, whether or not they are advertisements.

The main exemptions to the new financial promotion restrictions are set out in a statutory instrument.[52] In specified circumstances[53] the general restriction do not apply to deposits and general insurance contracts.

Many of the exemptions under the current regime are replicated under the new regime. The key additional exemptions include the following:

(a) promotions not directed at the UK;

(b) generic promotions (i.e. not relating to a particular investment);

(c) mere conduits;

(d) high net-worth individuals.

There are also proposals to exempt from the new regime certain promotions directed at particular audiences, that become available to a wider audience, where systems are in place to prevent participation from the investors outside the target group.

Key areas currently not covered by the FS Act that will fall within the new regime are:

(a) certain types of solicited calls that do not fall within the generalised exemptions;

(b) the regulation of financial promotion out of the UK by unauthorised persons.

14.11 Offers of securities

14.11.1 UK

There are two different regulatory regimes that apply to the offer of the securities in the UK. One regime applies to listed securities and the other to unlisted securities. Recently securities have been offered over the Internet (e.g. egg.com and lastminute.com) and these offers were required to comply with the relevant regulations.

---

52 FSMA (Financial Promotion) Order 2001.

53 Broadly, if restriction under the current regime are met.

14.11.2   *Listed*

UK listed securities include shares and debt securities which may be traded on the London Stock Exchange (the "Exchange"). These securities are regulated by Part IV of the FS Act and the FSA Listing Rules.[54] Generally, the issue of such securities requires the publication and filing of a prospectus or listing particulars.

Recently lastminute.com shares were offered to UK investors over the Internet. As part of the offering, investors were able to view and print the prospectus and application form directly from the Internet. In the case of the egg.com offering investors were able to submit their applications via the Internet and also supply their debit card payment details and so pay for their shares over the Internet.[55]

14.11.3   *Unlisted*

Unlisted securities, for example shares traded on the Alternative Investment Market ("AIM") will be subject to the POS. These regulations provide that securities offered to the public in the UK must be accompanied by a prospectus that complies with POS regulations, except where certain exemptions apply.

14.11.4   *Investment advertisements*

A prospectus or listing particulars that complies with the relevant UK requirements is not caught by the investment advertisements requirements[56] set out in Section 57 and is not expected to be caught by the new financial promotions regime. However, if the prospectus or listing particulars are posted on a website it is important to ensure that securities laws of other jurisdictions are not breached.

14.11.5   *Overseas*

The Internet may be used to offer securities in a number of jurisdictions. It is important to ensure that the offer complies with the relevant regulations or prohibitions in each jurisdiction where the offer is made.

Generally, registration under the US Securities Act 1933 is required before securities can be offered or sold in the US. Before an offer is made in the US filing of various documents is required and a declaration by SEC that the registration is effective. Care should be taken to comply with these requirements as the SEC has successfully prosecuted persons who have fraudulently offered securities on the Internet.

Fortunately, the SEC takes the view that offerors who design their websites and systems to prevent the sale of securities to US persons will not be deemed to be directing their offer at US persons. For example, in the case of a UK offer, the website could contain a prominent notice clearly stating that the offer is not directed at US persons and that only person resident in the UK should apply. In this case, it is unlikely that the offeror would not need to registered under Securities Legislation Regulation.

---

[54]   The Listing Authority function was transferred from the London Stock Exchange to the FSA on 1 May 2000.

[55]   The lastminute.com and egg.com offers were restricted to existing customers.

[56]   Section 58(10)(d) of the FS Act and paragraph 14 of the FS Act (Investment Advertisement) (Exemptions) Order 1995.

In Australia, a similar approach is adopted by the Australian Securities Investment Commission. Broadly, offerors that design their website and processes so that they do not accept applications from Australian residents will not fall foul of Australian securities regulation.

14.12   Information on the Internet

The Internet is a useful media to broadcast information about securities and investments. These broadcasts will be subject to regulation under the FS Act and by the Exchange and in future, regulations under FSMA.

14.12.1   *Misleading statements*

Section 47(1) of the FS Act makes it a criminal offence for any person to make a statement, promise or forecast (including recklessly) which he knows to be misleading, false or deceptive, or dishonestly conceals any material facts. The Section applies to a statement, promise or forecast made in or from the UK. Therefore all statements published on the Internet should be prepared with care because if the statement can be viewed in the UK it could be deemed to have been issued in the UK and therefore, if it is misleading as defined above, an offence would have been committed.

14.12.2   *False markets*

Section 47(2) of the FS Act makes it a criminal offence to create a false or misleading impression as to the market in or price of value of any investments. The person creating the false or misleading impression must do so whilst encouraging or discouraging another to acquire, dispose of, subscribe or underwrite investments. Share price manipulation in chat rooms, ramping and pump and dump are likely to caught by this Section. There are likely to be reputational risks for firms where they run chat rooms or provide newsgroup facilities which others abuse. The FSA has also indicated that it would expect firms who are notified of such material appearing on websites they run to remove such material.

14.12.3   *The new regime – market abuse*

Under the new regime the FSA will have power to impose unlimited penalties on those who abuse prescribed markets. The offence occurs "in relation to"[57] qualifying investments traded on a prescribed exchange. "In relation to" investments includes behaviour that relates to anything which is the subject matter of qualifying investments (e.g. silver for exchange traded silver future); or anything whose price/value is based on the qualifying investment's price/value (e.g bonds which are convertible into Exchange listed shares) or any investments whose subject matter is a qualifying investments (e.g. options on Exchange shares).

The new powers will complement the existing criminal offences relating to market manipulation and insider dealing that are covered by the FS Act and the Criminal Justice Act 1993. The FSA has described the existing offence as covering "a relatively narrow range of very serious misconduct".[58]

---

[57]   Section 118(6) FSMA.

[58]   FSA Consultation Paper 59, paragraph 2.10.

Section 118 of FSMA broadly defines market abuse in terms of the following three types of behaviour:[59]

(a) involves the misuse of non-public information;[60]

(b) is likely to give a false or misleading impression;[61] or

(c) is likely to distort the market[62]

and which also falls below the standard of behaviour reasonably expected of a person in that position in relation to that market by a regular user of the market (and does not fall within a safe harbour).

The offence can be committed by anyone, even by people who have no intention to abuse the market and by securities firms, banks, ordinary trading companies or other persons who are not authorised under the FSMA. The offence can be committed in relation to securities or derivatives quoted on stock markets or other investment exchanges,[63] which are in, or accessible electronically from, the UK. This is true even for behaviour that occurs outside the UK.

Under Section 119 FSMA, the FSA must prepare a code of market conduct which sets out guidance on whether behaviour amounts to market abuse. The code may specify behaviour the FSA considers is or is not market abuse. The FSA may also set out factors they consider need to be taken into account in determining whether behaviour is or is not market abuse.

Clearly material appearing on the Internet will be caught by these provisions. Yet again it highlights the need for systems and procedures, where firms are hosting newsgroups or chat rooms, to identify and prevent firms being seen to be a party to such activities. There are clear reputational risks here. Indeed avoiding being involved in a web of market abuse being carried on by others is difficult in the e-world, as, for example firms have little or no control over third parties linking to their sites.

---

[59]   Including action or inaction.

[60]   The behaviour is based on information which is not generally available to those using the market but which, if available to a regular user of the market, would or would be likely to be regarded by him as relevant when deciding the terms on which transactions in investments of the kind in question should be effected (Section 118(2)(a) FSMA).

[61]   The behaviour is likely to give a regular user of the market a false or misleading impression as to the supply of, or demand for, or as to the price or value of, investments of the kind in question (Section 118(2)(b) FSMA).

[62]   A regular user of the market would, or would be likely to, regard the behaviour as behaviour which would, or would be likely to, distort the market in investments of the kind in question (Section 118(2)(c) FSMA).

[63]   It is expected that the following exchanges will be prescribed for the purposes of Section 118: Exchange, LIFFE, LME, IPE, OM London Exchange, Tradepoint.

14.12.4   *Takeovers and mergers*

There has been an increase in the use of the Internet to disseminate information relating to takeovers. In the UK, in addition to company and securities law requirements (e.g. authorisation of investment advertisement), takeovers of public companies are subject to the City Code on Takeovers and Mergers (the "City Code"). The City Code contains rules and principles which aim to ensure fair treatment of shareholders in a takeover. It does not have the force of law but is accepted by the city and financial institutions as setting out guidance on the conduct to be followed during a public takeover.

A recent report from the Panel[64] indicates that the use of new media, including the Internet does not cause any particular concern to the Panel provided that the Code's principles of care, responsibility and availability of documents are upheld. However, if the Internet is to be used in connection with a takeover it is sensible to consult the Panel at an early stage.

---

[64]   1999–2000 Report.

Table A

Core Investment Services under the ISD – Section A

1 (a) Reception and transmission, on behalf of investors, of orders in relation to one or more of the instruments listed in Section B;

(b) execution of such orders other than for own account.

2 Dealing in any of the instruments listed in Section B for own account.

3 Managing portfolios of investments in accordance with mandates given by investors on a discretionary, client-by-client basis where such portfolios include one or more of the instruments listed in Section B.

4 Underwriting in respect of issues of any of the instruments listed in Section B and/or the placing of such issues.

Instruments under the ISD – Section B

1 (a) Transferable securities;

(b) units in collective investment undertakings.

2 Money-market instruments.

3 Financial-futures contracts, including equivalent cash-settled instruments.

4 Forward interest-rate agreements ("FRAs").

5 Interest-rate, currency and equity swaps.

Options to acquire or dispose of any instruments falling within this Section of the Annex, including equivalent cash-settled instruments. This category includes in particular options on currency and on interest rates.

Non-core services under the ISD – Section C

1 Safekeeping and administration in relation to one or more of the instruments listed in Section B.

2 Safe custody services.

3 Granting credits or loans to an investor to allow him to carry out a transaction in one or more of the instruments listed in Section B, where the firm granting the credit or loan is involved in the transaction.

4 Advice to undertakings on capital structure, industrial strategy and related matters and advice and service relating to mergers and the purchase of undertakings.

5 Services related to underwriting.

6 Investment advice concerning one or more of the instruments listed in Section B.

7 Foreign-exchange service where these are connected with the provision of investment services.

Chapter 15

BEST PRACTICE FOR COMPANIES IN THE USE OF EMAIL, INTERNET COMMUNICATIONS AND ACCESS TO WEBSITES

Heather Rowe
Partner
Matthew Redding
Lovells

15.1   Introduction

In recent years there has been a lot of publicity concerning the need for good corporate governance, such as the Cadbury and Greenbury Codes and various reports in this area. Clearly those reports were aimed at best practice in "corporate" matters for directors of companies, but directors of companies do need to consider generally how their companies use technology and what communications methods their employees are using, particularly when, for the first time, global (and fairly uncontrolled) written communications can be made over the Internet. Granting employees the use of email and the Internet is a somewhat different concept from enabling one's staff to make international telephone calls because it is very easy for the recipient of an email message to store and reproduce that message in a way which would be admissible in legal proceedings or for employees to attach executable files to a message over the Internet containing a virus which could have a devastating effect on the recipient. Indeed, employees could also receive and open such messages. The recording of telephone calls is a more hit or miss affair, and is regulated in some jurisdictions so that the caller or employer is aware that recording or monitoring is taking place and would no doubt be more cautious about what they say if they were aware it was being recorded. This is almost certainly not the case with the use of email. Users are generally fairly naive as to how email works and any security risks involved.

A more simple danger is that use of the Internet does encourage users to send messages in a rather colloquial form, which can lend itself to misinterpretation. The Internet even has its own "Netiquette", which some take very seriously, so an email in capital letters would cause offence.

It is, therefore, in the broadest sense a matter of good corporate governance that directors of companies need to be aware of what liabilities their company could incur if their employees are permitted wholesale (and unfettered) use of the Internet. Good corporate governance requires policies to be established in areas such as Internet use.

Interestingly, the original Cadbury report suggests that "the directors should report on the effectiveness of the company's systems of internal control" and their findings should be reviewed by the auditors. Quite what this means is uncertain but, if wholesale use of the Internet and access to, say, pornographic websites or websites carrying terrorist information could be made by employees without any proper restrictions and the company has no guidelines about how their employees should use email and the Internet, does it suggest a lack of internal controls? Subsequent reports from Cadbury have suggested that the word "effectiveness" should be dropped, but that still requires directors to report on the company's systems of internal control.

To give a specific example, the Bank of England has issued various guidelines to banks that their directors should understand the implications of the computer systems that banks use and, in particular, states that "adequate controls in banks' computer and telecommunication systems are of particular importance in the light of the increasing use of such technology in areas such as lending". In addition, banks in general are required by statute to conduct their business in a "prudent" manner with "adequate accounting and other records of business and adequate systems of control of its business and records".[1]

The Financial Services Authority's (the "FSA") Guide to Banking Supervisory Policy sets out the FSA's prudential policy for its supervision of institutions, as authorised under the Banking Act 1987. This is constantly being updated. It contains a specific section called "Controls in an Information Technology Environment". This recognises that there are "additional risks associated with electronic environments" and that "it is the responsibility of management to understand the extent to which an institution relies upon electronic information to assess the value of that information and to establish an appropriate system of controls".[2] It is therefore clear that regulators are taking an increasingly close look at how information is protected and processed.

A number of former financial regulators such as the Securities and Futures Authority and the Personal Investment Authority (now within the FSA) each had express rules as to how their members might use both email and electronic records in the course of their business to deal with clients.

This Chapter is intended as an aide-memoire for the management of companies as to some of the legal issues relating to email and Internet use and how to ensure that they discharge their duty of care adequately in relation to their company's business, bearing in mind the adverse effects that employees could cause to that business. It touches on the use of websites by companies in the course of their business, but not in substantial detail as this is dealt with elsewhere in this Guide.

15.2 The law of confidence

There is no general law of privacy in the UK entitling an individual to say that information about him is private, although there are certain specific pieces of legislation that address the privacy area. Moreover, the European Convention on Human Rights does provide a right to privacy (Article 8) and this was incorporated into English domestic law on 2 October 2000 by the Human Rights Act 2000 (*see* Section 15.3 below).

There is, however, a general law of confidence, the breach of which may be actionable. A breach of confidence could be made easily over the Internet and the global nature of the Internet could lead to the breach of confidence being multiplied many times, particularly if confidential information finds its way onto a company's website or onto a bulletin board. Employees should be made aware of the restrictions on the use of confidential information and what constitutes such information.

---

[1]   *See* Schedule 3 (7) of the Banking Act 1987.

[2]   Section 4.3.6, "Accounting and Other Records and Internal Controls Systems" available at www.fsa.gov.uk/pubs/supervisor.

The converse is that a company may take positive steps to collect information of a confidential nature (say, to its website by inviting customer or user emails containing information of a confidential nature) – perhaps in response to a questionnaire marked as confidential and containing questions of a sensitive nature, and then use it in breach of confidence. Proper procedures need to be in place to prevent misuse of that information.

As a first step one has to establish that the information is confidential – then ensure that it is kept so. Three elements must be established for an actionable breach of confidence to exist:

(a) the information must be of a confidential nature, which has been further defined in case law (e.g. *Coco v. A.N. Clark (Engineers) Ltd* 1968 FSR 615);

(b) the information must have been imparted in circumstances creating an obligation of confidence. This can be either where the confider has agreed with the recipient that the information supplied will be kept confidential (e.g. by a statement in a loan application form) or where a confider supplies the information in circumstances where the confidant knows, or should realise, that it must be kept confidential. For example, where personal or financial details are given for a specific purpose (such as opening an account) there will be an implied obligation that they will not be used for a very different purpose. A duty of confidence may even arise independently of any contractual or other relationship between the parties if, for example, someone receives confidential information in complete error and he knows or should know that it would be "unconscionable" to publish (*see* Lord Goff in *Spycatcher* 1990 1 AC at p.281); and

(c) there must be an unauthorised use of that information to the detriment of the confider, although later case law suggests that this may not be necessary at least between private litigants.

Breach of the duty of confidence may entitle the aggrieved party to obtain an injunction to prevent further misuse and/or to claim damages. The possibility of an injunction could be a significant problem for a website owner and it could adversely affect the operation or structure of its databases where data collected via a website is subsequently held and processed.

There are two basic defences to actions for breach of confidence:

(a) if the information is in the *public domain* – generally known or accessible to the public. However, the initial confidence breaker and those assisting him may still be restrained to prevent them from profiting from their wrongdoing (*see Spycatcher*) again; and

(b) if it is in the *public interest* that the information should be disclosed, although in some cases this may only be to the appropriate authorities. The leading case is *Lion Laboratories Limited v. Evans* [1985] IQB 526.

This general law of confidence will apply both to data held on a computer system and to manual data. It will apply to confidential data sent, say, by email or over the Internet to a website if this data is then used without the authority of the information provider. It may well have been sent for a specific purpose but the website owner or email recipient might use that data for a purpose beyond the authorised use. It is therefore important, if soliciting information over the Internet, to establish what use it will be put to and to ascertain whether the information could reasonably be regarded by the sender as confidential – and/or to make clear what use that information will be put to. If it is clear from a company's on-line application form for insurance what uses an individual's health data will be put to *and* the subject nevertheless sends the information, this ought to be sufficient implied consent to use it for *those* purposes only.

The general law of confidence is not restricted solely to data about living persons, unlike the UK Data Protection Legislation. It therefore protects corporate confidential information as well. Most importantly, the aggrieved party may be entitled to damages for breach of confidence.

15.2.1   Examples of confidential information

There are duties of confidence imposed on (amongst others) solicitors, doctors and banks. In relation to banks, this duty (sometimes referred to as one of secrecy) was considered most carefully in the leading case of *Tournier v. National Provincial and Union Bank of England* [1924] 1KB 461.

The judgment in *Tournier* establishes that the duty arises out of the banker/customer contract. Breach of the duty could give rise to a claim for substantial damages, if loss has resulted from the breach. The duty extends to all information acquired by a bank regarding its customers. This case also sets out four exceptions under which a bank could legitimately disclose information about its customers. These are where:

(a) a disclosure is under compulsion of law;

(b) there is a public duty of disclosure;

(c) the interests of the bank require disclosure; and

(d) disclosure is made by the express or implied consent of the customer.

(It can be seen that (a) and (b) are examples of a public interest defence.)

Point (c) above cannot be used where disclosure is simply of benefit to the bank in question. Otherwise it could be used to drive a coach and horses through the *Tournier* exceptions.

Clearly, confidential information can be disclosed by email just as it can by any other method. The danger is that it is very easy to send email inadvertently – it is a lot easier to hit "send" and regret it than to type a letter, read it, sign it, and then fold it and put it in an envelope. Indeed it is all too easy to receive a confidential email and then to forward it to someone (quite legitimately) only to find that you have circulated it to the wrong circulation group. Companies really should have simple guidance in place to remind their employees to take care in using email.

It is clear that the most common form of disclosure of customer information collected by website owners on third parties via their website will be where the confider has consented to the disclosure. Consent will be necessary even where the information is to be supplied to companies in the same group. Where consent has been obtained, any disclosure, as long as it is within the terms of the consent, will be lawful. Consent from a customer to send him details of offers from associated group companies will not be sufficient consent for details of offers from third parties to be sent to that customer or vice versa. In practice, there will be written terms and conditions for on-line banking, say, as for other banking services, so consent could be included in those terms and conditions. A number of banks and building societies in the UK are already running Internet banking services. No doubt their terms and conditions for such services address customer consent to use of their data. Banks are in a slightly different position to other companies insofar as the Banking Code of Practice (4th edition, March 1999, to be replaced by the 5th edition in January 2001),[3] in relation to those banks that subscribe to the Code (over 99 per cent of relevant banks in the marketplace), requires consent from personal customers to disclose their information even to members of the same banking group if the disclosure is for marketing purposes.

15.2.2 *Protective steps*

15.2.2.1 *Consent*

The consent referred to above must be given voluntarily and the provider of the information must not be forced to give it. In addition, the provider must be fully aware of what he is providing for it to constitute proper consent.

This raises the question as to whether such consent clauses, extracted from a customer, will breach any other legislation, such as the Unfair Contract Terms Act 1977, the EC Directive on Unfair Contract Terms and the UK Regulations passed to give effect to that Directive in English law.[4] Such clauses if held to be "unfair" could be voidable. Such consent must also comply with the requirements of the Data Protection Act 1998 (the "DPA 1998") (*see* Chapter 7). Consideration should be given to these laws when drafting consent provisions.

15.2.2.2 *Confidentiality notices*

Communications sent by email can be intercepted (or perhaps even misdirected) and read by strangers. Therefore, it is suggested that, if it does not already do so, every company should provide a macro to its staff which they are required to use when sending emails externally. The macro should contain a confidentiality warning, in similar form to the wording which typically appears on faxes. The macro should also contain the information that is required by the Business Names Act 1985 to be included on business letters. In practice, one suspects such a warning would not put off a serious hacker or blackmailer. Such a warning might be drafted to read something like:

> "CONFIDENTIALITY This email and any attachments are confidential and may also be privileged. If you are not the named recipient, please notify the sender immediately and do not disclose the contents to another person, use it for any purpose, or store or copy the information in any medium. [Widget Ltd] (reg. no [10101010]) is a limited company, registered in England and Wales at [10 London Street, Borough of London, London EC1A, 1AA]."

This is a prudent step to protect not only any confidential information about third parties that such a company may be transmitting but also a company's own confidential information. If the unauthorised recipient is made fully aware of the confidential nature of the contents of an email it is far easier (assuming one can find that person in the first place) to take action against them.

---

3   The Banking Code of Practice can be downloaded from www.bankingcode.org.uk.

4   Unfair Terms in Consumer Contracts Regulations (SI 1999 No. 2083, replacing Sl 1994 No. 3159).

15.3   The Human Rights Act 1998 (the "HRA 1998")

The Human Rights Act 1998 ("HRA"), took effect on 2 October 2000, and incorporated the European Convention on Human Rights (the "Convention") directly into our domestic law. This means that "public authorities" (basically anyone carrying out functions of a public nature) have to comply with the Convention. However, the HRA is supposed only to have "vertical" application, that is, apply to "public authorities", which would not include most companies. However, there is a lively discussion taking place at the moment between judges, academics and public law practitioners as to whether the HRA will also have "horizontal" effect, that is, also apply to private entities such as public and private companies. The safe view must be to assume that it could and, therefore, that such companies should comply with the Convention.

For present purposes, the most relevant article of the Convention is Article 8 which provides as follows:

> **"Article 8**
>
> Everyone has the right to respect for his private and family life, his home and his correspondence.
>
> There shall be no interference by a public authority with the exercise of this right except such as is in accordance with the law and is necessary in a democratic society in the interests of national security, public safety or the economic well-being of the country, for the prevention of disorder or crime, for the protection of health or morals, or for the protection of the rights and freedoms of others."

In summary, therefore, privacy must be respected unless it is necessary to override this for one of the stipulated public interest reasons in Article 8.2 and the interference must be proportionate in all the circumstances.

The European Court of Human Rights has held that employees have a legitimate expectation of privacy at work, which would include when sending and receiving emails. So, if a company viewed a private email as part of its monitoring system, this could give rise to a claim under the HRA or, if that does not have "horizontal" application, by the employee directly to the European Court of Human Rights. The company would then have to show why it was necessary, on one of the Article 8.2 grounds, to have invaded the emailer's privacy. However, this legitimate expectation of privacy could be removed by notifying all employees, clients and contacts that all incoming and outgoing emails may be reviewed.

15.4   The Data Protection Act 1998

The primary purpose of the DPA 1998 is to enable the UK to comply with the EC Data Protection Directive,[5] which had to be incorporated into the national law of the Member States by October 1998. In one way the DPA 1998 is to be welcomed because it simplifies some of the more bureaucratic procedures of the Data Protection Act 1984 (the "DPA 1984"), which it replaces in full. Companies will need to ensure, when setting guidelines for Internet use for their employees, that data protection considerations are taken into

---

[5]   EC Directive 95/46 on the protection of individuals with regard to the processing of personal data and on the free movement of such data (Section 70(1) of the DPA 1998).

account in drawing up those guidelines. This is particularly so as the subject of the data may be able to claim damages for any breach of the DPA 1998 by the data controller, which is wider than under the DPA 1984. Some examples of possible breaches that can arise are:

(a) changes in their use of personal data and/or establishment of a website will not breach the terms of their "notification" of "registrable particulars" (the new procedure under the DPA 1998 which replaces the registration procedures under the DPA 1984) – this requires broadly similar categories of information to be notified to the Data Protection Commissioner;

(b) employees should be made aware of the requirement under the DPA 1998 that personal data cannot be transferred outside the EU to a country that does not provide adequate protection for personal data except with the consent of the data subject or in certain other specified circumstances. Companies need to ensure that the appropriate consents (or other exceptions to the prohibition on transferring data) are in place. Otherwise even sending an email to such a country containing personal data may potentially breach the DPA 1998 unless an exception in the DPA 1998 applies;

(c) staff collecting data on and from websites must be aware that this information will be subject to access by the person about whom the data is held and that appropriate systems to enable subject access must be in place;

(d) when the data controller collects data, Schedule I to the DPA 1998 requires individuals to be given certain information:

    (i) the identity of the data controller;

    (ii) the identity of a nominated representative (if any) for the purposes of the DPA 1998;

    (iii) the purpose or purposes for which the data are intended to be processed; and

    (iv) any further information which is necessary, having regard to the specific circumstances in which the data is to be processed, to enable processing in respect of the data to be fair.

The timing of such notice may differ when data is collected from a third party and not directly from the subject of the data.

(e) the first data protection principle has been expanded so that the procurement and processing of data will often not be fair unless consent is obtained for such processing (there are exceptions to this prohibition); a guideline explaining how data can be fairly processed should cover the steps required to deal with this;

(f) the DPA 1998 requires that (again, with exceptions) certain types of data will need to be collected and processed with "explicit consent" – where that data is "sensitive data", including data in relation to religious beliefs, trade union membership, health and criminal convictions;

(g) an individual has the right to block use of their data for direct marketing purposes (even, it would appear, if a prior permission is in place). Companies need to consider how databases are created so that they can, if necessary, suppress data on such individuals;

(h) an individual also has the right to prevent that processing if it is likely to cause substantial damage or distress to the subject of the data or to another.

The Seventh Principle of the DPA 1998 provides that "Appropriate technical and organisational measures shall be taken against unauthorised or unlawful processing of personal data and against accidental loss or destruction of, or damage to, personal data". The DPA 1998 gives some further guidance on matters which should be taken into account in deciding whether security measures are "appropriate". These are:

(a) taking into account the state of technological development at any time and the cost of implementing any measures, the measures must ensure a level of security appropriate to the harm that might result from a breach of security and the nature of the data to be protected; and

(b) the reliability of staff having access to the personal data.

The DPA 1998 introduces express obligations upon data controllers when the processing of personal data is carried out by a data processor on behalf of the data controller, giving the data controller responsibility for ensuring that the data processor's operations are sufficiently secure.

As long ago as in her 11th Report of 1995, the Data Protection Registrar (as she then was) stated that maintaining privacy of information is a key consideration in the development of the information superhighway. She stressed the problems for individuals using the Internet in terms of users having their data captured in transit. Whilst many of the problems relating to unauthorised data capture in transit will, no doubt, be solved by developing privacy enhancing facilities and services on the Internet, users should be told what risks are involved in using the Internet.

To quote the Data Protection Registrar "the Internet is an inherently insecure environment, and you cannot rely on the network itself to provide protection from unauthorised access to, or disclosure of, personal data. The measures you should take to safeguard personal data will, of course, depend on the use you intend to make of the Internet and the sensitivity of the data involved. A stand-alone system merely to allow internal users to send (presumably authorised) email to contacts elsewhere in the world may need little more protection than an encryption facility for sensitive mail. On the other hand, if you contemplate connecting the whole of your internal network so as to provide an integrated internal and external email facility and to allow external access to a major information resource which you hold, you will need to take expert advice on the security techniques to use".

Broadly, the Data Protection Registrar recommended that if you are asking someone to send you information by an insecure transmission medium like the Internet, the risks involved should be brought to their attention. Many websites contain a warning that individuals should consider whether they wish to send personal data by such an insecure medium, before doing so. Whether this is necessary using an intranet, which one hopes is inherently more secure, is more questionable; if using encryption to "scramble" messages, a warning is probably unnecessary.

It cannot be stressed too strongly that the panoply of the data protection legislation applies as much to information collected by Internet use or to emails which one captures and stores as it does to information collected by more traditional channels.

15.5   **Privacy and surveillance – monitoring communications**

The UK has no privacy law, as such, but a number of pieces of recent legislation do protect an individual's privacy.

15.5.1   *Regulation of Investigatory Powers Act 2000*

A business which records or monitors employee or other emails or business calls must either ensure that both sender/caller and receiver have consented or bring itself within the regulations under the Regulation of Investigatory Powers Act 2000 (the "RIPA 2000"). The RIPA 2000 obtained royal assent on 25 September 2000. Its various provisions are being brought into force, with many provisions having come into force by late October 2000.

In the past, businesses and others operating private email and telecom systems were not specifically prohibited from intercepting communications on their own systems (though they were, of course, subject to provisions in their telecommunications licenses and data protection legislation). One of the effects of the RIPA 2000 is that, in future, businesses that intercept communications through their own post or telecommunications system will need to be sure that their actions are legally authorised. "Telecommunications system" has been given a broad definition by the RIPA 2000, as including systems that exist for the purpose of facilitating the transmission of communications by any means involving the use of electrical or electro-magnetic energy. Communications over such a network include email or other Internet-based communication, as well as voice telephony. If intercepted unlawfully on such a system, the sender or recipient of the communication may be able to obtain an injunction or sue for damages. Interceptions are generally authorised if there are reasonable grounds to believe consent to the interception has been obtained from both the sender and the recipient. The Lawful Business Practice Regulations[6] (regulations enacted pursuant to the RIPA 2000) authorise businesses to intercept communications on their own private network without consent for certain purposes.

15.5.1.1   *Consent*

Interception is lawful if both the sender and the recipient have consented or there are reasonable grounds for believing that they have done so. A business which monitors employee calls or emails may be able to obtain the express consent of employees in their employment contracts or otherwise, though it is likely that the consent could be withdrawn at any time in respect of future communications leaving the employer with a dilemma about whether they could dismiss on these grounds. Dismissal in those circumstances could be very difficult but much will depend on the circumstances.

Obtaining the consent of the other party to the communication will often be more difficult. In some cases it may be possible to obtain consent in customer terms and conditions as a click box on screen on a website, when loading software or in connection with setting up security arrangements for telephone services. In others it may be possible to rely on implied consent by conduct. If clear notification of the fact that communications are being intercepted is given in customer literature, on-screen or as a recorded message played to all callers immediately on connection, then people going on to send the message or make the call may be regarded as having impliedly consented. However, the sufficiency from a legal point of view of obtaining consent in these ways and their commercial acceptability will vary from case-to-case.

---

[6]   Telecommunications (Lawful Business Practice) (Interception of Communications) Regulations 2000 which came into force on 24 October 2000.

15.5.1.2   Monitoring/recording business communications without consent

The Lawful Business Practice Regulations came into force on 24 October 2000. The regulations authorise businesses to intercept communications (e.g. emails and telephone calls) on their own systems in certain circumstances without obtaining the consent of the sender and recipient.

The regulations authorise conduct by businesses (in a wide sense of the word, expressly including activities of a government department, of any public authority or of any person or office holder on whom functions are conferred by or under any enactment) that involves monitoring or recording communications transmitted over their systems without consent for the following purposes:

(a) establishing the existence of facts;

(b) ascertaining compliance with regulatory or self-regulatory practices or procedures;

(c) ascertaining or demonstrating standards which are achieved or ought to be achieved by persons using the system;

(d) preventing or detecting crime;

(e) investigating or detecting unauthorised use of the business's communications system;

(f) ensuring the effective operation of the communications system.

The Regulations will also authorise businesses to monitor (but not record) communications for the following purposes:

(a) checking whether or not communications are relevant to the business;

(b) monitoring calls to confidential, counselling helplines run free of charge.

The Regulations will also authorise public authorities to monitor or record in the interests of national security in certain circumstances.

This covers detecting fraud or hackers or monitoring of email to prevent the sending of material prohibited by office rules such as pornography. Checking emails and voicemails to see if they are business communications may be an important right when staff are on holiday.

However, it does not cover monitoring or recording for marketing or market research. The Department of Trade & Industry (the "DTI") has stated that the regulations are going to be reviewed after one year to ensure that they are working effectively.

Even where the Regulations are relied on, businesses are required to make all reasonable efforts to inform every person who may use the telecommunication system in question that communications transmitted by means thereof may be intercepted. Informing employees can easily be done in the office. Email policies should be made immediately apparent to employees and companies that do not currently have a formal policy should certainly adopt one now, perhaps even incorporating it (e.g. by reference) into employees' contracts of employment. If phones are made available to non-employees, for example in a waiting area, users should be warned, for example by a notice near the phone, of potential monitoring.

15.5.1.3 *Employees who do not consent*

Where an employer requires consent from his employees to monitoring (e.g. because that monitoring is not for one of the purposes set out in the Regulations) and an employee either refuses to give that consent or subsequently withdraws it, the employer's first course should be one of consultation and negotiation. If the consultation and negotiation process is exhausted and the employee has adopted his final stance, an employer has two options.

The first is to allow the employee to continue in his employment but to refrain from monitoring that employee's telephone conversations or emails for the specific purposes for which consent is required (and has not been given). This may often be impossible in practice.

The second is to dismiss the employee. For an employee with less than one year's continuous service (and who has not therefore acquired the statutory right not to be unfairly dismissed), this should not give rise to any particular claims, provided that the employee is allowed to work out his contractual notice period (or is paid in lieu of it). That said, public sector employers would need to be very wary of a claim that, in treating the refusal or withdrawal of consent to monitoring as a reason to dismiss, the employer had breached the employee's rights under the HRA 1998 (*see* Section 15.3 above).

If the employee has one year's continuous service or more, that employee will have the right not to be unfairly dismissed under the Employment Rights Act 1996 (the "ERA"). The employer will therefore have to establish that the reason for any dismissal is one of the five "potentially fair" reasons under the ERA and that it was reasonable in all the circumstances to treat that reason as sufficient to dismiss the employee.

For present purposes the relevant reason will be the "catch-all" under Section 98 of the ERA of "some other substantial reason such as to justify the dismissal of an employee holding the position which this employee held".

In deciding whether an employer has acted reasonably in dismissing for "some other substantial reason" an Employment Tribunal will balance the needs of the employer in (for example) requiring consent to monitoring of the sort in question, against the disadvantages to the employee in refusing or withdrawing that consent (i.e. dismissal).

This will be a question of fact in each case and will depend on the nature of the employer's business, the capacity in which the employee is employed, the sort of monitoring in question and the purposes for which it is to be carried out. An employer might be able fairly to dismiss an employee for "some other substantial reason" if, for example, the employer can show that (for this employee in this job) monitoring is necessary to protect the employer's business interests or necessary for the employees' proper performance of his duties. However, it is arguable that any such monitoring would be covered by the Regulations and therefore not require consent in the first place.

In addition, if an employer concludes that a particular employee cannot properly carry out his job in circumstances where he has refused or withdrawn consent to monitoring, the employer will have to consult with the employee and look for other suitable vacancies within the organisation (which the employee could perform without giving consent to monitoring) before dismissing the employee. Failure to do so is likely to render any dismissal unfair.

It will therefore be most important for an employer to consider all the circumstances of the individual's particular case (including representations on consultation) before deciding what action to take.

Any claim of unfair dismissal is also likely to be accompanied by a reference to article 8 of the HRA. Although the Act does not give a direct claim against a private sector employer, an employee dismissed in the circumstances set out above is likely to claim that his dismissal is all the more unfair because it stemmed from the employee's refusal to compromise his rights under the Act. As mentioned above, employees in the public sector have the additional protection of a direct claim under the Act against their employer for breach of its provisions.

It is possible, therefore, that if an employer has cogent evidence that the advantages to the employer of requiring and receiving consent to monitoring outweigh the disadvantages to an employee of dismissal for refusal or withdrawal of consent, that dismissal may be considered fair by an Employment Tribunal. However, in practice, employers should avoid this situation unless they consider it strictly necessary and have exhausted all other practicable options.

15.5.1.4   *Warrant to intercept*

Companies should also be aware that they may have to comply with a warrant to intercept communications over a private network. If the material is encrypted or otherwise protected, the recipient may be forced to hand over either a legible copy of the material or the decryption key or other device to remove the protection. Such a warrant would normally be obtained by either the police or customs and excise and it would be a criminal offence not to comply with it.

15.5.2   **Telecommunications licences**

Businesses recording or monitoring telephone calls must also comply with the relevant telecommunications licences. The class licences applicable to office switchboards generally require the operator to make every reasonable effort to inform the parties to the call beforehand that it may be monitored or recorded. OFTEL, the regulatory body of the telecommunications industry, also strongly recommends that where employee calls are being monitored or recorded a separate, unmonitored pay phone is provided for employees' private use.[7]

15.5.3   **Data Protection Act 1998**

Monitoring or recording of telephone calls and emails will often involve the processing of personal data. This must be included in the business's notification under the DPA 1998. The data must also be fairly obtained. Data will not be fairly obtained unless, so far as reasonably practicable, the individuals in question have been informed, among other matters, of the purpose for which the monitoring or recording takes place.

---

[7]   Recording telephone conversations on private networks; guidance published by OFTEL 19 August 1999, available at www.oftel.gov.uk.

The Data Protection Commissioner's Office has recently released a draft code of practice concerning the use of personal data in the employer/employee relationship.[8] This emphasises the requirement that monitoring must be proportionate between the adverse impact and the benefits and that, apart from in exceptional circumstances, the staff must be aware of the extent and the purpose for the monitoring. Exceptional circumstances would normally only arise if targeted and limited covert surveillance becomes necessary to investigate specific criminal activity (normally with police involvement). Even in these circumstances, information that is obtained as a result of the monitoring other than that targeted should be discarded (unless it involves gross negligence that a reasonable employer should not ignore or other criminal activity).

Notification of the extent and purpose of monitoring might easily be incorporated into an office email policy. However, one should be aware that if the policy is not enforced, the Data Protection Commissioner has indicated that it is the practice rather than the stated policy that will be used to assess whether monitoring is proportionate.

Commentators have noted that the limits of permissable monitoring in the draft code of practice are significantly narrower than those contained in the Lawful Business Practice Regulations 2000 (*see* Section 15.5.1 above). The draft code was consulted upon from 6 October 2000 to 5 January 2001, but the results have not been published at the time of writing.

15.5.4 *Human Rights*

The European Court of Human Rights case *Halford v. UK*[9] established that the interception of a person's office telephone without their consent can constitute an interference with the right to respect for private life established under Article 8 of the Convention on Human Rights. The decision was more recently upheld in *Kopp v. Switzerland*[10] where a lawyer's telephone was unlawfully tapped by a Post Office official. The Convention was given effect in the UK when the HRA came into force on 2 October 2000. These principles may be applied in respect of other forms of communication, such as email. If an employee has been warned that his communications may be monitored (as should be the case under the Regulation of Investigatory Powers Act (above)), it is submitted that he would have a weak case under the HRA, though this area of law is yet to develop.

15.5.5 *Harrassment*

The Protection from Harassment Act 1997 (the "PHA 1997") was enacted to deal with the problem with stalkers. However, it was broadly drafted enough to encompass harassment in the workplace. It has been suggested that close monitoring of employees, such as keyboard monitoring (monitoring the number of keystrokes) may constitute harassment under the PHA 1997 or even sexual harassment (if mainly female staff, for example PAs and secretaries, are being monitored).

---

8   Available at www.dataprotection.gov.uk.

9   *Halford v. UK* (25/06/97) 24 EHRR 523, [1997] IRLR 471, *The Times* July 3, 1997.

10   *Kopp v. Switzerland* (25/03/98) 27 EHRR 91, [1998] EHRLR 508.

15.6 **Potential liability of a company for defamatory communications**

In principle, a company's potential liability for defamatory email messages sent by its staff does not differ from its potential liability in respect of any other communication written by its employees. Although the legal status of an email message has not been determined (either by the courts or by Parliament), the generally accepted view is that a defamatory email message is actionable as a libel – that is to say, as a publication made in permanent form. This is because email messages (although often seemingly transient) are invariably stored on and retrieved from a computer's hard drive. Email messages will accordingly be treated in law as equivalent to letters, faxes and other paper written documents. In order to bring a claim for libel based on the publication of such a document, it is unnecessary to show that any loss or damage has been suffered; the law presumes that some damage will flow from its publication.

A company will have a potential liability on two levels:

(a) it may be held vicariously liable for the acts of its employees in themselves publishing email messages through the company's communications system; and

(b) in addition, as the owner and controller of the communications system through which email messages written by its staff are sent, the company may be directly liable for publishing those messages itself.

A company will be vicariously liable for defamatory email messages sent by a member of its staff, provided that the employee, when sending the email, was "acting within the scope of his employment". Any email that is sent by a member of staff as part of, or directly incidental to, the carrying out of his job will be deemed to have been sent while that person was "acting within the scope of his employment". This will be the case even if the member of staff was expressly forbidden from publishing defamatory material. A company will only escape the risk of vicarious liability if the sending of the email message was completely unconnected with the employee's job and could properly be regarded as a wholly private communication.

The fact that an email message is confined to the company's internal communications system will not prevent the company being held vicariously liable. The courts have held that a communication between two individuals, even where they are both employed by the same company, is capable of amounting to a "publication" for which the company can be held vicariously liable. This arose in the case of *Western Provident Association Limited v. Norwich Union Healthcare Limited and The Norwich Union Life Insurance Company Limited* (formerly The Norwich Union Life Insurance Society), reported in the *Financial Times* on 18 July 1997. This case did not result in a judgment as it was settled.

Norwich Union paid £450,000 in settlement to Western Provident and issued an apology admitting that its staff libelled the private healthcare group by internal email. This is believed to be the first libel action brought involving messages sent by email. Norwich Union staff spread rumours that Western Provident was being investigated by the DTI and that the group was close to insolvency. In a statement in open court Norwich Union admitted that the rumours were false and deeply regretted and sincerely apologised to Western Provident for the dissemination of the rumours. Norwich Union stated that it had made every effort to ensure that such unacceptable practices did not occur again. It also undertook not to repeat the allegations.

Although the potential for serious financial or other damage to a third party is greatly increased when emails are sent externally to outside bodies, such as clients or potential clients, a company should not ignore the fact that considerable damage can be caused by a defamatory allegation or rumour circulating internally. What is more, where it can be shown that an employee either intended or should reasonably have anticipated that the contents of his email would be passed on to others either within or outside the organisation in which he worked, the company will be held vicariously liable for those further communications.

The extent of a company's direct liability in respect of staff email communications is a more uncertain area of the law. In the case of *Riddick v. Thames Board Mills* (1977)[11] it was suggested that there cannot be direct liability for internal communications between staff members because a company cannot publish to itself, however, views on this case were mixed. Even in respect of external communications, there is the unresolved question of whether the mere act of providing staff with computers and a link to the Internet constitutes a sufficient act of publication. Assuming it does amount to publication, the Defamation Act 1996 provides a possible defence to a company whose only involvement in the publication has been the operation or provision of the system or service by which the message was retrieved, copied, distributed or made available in electronic form.

In such circumstances, the company would have a defence if it could show that it had taken reasonable care in relation to the particular publication and did not know, and had no reason to believe, that what it did caused or contributed to the publication.[12] It is not clear what steps, if any, a company would need to take to bring itself within the terms of this statutory defence, which has not so far been tested in the courts. Certainly, it would be prudent for the company to implement and enforce a strict office policy as to the use which staff make of the company's email facility. It is not, however, recommended that a company takes more active steps, such as monitoring the contents of email messages passing through its systems. Such action might take the company outside the statutory defence on the basis that it had ceased "only" to be involved in the operation or provision of the communications system or service. It also risks contravening legislation detailed above in Section 15.4.

Any company which is sued (as either directly or vicariously liable or both) over the contents of an email will be able potentially to rely on any of the defences which are normally available to a claim in libel. In particular, any email communication which is legitimately sent to a person who has a genuine interest in its contents will be protected by the defence of qualified privilege, provided that the sender was not acting maliciously and had reason to believe that the contents of the email were true. The defence would commonly apply where, for example, job references or credit ratings are communicated between persons by email for proper business or professional purposes. Where, however, an employee publishes material for an ulterior purpose, or without believing that it is true, that state of mind will be imputed to the employer, preventing it from relying on the defence of qualified privilege.

---

11   *Riddick v. Thames Board Mills* [1977] 3 All ER 677.

12   *See* Section 1 of the Defamation Act 1996.

The position becomes more complex where an email is sent to a recipient who is outside the jurisdiction of England and Wales. This is likely to occur frequently, particularly in the case of a multi-national organisation, which has offices or branches worldwide. The question of whether such a communication will be actionable here will probably depend not only on the position under the law of this jurisdiction but also on the position under the law of the country in which the email is received. In some circumstances limitations on liability imposed by the foreign law may have an effect here.

For these reasons, a company would be well advised to ensure that its staff are properly versed in the potential liability attaching both to themselves and their employer in respect of defamatory communications by email. The problem is accentuated by the fact that people have tended to treat email as a relaxed and informal mode of communication.

Where a company's employees make widespread use of email, it is recommended that a formal written corporate policy should be implemented, including the following:

(a) staff should be required to confine their communications by email to those which are properly required for business purposes;

(b) staff should also be expressly prohibited from publishing any material which is potentially libellous;

(c) care should be taken to ensure that statements are true, could not be misconstrued and are only sent to those with a legitimate interest in the subject matter;

(d) staff should be told to take steps to validate incoming emails, as it is possible to "spoof" the sender's address and change the contents *en route*;

(e) staff should be instructed that, if they receive a defamatory email, they should report it to their immediate superior (or to a designated person within the organisation); and

(f) on no account should staff repeat the libel, which could include forwarding it to others.

It is to be hoped that this will help both to instill a sense of responsibility amongst staff and minimize risks.

In addition to the above points, which are more specific to defamatory emails, it is important that any guidelines should cover one or two wider issues, such as:

(a) where staff have to communicate confidential material by email, they should use a prescribed macro including a confidentiality warning (*see* Section 15.2.2.2 above);

(b) staff should be aware that, although the speed and quality of email systems is improving all the time, the delivery of email items within a specific period of time or at all is not guaranteed and therefore it should not be relied on for time-critical dealings;

(c) hard copies of all important emails sent or received should be kept; and

(d) staff should also take steps to ensure that no email files are deleted which contain messages which may be relevant to actual or contemplated litigation.

Companies, whilst they will not escape the risk of vicarious liability for certain messages sent by employees, should contemplate an express direction to their staff not to use email other than for their business purposes – this may help to engender a sense of responsibility amongst staff in respect of the content of emails.

15.6.1 *Potential liability for other wrongs*

It is recommended also that there be similar restraints on the sending of material which is obscene, discriminatory or which might be regarded as amounting to harassment of another (*see* Section 15.9 below).

15.6.2 *Particular concerns in relation to employees*

A company that has set very clear guidelines on Internet use for its employees, perhaps, could even contemplate going as far as incorporating those guidelines either expressly or by reference into the employees' contracts of employment. It could be made clear that non-compliance might constitute a disciplinary matter and it should perhaps stipulate that, depending on the nature of the offence, failure to comply could entitle the employer to dismiss the employee in question.

15.7 The implications of disclosure obligations

Companies increasingly store their emails in the same way or for the same periods that they store paper files or to provide a useful database to check important email addresses in a hurry.

At an early stage in litigation, at least after the claim form is issued and possibly before, a party comes under an obligation not to destroy documents which might possibly be relevant to the action. If the company has in place a system for the deletion of email files after the expiry of a fixed period of time, it may find itself inadvertently in breach of this obligation. Procedures should be put in place to avoid the possibility of such an occurrence.

The obligation to preserve documents and to disclose them arises in any litigation, not just in relation to claims for libel, although Section 15.5 of this Chapter has deliberately focussed on that important area. Staff should, accordingly, be required to act with caution when sending emails, not simply to minimise the company's exposure to a claim for libel, or other action over the contents of the email, but also to avoid prejudicing the company's position generally with regard to litigation in which it is involved.

15.8 Watching for the use of the World Wide Web by others

In addition to watching what your own employees might be using the Internet for, it would perhaps be prudent to consider, for certain types of company, setting up a policy on what to do about the activities of others on the Internet. For example, should one regularly search to locate, on the Internet, information about your own company which is defamatory or otherwise damaging to its business interests; this could occur, for instance, on worldwide websites, in news groups or on computer bulletin boards. Companies should certainly consider setting up a procedure to follow should they be notified that such a message may exist. The company's own employees, however, should not access or otherwise monitor material on the Internet which might be damaging to the company in case to do so might "signpost" the fact that the company was monitoring that information and might positively encourage the posting of further material of that kind.

One reason why it might be appropriate to prevent employees visiting a website linked to the company, which makes statements about the company, is that it could be used against you. Something called the "Mock Information Network" was able to embarrass McDonald's, the fast food company, with the fact that McDonald's had accessed its website

1700 times (clearly, interested employees) in the first week after the launch of that site, which contained materials potentially damaging to McDonald's. The reason for this is that it is very difficult to access a website without the website being able to identify the address of the computer accessing the site.

15.9 Harassment

It is unlikely that harassment issues should arise except where there is use of, for example, bulletin boards or "live chat". However, it is perhaps more likely to arise, say, within a corporate's own intranet used by its employees. There are already cases pending in the US (in which the damages being claimed are astronomical) where, for example, employees of companies are claiming that they are being harassed by sexually or racially discriminatory email.

Probably the most publicised of these actions is *Owens v. Morgan Stanley & Co.*, which has been before the New York Courts. A law suit was filed by two African-American employees of the investment banking firm who claimed they were subjected to a hostile work environment. The original complaint which alleged violations of various statutes, including the New York Human Rights Law, sought $5 million in compensatory damages and $25 million in punitive damages per claimant. It is clear that the sums involved were pretty vast.

The basis of the suit was a racist email message which became the subject of office jokes and of ridicule of the claimants, as well as other African-American employees at Morgan Stanley. The claimants even suggested that they were denied promotions despite demonstrating ability although, perhaps, this issue is not linked to the email campaign. The claimants argued that it was directly related to the email campaign. In the allegations, the alleged author of the email message was named in the law suit as well as other Morgan Stanley employees who were accused of further distributing the offending email in question.

Since the terms of the settlement of this case are confidential, it is difficult to know how significant this case really is, although the figures initially bandied around were certainly fairly spectacular.

If a site owner considers harassment of any sort is a sufficient concern, a few extra words could be included in health warnings to make it clear to visitors and to staff that they are not allowed to post or circulate materials of that nature. This is perhaps something else to include in organisations' internal guidelines on the use of email generally.

Looking at English law, it is important for an employer to avoid harassment by email. If anything is carried out by a person in the course of his employment it is treated as carried out by the employer as well as by him, whether or not carried out with the employer's knowledge or approval, *see* Section 41 of the Discrimination Act 1975. What exactly is "in the course of employment" in the context of this Act is not entirely clear, but the employer could be liable, in certain circumstances.

Section 32 (1) of the 1976 Race Relations Act contains similar provisions in relation to racial discrimination. Article 14 of the HRA also provides for protection against discrimination on any ground.

It is prudent to have warnings covering both situations in place to assist the employer in attempting to avoid vicarious liability.

15.10 Copyright

Websites are undoubtedly going to contain material protected by copyright and, by their nature, websites are easy to copy. There is a great incentive to copy, because the copy will be a perfect digital copy. Websites should therefore set out the basis on which the user can copy the material in question although, in truth, as with many claims for breach of copyright, one has to be able to prove that an act of copying has taken place. The website owner may consent to some material being copied and circulated (such as a screen saver which is developed as part of a marketing campaign).

Users should be prohibited from altering or modifying material on a website unless the site owner permits them to do so. Under English law, it is a criminal offence under the Computer Misuse Act 1990 to cause an unauthorised modification of the contents of any computer. The legislation is drafted sufficiently widely to encompass the modification of a web page. However, a successful prosecution would depend on the extent that the user was "authorised" to access and modify the web page. Even if the website owner would not consider reporting a particular transgression to the police, its website should include a warning that persons accessing the website are not authorised to modify, adapt, delete or replace any pages or other data on, or accessible from, the website or to link or append to this site, or the data contained on it, any material or data. This will help in establishing the offence of unauthorised access or modification.

Where the website includes an electronic bulletin board, the warning would need to be modified to take that into account; liability for bulletin boards has been addressed in Section 15.12.1 below.

Recent developments indicate that there are technological ways to protect your copyright, including some form of indelible message embedded, unseen, in the text (rather like a watermark) that would need sophisticated methods to avoid it or delete it.

15.11 Liability – health warnings and disclaimers

In using the World Wide Web to promote themselves, companies need to be aware of a number of legal obligations arising as a result. For example, in the UK, advertising is administered by the Advertising Standards Authority (the "ASA"). They have made it quite clear that advertising on the Internet comes under the codes of practice that they publish, in the same way that advertising in a newspaper would. On that basis, to the extent that the Code of Advertising Practice and the Code of Sales Promotion (the 10th edition of both codes, produced by the ASA, came into force on 1 October 1999 with Addendum 1 added on 23 April 2000)[13] require certain information to be contained in advertisements, the same will apply in relation to advertising on the Internet.

There are also certain health warnings which regulators and regulatory bodies recommend that companies under their regulation should observe. These should therefore appear on a company's website in the same way that they would appear in a newspaper advertisement. For example, certain financial services companies are required to state which regulatory body they belong to.

---

13   The British Codes of Advertising and Sales Promotion are available at www.asa.org.uk.

There are also obligations to give certain information when selling goods and services at a distance under The Consumer Protection (Distance Selling) Regulations 2000, which were made on 31 August 2000 and came into force on 31 October 2000 after a two month transitional period. These regulations implement into UK law the European Directive 97/7/EC on the protection of consumers in respect of distance contracts.

The regulations will entitle consumers to receive clear information about goods or services before purchasing, confirmation of this information in writing (or fax or email), a cooling down period of seven days and delivery within 30 days of purchase, unless agreed otherwise. The regulations do not apply to all distance contracts, the most important exception is for financial services (a separate proposed Directive on the distance marketing of financial services is currently under discussion).

For example, when a supplier cold calls someone at home there is often confusion over what is on offer and who is behind the call. This can lead to consumers agreeing to something they don't want or need and in the worst cases spending money without realising what they are committing to. Under these regulations suppliers who "cold call" consumers at home must identify clearly the company they represent and the commercial purpose of their call at the beginning of the conversation. If a supplier fails to comply with the regulations consumers will be able to cancel the contract and have any money they may have paid up front refunded by the supplier. Where suppliers fail to refund the consumer's money or fail to meet their statutory obligations the Director General of Fair Trading and Trading Standards Departments will be able to take proceedings for an injunction. This would apply similarly to an unsolicited, direct-marketing email (for further details, *see* Chapter 9 of this Guide).

15.11.1 *Enforceability of health warnings*

For the reasons set out earlier in this Chapter, a website owner may wish to impose terms and conditions on those accessing its website or to ensure certain facts or disclaimers are brought to the attention of visitors or users before they visit. Those familiar with the Internet will appreciate that many different methods are employed to try and impose terms and conditions on website users. Unless terms and conditions or disclaimers are brought to the attention of the user in question, the chances of them being enforceable must be remote.

A link to a company's standard terms and conditions, or a disclaimer or "health warning", hidden at the bottom of the home page in small print are less likely to be enforceable than those in which a user must scroll through the text (with unusual and onerous provisions highlighted) and click on an "Accept" icon. However, the latter may be unpalatable from a presentational point of view. In the end, a balance must be struck based on a sensible risk assessment which takes into account the nature of the website, the target audience, and any legal requirements to use a health warning or disclaimer and the harm that could be done if the health warning was omitted or could be circumvented.

15.11.2 *Jurisdictional issues*

Whilst a number of the key issues specific to Internet/intranet/extranet health warnings are dealt with in the following Section, how to impose your general terms and conditions (such as limitation and exclusion of liability provisions), and "contracting" on the Internet are not dealt with in detail here (*see* Chapter 6 of this Guide). To summarise, general legal principles would apply (in particular consumer protection legislation) and local legal advice would need to be sought regarding the precise method of incorporating the contract to be used for each website. If the website server is located overseas, clearly the laws of that country should be complied with. As a website could be downloaded anywhere, it is not feasible to check the law in all countries as to what liabilities could arise. But, to avoid defamation or breach of local advertising requirements, it might be prudent to check legal liability issues in countries where the website owner has a substantial presence or assets, as those are the countries where someone is more likely to "have a go". Alternatively, one could check the liability issues in those countries considered most likely to access the website.

A website owner may well wish to disclaim all liability should a user rely on any information contained on a website. Whether or not a court would be prepared to uphold such an exclusion would depend on the circumstances. Again, this is outside the scope of this Chapter.

The steps which a website owner should take to ensure that its disclaimers/health warnings have the greatest chance of being effective will very much depend on the nature of the website in question and the risks associated with it.

The warning would need to be modified to take into account the specifics of any site. Given the fact that it may be possible to circumvent the home page of a website (by use of a bookmark or by accessing the page's IP address), the warning should be displayed automatically (if possible) on each access to the website or perhaps referred to in a footer on each page of the site. In addition, should it be technically possible to filter out users who are attempting to access the site from outside the "approved" countries, this should be done.[14]

Another option would be to use a form of registration screen which requires the users to supply relevant details (such as their address) before access to the website is permitted. The details could be screened to reject access to those with an address in a jurisdiction that should not access that site for legal reasons in the relevant jurisdiction. Clearly this too would not be foolproof if a user is dishonest in completing the on-line registration form, but it is to be hoped that Internet use will not be more heavily regulated than its hard copy equivalent (e.g. newspaper advertising).

15.12 Health warnings and disclaimers – specific issues

This Section considers specific issues and provides various warnings and disclaimers which, if relevant, website owners could consider adopting.

15.12.1 *Disclaimers regarding copyright infringement, obscene and offensive material*

Where a user is able to access and place information on an electronic bulletin board, users should be informed that they are prohibited from posting on the bulletin board any materials that are obscene, offensive or otherwise in bad taste, or which would infringe the rights (including copyright) of any third party. The website owner should also reserve the right to withdraw access to the board at any time for any person and may remove any posting at its sole discretion for any reason whatsoever.

---

[14] The obvious problem here is that one can only determine the last leg of the user's path. He may have accessed the site having gone through several countries, a fact of which even he may be unaware.

15.12.2 Copyright licences

Material that is not to be copied freely should only be copied to the extent necessary to access the website. Although, admittedly, breach of copyright is difficult to police, the site should contain a statement setting out the basis on which material may be copied, altered and disseminated. For example:

> "Copyright in information contained on this website is owned by [   ] . You may use this information and reproduce it in hard copy for your own personal reference use only. The information may not otherwise be reproduced, distributed or transmitted to any other person or incorporated in any way into another document or other material without the prior written permission of [   ]."

In addition, the appropriate copyright symbol with the name of the entity that owns the copyright should appear on the website, with the year in which the copyright came into being; including the copyright symbol in some sort of footer, which would appear on every page, would be preferable, if it could be achieved.

15.12.3 Defamation

Following on from what has been said above, one cannot assume that a statement (which is not defamatory under English law) posted on an electronic bulletin board run by a company in the UK would not be actionable, and a website owner held liable, in another country from which the bulletin board was accessible and where the defamation laws are more strict. In addition, in certain jurisdictions, such as the US, current case law indicates monitoring or vetting postings could actually increase the possibility that a site owner would be liable for defamatory statements which were posted, notwithstanding the monitoring and vetting process.

Changes to English law (in the Defamation Act 1996) have altered the liability of Internet Service Providers for defamatory material; these changes may affect a company's liability under English law for defamatory statements posted on a website run by a bank, say, where the statement was made by a person over whom it had no effective control.

At the end of March 1999, the Honourable Mr Justice Morland handed down a decision in the Queen's Bench Division in the case of *Laurence Godfrey v. Demon Internet Limited*. This was probably the first defamation act involving the Internet for a judicial decision in the UK. For that reason many US cases were cited in the proceedings.

The claimant was a lecturer in sciences resident in the UK and the defendant was an Internet Service Provider. Demon had certain bulletin boards, and an unknown person posted something defamatory about Dr. Godfrey. Dr. Godfrey then contacted the service provider requesting the removal of the posting.

The point in this case is that the claimant had written to the service provider drawing to their attention the scurrilous nature of the anonymous posting about him. Therefore, the statutory defence under the Defamation Act was not available. They had been notified by the claimant that the material was defamatory and, thereafter, they could not avail themselves of the protection provided by Section 1 of the Defamation Act. In fact, the case only really confirms what many felt the position of a service provider to be – that they have a defence regarding the content they transmit or host on a website until they have knowledge of the possibility it is defamatory.

This matter was only decided in a pre-trial action. The defendant settled the case on 30 March 2000, three days before it came to full trial and the decision should therefore be regarded as indicative, rather than definitive.

The decision in the case causes difficulty, in that vetting or monitoring information may be construed as taking on an "editorial" capacity, denying a company the benefit of a defence under Section 1 of the Defamation Act 1996. Where large volumes of information are being posted on a website, it would be impractical to monitor this information anyway. Mechanical filters searching for particular or undesirable words, however, could amount to the same thing. There has been no English decision on this.

As a result, vetting or monitoring should be applied consistently to information that the company controls or edits in one way or another. Where large volumes of information that are impractical to check are being made available (e.g. on a bulletin board), it would be preferable not to monitor for potentially defamatory material. In either case, site owners will also need to put into place a policy regarding complaints and ensure that processes are in place should a complaint be made. Failure to do so could affect an owner's ability to rely on the statutory defences contained in the Defamation Act 1996.

A safe course of action might be to ensure that a process is in place for the immediate removal of material that is alleged to be defamatory in nature, at least until the material can be reviewed. However, in establishing such a policy, it should be borne in mind that a right to free speech is enshrined in the HRA, which came into force on 2 October 2000. Deleting messages without investigation may be a violation of the right to free speech. It may be less violatory if the material is quickly and properly investigated and re-posted if there is no serious claim. This may put the company in the difficult position of deciding when something is defamatory and, again, may also constitute action in an "editorial" capacity, denying the company of the section 1 defence. However, it remains to be seen to what extent the right to free speech will influence this area of the law.

Where users can access and place information on a company's electronic bulletin board, they should be warned along the following lines:

> "Users are prohibited from posting on this bulletin board any materials that are defamatory (or potentially defamatory) of any person, obscene, offensive or are otherwise in bad taste or which would infringe the rights (including copyright) of any third party. [   ] reserves the right to withdraw access to this board at any time for all and any person(s) and it may remove any posting at its sole discretion for any reason whatsoever. In the event that you breach the above restriction, you shall indemnify [   ] against all and any costs and liabilities which arise out of or relate to such breaches. Please press the 'Accept' button to acknowledge your acceptance of these terms or the 'Cancel' button to cancel this [your visit to the Bulletin Board] transaction."

There is no guarantee that the above disclaimer would prevent a claim being brought against a company by a third party who has been defamed, for example, but it would at least make it difficult for the user to argue that he did not know that they could not post certain types of material.

Whilst the website owner could, in theory, include indemnity wording on the website for any breaches of this particular provision, in practice such an indemnity will probably be of little or no value.

15.12.4   *Data protection*

As mentioned in Section 15.4 of this Chapter, if unencrypted email is being used to send personal data to a website, the Data Protection Registrar recommends the use of a health warning.

15.12.5   *Accuracy of content and information*

As a standard practice, many reports, brochures and other publications generated by website owners carry a health warning in relation to accuracy, reliability and fairness. Text on a website should be treated in the same way. This is particularly so when the target audience is not the chosen persons to whom one might post a copy of a brochure, but it is potentially anyone with Internet access.

A sample clause regarding accuracy might read:

> "Information on this [website] [home page] is given by us in good faith and has been taken from trade and other sources believed to be reliable. We do not represent that the information is accurate, complete or fair and it should not be relied on as such. We have not verified all of the information which may not be complete or accurate for your purposes. Any opinions and estimates expressed reflect our judgement at this date and are subject to change [without notice]."

If it is intended that the access to such material should be restricted, then the more appropriate procedure would be to create restricted access to the website (e.g. by use of password protection).

15.12.6   *Contracting over the Internet*

Employees should take great care using the Internet to avoid committing themselves or their employers to a binding contract; there should perhaps be a statement clarifying in what circumstances a binding contract can be made over the Internet.

Many companies still prefer to consummate contracts off-line even though the product is advertised on-line.

15.12.7   *The Companies Act 1985 and The Business Names Act 1985*

Section 349 of the Companies Act 1985 provides that:

"(1)   Every company shall have its name mentioned in legible characters:

(a)   in all business letters of the company;

(b)   in all its notices and other official publications;

(c)   in all bills of exchange, promissory notes, endorsements, cheques and orders for money or goods purporting to be signed by or on behalf of the company; and

(d)   in all its bills of parcels, invoices, receipts and letters of credit.

(2)   If a company fails to comply with subsection (1) it is liable to a fine.

(3)   If an officer of a company or a person acting on its behalf:

(a)   issues or authorises the issue of any business letter of the company, or any notice or other official publication of the company, in which the company's name is not mentioned as required by subsection (1); or

(b)   issues or authorises the issue of any bill of parcels, invoice, receipt or letter of credit of the company in which its name is not so mentioned, he is liable to a fine."

The Business Names Act 1985 extends a further obligation to individuals, partnerships and companies who carry on business in the UK. They must display the individual's name, partners' names and corporate name respectively and relevant addresses for service on all business letters, written orders for goods or services to be supplied to the business, invoices and receipts issued in the course of the business and written demands for payment of debts arising in the course of the business.

Email could be used as a notice or receipt, for example; the company's name should therefore appear in "official" email.

15.12.8   *Hypertext links*

It is possible, on the World Wide Web, to put in place "hypertext links". To create a hypertext link, a web designer inserts a particular command that specifies the Uniform Resource Location (the "URL") of the site that it wishes to link to. When the user selects the hypertext link (e.g. by clicking on an icon which indicates the name of the proposed site), the command in question then instructs the browser of the user to make that connection. Once that has happened, the browser ceases to display one site in favour of the other. Rules should be put in place to ensure that hypertext links are only installed by employees with appropriate authorisation within the organisation.

The prudent reason for this is that, for example, the site may be one which contains material which could be defamatory or could perhaps be taken as a recommendation of a product available on that site which might breach particular regulations. It should be noted that certain regulators (e.g. within the financial services industry) insist that when a hypertext link is used it is made clear, when leaving the first site, that the user is leaving a regulated environment and that the controller of the first site takes no responsibility for anything that might occur as a result of visiting the second. This sort of warning is probably prudent for any organisation.

15.12.9   *Internet Frames*

A frame is a frequently used device that allows a third party's website to be displayed within a box (the "frame") on a company's website, without the person viewing the frame necessarily realising that the content of the frame is from another website. The surround to the frame remains in the control of the first company. A company that provides access to third party websites through the use of a frame, potentially risks an accusation for trade mark infringement, passing off or copyright infringement.

In order to eliminate risk from the third party site, express consent should be sought. Where this is impractical or undesirable, to minimise the risks, the first company should determine if there are any restrictions on framing or linking in the terms and conditions of the site to be framed.

In order to minimise the risks of trade mark infringement, the company should not use third party trade marks or logos except in links to the third party site where the trade mark is used in the heading of that party's web pages.

If the first company's content was not distinguishable from the third party's content, the first company may be accused of passing itself off as part of the third party company. This may be avoided by demarcating the extent of the frame clearly, perhaps with an individual style.

A third party might complain that it is associated through the frame with any advertising on the first company site. Thus, it would be preferable not to have any advertising in the surround to the frame. If this is not practical, the risk of complaint might be reduced by minimising as far as possible the risk of any advertising held on the surround to the frame from conflicting with the third party site's goods, services or advertising.

The first company should avoid altering the content of sites that are displayed through a frame and avoid framing competitor sites, as both of these acts would be seen as very aggressive and significantly increase the risk of complaint.

If the first company were to copy the third party site and make that available to its users, there would be a clear case of copyright infringement. Thus, it is important that the frame content stored on the first company's server is no more than the third party site's URL and the command to insert the information from that URL into the frame on the user's screen. The Swedish Court of Appeal recently ruled that the creation of a link could not be regarded as unlawful reproduction nor distribution.

As with a hyperlink (*see* Section 15.12.8) a user may hold the first company responsible for the content held on a third party's website but which is accessible through a frame. It would therefore be wise to specifically state that the company is not responsible for third party content accessed by way of a frame before the framed site can be accessed, or at least include such a statement in the company's website terms.

15.13   **Conclusion**

The Internet is useful, provides huge benefits and is here to stay.

Company directors, however, need to be aware of the possible pitfalls of Internet use by their employees and must act in the company's best interests. This includes ensuring that Internet use could not result in additional liabilities for the company and may well necessitate internal procedures and guidelines being put in place so that they can feel satisfied that they have fulfilled their responsibilities as directors.

To finish with some statistics:

In a survey in 1999, the majority of British websites did not have an email management strategy in place, according to a survey conducted by Buchanan E-mail Ltd. Further, the current email culture is one that encourages one way contact, where the consumer is submitting personal information, with minimal feedback from the sites.

The findings are based on a survey of 361 websites in the UK, across a variety of sectors. There were three steps in the methodology. First, it was established whether the site had a contact email address, second a simple email query was sent to the site, and finally the site was questioned about its privacy policy. Sites were given 28 days to respond.

90 per cent of sites provided an email contact address. Of these, a response was received from 62 per cent of sites. Buchanan calculated that 91 per cent of sites delivered a personalised human response, with nine per cent delivering an automated reply. On average, replies were received within two working days, five hours and 11 minutes. In the fastest 50 per cent of sites, the average time of reply was one working day and 34 minutes. The fast responses ranged from eight minutes to just under two hours, with the slowest from one to three working days.

The survey also looked at the quality of the responses. 40 per cent referred to two questions, with 22 per cent answering one. In 28 per cent of cases, none of the consumer's questions were addressed. 58 per cent referred to the privacy policy of the site.

On a different note, a new study in August 2000 found that the use of electronic communications tools at work has increased in both North America and Europe, with North American workers using the Internet more than their European counterparts. Almost 97 per cent of US workers use the Internet on a daily basis, compared with 61 per cent of German and UK office staff.

The study, by Pitney Bowes Inc., analysed the adoption and usage rates of messaging tools among knowledge workers in the US, Canada, France, Germany, and the UK. Internet usage has increased by an average of 18 per cent, while intranet usage has risen by 12 per cent.

Email messages received and sent by all five countries surveyed has increased by 10 per cent, and this is indicative of the increasing use of desktop and laptop computers as the principal working tools.

Email has emerged as the most-used communications tool in the US and Canada, with 97 per cent of workers using it every day or several days a week. In the UK, email and desktop personal computers ("PCs"), at 96 per cent, share equal ranking as the best tool for office communications. The desktop PC is also a popular tool of choice in France, with similar figures to the UK. In Germany, the fax machine is still the most frequently used tool, with 93 per cent of office staff sending faxes on a daily basis.

Workers gain a lot of value from text messaging and knowledge management tools and with the increase in their use, companies in both North America and Europe can deliver more value to their employees via intranets, and to their customers via the Internet.

INDEX

NB: All references are to chapter number followed by paragraph number, e.g. 2.4.12 refers to Chapter 2, paragraph 4.12.

Other titles in the *Practitioner's Guide* series:

A Practitioner's Guide To The Financial Services Authority Listing Rules

"As part of our overall effort to make the FSA Listing Rules as accessible as possible to its users, we welcome the publication of this guide to help practitioners keep up-to-date with the latest changes to the Listing Rules."

Paul Geradine, Director of Listing, The Financial Services Authority

A Practitioner's Guide To The City Code on Takeovers and Mergers

"… widely used as a practical guide to the rules governing the conduct of takeovers in the United Kingdom. The publication of a new edition of the guide each year is welcome recognition of the fact that the Code is not a static body of rules, and that it is important to keep the contents of the guide up-to-date."

Patrick Drayton, Director General, The Panel on Takeovers and Mergers

A Practitioner's Guide To The Acquisition of Private Companies in the European Union

Provides a thorough examination of the legal and regulatory aspects of acquiring private companies in fifteen EU countries. It is written by a leading team of practitioners.

A Practitioner's Guide To Takeovers and Mergers in the European Union

Completely revised and up-to-date, this handbook provides clear, comprehensive and practical guidance on takeover regulation and practice in the European Union. It is written by a leading team of practitioners from fifteen EU countries.

A Practitioner's Guide To The Alternative Investment Market Rules

This easy-to-read guide provides practical analysis of the rules and expert commentary from a specialist team of practitioners. It includes model documentation as well as a clear explanation of the admission rules, on-going obligations, and the principles of corporate governance.

A Practitioner's Guide To The EASDAQ Rules

Simple, practical analysis of the rules and unique guidance to companies applying for admission to EASDAQ. It examines the application of offering laws and the continuing obligations issuers must comply with. It also takes you through the rules and procedure for listing securities on EASDAQ and Nasdaq (dual-listing securities) and discusses the impact of technological developments.

A Practitioner's Guide to SEC Regulation Outside the United States

Written by an expert team of former SEC officials and prominent US and UK lawyers, this guide examines the US legislative and regulatory regime and provides comprehensive guidance to non-US companies on SEC operations, rule-making and enforcement.

A Practitioner's Guide To The Role of Directors Their Duties and Responsibilities

"As higher standards of knowledge and skill are required of directors, this will be a valuable Guide to those directors who want an informed view of their responsibilities. This Guide will also be an indispensable source of information for lawyers and other practitioners who are called upon to advise directors. Each set of issues is written by a leading practitioner in the relevant field."

Peter Holland, Partner, Allen & Overy

Professional Partnership: A Practitioner's Manual

Written by acknowledged experts this brand new book and CD package provides guidance, clarity and solutions to many of the problems facing all accountants in practice. The book is split into two parts. Part one provides a thorough training programme of new skills required to compete effectively for new clients and to retain existing clients. Part two provides commentary and review of the latest developments to affect partnerships themselves as well as looking at financial planning and the options available to partners

For further information on these titles visit our website at:
www.cityandfinancial.com

ORDER FORM

How to order

By fax...if you wish to pay by credit card or BACs, or if you require an invoice, fax the completed order form on the number below:

 00 44 (0) 1483 727 928

By internet...www.cityandfinancial.com

By post...send the completed form, along with your payment to the address below:

8 Westminster Court
Hipley Street
Old Woking
Surrey GU22 9LG

Customer details *(BLOCK CAPITALS PLEASE)*

Mr/Mrs/Ms:	
Full Name:	
Job Title:	
Company Name:	
Address:	
Postcode:	Email:
Tel:	Fax:

City & Financial Titles

	PRICE	QTY	TOTAL
A Practitioner's Guide To:			
The Regulation of the Internet	75.00		
The City Code on Takeovers and Mergers *(now includes the Code)*	80.00		
Takeovers and Mergers in the European Union	75.00		
The Acquisition of Private Companies in the European Union	75.00		
The Financial Services Authority Listing Rules	75.00		
The EASDAQ Rules	70.00		
SEC Regulation Outside the United States	70.00		
The Alternative Investment Market Rules	65.00		
The Role of Directors Their Duties and Responsibilities	75.00		
Professional Partnership: A Practitioner's Manual *(including CD-ROM)*	80.00		

Postage and packaging

The following amounts should be added up to a maximum of £15 for UK and Europe and £25 for the rest of the world:

UK: £4 per copy
Europe: £6 per copy
Rest of world: £8 per copy

Postage & Packaging £ _____

Total Amount Due £ _____

Payment details

(Please tick your preferred method of payment)

☐ Cheque made payable to : City & Financial

☐ Bacs: A/C No. : 23026324
Sort code : 56-00-23

☐ Please tick if you require an invoice

Please debit my: VISA MasterCard AMERICAN EXPRESS

Account No: ☐☐☐☐ ☐☐☐☐ ☐☐☐☐ ☐☐☐☐

Expiry date: ☐☐☐☐

BPRINT2

Prices and postage charges are subject to change
☎ 00 44 (0) 1483 720707